Colley Cibber

Colley Cibber

A Biography

HELENE KOON

THE UNIVERSITY PRESS OF KENTUCKY

Frontispiece: Colley Cibber by J.B. Vanloo, William Andrews Clark Memorial Library, University of California, Los Angeles. Photographed by Nicholas Koon.

Library of Congress Cataloging-in-Publication Data

Koon, Helene, 1925–
  Colley Cibber.

  Bibliography: p.
  Includes index.
    1. Cibber, Colley, 1671–1757—Biography.
  2. Dramatists, English—18th century—Biography.
  3. Actors—Great Britain—Biography. 4. Theatrical
  managers—Great Britain—Biography. I. Title.
  PR3347.K58 1985   828'.509 [B]   85-17899
  ISBN 0-8131-1551-5

This book is for
CHARLES
who lived through it
from the beginning

Contents

Preface

THIS BOOK is the result of two encounters with Colley Cibber, "Comedian and Late Patentee of the Theatre Royal," as he identified himself in his famous *Apology*. My first encounter with him was in the theater, where he was known as a brilliant comedian, a popular playwright who introduced a new mode into English drama, and an expert manager whose history of the theater is regarded as one of the best primary sources for eighteenth-century theater research—in short, the Compleat Theater Man. At my second encounter, in the literary world, the image changed to that of a vain pretentious fool, a writer of worthless plays and the worst poet laureate in history, whose sole claim to recognition was his coronation by Pope as King of Dunces. The extraordinary discrepancy between the two images intrigued me. What kind of personality could have caused such widely divergent views? Which was the "true" Cibber? I felt I had to know.

The resulting search led over mountains of books and documents: through parish records, legal papers, journals, diaries and correspondence in libraries from the Huntington in California, the Folger in Washington, London's British Library and the Parisian Bibliothèque Nationale. Sometimes, the path was well-trodden, more often it seemed a trackless waste.

At length a picture began to emerge. It was neither the kind-hearted creature of his self-portrait nor the grotesque clown of his enemies' caricatures, and it did not always agree with previous scholarship or with my own expectations, but it was coherent, logical, and it answered my questions.

First, Cibber was, above all else, an actor—that is to say, he was sensitive, eager to please, unsure of his place in his ephemeral, ever-changing world, and extremely vulnerable to criticism. Actors often protect themselves by playing a character off the stage as well as on, and Cibber created such a one early in his career: Lord Foppington, the vain, self-centered laughing fool. He played it so long and so well that eventually it was almost indistinguishable from the man himself.

Yet no fool could have remained in his position of power for the twenty-five years that his voice was the most potent in English theater. Those well-fashioned plays, so popular in his own time and for a century to follow, are not great (a quality he never claimed), but they are the work of a skilled and knowledgeable craftsman. Under the management of the triumvirate, Drury Lane was prosperous, its company content, its repertory admired. As the manager who selected new plays, Cibber's voice shaped the theater of his time and after, and his change of emphasis from the page to the stage was a very real contribution to the development of English drama as we know it today.

Like most actors, he made friends easily, and his circle included most of the important people of his day, but it was not restricted to them. Actors, writers, painters, musicians, politicians, aristocrats, and royalty applauded him in the theater, bought subscriptions for his books—and made him poet laureate. That is not to say he had no enemies. Yet the view that he was widely and personally disliked is not sustained by the evidence. Until his politically biased *The Non-Juror* (1718), he suffered no more attacks than any other man of his prominence, but the success of that play brought him the open enmity of the Tories. Since Cibber was, by heritage and training, a thoroughgoing Whig, they saw him as a symbol of Walpole's hated administration and an easier target than the prime minister. Unfortunately, the major satirists of the century were Tories, and the words of Pope and Fielding not only damaged Colley's reputation, but provided material for biographers and critics who scarcely troubled to consider the source.

Separating the image from the man has been a complex task. For obvious reasons, he carefully kept his private life out of public view—in his *Apology*, he does not even give his wife's name—but I have tried to set the record straight and present his character without judgmental bias. Often it has been necessary to look at what he did rather than what he said in order to see the pattern of his life. But the pattern is there, and after more than a decade of climbing the mountains of commentary, it is a pleasure to find that familiarity has not brought contempt, and that at the end of the journey Colley Cibber remains as charming, delightful, and worthwhile a companion as when we set out.

Acknowledgments

I SHOULD LIKE to express my gratitude for the assistance and cooperation of the Huntington Memorial Library, the William Andrews Clark Memorial Library, the Folger Library, the British Library, the Bodleian, the Bibliothèque National and the Bibliothèque de l'Arsenal. I am most particularly grateful for advice, encouragement, and patient reading of the manuscript to Professors Esther Landon, Maynard Mack, David Mann, and Paul Zall.

Prologue

LATE ON a chill January afternoon in 1696, Colley Cibber stood in the wings of the Theatre Royal, Drury Lane, shivering with excitement. His first play, *Love's Last Shift*, was about to open, and he had one of the leading roles. He checked his costume for the twentieth time—his magnificent blond full-bottomed wig, elaborately curled, was a masterpiece of overdone elegance, and his fine new coat with its oversized buttons and extra-long sleeves was perfect. So were his snowy shirt with its thick lace ruffles, his brocaded waistcoat, and his satin kneebreeches, while his immaculate white silk stockings and gaudy silver shoe buckles gleamed in the backstage half-light.

He could see well enough. Although at five-thirty in the afternoon the glass dome in the roof showed only a wintry night sky, the "rings" (chandeliers) and sconces had been filled with fresh candles, lit just before the house opened. Except for the footlights around the rim of the forestage and the three chandeliers above it, both actors and audience were equally lighted. The hypnotic effect of a darkened auditorium would not be possible until the invention of electric lights, and actors had to depend solely on their own skills to command the attention of their restless patrons.

Colley knew the part of Sir Novelty Fashion was splendid and that the play had every chance of success, but for all his seeming nonchalance, his palms were sticky, and he was far less assured than he appeared. He began to tremble but not with cold, for the nearly one thousand bodies packed into the narrow confines of Drury Lane had warmed the air considerably. They had ripened it as well, and the atmosphere was thick with the scent of exotic perfume, burning candlewax, stale fruit peelings, and sweat. He scarcely noticed—the odor was part of every audience. Beyond the curtain, he could hear the muffled roar of their voices rising and falling like the waves of the sea and broken from time to time with ripples of laughter,

1

angry growls, and the cries of orange girls selling their wares. The familiar sound sent the blood pounding through his veins.

The loudest voices came from the pit just beyond the deep forestage. It was crowded with young gallants and "vizard masks" (prostitutes) pushing and shoving for places on the backless benches and at least as interested in assignations as in drama. At one side, "Fop Corner," the area claimed by self-styled critics, was warming up for its running commentary on the action. Such critics could be merciless if a play—or player—did not suit them, and they took a cruel pleasure in shredding reputations. Above the pit, at the sides and back, were two tiers of boxes for the more respectable, but hardly less vocal, prosperous tradesmen and gentry. A few aristocrats sat in the boxes nearest the stage, and a scattering were on the stage itself. Furthest away, at the back of the house, were the upper galleries for apprentices and footmen, who would see the play while waiting for their employers below, and who often made their reactions known by drumming their feet noisily or by shouting rude comments that could be clearly heard above all other sounds and could unnerve the most experienced actor. In the next few hours, these varied and various strangers would determine Cibber's future both as actor and as author.

First and Second Music had been played, and Colley waited impatiently as the prompter busily checked that the stage properties were in order and that the scene shifters had put up the first act "Park" flats correctly. At long last the prompter jingled the little bell at his wrist and signaled the musicians in the pit to start the Third Music that would end the preliminaries and cue the prologue. Colley jumped as a hand touched his shoulder, and he turned quickly to find Tom Southerne standing beside him. Southerne was an established and popular author whose tragedy, *Oroonoko*, produced by Drury Lane the previous month, had been a great success. Colley's first speaking role had been in Southerne's *Sir Anthony Love*, and he liked the gentle, kindly playwright. Now, almost invisible in his rich black suit, his silver sword flickering in the dim light, Southerne took Cibber by the hand and offered a few words apparently meant as encouragement. "Young man," he said with fatherly affection, "I pronounce thy play a good one; I will answer for its success, if thou dost not spoil it by thy own action."

Cibber thanked him, taking the words as a compliment, but he was hardly reassured. At twenty-four, he had served his seven years of apprenticeship, starting as a wordless spear-carrier, graduating to small roles and an occasional substitution in more important parts, but he had never been given a real opportunity to show what he could do. He had written the part of Sir Novelty Fashion for just this purpose. The character was a fop of the first order, and Colley's slender body, mobile face, and light voice were ideal for it. He had studied the type thoroughly; he knew precisely how to mince across the stage with peacock gravity, how to lift an eyebrow or flip the ruffles at his wrist to emphasize a point, how to turn an inflection for a laugh; and his timing was flawless. Still, certainty warred with doubt, and Southerne's words troubled him more than he would admit.

Katharine, his wife, slipped close to him, kissed him lightly, and wished him luck. She and the vivacious Susannah Verbruggen would be playing Hillaria and Narcissa, the two coquettes. Katharine was not a particularly good actress, but she sang well and she would do quite nicely in the part. After three years of marriage, she still looked like a girl, he thought, decidedly pretty in her ribbons and laces as she tripped lightly across the stage to her place beside Susannah. He loved her very much.

The Third Music seemed to go on forever, and then suddenly it was over. The musicians did not leave their narrow kennel between the edge of the forestage and the first benches in the pit, for they would be wanted throughout the play as well as between the acts. Cibber, who was fond of music, had threaded songs and dances into the action, concluding the play with an elaborate miniature masque.

He became aware that John Verbruggen was standing next to him. They had been friends since the days when seventeen-year-old Colley hung about backstage, willing to do anything for a chance to set foot on the Drury Lane boards, and John had introduced him to the company. Verbruggen was playing Loveless, the leading role, and now he was about to deliver the prologue. For once, Cibber had made no claim for this prized solo spot, content to stand by, in case Verbruggen needed prompting, and wait for his own splendid entrance in the second act.

Verbruggen strode forth, silenced the audience with a gesture, and began the opening lines:

> Wit bears so thin a Crop, this duller Age,
> We're forced to glean it from the barren Stage:

He finished to loud applause and made his exit, smiling with satisfaction. The curtains opened, and he was back onstage again with funny little Will Pinkethman, who played his raffish servant, Snap. The forestage, where most of the action took place, was out of Colley's sight. He could, however, hear the laughter, and before the first scene was over, he knew the play was going well.

What Cibber did not know was that *Love's Last Shift* heralded a new era in the theater, an era that later critics would call "sentimental," meaning a kind of drama that appealed to the emotions rather than the intellect. The term, as used by critics, was neither complimentary nor accurate and became a derogatory epithet for plays that appealed more to theatrical than literary audiences. Cibber's approach, new in 1696, marked a sharp diver-

3

gence between stage and page whereby theatrical values took precedence over language as an end in itself. He had set out to write a good stage piece without regard for theories or rules; his knowledge had come from experience in front of an audience, and he had no words to define it. For him, the art of the theater was an ephemeral but intense experience that could neither be duplicated nor repeated, for each performance included a new and unpredictable variable in the audience. A play, he thought, was not an object to be dissected and examined; it was a creation to be shared at a level too profound for analysis.

He had learned that for the kind of wide appeal which keeps the theater doors open, the humor had to be broad, the story easily understood, the characters recognizable, and the references based on knowledge common to all. He had also learned an even more important lesson: actors had to be given the chance to create memorable *moments*—the kind that pass quickly in the theater but remain in the mind long after the curtain has fallen. He may not have been able to state his ideas, but he had put them into a visible form that was even now taking place a few feet away from him.

The first act came to an end, and the scene shifters rushed to change the park into a garden. Cibber's pulse began to race, his vision blurred, and for a second or two he could not catch his breath. Katharine and Susannah joined him for their entrance, and the stage, warm and bright, beckoned to him as it always had, and as it would for the rest of his life. He straightened his shoulders, flicked his irreproachable lace, and stepped forth to glory.

ONE

Apprenticeship

NO TRUE Londoner doubts that he lives at the center of the world. Other cities may be larger, more beautiful, or even older, but none has more varied charms. London is a city of contrasts. Ancient stone structures stand between contemporary buildings, narrow winding lanes open suddenly into broad avenues and gracious shady squares; its streets are crowded with people as changeable as its weather, yet it has an underlying sense of permanence. It is a monument of history housing a vital present, a focus of trade and industry, a mecca for the artist and the artisan, the core of national power, and its heartbeat sets the pulse of the country.

Colley Cibber was a Londoner, blood and bone, irrevocably locked into its shifting moods, its art, its politics, and its irrepressible spirit. He was born on Monday, 6 November 1671, in Southampton Street, near Southampton (now Bloomsbury) Square. Dominated by the earl of Southampton's great mansion, finished just ten years before, it was already a fashionable residential area. To the north, open fields stretched toward Highgate; convenient to the City, now busily raising itself from the ashes of the Great Fire of five years earlier, it was an ideal location for the family of a rising young sculptor like Caius Gabriel Cibber.

The City and its surroundings bustled with activity. Little more than a decade into the Restoration, Charles II kept a tenuous hold on his throne with a skillful combination of political legerdemain and charm while he and his court continued their relentless pursuit of pleasure after the long years of exile. The country at large, plagued by political and religious questions and still guilt-ridden by the execution of Charles I, deplored, condoned, and imitated. Court and commons alike drank, danced, gambled, kept mistresses, and supported the theater, laughing heartily at Wycherley's indecently witty comedies even as they proclaimed their admiration for Dryden's tragic heroics. The sincerity of that proclamation was somewhat undercut by the extreme popularity of the duke of Buckingham's wicked parody, *The Rehearsal*, which had its premiere a month before Colley's birth. Like a portent, the play in which he would one day act the leading role combined the two major shaping forces of his life, the court and the stage.

He was baptized at the elegant St. Giles-in-the-Fields on 20 November 1671, by Robert Boremann, who had officiated at his parents' wedding in the same church, and his christening signified a double heritage.[1] "Colley" was his mother's maiden name, probably given because it was in imminent danger of dying out, since Jane Colley's only brother, Edward, had no children. English as the oak, it stood for generations of conservative, respectable country gentry. "Cibber," on the other hand, was an invented name with no history at all, although the "Gabriel" part of his father's name went back through generations of artists. When the two lines converged, young Colley Cibber received from his mother the values of a gentleman, from his father the soul of an artist.

Caius Gabriel Cibber was a romantic figure. A handsome man with dark eyes and hair, clean-shaven except for a neat mustache and small goatee, he was improvident, restless, impulsive, and gifted. His English was accented with the German of his birthplace in Flensburg, Holstein, where his own great-grandfather, Peter Gabriel, had settled in 1576.[2] The origins of the family are not known, but they may have been a Huguenot branch of the French Gabriels (also sculptors and architects), who fled after the persecutions following the St. Bartholomew's Day massacre of 1572. In Flensburg, they were clearly Protestant, members of the Lutheran church.

They were all artists. Peter Gabriel was a master mason; his son, Hans, a master painter; his grandson, Claus (father of Caius), a master woodcarver whose career, filled with hostility and struggle, paralleled that of *his* grandson, Colley. Claus served his apprenticeship in Copenhagen, but when he returned to Flensburg, the local guild refused to admit him to membership. After more than ten years of legal battles that sometimes spilled over into physical confrontations, he won acceptance, but only after he enlisted the aid of the powerful local Landrat Kai von Ahlenfeldt zu Mehlbek, godfather to his second son, Caius.

An even more important patron was the heir to the Danish throne, Prince Friedrich; when Friedrich became king, Claus Gabriel was appointed court joiner. The appointment entailed moving to Copenhagen, but before the family's departure, Claus thoughtfully inscribed his three sons in the Flensburg Joiners Guild, hoping, no doubt, they could avoid the kind of struggle he had undergone. It was an unnecessary precaution, for the family never returned to Flensburg. Claus died in 1654; his son, Hans, succeeded to the court appointment; his youngest son, Peter, continued to work in and about Copenhagen; and in 1655, King Friedrich sent Caius off to study in Italy.

Precisely what Caius Gabriel did in Italy is unrecorded, but his later sculpture suggests that he may have studied with Bernini or Giovanni da Bologna, and there is a curious connection with the important Cibò family. He may have worked for or been assisted by the noted art patron, Cardinal Alderano Cibò, for the name is similar to the "Cibber" he added afterward, and he adopted the Cibò crest when he came to England.[3]

About 1658, he worked briefly in Amsterdam for the Dutch stone-carver, Peter de Keyser, before moving to the London workshop of Keyser's English nephew, John Stone.[4] Just before the Restoration, Stone, a lifelong Royalist, visited Holland, where Charles II was preparing for his return to England. Stone intended to ask for an appointment in the new court, but before he could succeed, he suffered a stroke, and Caius Gabriel, now a trusted workman, went over to bring him home. Stone never fully recovered, but his workshop continued to operate until his death in 1667.

Caius stayed on in England. He was thirty-two years old and established in his profession, and London offered more opportunities than any other place in Europe. The devastation of the Great Fire had created such a need for skilled craftsmen that the City had given qualified foreigners permission to work within its Liberties (those areas, inside and outside the Wall, under its jurisdiction) for five years or until the reconstruction was finished. Cibber, as he now called himself, was well qualified, and his work was known to important people; the lord chamberlain himself, the earl of Manchester, recommended him to the Gresham Committee for the new statues at the Royal Exchange.[5] He took steps to ensure a more permanent residence and, like his former master, Stone, joined the Leathersellers' Company, one of the oldest and wealthiest guilds in the City, by redemption.[6] The annual "fine" of twenty-five pounds was high, but it gave him certain rights, not the least of which were the elimination of the five-year restriction and the right to work where he chose.

Around 1667, he married an Englishwoman named Elizabeth, and in September 1668, a son, Gabriel, was born but apparently did not survive, and in two years Elizabeth too was dead. A few months afterward, Caius Gabriel married Jane Colley, who brought him a large dowry, gentle connections, and, in due time, a strong and healthy son.[7]

Little is known of Jane Colley, except for the gibe of the anonymous *Laureat* that she was "a very carking, sparing Housewifely Woman," but a good deal is known of her family.[8] Country gentry who traced their lineage back to William of Wykeham, the Colleys had been in Rutland since the time of Henry VII.[9] In 1481, John Colley had been awarded the manor and advowson of Glaston and the Castle of Okeham "by Knight's Service,"[10] and his descendants became prosperous squires, living comfortably in their imposing home at Burley-on-the-Hill. Servitors to the earls of Rutland for nearly two hundred years, they were substantial residents, providing a steady succession of soldiers, sheriffs, and members of Parliament.

In 1591, Jane's grandfather, Sir Anthony, then aged three, came into a sizeable inheritance. Like his forefathers, he served the Crown well, was knighted in 1621, and remained so staunch a Cavalier that he "sunk his Estate from three Thousand to about Three Hundred *per Annum*" for his king.[11] In 1640, near death, he sold off a large portion; seven years later, his son, William, sold the rest and moved the family to London.

By their former standards, the Colleys were poor, but they were not reduced to beggary. In keeping with the family tradition, William's son, Edward, went to Winchester in 1654, where he was admitted as "founder's kin," going on to New College, Oxford. He received his degree, became a Fellow, and remained there until his father's death in 1670, when he returned to London as head of the family. When his sister, Jane, married Caius Gabriel Cibber later that year, her dowry was six thousand pounds, probably her share of the estate.[12]

If she was, as the *Laureat* claimed, "sparing," Jane had good reason. Within six months of their marriage, the Cibbers were in financial straits, and Caius was borrowing forty pounds from a Thomas Minshall. He was drawn into gambling and ruined, it was said, by a "gentleman" who lodged with them. Whoever he was, the gentleman had little mercy, for Colley was barely a year old when the debt landed his father in Marshalsea prison. During the next three years, the family's fortunes grew worse. Two more children were born and died, and debtors' prison became a familiar place.[13] When Christopher Wren received court permission for Cibber to carve the base of his monument to the fire, it was on condition that the sculptor spend his nights in Marshalsea. The elaborate allegorical relief on the monument enhanced his reputation but did not entirely free him from debt.[14]

It would be easy to assign the mature Colley's giddy mask to an attempt at concealing a childhood of privation and shame, but it would not be accurate.[15] It is not likely that he was aware of his parent's financial problems, for the worst was over before he was five years old, and there is no record that Caius Gabriel was ever again incarcerated for debt.[16] After he finished the monument, he was commissioned to carve coats of arms and statues for Newgate prison, and when a debt for thirty-six pounds brought him back into court during the Easter term of 1677, he was just completing his most famous work, the paired Raving and Melancholy Madness to be set over the gates of Bedlam Hospital.[17]

Colley was an attractive child, blond, blue-eyed, and bright, and his parents adored him. With prudent foresight, they put aside a bit of Jane's dowry to provide a tiny income when he came of age, and they tended to spoil him, indulging his whims and taking him on special outings. Sixty years later, he would remember his father taking him to the royal services in Whitehall Chapel and at least once to see Charles II feeding the ducks in St. James's Park.

When Colley was six years old, Caius Gabriel was offered his first commission outside of London, the Sackville tomb at Withyam, Sussex, family seat of the earl of Dorset.[18] Possibly Jane's family had some influence here, for one of the earl's ancestors had married an early John Colley. The commission was important to the Cibbers, for in a world where rank counted more than law, the patronage of a Dorset was valuable protection for a foreigner. In 1678, Titus Oates emerged from obscurity to infect the country with the fever of the Popish Plot. Much of the anti-Catholic sentiment Colley later expressed in his plays may be rooted in the violent controversies that shook the country during his childhood. Religious allegiances frequently became political alliances as the newly formed Whig and Tory parties struggled for supremacy. To forward their own designs (the succession of the king's illegitimate son, the duke of Monmouth) and consolidate their power, the predominantly Protestant Whigs fostered Oates's tale that Rome was planning to place England under papal rule, and Plot Fever soon erupted into an open witch hunt for Catholics. Two years elapsed before it ran its course and two centuries before the repercussions subsided.

The Cibbers were safely Protestant—Caius Gabriel's moderate Lutheranism had easily converted to Anglicanism—but they must have been well aware of the fury. By 1679, they had moved to Bennet's Court, St. Margaret's parish, not far from Monmouth's London residence.[19] Young Colley may have witnessed the street riots sweeping past their house; certainly he heard the shouts and clamors, and the effect was indelible. Even after Oates was proved a charlatan and the intensity of the fever abated, anti-Catholicism remained just below the surface, breaking out at the slightest pressure.

In spite of the public crisis, the private lives of the Cibbers seem to have become relatively stable by this time. When the Leathersellers accepted a fountain created by Caius Gabriel in payment of his livery fine, he was clear of debt and the company in possession of a bronze mermaid whose breasts spouted water in their courtyard.[20] His next commission was a great fountain for Soho Square, and when it was finished, he was summoned to Cambridge to carve four heroic-scale statues for the new library Christopher Wren had designed for Trinity College.[21]

In January 1680, while still at Cambridge, Caius Gabriel signed a contract for seven statues to be carved at Belvoir Castle, home of the earl of Rutland, and here again the Colleys, long associated with the earls of Rutland, may have been influential.[22] Early in 1682, when he finished at Cambridge and could travel north, Caius took his son Colley with him, entering him in the grammar school at nearby Grantham.

Founded by Richard Fox, the school was small and seldom had more than twenty pupils, but its standards were high, and among its distinguished alumni it boasted at least one member of the renowned Cecil family. It was expensive, however; the "Free School," as it was called, was gratis only for boys whose parents lived within one mile of the town. Since Colley was eligible for a scholarship at Winchester, it is a curious choice—unless Caius Gabriel wanted to keep his son near him.

School brought a drastic change to Colley's life. For nine of his ten years, he had been the center of his indulgent parents' world, but now his mother was occupied with his brother, Lewis, born in August 1680, and he was sent forth into a strange, unfriendly environment.[23] From his point of view, the little village could not compare with what he left behind. Grantham's main street, its church, and its school seemed insignificant compared with London's crowded lanes and great buildings, its constant motion, and its ever-present sense of past glories. Grantham, too, had its history—Richard III signed Buckingham's death warrant at the Angel Inn—but it was a sleepy place. Its only connection with London was the Skipwith family, who owned the stately "Hall's Place" at the edge of the village. The head of the family, Sir Thomas, was a City barrister; he had just purchased shares in the Theatre Royal Drury Lane, where Colley would spend most of his adult life.

Travel was arduous, dangerous, and costly. The boy probably did not see London again until his schooling was finished, and he must often have been homesick, particularly during the wintry weeks of leaden skies and winds that sent a North Sea chill to the very marrow of the bones. Summers, though short, were less depressing, and sometimes he could spend holidays with his father.[24] Just before Easter that first year, Caius Gabriel wrote Rutland's secretary that he had promised to let his son see Belvoir Castle during the holidays but that he had to collect a shipment of marble instead. He would, he said, send one of his workmen to escort the boy to the castle, adding as a special request, "pray take notis of him."[25] There must have been other such treats, for Caius Gabriel stayed as near Grantham as he could during the school years. He left Belvoir to become "Armorial Servant" to the earl of Kingston, working at the earl's country house, Thoresby Hall, only a few miles further away. Here he spent five months recuperating from a broken leg, and Colley could easily have visited him whenever he had permission.[26]

Grantham Free School was an oblong stone building, and lessons were conducted in a single room lighted by deep-set windows through which Colley could look out at St. Wulfram's Church on one side and broad green fields on the other. Former students had cut their names into the wide wooden casings, and if he looked closely, he might have seen a neatly carved "I. Newton" in one of them. The master was the Reverend William Walker, nicknamed "Particles" after his text, *A treatise of English particles . . . and how to enter them into Latine* (1673), a stern disciplinarian who did not hesitate to use the cane on erring students.

The curriculum was heavily weighted with Latin and Greek. Although few of the students would go on to a university, Grantham provided excellent preparation, and young Colley's quick mind was well trained as he progressed, not always smoothly, through the six forms. Clever, mischievous, and "always in full Spirits," he could never resist the temptation to perform, and Walker took a dim view of the talent that would one day make theaters ring with applause. Nevertheless, the master was fair, balancing a whipping for a poor theme with the observation that "what was good of it was better than any Boy's in the form" (I, 10).

Colley was probably not very popular with the other boys, but the assumption that some flaw in his character made him disliked even as a child is based solely on his own comments in the *Apology*, flimsy evidence at best. Yet there may be some basis for presuming he had few friends, for unlike most grammar schools, Grantham primarily enrolled local boys. From the start, the young Londoner's behavior, clothes, and speech marked him as an outsider. The majority of the pupils shared a knowledge of the village and its customs, and, like most close-knit groups, were not eager to accept a stranger, especially a clever one who surpassed them in their studies. The division remained when, at the end of the day, they went home to their families while Colley boarded with the master.

Separated from the others by background, experience, and daily life, Colley probably felt alienated, and it is unlikely he was quite as carefree as his stories in the *Apology* suggest. He needed protection from hostile schoolmates, and he found it in a way that already pointed toward the actor's profession. He became the class clown, laughing at himself and at them. The mask of laughter gave him an armor, and by the time he left Grantham, it was well developed.

Commentators have been fond of reading Cibber's recollections by the light of his enemies' lamps. Taking the words of Pope and Fielding at face value while discounting Cibber's own, they have cited his childhood recollections as "proof" of his unattractive personality.[27] Yet the memories of an aging eighteenth-century gentleman, long practiced in the traditional self-deprecatory pose, reveal more of the mature Cibber's values than of his popularity as a schoolboy. His tales invariably illustrate a moral point. He tells of boxing the ears of a boy who had insulted him. The boy, "near a Head taller," promptly knocked young Colley down, and the scuffle continued until another lad, whom Cibber had always considered a friend, cried out, "Beat him! Beat him soundly!" At that, Colley gave up the battle and burst into uncharacteristic tears. Afterward, he was amazed when his erstwhile friend explained it was "because you are always jeering and making a Jest of me to every Boy in the School." The older Cibber makes his point: "I deserv'd his Enmity by my not having Sense enough to know I *had* hurt him; and he hated me because he had not Sense enough to know I never *intended* to hurt him" (I, 11). It is an honest evaluation followed by a defense that applies as much to his later behavior as to the immediate instance.

In spite of such confrontations and his admitted "frequent Alacrity to do wrong" (I, 9), Colley was a good student, eager to please the master. He tried even harder after Samuel Burnet took over as master in 1684. More sympathetic to the lively boy than Walker had been, Burnet was an innovative educator, and when the death of Charles II was announced, he asked the students in Colley's form to write a funeral oration. It was an unexpected and unpopular assignment, and the boys tried to dodge it by claiming it was "above their Capacity." Burnet insisted, but they agreed among themselves to "decline" it, without, however, informing Colley. Not recognizing their ploy, the fourteen-year-old naively produced a eulogy that brought him to the top of the form. It was a "preferment dearly bought," for his classmates felt betrayed and refused to speak to him for some time (I, 31). Burnet must have understood what was happening; he gave Colley special attention, taking him out horseback riding and leaving the others to their lessons, an expedient that only exacerbated matters.

Three months later, a similar situation arose when the boys asked Burnet for a holiday to celebrate the coronation of James II. He agreed, on condition that one of them would write an ode for the occasion. Cibber does not say he volunteered or that the others refused to try, only that it "fell to my Lot," and in half an hour he produced a set of verses that earned the whole school a day's freedom from lessons. He admits he was so "vain" about his accomplishment that his infuriated schoolmates refused to invite him to their celebration. Secure behind his mask, he pretended to shrug off the disappointment, but it went deep enough for him to recall it fifty years later. He uses the story to answer a later charge against him, concluding with wry candor, "If I confess my Vanity, while a Boy, can it be Vanity, when a Man, to remember it?" (I, 34).

In 1687, Colley finished at Grantham and could return to London at last. Before setting out for home, he probably visited his father at Chatsworth, where Caius Gabriel was just beginning a series of sculptures for the earl of Devonshire.[28] The earl, a fiercely assertive Protestant, was currently under royal displeasure, having caned a Catholic courtier at Whitehall the previous year. For such rude behavior in the palace, he had been sentenced to King's Bench Prison and fined an exorbitant thirty thousand pounds, but he had escaped and fled to his country seat. Here he spent his time in remodeling the Tudor house built by his great-great-grandmother, Bess of Hardwick, and, on the advice of his kinsman, the earl of Kingston, hired Caius Gabriel Cibber to assist in his grand new designs.[29]

After visiting his father, Colley went back to London until time to enter Winchester College, for he was expected to follow the family tradition and go from Winchester to New College, Oxford, and on to a career in the church. At the moment, he had no other aim in mind, although the actor in him might have been discerned in his picture of himself as a cleric—not a humble servitor of God but in the role of bishop, with all its trappings.

While waiting, Colley discovered an amusement that soon became a passion, the theater. For a shilling he could suffer with Betterton in *The Maid's Tragedy* or laugh at Sedley's witty *Bellamira*, but, since it is likely that his mother kept him on a fairly short allowance, he probably followed the practice of other impecunious young gallants. With sufficient nerve and skill, he could see one or two acts and leave without paying, returning another day to see the rest. However he managed it, he saw as much as he could, and before he set off for Winchester, the stage was his "darling Delight."

At fifteen, he was a bit old to be entering a school that generally admitted boys only between the ages of eight and twelve, but exceptions were made for excellence in scholarship or for founder's kin, and Colley, with his "pompous Pedigree" in his pocket, should have had no difficulty. The examination was a formality, and his uncle Edward must have coached him that the proper response to the obligatory question, "Cantas?" was a rendition, melodic or otherwise, of the hundredth psalm, "Jubilate Deo, omnis terra. . . ." It was not enough. With no supporting recommendations from important personages, Colley's claim to kinship was insufficient and his entrance to the school denied.[30] The setback was more serious to his parents than to the boy, who took the next post back to London, congratulating himself all the way on his "happy Reprieve," and quickly arranged to see another play "before my Mother might demand an Account of my travelling Charges" (I, 57).

The failure at Winchester did not make Colley ineligible for the university, and he wrote to his father that he would like to go directly on to Oxford. Caius Gabriel, "who was naturally indulgent" to his son, acquiesced. He had evidently learned the value of influence, for he suggested Cambridge instead, since his work on the King's College Library had gained him "some Acquaintance with the Heads of Houses, who might assist his Intentions." He may also have learned of his son's theatrical predilections from a concerned Jane, for he directed Colley to meet him at Chatsworth. Together they would go back south to the university.

Colley might have entered Cambridge in October 1688 if history had not intervened as the brief, troubled reign of James II came to its close. His autocratic rule, coupled with his extreme Catholicism that raised the specter of Bloody Mary Tudor, had alienated too many. Only the fact that he had no male heir had kept the Protestants at bay, and when his queen gave birth to a son in June of this year, their passive resistance became open rebellion. Within a month, a delegation invited James's eldest daughter, Mary, and her husband, William of Orange, to ascend the English throne.

William fitted out an invasion fleet and landed at Torbay the day before Colley's seventeenth birthday.

The earl of Devonshire, one of the first to support him, raised his own regiment, and Colley, obediently journeying northward, met his father, riding under Devonshire's banner, at Nottingham. Their reunion was brief and fruitful. Caius Gabriel convinced the earl that the combined rigors of war and winter were too much for his fifty-year-old bones and offered his son as a substitute. Devonshire was agreeable and even promised to provide for the boy when the war was over.

For a brief time, Colley saw himself in a new role, dressed in the uniform of a cavalry officer and crowned with military glory. He had no real understanding of war, and the nearest he came to actual conflict was on 8 December, when he and six thousand other horsemen set off in haste to save Princess Anne. Her husband, Prince George of Denmark, had joined William, and she was reportedly fleeing her father's wrath, pursued by his soldiers. Devonshire's regiment found only a single coach with three frightened young women in it, but they led the princess and her ladies back to Chatsworth and celebrated as if they had won a major victory.

The majordomo at Chatsworth knew Colley from previous visits and asked him to assist at the banquet. Happily, if inefficiently, he waited table and briefly fell in love with the most beautiful creature he had ever seen, Lady Sarah Churchill, who would one day be the redoubtable duchess of Marlborough. His recollection of that evening is touchingly honest. When he wrote of it some fifty years later, he could easily have invented some sparkling repartee, but his words ring true by their very banality. "Some wine and water," commanded the future duchess, and the young soldier who leaped to obey treasured the request for the rest of his life.

The regiment took the princess to meet her husband at Oxford. The university town, which had been anti-James since he had replaced the Magdalen Fellows with his own priests, showered honors on the royal couple, and the army enjoyed the fringe benefits of warm beds and good food until William and Mary were proclaimed the rightful rulers of England. Devonshire went to London to assist in the new government, and his regiment returned to Nottingham. A few of the temporary officers were given permanent commissions, but most, including the inexperienced young Cibber, were released. He was not unhappy; soldiering for a few tense weeks had been exciting, but as the drama waned, so did his interest.

Colley still faced the problem of his future, and Caius Gabriel, remembering Devonshire's promise, kept his son with him until the earl returned to Chatsworth. At the first opportunity, he made the boy demonstrate his learning with a long petition in Latin, and the earl was so impressed he offered to find a post if Caius Gabriel would send the boy to London. Colley was overjoyed, but his father might have been less pleased if he realized how long it would take. Hundreds of petitions for places in government, church, university, and court besieged every aristocrat, and finding a place for an untrained alumnus of a grammar school was not a simple matter. Colley himself later confessed, "I believe it was then harder to know what I was really fit for, than to have got me anything I was not fit for" (I, 73).

At eighteen, Colley was more sanguine about his ability, and when he returned to London in September of 1689, he had a brief vision of himself in the role of the compleat courtier. There was no more substance to this image than to his previous dreams of church and army, and he exerted very little effort to realize it. If he had been serious about a career in government, he would have spent his days among the crowd of place-seekers at Devonshire's London residence, stopping the great lord on his way to or from Whitehall, making certain his face and name were remembered. He did nothing; indeed, when one of Devonshire's household told him the earl planned to recommend him to the earl of Shrewsbury, then secretary of state, he was "afraid of succeeding to the Preferment." It would have given him too little time for the theater.

Whether Colley was conscious of it or not, he had already determined his future, for he was irresistibly drawn to the stage. He was a daily visitor to the Theatre Royal in Drury Lane and soon knew every actor by name and specialty. He learned where they congregated before and after performances, and he haunted the Rose Tavern, listening to their talk, pretending to be one of them. He made a friend of young John Verbruggen, not much older than himself but already in his second season with the company.[31] Tall, ruggedly handsome, Verbruggen was ambitious to play Alexander the Great in *The Rival Queens*, a role that belonged to the brilliant young leading man, William Mountfort, but that Verbruggen wanted so badly he listed himself simply as "Alexander" on the playbills. He enlightened Colley on the conditions of an actor's life and gave him his first entrée to the backstage world by introducing him to the prompter, John Downes, who often hired the "walk-ons," those who made up crowds and armies but spoke no lines. Colley ran errands for Downes, "walked" when he could and watched when he could not. Hopelessly stagestruck, he "saw no Joy in any other Life than that of an Actor" (I, 73).

Colley did not tell his parents for some time. He knew they would be dismayed by his choice of career, that his father, who counted on Devonshire's assistance, wanted a gentleman's career for him, and that his mother would feel disgraced, but he could no more forget the theater than he could stop breathing. It was not just a parent-child conflict, it was a conflict within himself as well, for his two heritages were in direct opposition to each other. On the one hand, his background, education, and family tradition pointed toward a respectable profession; on the other, his creative spirit and artistic sensitivities drove him toward the stage. In the end, of course, there was no contest at all. He would behave like a gentleman— but he *had* to be an actor.

Cibber faced his parents, "determin'd, let Father and Mother take it as they pleas'd, to fix my *non ultra*" (I, 79). This time his ambition was no vague and shadowy image of future glory but a vivid and immediate reality based on firsthand experience. He even knew the disadvantages of the profession: the poor salaries, the lack of security, the social stigma. They did not matter. He had found where he belonged, and he would never change his mind. At the end of a long and turbulent career, he would still insist, "The Allurements of a Theatre are still so strong in my Memory, that perhaps few, except those who have felt them, can conceive" (I, 74). His commitment was complete when, in September 1690, he was accepted as a member of the company at Theatre Royal, Drury Lane.

Young Cibber approached the theater with the reverence of a novice taking religious orders; for him, the playhouse was a temple and its high priest, Thomas Betterton. Colley's own disapproving father was still far away at Chatsworth, and Betterton provided a substitute image at once paternal and inspiring. The same age as Caius Gabriel, Betterton was the foremost actor on the English stage and an imposing figure. He was six feet tall, thickset, and so broad of shoulder that his arms seemed short, while the thick dark curls of a full-bottomed wig made his head look disproportionately large for his body. His pockmarked face was not handsome, but the strong features were expressive with a sweetness in repose that revealed his gentle nature. His power on the stage was extraordinary; his majestic dignity commanded attention, and his rich baritone silenced even the orange girls. He was extremely versatile, playing the raffish humor of a Dorimant as skillfully as the tragic grandeur of Othello. Even more impressive was his ability to enter into a character; he actually turned pale at the sight of the ghost in *Hamlet*, when "his whole body seemed to be affected with a tremour inexpressible . . . and this was felt so strongly by the audience that the blood seemed to shudder in their veins like-wise."[32]

Betterton was not only a superb actor but a skilled and devoted teacher of acting. As one "knows" the correct pronunciation of words from the way one first learns them, so Colley "knew" acting as he learned it from Betterton. Another generation would find the style too mannered, but the audiences of 1690 regarded deliberate gestures and formal speech as realistic. Art was not life, it was, as in Pope's words, "nature methodiz'd," with a code of interpretation that borrowed freely from other forms of expression. Actors consulted paintings and sculpture for visualizations of emotion, incorporating such "attitudes" into their performances, and the audience's recognition of a "Dying Gaul" enhanced its appreciation of the dramatic moment. Society itself struck attitudes, wearing its satins, velvets, and laces with full consciousness of their effect. Beruffled men sat, stood, and walked with an ever-present awareness of their swords, and tightly laced women learned to move gracefully under layers of heavy petticoats. If thick ruffles and wide skirts disallowed easy embraces, the touch of fingertips had greater impact; the stage reflected a code that established social, emotional, and psychological implications by the depth of a bow or the snap of a fan. Any noticeable variance from the code brought hisses from the pit and a general conviction that the actor did not know how to behave in or out of the theater.

Like the arabesque of the ballerina, however, the "attitude" was the culmination of a series of movements, and the actor's reputation did not derive from the beauty of his poses but from the concept that determined them. Betterton anticipated Stanislavski in his view that "the Actor ought to be thoroughly acquainted with the whole Nature of the Affections and Habits of the Mind," and that life experience was the basis of interpretation, since "every Passion or emotion of the mind has from Nature its proper and peculiar Countenance, Sound and Gesture; and the whole Body of Man, with all his Looks, and every Sound of his Voice, like Strings on an Instrument, receive their Sounds from the various Impulse of the Passions." Colley was told to rehearse in front of a mirror, "so that you may thus easily discover any *Habit* or *Gesture* that wants Grace, and Agreeableness, and any Action which may add them to your Person," but he was warned to be cautious about this. The best check was "some Friend, who is a perfect Master in all the Beauties of *Gesture* and *Motion*, and can correct your Errors, as you perform before him."[33] He had found such a friend in Betterton, and to the end of his life, he acted and judged acting by that standard.

"Master Colley," as he was known, may have felt himself dedicated to the theater, but he neither looked nor behaved as if he were. His very appearance was unprepossessing. Of average height and small-boned he was so slight that he was teasingly called "Hatchet Face." His immature features, regular but not handsome, were colorless and hardly carried beyond the footlights. His voice posed a serious problem, and his dream of one day playing leading roles opposite the beautiful Anne Bracegirdle was shattered when he realized his reedy tenor would never have the power or the richness required for such parts.

A closer look, however, would have revealed more positive factors. Colley's figure may not have been impressive, but at least it was straight and did not restrict him, like Samuel Sandford's crooked little body, to the playing of villains. His face was expressively mobile, and the lack of distinctive features allowed him to transform and vivify his appearance with a bit of makeup. If his voice was poor, his articulation was clear, and he easily managed the fine-tuned cadence of blank verse. His ear was good; he could hear the subtlest nuances of speech and, within the limits of his vocal powers, imitate them with startling accuracy.

The young actor was also ambitious, but at nineteen he had not yet learned his limitations, and he often appeared vain, self-centered, spoiled, and superficial, a boy who had taken it into his head to go on the stage with little to recommend him. His ambition, his dedication, and his desire to do well made him extremely vulnerable to mockery. He protected himself with the pert mask he had worn in his schooldays, but his flippancy offended as often as it amused. Not many could, or would, see beneath it, and actors like George Powell regarded him with contempt. Powell, a player's son, had been acting since boyhood and was so at home on the stage that even staggering drunk he could give a fine performance. He had no patience with beginners, and he took particular delight in tormenting the brash young Cibber. Colley's laughing bravado hid his wounds, but he may well have been remembering Powell's sarcastic gibes when he wrote in his old age, "The inward Wounds . . . are as dangerous as those given by Oppression to Inferiors; as long in healing, and perhaps never forgiven" (I, 13). Certainly he was hurt by Powell, and if he did forgive, he never forgot.

But Colley found a genuine friend in William Mountfort, who gave him his first speaking part, the "Servant to Sir Gentle" in Thomas Southerne's comedy *Sir Anthony Love*. The handsome Mountfort was the antithesis of Powell; an excellent, versatile actor and as conscientious as Betterton, he danced and sang well, wrote popular plays, and managed the delicate art of play doctoring so diplomatically that authors thanked him publicly for his assistance. Like Betterton, who was grooming him as a successor, Mountfort took pains with the younger actors, training them carefully in technique and style.

Cibber learned quickly and well, but he had little chance to display his knowledge. Apart from his role in *Sir Anthony Love*, and two other minute parts, his acting that first year was still confined to crowd scenes.[34] His enthusiasm was undiminished. He continued to spend all his time at the theater where, as a nominal member of the company, he could observe actors in the process of creation from the time they received their lines to the finished performance. He heard Dryden read *Amphitryon* for the company in "so cold, so flat, and unaffecting a manner" that he scarcely believed it could be acted, and, a few weeks later, saw James Nokes bring roars of laughter with those same lines. He studied Edward Kynaston, who had begun his career when boys were still playing women's roles and whom Pepys called "the prettiest girl and the handsomest man" on the stage. Kynaston, whose magnetic vitality and piercing glance roused "trembling Admiration" in the audience, sometimes used a kind of comic inflection in his delivery of tragic lines, a technique Cibber would recall and use one day.

He absorbed it all—the gestures, the timing, the movements, the intonations, the facial expressions—and he stored them away in his retentive memory.

At first Cibber approved of everything, but gradually, as he became more familiar with the "rules" of acting, he grew critical of his colleagues. Like all young actors who have just learned the rudiments, he began to see flaws in their performances. Verbruggen's delivery was rough and lacked subtlety, Powell's expertise in ad libbing did not conceal his lack of discipline on and off the stage, and the marvelous mimic, Ned Estcourt, who filled his script with notes and observations on character, seemed to forget all his ideas once onstage, where he "labour'd under a heavy Load of Flatness" (I, 115). Only Betterton, the matchless ideal, was immune from young Cibber's developing critical faculties, and although the older actors had passed through the same stage, they did not appreciate such comments, especially when laced with humor, from an unpaid apprentice.

Beginners were not paid until they had proved themselves, and Cibber served most of his first year without wages. It was not as much of a hardship as it might seem—he still lived at home and was under no obligation to support himself—but a salary meant full acceptance into the company. His chance may have come at the premiere of Dryden's opera *King Arthur*, in May 1691. It was a lavish production using the entire company, and he probably had a small, nonsinging role in it.[35] According to theater gossip, he was to give a message to Betterton, but when he made his entrance he became so flustered (possibly stage fright at the idea of appearing with his idol) that he disrupted the scene. Afterward, an irate Betterton demanded to know who had blundered, and Downes answered, "Master Colley, sir."

"Master Colley!" Betterton exclaimed. "Then forfeit him!"

"Why, sir, he has no salary."

"No? Why then, put him down for ten shillings a week and forfeit him five."[36]

The story may be apocryphal, but it is typical of Betterton's kindness toward young actors. He evidently understood Cibber's stage fright, and he took the boy seriously, treating him not as a schoolboy, a refractory son, or a silly amateur but as a fundamentally serious young artist. Colley, just beginning to comprehend the depth and breadth of the actor's art, asked no more.

During the summer that followed, Caius Gabriel finished at Chatsworth and returned briefly to London before going on to Hampton Court and his last commission outside the capital.[37] He probably had little opportunity to see Colley, for as soon as the London season ended, the company went to Oxford, where it played for the "Act," the celebration that accompanied the conferral of degrees. It meant a strenuous two performances a day, but it was remunerative, for the actors were paid double their usual salaries. The extra income served to tide them over the long summer hiatus.[38]

On 19 October 1691, Drury Lane opened its doors to a city filled with bonfires and illuminations, ringing with the sound of bells and the guns of the Tower as William III announced a firm peace in Ireland and an end to James II's last abortive attempt to regain the English throne. It was a splendid way to begin his second season in the theater, but Cibber had little reason to be complacent. His position, like that of all actors, was extremely precarious. Even the great Betterton was not secure and this season exchanged his position as a shareholder for that of salaried performer, partly because of the theater's financial problems, partly because of his own.[39] After a lifetime on the stage, the greatest actor of the day was scarcely more prosperous than the rawest newcomer.

Financial security meant little to young Colley. His small salary did not preclude his dressing elegantly or following the gentlemanly pursuits of the day. He haunted the coffeehouses, going to Will's to see Dryden hold court in his special chair (though never daring to speak to the great man); he drank with his fellow actors at the Rose Tavern; and he gambled at the Groom Porter's, which William III sometimes visited for the same purpose. But however much he amused himself, he arrived at the theater each day on time for rehearsal and ready to work.

Cibber's diligence was rewarded when Betterton gave him the small part of the Chaplain in a revival of Otway's *The Orphan*. His one brief scene precipitated the climax, and on his exit he received his first applause, doubly satisfying because Queen Mary and her maids of honor were present. Cardell Goodman's compliment the next day meant even more. Goodman, a picaresque figure with a taste for fine living and fine ladies, had been a popular actor until he retired from the stage to live with the duchess of Cleveland. The morning after the opening of *The Orphan*, Goodman visited his former colleagues and, during the course of the conversation, asked about the "new young Fellow" who had played the Chaplain.

"That's he, behind you," Mountfort told him.

Goodman turned around, looked earnestly at Colley for a moment, then clapped him on the shoulder, "If he does not make a good Actor, I'll be d———d!" (I, 188).

The words brought tears to Cibber's eyes. He had so carefully concealed his deep longing to be a "good Actor" beneath the mask of gentlemanly fool that he was well protected from ridicule, but he had no defense at all against praise.

Actually, aside from George Powell, few people ridiculed Cibber in these early days. The older players might laugh at his pretensions and his ambition, and there was no doubt a large portion of the good-natured teasing common among actors who know each other well, but there was little or none of the kind of mockery Cibber would meet later. On the contrary, once he had proved himself, he was probably rather well liked because of his friendliness and his easy flow of light conversation, for his circle of acquaintances noticeably widened. He kept up his contacts with aristocrats like the duke of Dorset and the earl of Devonshire—not, as has been charged, because he was a snob, but because he was a man of his time.[40] The patronage of the "quality" was the accepted, and only, hope for professional or social advancement.

A good many of his friends were musicians, for he loved music and, although he could neither sing well nor play an instrument, he listened intelligently and had intuitive taste. He was drawn to John Shore, Drury Lane's peppery young trumpeter. Shore's father, Matthias, was a royal "sergeant trumpeter"; his older brother, William, also held an appointment at court, and John himself was so gifted that Purcell wrote obbligatos expressly for him. One evening after the show, he invited Colley to his home for a visit that had a profound and lasting effect.

As they passed the Shores' music room, Colley was "immediately charmed" by the sound of a woman singing. He begged an introduction and was presented to John's sister, the gentle, attractive Katharine. She, too, was a musician, with a lovely voice which, as a student of Henry Purcell, she could accompany with a well-trained touch on the harpsichord. Impulsive as always, Cibber fell in love with her at once and began to court her in secret. Both felt secrecy was necessary, since Katharine was four years older and the daughter of a prosperous householder, while Colley had still to make any kind of respectable advancement in his career.[41]

Although he was rehired for the 1692-93 season, Cibber was given no new parts, and his status was no higher than before. It was a discouraging beginning, but worse was to come. On Saturday, 10 December, he came to Drury Lane ready to play in *Bussy D'Amboys*, scheduled for that afternoon, and found the company in a state of shock. Weeping actors told a tale of horror about Mountfort and two young men, Charles, Baron Mohun and Captain Richard Hill, veteran of the Irish wars. Fifteen and seventeen years old, respectively, they were the kind of dissolute young rakes who made the streets perilous at night and started swordfights in the theater. Like most London males, Hill had fallen under the spell of Anne Bracegirdle, but when she did not respond to his ardor, the frustrated and angry young man decided she must be having an affair with Mountfort. That Mrs. Bracegirdle was famous for her chastity and that Mountfort was perfectly happy with his wife, Susannah, now expecting their second child, did not in the least alter his opinion, and he persuaded Mohun to help him take his revenge. On the night of 9 December, well fortified by alcohol, they waylaid Mountfort on his way home from the theater. As Mohun spoke to him, Hill came out of the shadows and plunged his sword into him. Mountfort, bleeding profusely from a twenty-inch wound, staggered the few steps to his own door and collapsed in Susannah's arms. He died the next afternoon.[42]

Mountfort's death was a terrible blow to the company, for he was not only Betterton's right hand but beloved by all. Two weeks later, the ailing character actor Anthony Leigh died, his illness aggravated, it was said, by his grief for Mountfort. The theater closed until the two actors' roles could be redistributed and rehearsed. A few actors profited with new and better parts, but Colley gained nothing. He was not even considered for William Congreve's first comedy, *The Old Batchelor*, which played an unprecedented fourteen consecutive nights that spring. He longed to play Fondlewife, but the part went to Thomas Dogget, a lively little comedian who had joined the company the previous year, earning an immediate and impressive reputation as "Solon" in Durfey's *The Marriage-Hater Match'd*.[43]

Colley consoled himself by courting Katharine Shore. On his twenty-first birthday, he came into his inheritance of twenty pounds a year; with the security of that income and his twenty shillings a week at the theater, he proposed to her, and on 6 May 1693, they were married at St. James's, Duke's Place, Aldgate.[44] It was a love match in the beginning, and it remained so for more than forty years. Some have claimed that Katharine's parents disapproved and that Matthias Shore was so enraged he put the money he had set aside for her dowry into building a Thames pleasure barge, but the evidence does not bear this out.[45] The Cibbers' opinion is not known; Caius Gabriel, at least, was concerned with other matters. That month, at the request of the duke of Dorset, he was appointed sculptor-in-ordinary to the Crown.[46]

Another engagement at Oxford helped the newlyweds through the summer of 1693, but when Drury Lane reopened in the autumn, their livelihood was immediately and seriously threatened. The cause was Alexander Davenant. Having inherited some of the Drury Lane shares from his father, he had later bought those of his brother, Charles, and paid for them with money secretly borrowed from Sir Thomas Skipwith. The barrister from Grantham was uninterested in theatrical operations and "farmed" the shares back to Alexander for active management. Davenant's constant speculations and extravagant productions lost so much money that by 1690 he had to sell his own shares to another lawyer, Christopher Rich, who also farmed them back to him. After three more years of rash investments and costly failures, with the threat of bankruptcy looming, Alexander gathered all the available cash and sailed away to the Canary Islands, leaving the company to face an avalanche of debts and chancery suits.

Rich and Skipwith took the only possible course; they foreclosed on Drury Lane and officially took over the management themselves. Skipwith died shortly after, and his son became Rich's partner, working sub rosa in order to preserve his status as a gentleman.[47] Rich, who used his power openly, was neither scrupulously honest nor knowledgeable about the theater, but he knew the principles of commerce, and he applied them toward putting Drury Lane on a sound financial basis. Insensitive to the artistic and human elements, he regarded plays as products to be sold and actors as hired workmen, and within weeks he infuriated the entire company. The actors seethed with anger and talked of rebellion, but they were helpless. If they refused to act, they were fined or dismissed, and Drury Lane was the only theater in London.

The young Cibbers were among the least secure, for Katharine was now pregnant with their first child, and Colley, if not at the very bottom of the theatrical hierarchy, was very near it. With no promise he would be hired next year, he had to seize every chance to prove himself. When Kynaston was suddenly taken ill the day before a command performance of *The Double Dealer* and Congreve unexpectedly suggested him as a replacement, Cibber was ready. From his habit of constantly observing rehearsals and performances, he knew the stage business well, and he memorized the lines before he slept that night. The next day, his imitation of Kynaston was so impressive that Congreve persuaded Rich to raise his salary.[48]

It was only a small step upward, and it was soon tempered by the death of a newborn daughter.[49] They could not afford to indulge in a lengthy mourning; Katharine, who was singing at Drury Lane this year, was back at work a month later. Colley acted in two new plays before summer, but he received no further recognition, and when the 1694-95 season began, his rank in the company was unchanged.[50] It was a bitter realization for a young man good enough to replace Kynaston.

Others became bitter, too. As the holder of a patent, Rich was responsible only to the Crown. Eager for profit, he acted ruthlessly, taking 20 percent of the box office receipts and all of the after-money for himself. He paid salaries irregularly, exacted fines which had long been overlooked, and tricked actors into agreements soon broken without compunction.[51] When Betterton and Elizabeth Barry, their star tragedienne, protested on behalf of the others, Rich offered their choicest roles to George Powell and Anne Bracegirdle. The latter, a good friend of Mrs. Barry, refused and became one of Rich's "enemies," but Powell fancied himself Betterton's equal and had no such scruples. The talk of rebellion became open; Betterton gathered the veteran actors, and together they filed such a list of complaints with the lord chamberlain that he called a meeting of the patentees and the players.[52] On 17 December, the actors presented their grievances as Rich, representing the patentees, dodged, denied, and countercharged. The meeting ended in a deadlock that was still unbroken two weeks later when the death of Queen Mary officially closed the theater until Easter.

While Betterton and his cohorts sought permission to establish a separate company, the lesser lights did whatever they could to survive. A fortunate few had other trades, but the Cibbers faced a dismal winter made bleaker by the death of a second child.[53] Colley's small annuity was not enough to support them, and his grammar school education had not prepared him for a trade. It had made him literate, however, and when elegiac poems on Queen Mary began to appear, he tried his hand at writing. He dedicated *An Ode on the Death of our Late Sovereign Lady Queen Mary* to his father's former patron, the newly created duke of Devonshire, and published it in June. It was not a very good poem, but it was no worse than most, and it brought sorely needed cash. It served another purpose as well, for it turned his mind toward writing, and it may have been about this time that he first thought of creating a play with a part for himself.

Meanwhile, Dorset granted Betterton's company a license to perform at the old Tennis Court in Lincoln's Inn Fields. It was a blow to Rich, for with the exception of George Powell, Joseph Williams, and Susannah Verbruggen (formerly Mountfort), Betterton had all the best actors in London.[54] Furthermore, he had Congreve's new comedy, *Love for Love*, for his opening, along with the playwright's promise to supply an additional work each year.

Either because he was not invited or because he did not have the capital to buy a share in the dissidents' company, Cibber remained at Drury Lane. The situation had some advantages; his salary was raised, and more important, he had fewer rivals for parts. There were, however, distinct disadvantages. Rich's power was now absolute, and he put Powell in charge of the productions. Cibber could deal with Rich's deviousness, but he could not overcome Powell's contempt.

Rich was eager to reopen Drury Lane before Betterton could get his company underway. At Powell's suggestion, they chose Aphra Behn's old melodrama, *Abdelazar*, and began rehearsals at once. Too quickly, perhaps, for in the last week they discovered that a new prologue was urgently needed. Of several offered, none seemed right for the occasion until Cibber, sensing an opportunity, wrote an acceptable one. Modestly, he asked no payment on condition that he be allowed to speak it, but when Powell sneered that it "would be as bad as having no prologue at all!" he demanded two guineas, which he pocketed with a sigh. The pain went even deeper when he heard the applause and "reflected that the same Praise might have been given to my own speaking" (I, 196).

Powell was certain he could attract audiences, but he misjudged his own popularity and the strength of the company, as he soon learned when *Love for Love* opened to "extraordinary Success." Drury Lane's nearly empty houses were disheartening; Powell's drinking and arrogance increased, rehearsals became intermittent, and discipline utterly vanished.

On a Saturday in May, when Betterton's playbills announced *The Old Batchelor* for the following Monday and *Hamlet* on Tuesday, Powell decided to challenge the new company by giving his own *Hamlet* on Monday. Lincoln's Inn Fields, however, reversed the order Monday morning, panicking Drury Lane's company. Someone suggested that Drury Lane give *The Old Batchelor*. Powell seized on the plan. It would be a wonderful joke, he thought, and he would imitate Betterton down to his gouty limp. The decision was hasty and ill-considered. Drury Lane did not even have copies of the script, and not until the books arrived did they discover there was no one for Dogget's role, Alderman Fondlewife. Someone knew how much Cibber had yearned for the role and suggested him. Powell was reluctant but so determined to have his own fun that he finally gave in with a sour, "If the Fool has a mind to blow himself up, let us e'en give him a clear Stage for it" (I, 207).

Colley, coming tardily to the theater, found the rest of the company already studying their parts. He had studied Dogget's every nuance, every gesture, and after scanning the lines briefly, he went through the afternoon rehearsal with an ease that startled the doubters. At the performance, Powell imitated Betterton with some success, but the company as a whole was not prepared, and Cibber's polished portrayal stood out in relief. He had carefully applied a makeup that added forty years to his age, and his simulation of Dogget's walk, gestures, and intonations first surprised, then delighted, the audience. He finished the scene to a burst of applause that rose and fell three times over, and he savored it. As an actor, he needed approval as he needed air to breathe, not merely that of friends and colleagues but the vital approval of the audience with whom he shared the special moment of creation.

Cibber imagined that the triple round of plaudits proved his worth beyond all doubt, but when he tried to build on it, he was again turned back. He volunteered for all kinds of parts; Powell said they were not in his line. Quoting Betterton, he answered crisply that "any thing naturally written ought to be in every one's Way that pretended to be an Actor" (I, 209), but Powell either sneered or ignored him. After six long years, Cibber had made almost no progress toward the heights, and he began to visualize a lifetime of unremarked and unremarkable roles. He responded with a pretended lack of interest in the company, became careless with his lines, and fell back on hackneyed tricks until he was in danger of dismissal. By the end of the season, the problem was critical, and Katharine was pregnant for the third time.

The only way Cibber could break through the barrier was to write a play for himself. It was not an unprecedented idea. Betterton, Mountfort, even Powell, had written plays tailored to their special talents.[55] Cibber had more education than any of them and more practical experience on the stage than professional writers like Southerne or Congreve, and that summer he set to work with the same determination that had made his Fondlewife so memorable.

Cibber needed a special kind of character, a role that would display his unique comic gifts and not be automatically assigned to anyone else. In spite of his claims of versatility, he knew he was an unlikely romantic leading man. His talent lay in comedy—not the low comedy of Will Pinkethman, at his best in wildly physical farce—but the kind that demanded skillful inflection and precise timing of lines. He found the perfect role in a slight exaggeration of his own public mask. He *was* something of a dandy (although he knew to a fraction of a millimeter the unstated line that divided the beau from the fop), and he didn't mind making that image the butt of laughter. He had learned it was the quickest way to amuse without offending.

The brilliantly idiotic Sir Novelty Fashion owes much to Shakespeare's Le Beau, Etherege's Sir Fopling Flutter, and Crowne's Sir Courtly Nice, but he is nonetheless original. Earlier fops had been froth floating on the periphery of the main action, vain, self-centered fools whose sole redeeming feature was their capacity to serve as butts of ridicule. Sir Novelty, however, is closely knit into the main fabric of the play and, while he has the usual vanity and concentration on clothing, he has one quality his forebears lacked, a good heart. He relinquishes the desirable heroine with exceedingly good grace and rids himself of a troublesome mistress by endowing her with a generous three hundred pounds a year and giving her a handsome captain for a new lover.

Cibber called his play *Love's Last Shift; or, The Fool in Fashion.* The main story concerns the adventures and reconciliation of a young married couple, Loveless and Amanda. Ten years previously, Loveless, unready for the responsibilities of marriage, abandoned his beautiful and virtuous wife in favor of a long, fruitless search for pleasure on the Continent. When the play opens, he has returned to England exhausted, disillusioned, and penniless. Amanda, who still loves him and has remained true to him, wants him back. With the assistance of Young Worthy, she arranges an assignation with Loveless, who mistakes her for a prostitute. They spend the night together, and in the morning she reveals her identity. Recognizing her worth at last, Loveless repents, explaining:

> 'Twas heedless Fancy first that made me stray,
> But Reason breaks forth and lights me on my way.

Now ready to accept the reasonable state of matrimony, the love story ends happily as the pair are reunited.

The subplot, the Worthy brothers' pursuit of the coquettes, Hillaria and

Narcissa, is closely tied to the main line. Their story has the familiar Restoration trappings of elegant young rakes wooing beautiful women and the love chase frequently obstructed by an irascible and ridiculous father or by Sir Novelty, who is also courting Amanda.

Cibber said later the play "introduced a new Style of Acting" (I, 301). In truth, it was a new style of drama for the time. Although, as Maureen Sullivan has pointed out, it is within the romance tradition, its theme and tone marked a sharp departure from the Restoration pattern.[56] The central love theme deals directly with life after marriage, and the tone, although ironic, lacks the sharp satire of the earlier wits. Cibber, the actor, wanted to please his patrons, not provoke them.

The irony is light but all-pervasive. The subtitle suggests Sir Novelty is the fool, but in practice he is no more foolish than the Worthy brothers, who pursue empty-headed coquettes, or Loveless, who wastes ten years of his life in a vain search for a love he already possesses. Fashionable life, love games before and after marriage, and the emphasis on decorum at the expense of truth are gently mocked. Cibber's lines, understood and applauded in his own time, have been regarded as slyly hypocritical by later generations, who missed the point of the irony, but his tongue remained firmly in his cheek as he teased the pit in the epilogue:

> An Honest Rake forego the Joys of Life!
> His Whores, and Wine! t'Embrace a dull Cast Wife;
> Such out of fashion stuff! But then agen,
> He's Lewd for above four Acts, Gentlemen![57]

The single element untouched by irony is married love. His own marriage was happy, and he found nothing ridiculous in the state. For him it was not the last refuge of an impoverished rake, the inevitable result of a spent courtship, or the enchainment of two free souls, but the proper culmination of love. When Loveless recognizes this, he is ready to reform,[58] and in the winter of 1696, the "honest tears, shed by the audience at this interview, conveyed a strong reproach to our licentious poets, and was to Cibber the highest mark of honour."[59] With it, he ushered in the age of the sentimental, in which emotion replaced wit as the governing factor in stage comedy. His characters were charming and vulnerable; unlike their Restoration forebears, they fell in love openly, without reservation, and what they lost of the audience's admiration they gained in its affection.

As much as anything Cibber ever wrote, *Love's Last Shift* reveals its origin in an actor's brain, and much of the substance not apparent to the reader is clear in the theater. The structure is sound, every element contributing to the whole. The story is told through situation, and the succession of scenes is richly varied in tempo, tone, and type. Cibber relies heavily on audio and visual effects. Music throughout serves to link scenes or provide atmosphere, and the masque at the end explicitly demonstrates his theme. Costume defines character: Sir Novelty's exaggerated clothing makes him ridiculous from the beginning; Loveless is a rogue in rags, a gentleman when well dressed in act 5. True to the actor's approach, Cibber's dialogue is subservient to the action.[60] Language, the very essence of the work to the literary critic, is only one of the tools in the theater, where the lines are spoken once in the brief "two hour traffic," where actors are only too likely to forget, ad lib, or change speeches. Cibber knew intuitively that the totality of a scene was more important than any single element, and if his words, as Congreve noted, are only "like Wit" (I, 220) but not witty, they nonetheless serve the first principles of the theater: they are easily understood, and they further the action. He trusted his players to make them sparkle.

Never for a moment does Cibber forget he is writing for actors. From the lightly sketched stock figures in the subplot to the more fully drawn central figures, his characters depend on actors' interpretations to give them reality. It is here, perhaps, that he has suffered most from critics who base their opinions solely on the printed page.[61] The clearest example is the scene in which Loveless, after a decade of dissolute living, realizes he loves his wife after all and swears eternal fidelity in the future. Post-Freudian critics universally take exception to this and regard his "regeneration" as psychologically invalid. Yet Cibber is obviously practicing long-established theatrical principles and exploiting the conditions of performance. First, he takes full advantage of the onrush of time that precludes the careful analysis and reflection of a reader, knowing the audience responds to the moment. Second, he is aware the audience *wants* the love story to end happily. Critics have spent much time analyzing Loveless in the first four acts, but they have paid little attention to Amanda. During that time, sympathy for her builds up considerably, and whatever the cost, the audience wants her happiness. Loveless's conversion is the answer, and probable or not, it is the anticipated and desired climax to the action. Here the actor's interpretation is crucial, for only he can prepare the viewer for his about-face. Cibber has given several clues: significantly, Loveless returns to London only after hearing Amanda is dead, revealing a definite, if rudimentary, conscience; he speaks gently of her to Young Worthy, "Why, faith! she was a Good-natur'd Fool, that's the truth on't: Well! rest her soul" (I, i, 83-84). He is strongly attracted to her at the assignation, and by the time he enters "in new Cloaths," we should be ready to believe in his change. The third principle is pure theater. The play ends like a fairy tale, with the hero and heroine living happily ever after. This wished-for conclusion, however achieved, is essential to the comedy. What happens after that is neither Cibber's nor our concern. The curtain has fallen.

Cibber worked on the play through the summer of 1695, and when it was finished, he knew it was good. He also knew better than to present it unheralded. He showed it to influential friends, to the lord chamberlain, Dorset, and to Thomas Southerne, and they approved it heartily. Southerne himself gave it to Rich, and late in November, Cibber read the script before his assembled colleagues with all the comic inflections he could muster. They liked it, except for Powell, who gave Verbruggen the leading role and took no part for himself. Rehearsals began at once, and if Cibber believed in omens, he might have seen a promising one early in December, when Katharine gave birth to a daughter, Catherine, their first child to live.[62]

Verbruggen was ideal for the rough profligate in *Love's Last Shift*, a perfect contrast to the virginally beautiful Jane Rogers, who played his wife, Amanda. The rest of the cast was excellent: Susannah Verbruggen was dazzling as the frivolous Narcissa, and Katharine Cibber was her charming and giddy companion, Hillaria, while the low comedians were played by William Bullock and Will Pinkethman, both of whom would eventually become comic stars in their own right. They were energetic youngsters acting in an energetic young play, and their enthusiasm was infectious.

But it was Colley Cibber who astonished and delighted. His peacock Sir Novelty, gravely spreading his foolish feathers in wholehearted foppery, caught everyone's fancy, and from the moment he entered, it was evident he would carry the day. Even the fops in the pit laughed and applauded uproariously, seeing not their own but each other's vanity. For Cibber himself it was more than a satisfaction, it was a vindication; his ambitions, his hopes, his dreams, had come true. After seven years of struggle and disappointment, his first play had installed him as a high priest of comedy.

TWO

Journeyman to Master

Love's Last Shift was "the Philosopher's Stone" that transmuted the age into gold. On the third night, Cibber had the usual "author's benefit," for which he received all receipts over the house expenses. His benefit night was crowded with the fashionable, and Drury Lane enjoyed full houses for some time. His parents could see that his faith in himself had been justified, for Caius Gabriel was now permanently in London, and the Shores' animosity (if, indeed, there had been any) was forgotten in the celebration of his triumph.[1]

And it was a triumph. Cibber was recognized in the coffeehouses and on the streets. He dined with Caius Gabriel's former patron, the duke of Dorset and savored his remark "that for a young Fellow to show himself such an Actor and Writer in one Day, was something extraordinary" (I, 214). At Skipwith's table, he traded stories of Grantham and met Cardell Goodman again. Goodman no doubt recalled his prophecy that Colley would make a good actor, although his vatic skill did not reveal his own arrest for treason.[2]

Cibber reveled in the unaccustomed praise, forgetting that an obvious relish of success breeds enemies. John Dennis bitterly remarked that *Love's Last Shift* was plagiarized, that Colley had neither the experience nor, he implied, the intelligence to write it.[3] Cibber had not forgotten how to deal with animosity. He maintained his mask of indifference, dropping it only briefly for the dedication in the printed edition of *Love's Last Shift*, where he assured Richard Norton that "the Fable is intirely my own; nor is there a Line or Thought, throughout the Whole, for which I am wittingly oblig'd either to the Dead, or Living."[4]

The golden age was quickly over. In *The Lost Lover*, written by Skipwith's mistress, Delariviere Manley, he was relegated to the part of Smyrna, an old "Turkey-merchant" reminiscent of Wycherley's Pinchwife, while Powell, who almost always played romantic leads, took the fop role for himself. Both the play and Powell failed, as did a string of others, and their tribulations were compounded by the death of young Hildebrand Horden who had seemed another Mountfort.[5] The company was plunged in gloom, audiences diminished, Rich again paid salaries irregularly, and the season ended on a grim note.

Powell's steadfast hostility stopped Colley, who had known too much frustration as an acolyte to bear it easily now. During the summer of 1696, with a proven success behind him and an idea for a new comedy in his head, he joined Betterton's company.[6] The transfer of allegiance was brief and unofficial. Betterton was considerate of his actors and tried to manage democratically, but when everyone had a voice, no one was satisfied, and in the resulting chaos, debts rose as salaries fell. Cibber's new play was less than half finished when, realizing he was worse off at Lincoln's Inn Fields than at Drury Lane, he returned to home ground.

The prodigal was welcomed with a splendid character created just for him, Lord Foppington, in *The Relapse* by John Vanbrugh. The young soldier-architect-courtier had been so amused by *Love's Last Shift* that he had written a sequel, picking up the story six months later. He kept the same relationships, sharpened the wit, ennobled Sir Novelty into Lord Foppington and gave Loveless a spectacular fall from grace with Amanda's cousin. Vanbrugh insisted Cibber play the fop, and Powell, given the straight role of Elder Worthy, was furious; on the first night he dipped so deeply into his favorite Nantes brandy that his passion in the love scenes led Vanbrugh to claim in his preface he once "gave Amanda up for gone."

Cibber's Lord Foppington was a masterful contrast, the essence of polished imbecility. From Mountfort's Sir Courtly Nice, he borrowed the business of preening himself before a large looking glass in the first scene, but it was entirely his own idea to have his huge elaborate wig carried on in a sedan chair, an entrance that stopped the show. Splendidly vain, he strutted and posed, drawling lines in an elegant "Court tune," that slightly nasalized singsong with its long open vowels: "I rise, madam, about ten a'clock. I don't rise sooner, because 'tis the worst thing in the world for the complexion; nat that I pretend to be a beau, but a man must endeavour to look wholesome, least he made so nauseous a figure in the side bax, the ladies should be compelled to turn their eyes upon the play."[7]

Lord Foppington is a harsher and less lovable character than Sir Novelty, and the distinction between the two portraits defines two perceptions of Cibber's public personality. Sir Novelty is silly and vain, but his pretense to good taste stems from ignorance rather than hypocrisy, and his preoccupation with trivialities covers a good heart. Lord Foppington, however, is essentially vicious. He has all of Sir Novelty's flaws without the central redeeming virtue; vanity becomes pride, pretense is hypocrisy, and greed outweighs morality. Cibber saw himself as a more intelligent Sir Novelty, his shrewd judgment and pulsing ambition well concealed beneath the frothy wig and beautifully cut waistcoat, but fundamentally a good man, too pleased with his own lot to envy others. His friends accepted the picture, but those less well disposed viewed him as a Foppington and assigned the basest motive to his every act.

At the moment, gratified by popular acclaim, Cibber could afford to dismiss his enemies as incidental to a success that encompassed his family as well. His father had designed a Danish church in Wellclose Square, and it was dedicated on 15 November;[8] *Love's Last Shift* went into its second edition, and Katharine was again expecting a child. Cibber worked on his second play with every assurance it would add to his laurels.

Meanwhile, Vanbrugh's second comedy, *Aesop*, opened with Cibber in the title role, and its popularity at once assured it a place in the repertory.[9] The grotesque, satiric, and genuinely clever Aesop, the very antithesis of the highly wrought fop, is a remarkably complex character, sometimes seeming a fool, at other times showing an unorthodox wisdom. The character dominates the action, and in it, Cibber proved he was much more than a mere Foppington.

It is not surprising that Rich now regarded Cibber as a young miracle worker whose touch made any play succeed, and he welcomed Cibber's finished comedy with a generous contract.[10] But *Woman's Wit; or, The Lady in Fashion* is a huddled conglomeration of Carlisle's *The Fortune Hunters*, Otway's *Dare Devils*, and Mountfort's *Greenwich Park* and is chiefly noteworthy as evidence of Cibber's voracious play reading. Originally designed for Betterton's company, the revision for the less experienced Drury Lane players did not work, and the play shows evidence of his haste in the weakness of its structure.

The main plot is a battle of wits as Longville (played by Cibber) attempts to extricate his friend Lovemore from the clutches of the coquette, Leonora. Man's mind, however, is no match for a woman's cleverness, and she outwits him every time. When he pretends to make love to her as the concealed Lovemore listens, she responds, but confronted by her lover, she turns the situation to her advantage. Furious at the trick, she revenges herself by convincing Longville's fiancée he is false to her. She very nearly succeeds, but she loses the war, and when the truth is known, virtue triumphs.

This part of the story fills only three acts, and the subplot, which supplies the other two acts, is not integral to the whole. The subplot is Cibber's own, and he said he added it to give Dogget a good comic role as the "Disobedient School-Boy," Master Johnny, a curious ancestor of Goldsmith's Tony Lumpkin.[11] He is clearly aware of the play's weakness, for in the preface he confessed that, had it been performed at Lincoln's Inn Fields, he would have "proposed some Scenes more of a Piece with the former Acts."[12] A loose connection is made through Leonora's mother, Lady Manlove, Major Rakish, and his son, Jack, all of whom appear peripherally in the main story, but the central character is completely unrelated. All four characters lie, cheat, and deceive through a series of farcical scenes that have nothing to do with the Longville action.

In spite of its weaknesses, the play has some interesting elements. Deception and the consequent unmasking are used effectively; all the characters dissemble at one time or another—the good for moral ends, the bad for selfish reasons. The revelations are dramatic: Master Johnny's tutor is discovered to be a Jesuit priest,[13] and Leonora is unmasked before all the main characters. Cibber deplores the pretense of "fashion" as practiced by the Manloves and Rakishes, and the bad blood of the parents persists in their offspring. Leonora detests men and uses her wit to lead them on while privately saying, "Marriage is a mere Cessation of Arms;" she is pleased with the duels fought over her, "for both the Victor and the Victim were *Leonora's* still" (II, i).

Cibber considers her views immoral, but he does not explore the implications nor does he pursue the morality of the deception pattern. The greatest weakness of the play, however, lies in his sacrifice of substance for the sake of a momentary effect. He cannot overcome the temptation of the theatrical moment; he strains credulity with what may be the first onstage pistol duel: Lovemore shoots and ostensibly kills Longville, but his instant and abject remorse ends when Longville sits up and says the pistol wasn't loaded. It is an outrageous trick, and it gains a laugh at the expense of credibility even in the playhouse.

This time the glittering prize escaped him. If he did have a third night, it probably did not pay the house charges, but it was not a total loss, for he published the play. The preface is in striking contrast to the usual author's commentary on a failed work, complaining about poor management, the inadequacy of the cast, or the inclement political weather. Cibber humbly took full responsibility for the disaster: "I am so far from that vanity of thinking my self considerable enough to have received any Prejudice from my Enemies, that I am ready to acknowledge 'twas want of Merit in the Play, not understanding in its Audience, that made it meet with no kinder Reception." He pretended the failure didn't matter, but he was stung by it. Twenty-five years later, when he collected his works, he allowed *Woman's Wit* to rest quietly in its grave, and twenty years after that, he did not even name it in the *Apology*.

The remainder of the season went poorly. In January, Verbruggen went over to Betterton, Rich played games with salaries (Cibber says he once went six weeks without seeing a penny), Powell was constantly drunk, and to add to the company's misery, Dorset resigned as lord chamberlain. He was succeeded by the brilliant, disagreeable earl of Sunderland, who made everyone uneasy with his stated determination to moralize the stage.

Cibber's private life was no better. In May, a newborn son died, and sometime during the year Cibber's mother died as well.[14] She was buried in the Wellclose Square churchyard, and Caius Gabriel carved a monument to her memory.[15] Thirteen-year-old Lewis was sent to live with a relative, Samuel Adams of Wolverton, while Caius Gabriel completed a statue of William of Wykeham for Winchester College, where Lewis was enrolled in October.[16]

There was more to come. In late July, Cibber was arrested when Jane Lucas, who had played Amanda's maid in *Love's Last Shift*, charged him with assault. He wrote at once to Sunderland:

> That your Petitioner was on the 16th instant without any leave from your Lord-ship arrested at the suit of Jane Lucas and carried to the prison of the Gate-house where he now remains a Prisoner at her suit.
>
> That your Petitioner having always & still being willing to submit to such Or-der as your Lordship shall think fitt to give, and att the same time (as far as in him lyes) to justify the Priviledge of his Majesties Servants.
>
> Your Petitioner therefore humbly prays that the said Mrs Lucas and her Attor-ney may be brought before your Lordship to answer their Contempt and show cause why they refuse to discharge your Petitioner from Prison.[17]

He was ordered to appear at the next Westminster Sessions in August, but the case never actually came to court, and the charges were probably dropped. It is not likely there was much substance to them, for Cibber was an unusual man of his time. His marriage was clearly a happy one, and there is no evidence that he ever kept a mistress. Certainly his enemies would have made much of such matters, but the assault case is mentioned by no one, and Mrs. Lucas herself continued to play minor roles in the Drury Lane company until 1702.[18]

As the 1697-98 season opened, Sunderland made the weight of his office felt by enforcing the rule that every new play be reviewed by his office, to eliminate "all scurrilous sentiments and profanity." In December, to the actors' relief, he resigned, but their easement was short-lived, for his re-placement was the even harsher earl of Shrewsbury, appointed, fittingly enough, during one of the coldest winters London had ever known. The Thames was frozen solid for three weeks, and the icy chill kept audiences away from the theater as the new lord chamberlain opened an intense cam-paign to clean up theatrical morals. When he began to enforce edicts dredged up from the time of James I, Cibber must have congratulated him-self that Devonshire's efforts long ago had not landed him a post in Shrews-bury's service.

The lord chamberlain's campaign reflected a concern for public decency that had been growing under the sober reign of William III, a concern Cibber himself may have sensed when writing *Love's Last Shift*. The Society for the Reformation of Manners, initiated in 1692, had called for reform, and now, six years later, its views were substantially reinforced by Jeremy Collier's *A Short View of the Immorality and Profaneness of the English Stage.* Collier was a nonjuring clergyman who disliked the theater, and he marshaled a formidable array of carefully selected authorities from the Greeks to Shakespeare for his attack. Asserting that "the business of Plays is to recommend Virtue, and discountenance Vice," he charged that modern playwrights did just the opposite and cited long lists of examples from almost every work in the repertory. *Love's Last Shift* was exempt, but *The Relapse* was severely censured. Oddly enough, Collier defended the one character nearest vice, Lord Foppington: "'Tis true he was formal and Fantastick, Smitten with Dress, and Equipage, and it may be vapour'd by his Perfumes; But his Behaviour is far from that of an Idiot!"[19] Possibly his criticism was softened by Cibber's portrayal.

His words did not, as he no doubt wished, close the theaters, but they had an immediate and visible effect as a paper war began, with the playwrights issuing blasts in defense and Collier's supporters shooting back. Nevertheless, the stage suffered, for not one of the eight new plays that season was a success, and concerts replaced dramas with alarming frequency. The courts agreed with Collier and publicly chastised the playhouses as "nurseries of debauchery and blasphemy," a charge that seemed somehow justified when Ralph Davenant, the Drury Lane treasurer, was murdered on his way home from the theater.[20] Powell was suspended for wounding a "gentleman" in a tavern quarrel, and when Rich, desperate for an audience, let him perform, Drury Lane was summarily closed for a day while the House of Lords debated about forbidding actors to wear swords.

The Cibbers' daily life was so closely intertwined with that of the theater that every event affecting it affected them directly. They had their own troubles as well; in March, a second son scarcely lived long enough to be christened.[21] A saddened Colley slogged on through the dreary season, and when it was over, he spent the long summer vacation working on a new play, *Xerxes*, a tragedy in keeping with the prevailing mood.

The impact of Collier is clear in Cibber's prologue, where he agrees comedy has not reformed the town, and he claims a moral purpose for his work:

> Warn'd by the dangers painted, wou'd you learn
> To shun abroad what's here the wise man's scorn.[23]

But he did not like Collier's antitheater views, and he could not resist at least one jab at him:

Girls may read him, not for the Truth he says,
But to be pointed to the Bawdy plays.[23]

Xerxes, a villain of unrelieved wickedness, is determined to possess Arta-banus's wife, the virtuous Tamira. In his pursuit, he robs, rapes, and murders until even his most loyal followers repudiate him. The conclusion is a melodramatic bloodbath that leaves the stage littered with bodies.

Cibber may have appreciated tragedy, but he was unable to create it. He imposes stage tricks: in act 1, the stage darkens for "A Shower of Falling Lightning"; in act 2, he interpolates a masque; in act 4, magicians cause a ghost to appear, but none of these moments rises from the action. He exaggerates evil into grotesquerie; Xerxes rejoices in his villainy and tortures Tamira physically and mentally, his lust for her fanned by her immovable virtue. The blank verse is flat, the "noble sentiments" are platitudes, and Tamira's dying words sound like a motto from a sampler:

Yet to our Woes, the Gods this Comfort give;
From those that die, the Living learn to live.[24]

The climax has nothing of tragic inevitability but is brought about by a series of coincidences that destroy vice and virtue alike. Cibber's metier, whether he perceived it or not, was comedy. He firmly believed that sooner or later things had to work out happily, and when he spoke otherwise, his words rang false.

Cibber may have offered *Xerxes* first to Rich, as his contract for *Woman's Wit* required, but it was produced at Lincoln's Inn Fields in February 1699, with Betterton himself as Artabanus and the great tragedienne Elizabeth Barry as Tamira. Even their talents could not bring the play to life, and possibly it played only once.[25] He published it in April 1699, dedicating it to Samuel Adams with the wish that he "had a more effectual way" of thanking him for his care of Lewis, and never mentioned it in public again.[26]

However bleak the times, the magic of the theater never failed the young actor-playwright, and in spite of disappointed hopes, personal losses, and sorrows, the moment Cibber stepped on the stage, his face glowed with a good humor that seemed to permeate his very being. And, indeed, the theater was his solace and his retreat. Behind the facade of a Foppington, he could escape for a few hours into a world where everything was sure to end well. It was, perhaps, this certainty in his make-believe world that led him, after two resounding failures, to begin another play in the summer of 1699. It may also, of course, have stemmed from a desire for security in his tumultuous "real" world. Between the lord chamberlain's harassment and backstage politics, Cibber's professional life was not going well. He needed a good leading role.

Since comedies were out of fashion, Cibber worked on another tragedy through the summer and into the fall. It was painfully obvious he could never play a traditional tragic hero, but a villain with a touch of the grotesque might be within his range. As he had created a type for himself in comedy, so now he must create a tragic figure that would fit him. He found his inspiration in what was then one of Shakespeare's least popular plays, *Richard III*; he may have seen Sandford play the title role in the 1692-93 season, but it had not been performed since. Richard was a character he could tailor to his own style, since "where there is so much close meditated Mischief, Deceit, Pride, Insolence, or Cruelty, they cannot have the least Cast or Profer of the Amiable in them; consequently, there can be no great Demand for that harmonious Sound, or pleasing round Melody of Voice. . . . So that, again, my want of that requisite Voice might less disqualify me for the vicious than the virtuous Character" (I, 222-23). His approach was characteristically pragmatic. The deep-dyed villainy of Richard lent itself to his kind of exaggeration, the ironic speeches were ideal for the sort of comic inflection he had heard Kynaston use in serious roles, and if his habitual "court tune" led him to cry, "A harse! A harse! My kingdom for a harse!" it was at least consistent with the aristocratic accent as he knew it.

Although the role suited Cibber, the play was diffuse and heavy with historical allusion. He simplified it considerably, beginning the action just before the battle of Tewkesbury. He cut Shakespeare's 3,620 lines to 2,170, (1,102 of which were his own), eliminated several scenes and twenty-four characters, added bits of *Henry VI*, *Richard II*, *Henry IV (Part 2)*, and *Henry V* to structure the action tightly about the central figure of Richard.[27]

Cibber's adaptation was less audacious than some critics have claimed, for bardolators had not yet canonized the Swan of Avon, and throughout the Restoration and eighteenth century his plays were routinely altered to suit contemporary taste.[28] If Cibber's characters suffered from oversimplification and much of Shakespeare's subtle delineation was lost along with the poetry, his version is still wonderfully playable, and it held the stage for 150 years, the vehicle for every major actor from Garrick to Edwin Booth. Several attempts to present the original were made in the early nineteenth century, but it did not return to the stage until William Poel's production inspired Irving to mount it in 1887. Even today, parts of Cibber's work are often included in productions of the work, the most noteworthy being the Olivier film of 1955.[29]

It was nearly finished when the season began again, and his hopes for it should have been reinforced when Cibber's second daughter, Anne, was born and lived—after all, her sister, Catherine, had been born just before *Love's Last Shift*.[30] Another hopeful note sounded when Horden's replacement, tall, handsome Robert Wilks, arrived. Cibber knew him already, for the Irish actor had been at Drury Lane briefly in the 1692-93 season when he, too, had been only a raw beginner. His stay in London had been brief, and he had soon gone back to Dublin where he had more opportunity for leading roles.[31] Now, after years of tutelage by the legendary John Ashbury, he returned as a highly skilled artist.

Sensing a rival, Powell was suspicious of Wilks, but he pretended generosity and offered him a choice of Mountfort's roles which he had appropriated. Wilks diplomatically chose one of the few Dryden plays in which Mountfort had not acted and made his debut as Palamede in *Marriage a la Mode*. His Irish charm captivated the audience, and Cibber saw that Rich had made a wise choice in bringing Wilks into the company. Powell, on the other hand, soon realized how formidable was his competitor. Wilks was not only gifted but extremely diligent. He never missed a rehearsal, never came drunk, and he knew his lines (as well as everyone else's) perfectly. He infused a spirit of vitality into the company, and when he appeared as Sir Harry Wildair in the premiere of George Farquhar's *The Constant Couple*, he became the toast of the town.

When rehearsals for *Richard III* began, Powell was cast as Buckingham, giving Cibber an extra relish for the words "Off with his head—so much for Buckingham!" Literary critics regularly cite the line as a sin against Shakespeare, but actors as regularly include it for its theatrical effect. Wilks would have made a graceful and elegant Henry VI, had not Charles Killigrew, master of the Revels, cut out the entire first act—all of Wilks's part and, ironically, almost pure Shakespeare. Cibber pleaded for even a few expository lines, but for once in his life, his persuasive powers failed. With Shrewsbury's backing, Killigrew stood firm on the grounds that "*Henry* the Sixth being a Character Unfortunate and Pitied, wou'd put the Audience in Mind of the late King James" (I, 276). In December, the decapitated play had its premiere with four acts rough-hewn into five. To give the audience full measure, Cibber added the scene in which the young Princes were murdered,[32] but the damage had been done, and his third night brought him less than five pounds.

Hoping for more than the meager profits of his author's night, Cibber published the play, dedicating it to Henry Brett "for the many handsom [*sic*] Obligations you have laid on me." Cibber and Brett had been close friends since the night Brett had come backstage after a performance of *Love's Last Shift* and, proclaiming his "sincere passion" for Sir Novelty's extravagant wig, offered to buy it. Cibber was charmed, and a lifelong friendship began. The two young men shared an appreciation for the amusements of London and were frequent companions at the coffeehouses, the taverns, and the gambling clubs.[33] The dedication made a graceful reference to Brett's pursuit of Anne, the recently divorced countess of Macclesfield, for Cibber had a personal interest in their courtship.[34] One evening, when Brett stopped by the theater just before a performance of *Greenwich Park*, Colley teased him for not spending the time with his countess, and Brett replied that his only shirt was too filthy for a social call. At once Cibber led him to his dressing room where, stripping off his own immaculate linen, he insisted Brett wear it, for their roles were "not of equal consequence" that day (II, 45). Not long after, Brett married the countess. Cibber laughingly took credit and was rewarded with a standing invitation to their home in Gloucestershire, where he was their houseguest for the next few summers.

The failure of *Richard III* receded into the background when Vanbrugh brought the company *The Pilgrim*, which he and Dryden had altered from Fletcher's play. They offered Cibber his choice of parts. Neither the title role nor the villain was suitable, and he chose two small but showy roles, the Stuttering Cook and the Mad Englishman.[35] Vanbrugh, loath to waste such a popular player, also gave him the epilogue to speak, and Dryden, hearing him deliver it at rehearsal, insisted that Colley speak the prologue as well. Pleased as he was, Cibber quickly discovered that Wilks's admirable diligence was matched by a fiery temperament, for Wilks dearly loved the solo prologues and complained that it was "an Affront to all the rest of the Company, that there should be but one out of the Whole judg'd fit to speak either a Prologue or an Epilogue!" (I, 27). In a confrontation destined to become familiar, Cibber sought to pacify him with the offer of either or both, but Wilks refused to listen.

Fortunately, his anger, however intensely expressed, passed quickly, and *The Pilgrim* was a great success. It was soon shadowed, however, by the death of Dryden. The theaters closed on the day of his funeral, and all the actors walked in the procession to Westminster Abbey. About the same time, the Cibbers suffered a more personal loss when Katharine's father, Matthias, died after a short illness.[36] A few months later, Caius Gabriel also succumbed, leaving his sons only a respected name, an affectionate memory, and a few personal articles.[37]

During the long vacation, Cibber probably took his wife and two little girls to visit the Bretts at Sandywell Park. The quiet countryside and fresh Gloucestershire air were beneficial to Katharine, who suffered from asthma, and Colley took advantage of the long pleasant days to work on a new play. The Bretts were excellent hosts and provided a friendly audience for the finished scenes, making perceptive suggestions for improvement and enthusiastic prophecies of success.

This idyllic retreat was scarcely touched by news from London, but one event that was to have far-reaching consequences must have been reported. The duke of Gloucester, Princess Anne's only son, died on 29 July 1701, one week after his eleventh birthday, and his death marked the end of hopes for a continued Stuart line. The Whigs began looking toward

Hanover where the Electress Sophia, granddaughter of James I, had produced an heir with all the necessary qualifications: male, legitimate, and Protestant. The Tories, the Catholics, and the Scots were less enthusiastic about a foreign sovereign, and some wondered openly if the country would not be better served by James II's son, now growing up on the Continent. The question was not crucial at the moment, since William III was very much alive and could still ensure the present line with a child of his own, but the division of sympathies that began now would not be ended until the bloody battle of Culloden half a century later. Like his friend Brett, who was about to enter Parliament, Cibber was a strong Whig, and his politics would play an increasing part in the direction of his career.

Cibber enjoyed the country retreats, but he loved the city with all its noise and dirt and restless hordes. He came to life in the hothouse of the theater, and he bloomed under the lights and applause of performance. This year, however, he may have wished for a longer respite. During the summer, Shrewsbury had been replaced as lord chamberlain by the earl of Jersey, who was even more determined to "moralize" the stage.[38] Actors were frequently arrested for using "profane" or "immoral" expressions, and the ten-pound fine for such language, half going to the Crown and half to the accuser, brought forth many charges by venal theatergoers eager to collect, a sharp reminder that actors performed at the *pleasure* of the audience.

Cibber was no happier to discover that Rich had taken advantage of the six-week mourning for the duke of Gloucester by remodeling Drury Lane. The most drastic change, cutting back the forestage by ten feet, meant more seats but put an added strain on the voice, requiring a change of technique he found distasteful. Acting, as he had learned it from Betterton, was stylized but not broad; it had developed from an intimate relationship between actor and audience, a physical proximity that allowed the subtlest nuance to be seen and heard. Grand, sweeping, arm-length gestures would not come into use until the huge theaters and picture-frame stages of the nineteenth century made them necessary.

Colley had made good use of his time and now, not yet thirty, he was a mature artist, trained in the arduous school of repertory. Every season began with the company's regular plays, a different one each night, while the actors rehearsed the first new one. The system had given Cibber the opportunity to augment his strong points and minimize the weak, to develop a wide range of characters, to experiment with new ideas and test them against hundreds of audiences, to perfect details, and to polish his characterizations to the highest degree.

Proud of his profession, Cibber was angered when Rich disregarded actors' needs. No one knew better than Cibber how important it was to keep the doors of the theater open, but as he understood the distinction between beau and fop, so he also understood the difference between pleasing an audience and pandering to its lowest taste. Rich was concerned with the theater only as a business and would happily have sacrificed any *Hamlet* for an elephant show if he thought it would draw a larger crowd, but Cibber had more respect for his art and, on one occasion at least, had the last word. Rich brought in ropedancers as an entr'acte for a tragedy. When Colley's protests went unheeded, he went down into the pit and announced loudly that he would not play, giving his reasons. Supported by the audience and the other players, he won his point, and Rich never tried that particular experiment again.

This kind of maneuver made Rich heed Cibber more than other players. Powell got drunk, Wilks threw tantrums, and both maintained an adversary relationship with the management. Colley deftly turned the tables without losing his good humor; Rich listened and began to seek out his advice. The wily old lawyer played Powell and Wilks against each other until their rivalry grew so intense that Powell challenged Wilks to a duel, backing down quickly when Wilks reached for his sword. At last it was evident one of them would have to go, and Rich consulted Cibber about it.

Colley balanced their qualities and reached a considered judgment quite apart from his personal feelings. Powell was the better actor, with an intuitive stage sense that gave his performances a rare magic. Attuned to the audience, his timing was almost infallible, and he could play without analysis or reflection, supporting memory lapses with brilliant improvisation. He was, however, dissolute, overbearing, and undependable, a "martyr to Negligence." Wilks would never have Powell's innate gift, but the years of intense discipline had honed his talent to the finest of points. He drove himself incessantly, attended to every detail, and in learning lines was "perfect to such an Exactitude, that I question if in forty Years he ever five times chang'd or misplac'd an Article in any one of them" (I, 240). He had developed his own brand of magic, and although actors often complained he rehearsed them too rigorously, they rejoiced in the applause for smooth performances. Finally, Cibber pointed out that Powell's personal misbehavior had an adverse effect on the rest of the company, while he noted at the same time, "in how much better Order our Affairs went forward since *Wilks* came among us" (I, 255). Rich understood this kind of argument, and Powell moved over to Betterton's house. Cibber probably said nothing about his conversation with Rich, for that was not his way, but his influence was obvious, and Wilks never forgot the debt.

Swaggering about in his self-satisfied Foppington mask, Colley appeared wholly oblivious to backstage problems, but he was not as thick-skinned as the image suggested. That smiling facade concealed grief for his father's death, a deep devotion to his wife, and a somewhat envious pride in his brother, Lewis, who was admitted to New College, Oxford, on 17

December 1700.[39] He may not have wanted to change places with Lewis, but he was certainly aware how much smoother his brother's academic path had been made by their father's gift to Winchester.

That same month, Colley was beginning rehearsals for the new comedy he had brought back from Gloucestershire, *Love Makes a Man*, an amusing adaptation of two Fletcher plays, *The Elder Brother* and *The Custom of the Country*. His revised plot involves a pair of brothers and a girl. In acts 1 and 2, taken from the first play, the elder brother, Carlos, is a bookish scholar, the younger, Clodio (Cibber's role), a fop.[40] Their father plans to disinherit Carlos and give the entire estate to Clodio, along with a wealthy young heiress, but he is foiled when Carlos falls in love with the girl and elopes with her. The last three acts, drawn mostly from the second play, present a series of adventures spiced with a capture at sea, an overamorous lady, and a seeming murder, but the conclusion is happy for all. A special added attraction was Pinkethman's scene in which, according to legend, he devoured two chickens in ten seconds, a feat that never failed to bring round after round of applause.[41]

The two segments are cohesively knit together, and the action moves swiftly, the conclusion deriving logically from preceding events. Cibber has translated Fletcher's Jacobean verse into the colloquial prose of his own time, depending, as always, more on dramatic situations than on language to carry the story, but here his dialogue works well. Fletcher's ribaldry is replaced by overt moralizing that leaves no doubt as to the benefits of virtue: the true lovers, Carlos and Angelina, are united; Louisa, who has pursued Carlos for herself, gives him up and is rewarded with the honest Don Duarte; his sister, the lovesick Elvira, is fittingly provided with the foolish Clodio as her husband.

If Cibber's ending is more sentimental than Fletcher's, one reason may have been the continuing Collier controversy which had developed into a full-scale paper war and the fact that Collier's remarks on theatrical immorality found a favorable hearing from the lord chamberlain.[42] In the dedication of the printed text, Cibber reflected on the "Complaints and Hardships of the Stage" coming from "the formidable Zeal" of the courts. He openly attacked Collier for trying to destroy the theater, observing, with some acidity, that "the last time they pull'd down the *Stage* in the City, they set up a *Scaffold* at Court," a daring reference to the execution of Charles I. The stage had reformed, he claimed: "I doubt not, but we can produce Examples of some new Plays, Lawyers, and Pastors that have met with success without being oblig'd to Immorality, Bribery, or Politicks, and I dare offer this Play as one of the Number."[43]

He had a good third night despite a bit of unpleasantness when Rich's imported French dancers were driven from the stage by a young man who, moved by patriotism or alcohol, pelted them with oranges from the upper gallery. The audience objected, someone cried out "Fling him into the pit!" and a near-riot ended with the assailant's arrest. The next day, Cibber said later, the play "lagg'd" and was held up only "by the Heels of the French Tumblers," who drew the curious.[44] He published it with a dedication to Sir William Brownlowe, who had recently married Brett's sister; the dedication was a greater compliment than it appeared at the time, for *Love Makes a Man* soon became a repertory staple.

Cibber acted more this year than in any previous season, and it was a prosperous time for him. He may have used some of his newly acquired resources to move, for when his daughter Elizabeth was born in March, she was christened in a new parish.[45] It would be typical of his carefree attitude toward money, and he may further have played the spendthrift by going to France during the long vacation in order to study the French fops, although his knowledge of the language was so limited he was restricted to watching them from a distance.[46]

If Cibber did travel this summer, he returned to find Drury Lane in a precarious state. The master of the Revels, Charles Killigrew, knowing Rich's lease was soon to expire, tried to persuade the other shareholders to give Betterton the renewal, and there was talk the two companies might merge.[47] Killigrew had not reckoned on Rich's legal skills, however, and the battle went on until June 1702, when, as might have been predicted, Rich won. Trouble also flourished within the walls and the company grew mutinous as Rich grew ever more greedy, paid salaries capriciously, and dodged creditors with the skill of an impoverished aristocrat. The actor who complained was invited to share a bottle of wine, often discovering later he had been duped into a worse contract than before. By December, Rich was faced with the threat of another rebellion.

He was saved by Richard Steele's first comedy, *The Funeral*, which opened to unexpected success with Cibber in the leading role. Overnight, the atmosphere changed. Actors' spirits lifted, shareholders ceased complaining, and even Rich unbent enough to pay salaries "nine Days in one Week" (I, 263), but after the brief respite, players' grievances became so numerous that the vice chamberlain summoned Rich to answer them. In the midst of the turmoil, all charges were forgotten, and the nation was plunged into mourning for the death of William III on 8 February. The theaters were closed until the coronation of Queen Anne six weeks later.

Colley was now a principal member of the Drury Lane company and was fast becoming Rich's right-hand man. Consequently he was in a somewhat better financial state than he had been when Queen Mary died. Nevertheless, his income was not only reduced this season, but it was irregularly paid, and he undoubtedly felt the pinch severely. Once again he turned to writing, and during the long vacation he began work on a new comedy. His industry was necessary, for his family was still growing.[48]

It is not clear whether the failures of *Woman's Wit* and *Xerxes* turned him from writing original plays, but it is evident that *Richard III* and *Love Makes a Man* had shown him how much more easily and rapidly he could adapt the works of others.[49] At heart he was an actor, more interested in characterizations than concepts. He had not set out to be a playwright, and he freely admitted that the author in him served the actor. He did not lack originality—*Love's Last Shift* proved that—but he had opinions rather than ideas. A seasoned craftsman now, he had a fine sense of dramatic structure and was, more than most writers, extremely sensitive to his audience. With these two advantages and a facility for dialogue, he could create a memorable theatrical experience from the most outdated work. He would have been a fool if he had not used his gift to write good parts for himself. He knew his range was limited, but with a generosity not usual in actor-playwrights, he also wrote fine roles for his colleagues.

She Wou'd and She Wou'd Not is an adaptation of John Leanerd's *The Counterfeiters*, enriched with bits from a Spanish story, *The Trepanner Trepann'd*, and Cibber began his twelfth season on the stage with the finished play in hand. Briefly, it is the story of Hypolita who, having repulsed her lover, discovers he has ridden off to Spain to marry her brother's sweetheart. She disguises herself as a man and follows. In Spain she successfully courts the other girl and actually goes through a mock marriage, but she captures her man in the end. Cibber kept Leanerd's basic story, but he disentangled some of the complicated intrigues and mistaken identities and gave every actor at least one good scene. For himself, he wrote his first sizable character role, the crusty old father, Don Manuel; and he gave the role of the enchanting Hypolita, who would charm audiences for more than a century, to Susannah Verbruggen, taking advantage of her popularity in breeches parts.[50]

The play opened 26 November 1702, and the change in drama he had initiated in *Love's Last Shift* was more than ever in evidence, not as a matter of theory but of practice. Restoration dramatists had been concerned with literary matters: Aristotelian "rules," felicitous language, and that intangible quality they called "Wit." Cibber, the actor-playwright, was concerned with the "theatrical" qualities: a clear, uninterrupted plot line, distinctive characters, and striking situations. In the beginning he had proceeded from an intuitive stage sense, but now he was more certain of himself and stated his position clearly in the prologue to *She Wou'd and She Wou'd Not*. Rules, he said, were guidelines, not immutable laws, and he took a backhand slap at writers who put language before action: "His Wit, if any, mingles with his Plot, / Which should on no Temptation be forgot. . . . / From his Design no Person can be spar'd, / Or Speeches lopt, unless the whole be marr'd: / No Scenes of Talk for Talkings Sake are shewn; / Where most abruptly, when their Chat is done, / Actors go off, because the Poet—can't go on."

The fundamental principles are no different from those of any playwright whose first allegiance is to the stage, and Cibber's words are applicable to writers as dissimilar as Sophocles and Brecht. He recognized what few were ready to accept, that the brilliant Restoration comedy had come to a dead end, that on the stage the wittiest dialogue was lost unless it came from characters moving through well-defined situations in which a gradually increasing tension reached a climax.

Although the sixth night did not even pay the house charges, *She Wou'd and She Wou'd Not* was a mild success. Cibber had a good enough benefit on the third night and, like *Love Makes a Man*, the work stayed in the repertory for the rest of the century. He published it in February 1702, and, in a burst of patriotic fervor, dedicated it to James, duke of Ormonde, in honor of "the late happy News" from Vigo. The naval victory the popular duke had helped to win had been one of the few such in the War of the Spanish Succession.

With his income as an actor supplemented by the play and an extra salary for his management duties, Cibber probably did well this year, but he did not stop there. He also resurrected the subplot of *Woman's Wit* and reshaped it into a short afterpiece, *The School Boy; or, The Comical Rivals*, in which he played Master Johnny.[51] Another source of revenue may have come through the death of Katharine's mother, when the Shore inheritance was divided among her three children. For whatever reason, he was sufficiently prosperous to move his wife and three daughters (his new son, William, probably did not survive the winter) into the fashionable Spring Gardens and was able to offer a generous reward when he lost his watch and ring: "In or near the Old Play-house in Drury-lane, on Monday last the 19th of January, a Watch was drop'd, having a Tortoise-shell Case inlaid with Silver, a Silver Chain, and a Gold Seal Ring the Arms a Cross Wavy and Chequer. Whoever brings it to Mr. Cibber at his House near the Bullhead Tavern in Old Spring Gardens at Charing-Cross, shall have Three Guineas Reward."[52]

The spring of 1703, however, saw continued harassment by the lord chamberlain, the grand jury of Middlesex, and the Crown, all of whom demanded a higher standard of "decency" on the stage with the threat of arrest (occasionally carried out) for violations. Lincoln's Inn Fields, operating only under a license from the lord chamberlain's office, suffered the most, but although Rich's patent came directly from the Crown, it neither guaranteed immunity for his actors nor did they trust him to invoke it. He was more high-handed than ever, and a resurgence of complaints against him led them to petition Jersey's office again.[53] Wilks's name headed a list of signatures that included Rich's own assistant, Owen Swiney, recently arrived from Ireland. Their petition ignored, the company was soon distracted by the flurry of preparations for an expedition to Bath, where they were to entertain Queen Anne. Excited anticipation, however, was suddenly muted at the end of the season, when Susannah Verbruggen died in childbirth. The death of the superb comedienne not only saddened but seriously weakened the company, although grief did not prevent the other actresses from scrambling for her roles. Cibber sadly put aside a new comedy he had begun for her. None of the others, he thought, would be able to take her place.

Bath, as Cibber first saw it, bore little resemblance to the stylish resort he would know in later summers when it was under the benevolent dictatorship of Beau Nash. In 1703, it was not much more than a small cluster of uncomfortable houses around the cathedral, its Roman ruins poorly tended and its streets unpaved. Far from the sophistication of London, the only amusements were conversation and gambling. Although these were two of Cibber's favorite pastimes, he may have taken advantage of the comparative leisure to write *The Rival Queans*, a parody of Nathaniel Lee's *The Rival Queens*, in which Alexander was transformed into "Alec," commander of raffish beaux; Statira became "Statty," his sluttish wife; and Roxana, "Rocky," a prostitute of startlingly coarse vocabulary. Heroic tragedy had been losing popularity for some years, and Cibber, following the line of Buckingham's *Rehearsal*, mocked its high sentiments with wicked accuracy. It was not great art, but it was the kind of jesting likely to be written for a court on holiday.[54]

As the company began to rehearse *Sir Courtly Nice* for the Bath audience, Cibber was unhappy to find his leading lady was Anne Oldfield, who had inherited this least important of Susannah Verbruggen's roles. Anne, a striking beauty with lustrous dark hair and eyes, had been at Drury Lane since George Farquhar "discovered" her four years before. Vanbrugh had liked her well enough to give her the ingenue part in *The Pilgrim*, but Cibber was not impressed with her talent. He made no secret of his feelings and walked glumly through the rehearsal, although it was one of his best roles. Anne retaliated by muttering her lines in such a cold, ill-humored manner that he concluded "any Assistance I could give her would be to little or no Purpose" (I, 307).

At the performance, however, he was astonished to find himself playing opposite one of the most gifted comediennes he had ever met. Anne's lines sparkled brightly, her gestures were elegant, her expressions enchanting and her timing perfect. Without anyone particularly noticing, she had done precisely as Colley had a decade earlier—watched, studied, and practiced until, given the opportunity, she was ready. Cibber admitted his mistake and conceded unselfishly that "what made her Performance more valuable

46

was, that I knew it had all proceeded from her own Understanding" (I, 307), not from his coaching. He watched her carefully when they returned to Drury Lane. A series of benefits was needed to make up for the prestigious but unprofitable Bath engagement, and Cibber chose *Sir Courtly Nice* for his own. He was reassured to find that Oldfield's performance at Bath had not been merely a momentary inspiration but the flowering of a genuine talent.

Cibber needed his benefit, for once again his family was increased by the birth of a son.[55] In later years, Theophilus liked to say he was born on the night of the great storm that ripped the roofs from houses, tore ships from their moorings, and killed a host of people, but that was only his habitual dramatic license. He was actually born two days earlier, on 25 November, although the storm might well have presaged his turbulent career.

Cibber was extremely busy this year, appearing in eighteen of the first twenty-five plays, more than twice as often as in any previous season. Repertory did not require complete relearning of roles, and most actors simply refreshed their memories, but Cibber constantly polished his characterizations and tried new ideas so that even a negligible role like Osric in *Hamlet* was turned into a memorable portrait of a Frenchified dandy.

The young actor also assisted Rich, holding a critical position in the management. Rich, who thoroughly understood business practices, had no concept of the creative end of theater. His polar opposite was Wilks, an artist to his fingertips, but who, left to his own devices, would have bankrupted Drury Lane in a year. Cibber was the ideal middleman. His sympathies were with the actors, but he understood the economics of the theater and appreciated Rich's problems even when he disapproved of his methods. Conflicts were inevitable, but Colley was usually diplomatic enough to soothe all but the most ruffled feathers in and out of the theater. As a frequent mediator between Drury Lane and the lord chamberlain's office, he must have been pleased when Jersey's long persecution was ended in March and was supplanted by the genial term of the earl of Kent. The easing of restrictions was apparent at once, and Cibber promptly revived *Richard III* for his own benefit, playing his original version without objection from the master of the Revels.

That summer, while the nation cheered Marlborough's victory at Blenheim, Cibber went off to the Bretts at Sandywell Park. His heart was further lightened by the news that his brother, Lewis, despite a lamentable wildness, had earned his bachelor of arts degree and had been ordained by the bishop of London.[56] Colley did not attend the ceremony; he was completing the comedy he had put away on the death of Susannah Verbruggen, knowing he had found an able successor in Anne Oldfield.

The Careless Husband, considered his masterpiece, is an original work.

47

The story is simple, amusing, and moral; the main plot, an errant husband reformed by a patient and idealized wife, is combined with a subplot in which a flirtatious coquette learns the values of a good marriage. The two lines are tightly linked, and the story moves rapidly between them, one incident dictating the next. The famous scene in which Lady Easy discovers her husband "without his Periwig" asleep in an armchair, while their maid sleeps in another beside him, is the crisis that clearly demonstrates Cibber's moral point and is a good example of the distinction between the manners and mores of his age and those of later times. Two fully dressed people sleeping in armchairs—with or without periwigs—scarcely suggests infidelity to a culture accustomed to more graphic representations, yet Cibber's audience understood the symbolism perfectly, and it was so obvious to those at the end of the century that it was often cut as indecent, with added lines to explain what Lady Easy "sees" offstage.

The episode is supposed to be based on an actual incident in the Brett household. If so, the Bretts, to whom Cibber read each scene as it was finished, must have been both extremely tolerant and possessed of as imperturbable a sense of humor as Colley himself. Given Mrs. Brett's divorce scandal while she was still the countess of Macclesfield and the predilection for privacy common to the age, it does not seem likely that Cibber would expose his friends in this manner—or that the friendship would continue if he did.

This scene and its sequel, however, do give each character a moment of high nobility. Instead of falling into a jealous rage, Lady Easy shows her concern for her husband (and her marriage) by quietly covering his head with her scarf, "lest he catch cold," while pondering, with startling psychological insight, a possible reason for his unfaithfulness:

> Perhaps
> The Fault's in me, and Nature has not form'd
> Me with the Thousand little Requisites
> That warm the Heart to Love—[57]

When Sir Charles wakes and realizes he has jeopardized his marriage, his true moral nature asserts itself and he repudiates his temporary liaison. In context, the behavior of both is completely logical, resting on a belief in the innate goodness of humanity, but critics of a more sophisticated age have represented Lady Easy as a hypocritical prude and her husband as another Loveless whose reversion to type is inevitable. Cibber himself has been charged as a disingenuous sentimentalist playing to the gallery without regard for truth.[58] Yet in a time when marriage was a serious commitment and divorce nearly unthinkable, neither Cibber's nor his characters' sincerity was questioned. Certainly his views were consonant with the pattern of his life. As an actor, he reflected the taste of his aristocratic patrons, who laughed at the Society for the Reformation of Manners, but as a man he adhered closely to the conservative Protestant ethics of his middle-class childhood. His plays reflect this dichotomy; however amusing it is to laugh at morality, in the end, decent men and women practice it as faithfully as any Puritan.

The characters are clearly defined. The lighthearted Sir Charles Easy and Lady Betty Modish, the coquette, are paired with the sober Lady Easy and Morelove. The two lines of action are nicely balanced against each other, and precisely between them is Cibber's own character, the gilded coxcomb, Lord Foppington. Reflecting Sir Novelty's good-heartedness, he gives up Lady Betty with the graceful nonchalance of Cibber's own public pose: "Madam, I have lost a thousand fine Women in my time, but never had the ill Manners to be out of Humour with any one for refusing me, since I was born" (p. 168). There are no passages of burnished wit, but the dialogue has the colloquial elegance of the upper classes, and every line contributes to the comic structure. Cibber said he took some of Lady Betty's words directly from Anne Oldfield's conversation, but he may have been paying merely a gallant compliment, for he said the same of the duke of Argyle when he dedicated the play to him.

At the end of summer, he took *The Careless Husband*, amended by suggestions from the Bretts, back to London. There he read it to the duke of Argyle, who recommended it so enthusiastically that Cibber's third and sixth nights had full houses. His grateful dedication to the duke suggests he had taken the many attacks on the "indecency" of the stage to heart:

The Best Criticks have long, and justly complain'd that the Coarseness of most Characters in our late Comedies have been unfit Entertainments for People of Quality, especially the Ladies: And therefore I was long in Hopes, that some able Pen (whose Expectation did not Hang upon the Profits of success) wou'd generously attempt to reform the Town into a better Tast, than the World generally allows 'em: But nothing of that kind having lately appear'd, that wou'd give me an Opportunity of being Wise at anothers Expence, I found it Impossible any longer to resist the secret Temptation of my Vanity, and so ev'n struck the first Blow my self.

The moral pleased the town, and the play became a lasting favorite. Its appeal was enhanced by the brilliant performance of Anne Oldfield as Lady Betty, now firmly and finally established as a star in her own right, but the rest of the cast was excellent as well. Wilks's Sir Charles sinned as attractively as he repented, and Cibber's Foppington was perfection. George Powell, dismissed from Lincoln's Inn Fields for drunkenness and back at Drury Lane, was a charming Morelove. The play opened at the newly repaired Dorset Garden theater, for almost two decades the stage for rope dancers, contortionists, and other popular entertainers. It had been badly damaged in the previous year's great storm and was closed for repairs, but now, restored and refurbished, its smaller size gave a hospitable intimacy to Cibber's kind of comedy, and *The Careless Husband* ran for ten successive nights before going into the regular repertory.

Once again rumors circulated that Cibber was not the author.[59] He was becoming used to such attacks, and he dismissed them as the price of success. If he was hurt by them, the extravagant praises of friends like Joseph Addison and Richard Steele and the substantial profits from his author's nights provided a soothing balm for his wounds.

The rest of the 1704-5 season was not remarkable for success. Owen Swiney's comedy, *The Quacks*, failed, and Swiney left his job as Rich's assistant to take a position with the army in the north. Plump, irascible Dogget was back at Drury Lane again. A great favorite of the duke of Norfolk, he was the only actor allowed to change companies without special permission from the lord chamberlain's office, and he took full advantage of his privilege, moving back and forth whenever either manager displeased him. Despite his crustiness, he was welcomed wherever he went, for he always drew an audience. This season he inexplicably chose to play tragedy, taking the role of Phorbas in Dryden's version of *Oedipus*, and suffered one of his few failures. His line readings sounded, critics said, like the countrified comic in his own afterpiece, *Hob in the Well*. Cibber tried the same role a few days later and met the same fate on the grounds that he sounded like Foppington. It was an experience neither repeated.

In April, Vanbrugh opened Queens, the grand new theater he had designed especially for opera. Cibber had seen the duke of Somerset lay the cornerstone the year before and had concluded at that time that the Haymarket was much too far from the central part of the town to draw audiences. Just before the theater opened, Vanbrugh, realizing he knew little of practical theatrical operation, suggested that the Drury Lane company merge with the opera under Rich's management, but Rich had plans of his own. His refusal appeared wise when it was discovered Queens had an echo that made the opera sound as if it were being performed twice at the same time. Vanbrugh then turned to Betterton who, uncomfortable in the cramped quarters of Lincoln's Inn Fields, accepted the offer. Rich immediately and secretly took a lease on Lincoln's Inn Fields and sat back to wait until his plan to control both theaters could be effected.

Cibber probably knew more than most about the affair, but he could have had no idea how much Rich's machinations were going to affect his own life. At the time, his energy was focused on adapting Roger Boyle's *Parthenissa* into a new tragedy for the coming season, *Perolla and Izadora*. He liked to pretend he had read nothing since he left school, but Boyle's hefty six-volume saga is not the kind of frivolous literature a true Foppington chooses. It is a heroic romance set in the time of Hannibal, and Cibber excerpted the most dramatic elements of the subplot, defined a clear story line with good and evil in dynamic confrontation, gave his leading characters highly charged love scenes, and created a grotesque villain for himself. *Perolla and Izadora* is not a good tragedy; it is not even a good play. However sound the structure and cohesive the parts, the whole is ineffective. Cibber could invent plausible situations, but his characters remained simplistic and two-dimensional. His temperament, with its outward calm and unfailing good humor that belied the intensity of his ambition, was ideal for the comic mode, but its very coolness was antithetical to the tragic sense of cosmic doom.

With Wilks and Oldfield in the title roles and himself as the villainous Pacuvius, who is so offended by their intolerable nobility that he kills himself, the play had a good third and sixth nights and an additional performance in January before it sank into a well-earned oblivion. He published it with a dedication to Boyle's grandson, the earl of Orrery, for his assistance on the text: "Just before I hurry'd it upon the Stage, your Lordship did me the Honour of Adjusting its Garniture, the Expression: wherein I must own my Vanity was sufficiently mortified, to see after all my flatter'd Hopes and Care, how little I had been doing."

Colley might have been disappointed by the failure, but he had no reason to be disheartened. Three of his plays were standards in the repertory, and his reputation as an actor was secure. He was indisputably the most versatile comedian on the stage, much in demand by playwrights, and this spring he created the role of Captain Brazen in Farquhar's *The Recruiting Officer*, a character he would play until he retired. In public, he played the gentleman-artist, patronizing smoky coffeehouses, gambling late into the night, and gaily enjoying the fruits of his talent. In private, however, he was proud of his family and avoided any taint of scandal, though his social life often took precedence, and in the summer of 1706, not even the birth of another son, prevented him from making his annual visit to the Bretts.[60]

He was still in Gloucestershire when he learned of rapid changes taking place in the London theater. Betterton, feeling the effects of age and illness, wanted to retire from managing the Queens company, and Rich saw an opportunity for profit. He lured Owen Swiney back to London and persuaded Vanbrugh to hire him as manager of the combined opera and theater companies. Vanbrugh, relieved of the management problems, would receive five pounds each day as titular head of the company; Swiney was promised a hundred guineas a year, his choice of Drury Lane's actors and half the profits from Queens (the other half going to Rich, of course, who was to have final authority on all theatrical decisions). Vanbrugh was pleased with the arrangement, and Swiney, already in debt to Rich for two hundred pounds was grateful for the opportunity. Neither seemed to realize that, for no outlay of cash, Rich now had control of both theaters.

Swiney chose the cream of the Drury Lane company, but when he asked for Cibber, Rich refused. Swiney, rightly suspecting skulduggery, wrote to Cibber briefly outlining what had happened and pleading with him to join the others at Queens.[61] The letter, affectionate as it was, did not persuade Colley when he weighed the prospects. Queens would undoubtedly have the better actors (he had an unshakable belief that any company containing Betterton was bound to be superior), and most of his friends were there. On the other hand, the location and the acoustics of Queens were atrocious and the competition of the opera was strong. Moreover, although Cibber liked Swiney, he had little faith in his managerial talent. The only major drawback at Drury Lane was Rich's arbitrary dictatorship, which Cibber knew he could deal with, while the advantages were many: an excellent stage, an established audience, and considerable voice in the management.

On his return to London, Cibber went directly to Drury Lane where Rich escorted him through the warren of nooks and cupboards built during the summer. He evaded Cibber's repeated question, "But, master, where are your actors?" with detailed descriptions of lavish musical entertainments planned for the coming season. Cibber saw little place there for himself and, with a wife and five children to support, asked for a guarantee that his own salary would not be reduced. Rich responded with the promise that he could have his choice of roles. Colley was familiar with this kind of legerdemain. "You know upon what terms I am willing to serve you" (I, 334), he said coldly, and walked out to join Swiney at Queens.

Vanbrugh and Swiney were not distressed by the skeletal company remaining at Drury Lane. Business was so brisk that Swiney repaid Rich his two hundred pounds before the end of the year, and for a time the actors received full salaries. Rich, anxious to keep his interest in Queens a secret, advertised his productions as "by the *deserted* company of Comedians," and began a series of lawsuits, first against Cibber, then against the other "renegades."

Although the lawsuits were a forcible reminder of Rich's power, they were not a serious threat. Queens, however, soon had other problems, most notably the friction between the singers and the actors. Each group felt it was the mainstay of the theater and that the other side was receiving preferential treatment, but each had internal troubles as well. The singers, with their notoriously volatile temperaments, developed fierce rivalries among themselves, while the merger of two acting companies with roughly the same repertories was bound to bring conflicts in the casting of favorite roles. It was an impossible situation, and as Rich began to mount his promised extravaganzas, attendance at Queens diminished.

In January, to gain some peace, Swiney arranged for a subscription series of three plays, "For the Encouragement of the Comedians Acting in the Hay-Market," and "to enable them to keep the Diversion of Plays under a separate Interest from the Operas."[62] For three guineas, subscribers would receive tickets to *Julius Caesar*, *A King and no King*, and *Marriage a la Mode*. The third play was advertised as by Dryden, but the adaptation was by Cibber, an artfully patched set of the comic scenes from Dryden's *Marriage a la Mode* and *Secret Love* with a bit of *The Mock Astrologer* thrown in for good measure.[63] The whole effort, he confessed, took less than a week, and the result was an entertaining new comedy subtitled, *The Comical Lovers*. Tailored to the company, it set Wilks's gentlemanly Palamede beside Cibber's hilariously comic Celadon as they pursued two of the brightest female stars, Anne Bracegirdle and Anne Oldfield.

Cibber's play provided elegant and charming roles for both actresses, but it could not prevent the inevitable comparison between them. Whether they would or not, the beautiful, gifted Bracegirdle and the equally beautiful and gifted—but younger—Oldfield played the same roles. In the end, the audience gave Oldfield the honors, and on 20 February 1707, after a performance of *The Unhappy Favourite*, Anne Bracegirdle quietly and gracefully retired. For the next twenty years, "Nance" Oldfield would be the reigning actress on the London stage.

The bittersweet season continued. The rewards of benefits scarcely made up for the effort of playing in the echoing, barnlike Queens, even with the management taking only its legitimate deductions. In April, the smashing success of Farquhar's *The Beaux' Stratagem* was darkened by his death on the very night of his author's benefit.[64]

That summer, Katharine was pregnant again and may have been in poor health, for when Queens closed, Colley stayed with her instead of visiting the Bretts. An affectionate if inattentive husband, he was too deeply involved in the theater to pay much heed to domestic matters and was not a particularly good father. He disliked unpleasantness of any kind and was perfectly willing to leave the discipline of children to Katharine so long as they did not bother him. As usual, he spent the long vacation writing a play, *The Double Gallant*, and, with Katharine ill, the children were a problem. Katharine's brother, William, and his wife, Rose, took the gentle, sweet-tempered Elizabeth to stay with them; the others were probably boarded out, except for the baby, James, who was blind.[65] In October, Katharine had another sickly child.[66]

About the same time, Skipwith, a close friend of the Bretts (he had introduced them to each other), was staying with them in Gloucestershire. His visit was to have far-reaching consequences. He confided a long list of complaints about Rich, claiming somewhat untruthfully that he had received no income from his shares in Drury Lane for years, and that it was his fervent wish to be rid of them. Brett, now out of Parliament, had just handed over his army commission to his younger brother and was beginning to feel rather bored with country life. Jokingly he offered to take the shares off Skipwith's hands and, as he later told Cibber, "after a great deal of Raillery on both sides," Skipwith accepted his offer of ten shillings for the lot.

Once back in London, Brett went to Cibber for advice, and Colley's reply reflected his own approach to Rich. He assured Brett that the only way to profit from his bargain was to become personally involved in the management, to appear decisive and knowledgeable, and in any disagreement to force Rich into open confrontation. Longing to be back at Drury Lane himself, he urged Brett to press for a union of the acting companies there, leaving Queens for the opera. As Brett tried to follow his advice, Colley plunged into the new season, playing once or twice a week and rehearsing the first of his two new plays.

The Double Gallant was not the success he had hoped for, but it received "great Applause," and he had a good third night. In every sense, it is a play for actors, and he crafted it well. Deception is the keynote, and every character at one time or another appears to be other than the real self. The central character, Atall, is a wild young gallant who courts several ladies under various aliases and keeps his head in the most trying circumstances, a role peculiarly suited to Cibber's own personality. Atall's is not the only disguise; Clarinda dresses as a man, Careless as the "Prince of Muscovy," and an ex-footman poses as a respectable army captain. Pretense is mocked in the character he wrote for Anne Oldfield, Lady Dainty, a fashionable hypochondriac who admires "Swiss porters, French Cooks and Footmen, Italian Singers, Turkish Coach-men and Indian Pages."[67] Knowing that his audience came expecting laughter on the way to a happy ending, he gave them a succession of hilarious scenes, and not until the final curtain are the shams completely unraveled. Improbability is part of the fun from Atall's clever ruse convincing Sylvia he is actually two different men to the last-minute discovery that their marriage had been planned by their fathers all along.

Cibber's interwoven plot sources support his claim that he was merely "mending old linnen." Critics were quick to pounce on his borrowings from Susannah Centlivre and Charles Burnaby but slower to recognize the dramatic force of his reconstruction that would later make it a standard repertory piece.[68] He may have been sensitive to their comments, for he began his preface: "When I undertook to make the following Sheets into a Play, I only proposed to call it a Revis'd One, but some who had Read it were of Opinion that the Additions were of Consequence enough to call it a New one; and the Actors proposing an Advantage by it, the little Concern I had for it, made me comply with their Desire." He also denied that laziness was the reason for his writing so many adaptations, concluding with a reference to faultfinders: "I think it proper to prepare their favourable Thoughts of my Industry, by informing them, that I have a New Play now writing into Parts, which will be acted before *Christmas*, that has cost me two Summers hard Pains and Study, there not being one line in't, or Thought, either in the Dialogue or Design, but what's my own, and never seen before".

Six weeks later, *The Lady's Last Stake* opened, designed, Cibber said, as a "pendant" for *The Careless Husband*. More accurately, it is a parallel based on his favorite theme, the sanctity of marriage. Lady Wronglove is not unfaithful, but she has a passion for gambling, and in the dedication, Cibber explains why he considered it a dangerous flaw in a woman: "Gaming is a Vice, that has undone more innocent Principles, than any one Folly that's in Fashion, therefore I chose to expose it to the Fair Sex in its most hideous Form, by reducing a Woman of Honour to stand the presuming Addresses of a Man, whom neither her Virtue or Inclination wou'd let her have the least Taste to."[69] It was a preachment he did not practice, and at the first reading, Mary Porter, who was to play Lady Gentle, asked acidly, "How can you draw such admirable portraits of goodness and live as if you were a stranger to it?" Foppington bowed with exaggerated courtesy and smiled, adding one more touch to the image that hid the man, "The one, madam, is absolutely necessary, the other is not."[70]

For the subplot, Anne Oldfield donned breeches to reform and win the rakish Sir George Brilliant (Cibber), and their story produced another of his outrageous situations, often forgiven by an audience but never by readers. The disguised Mrs. Conquest is wounded by Sir George and pronounced dead by the doctor who is in collusion with her, but when Sir George is properly repentant, she revives at once. This time not even the audience was won over, and the play had only five performances in the whole season, although it too would be a repertory staple in later years.

The morality is self-evident; good is rewarded and evil punished, but it is of the fairy tale variety. Cibber's reordered world with its "happy ever after" is more a reaction against Restoration indecency than a crusade for virtue. Caught in a dilemma that reflects his own personality, he is amused by aristocratic wit that flouts the rules, but fundamentally his moral standards are those of the conservative middle class. Yet he is no Puritan in his judgment, and he forgives easily; he likes people, and as an actor he wants to please them. He detested Collier's humorlessness, and *The Lady's Last Stake* is no diatribe against gambling but an *exemplum* set forth in a disarmingly comic manner.[71]

During this time, Brett was sedulously following Cibber's advice in urging the lord chamberlain to merge the two acting companies. Cibber assisted as much as he could, and when he published *The Lady's Last Stake*, he dedicated it to Kent, reminding him that "without a Union of the best

Actors, it must have been impossible for it to have receiv'd a tolerable Justice in the Performance." In January, their efforts came to fruition when the Queens company joined Rich's group at Drury Lane.

Brett was less successful in his dealings with Rich, and he found his duties more complex and tedious than he had imagined. Rich had been stymied in his attempt to become the theatrical czar of London, but he had no intention of letting control of Drury Lane slip away. The union was barely under way when he began to subvert Brett's influence by suggesting that the other shareholders were not receiving proper returns on their investment, conveniently ignoring the fact that he had done no better. In a short time, Brett found himself besieged by demands for money, and by March, he was ready to retire from the field.

Again he turned to Cibber, but Colley, acting three or four nights a week, rehearsing and directing constantly, could not take over Brett's position by himself, and the weary Brett agreed to "farm" his shares to Cibber and Wilks. They asked Betterton to join them, but, past seventy and ill, he no longer had the strength, and Richard Estcourt was made the third partner. With Brett's tacit support, the three could stand against Rich, and they maintained the company to the end of the season.

Cibber probably spent the summer of 1708 working on a new comedy, but Rich would not let himself be dominated by the actors any more than by Brett. He used the summer months to regain his lost power, and when the fall season opened, he was in full charge again. He had barely reasserted himself, however, when the death of the queen's consort, Prince George of Denmark, sent the court into mourning and closed the theaters for six weeks. The Cibber household was soon in mourning as well for the death of Katharine's brother, William. They had been very close, and she felt his loss keenly. He left a sizable estate to his childless widow, Rose, and the Cibbers allowed her favorite niece, their daughter Elizabeth, to stay with her for some time.

In spite of his private sorrow, Colley's new comedy, *The Rival Fools*, opened on 11 January 1709. He said he had adapted it from Fletcher's *Wit without Money*, but he took little besides the basic premise of living by one's wits, and he need not have given Fletcher any credit at all. He carefully crafted it for the company's two principal low comedians, Bullock and Pinkethman, who romped through farcical situations that had no relation to the original play: Fletcher's witty widow became a modern coquette for Anne Oldfield and the silly beau a clever young Outwit for Wilks, but they had little to do. The only character that owed anything to Fletcher was Cibber's own, the coxcomb booby, Samuel Simple.

The Rival Fools was a failure, and for the first time in Cibber's life, he heard one of his own works booed by an audience. The cause was a pun many found unspeakably vulgar, a play on "Miller's thumbs," the slang term for bullheads and for the illegitimate son of James II. Cibber had one benefit and published the play two weeks later, but that was all.[72] It would not be performed again for a dozen years.

Outwardly, Drury Lane was doing very well in the spring of 1709. Kent had ordered the company not to play on Wednesdays and Fridays to give the opera better houses, but to everyone's surprise their own Thursday and Saturday audiences were full enough to offset the loss. Backstage, however, matters were in chaos. Rich had convinced Skipwith that Brett had taken unfair advantage of a gentlemanly jest, and Skipwith threatened prosecution. In disgust, Brett removed himself completely from theatrical affairs, leaving the actors without any protection from Rich's despotism.[73] The air was full of lawsuits on both sides, and even Cibber could not keep a cool head when he protested a 12 percent cut in salary and Rich replied coldly that he was earning more than Cardell Goodman ever did and *he* was a better actor than Cibber would ever be.

Rich's greed was insatiable. In addition to his other depredations, he demanded an "indulto"—one-third of all benefit proceeds above the legitimate house expenses. It was completely illegal and, because most actors relied on benefits to tide them over the summer, unethical as well, but when they rebelled, he announced that only those who signed the indulto agreement could have a benefit at all. Led by Cibber, Wilks, and Oldfield, the demoralized players devised a new strategy. The three signed the indulto and chose their roles from their most popular plays: *The Recruiting Officer* and *The Beaux' Stratagem* for Wilks and Oldfield, *The Alchemist* for Cibber, with a "new Epilogue representing the Figure of Nobody."[74]

The three stars played their benefits, accepted their diminished receipts and took their complaints straight to the lord chamberlain. Called to account, Rich presented the signed indulto agreements, but Kent ruled that the signatures had been obtained by unethical methods and ordered him to make restitution. Although Rich pretended to bow to authority, the actors knew he would find other ways to torment them, and it was soon clear that their fears were well founded, for neither Cibber nor Oldfield was given a new role for the rest of the season. Wilks had one, and that probably only because Rich was intimidated by the fiery leading man.

Other actors suffered as well, and they determined to end Rich's tyranny once and for all. With Kent's blessing, they sounded out Swiney about returning to Queens with a proposal that Cibber, Wilks, Oldfield, and Dogget manage the drama while Swiney continued with the opera. It was a delicate balance, almost destroyed at the outset by Dogget's flat refusal to accept a female in the partnership. Much as he admired Oldfield, he said, their affairs could "never be upon a secure Foundation" if "more than one Sex" were allowed in the management, and a somewhat shamefaced Cibber and Wilks offered to let Anne name her own salary, a proposal she received "rather as a Favour than a Disobligation"—or at least she made them think so—and with sound practicality agreed to two hundred pounds a year with a clear benefit.

The other sticking point was Rich. The holder of a royal patent, as he never tired of reminding the lord chamberlain, was responsible only to the Crown. For the revolt to succeed, he would somehow have to be stripped of his authority, and, since there was no legal ground that did not give him an insuperable advantage, the only possible way was to close Drury Lane and move the company to Queens. Neither Wilks nor Dogget had the social contacts or the diplomatic skills needed to negotiate such delicate matters, and during the next few weeks, it was Cibber who shuttled between Queens, Whitehall, and Drury Lane, arguing, persuading, and clarifying a myriad of details until at last the arrangements were satisfactory to all.

Rich must have realized that some sort of rebellion was brewing, but he could hardly have foreseen its extent until the morning of 6 June 1709, when Cibber arrived at the theater late for rehearsal and panting with excitement. The rest of the company, fully informed and breathlessly expectant, were silent as he calmly brushed aside a stern reprimand for tardiness. Angered, Rich refused to address him directly and made his usual threat to the assembly at large, "If he will not do his work, he will not be paid." At that very moment as if on cue, Kent's messenger appeared with the official order from the lord chamberlain's office: "I do therefore for the said Contempt hereby silence you from further acting & require you not to perform any Plays or other Theatricall entertainments till further Order; And all her Majesty's Sworn Comedians are hereby forbid to act any Plays at ye Theatre in Covent Garden or else where without my leave as they shall answer the contrary at their perill."[75]

In the hush that followed, only Cibber spoke. Knowing perfectly well that he was the center of attention, he started toward the door and, with a theatrical gesture, quoted one of Wolsey's lines over his shoulder, "Read o'er that! and now—to Breakfast with what Appetite you may!"

For Rich, it was the end of dominion, for Cibber, it was the beginning.

THREE

The Turning Point

WHEN CIBBER walked out of Drury Lane that June day, he did not know if he would ever return. Since Rich held the lease on Lincoln's Inn Fields, and the old Dorset Garden playhouse was being torn down this summer, Queens might very well be his professional home from now on. Vanbrugh's massive barn was far from ideal, but it was the only alternative, and the day after Rich was silenced, the three managers applied for and received official permission to move the company there.

Making Queens suitable for plays meant extensive changes, and the summer passed in a whirlwind of labor. Without sufficient time or money for a complete rebuilding, the company compromised. Temporary walls at the sides gave better sightlines, and a false ceiling under the dome eliminated the sepulchral echo, a benefit to singers as well as actors. The actors drove themselves without stint, and on 15 September, they opened the 1709-10 season with Betterton as Othello, probably played to Cibber's grotesquely villainous Iago, a role he now "owned."

His life had undergone as swift and drastic a change as it had with the success of *Love's Last Shift*. He was no longer a player subject to the whims of a capricious master, no longer merely a consultant on policy, but one of the masters who determined the direction of the theater. Wilks and Dogget listened to him as Rich never had, deferred to his judgment on new plays, and respected his talent on the stage. Outside of the theater, his power was recognized by playwrights, would-be actors, and the lord chamberlain's office. And with that recognition came enemies.

In the past, some had sniped at Cibber's plays, particularly the successful ones, but he could always chalk that up to jealousy. On the day after *Othello*, however, the *Female Tatler* carried a barb foreshadowing the kind of attack that would become familiar in the years ahead. "I lay aside *Ben* and *Shakespear*, when I but think of his Elaborate Piece, vulgarly called *Miller's Thumbs*" moaned the writer, claiming that "Captain Brazen" forced good plays to give way to "his Immortal *Xerxes*, and the *Double Dealer*, to his judicious sprightly unborrow'd *Double Gallant*."[1] This was not just a gibe at his work to be shrugged off and left to the decision of an audience. It was an attack on his principles and judgment, and it set a pattern that would be followed by others. Had he been Wilks, Cibber would have fired off an angry reply and precipitated a paper war that could only have harmed the box office. Colley pursued a more prudent course and made certain his private life was securely concealed behind his public mask, taking care not to expose Katharine and the children to hostile pens.

As Swiney prepared the first operas of the season, the three managers began to establish guidelines for themselves. They were experienced actors with strong beliefs as to what a theater should be and an intimate knowledge of daily practice, and they set about enforcing those beliefs in the most pragmatic fashion. The keynote, they felt, was discipline. They had all seen the shambles Betterton's democratic rule had produced, but they had also seen how adversely Rich's autocracy affected the players. The rules were firm but fair. Actors were to accept and prepare all parts assigned them and to be on time at the daily rehearsals and nightly performances of plays in which they appeared. They were to supply their own clothes unless the dress was unusual, and they were not to take costumes or properties away from the theater. They could be fined for violating any of these regulations, but in return, their salaries were regular, their benefits fair, and the management respected them as artists.

The day-to-day duties of the new regime sorted themselves out quite naturally. Wilks was everywhere, overseeing rehearsals, arranging for the mounting of new plays, and writing out advertisements for the newspapers and playbills (for which he received an extra fifty pounds a year). Dogget watched over expenditures with a frugal eye and saw to it that resources were not wasted. Cibber, more flexible than either, read and judged new plays, dealt with Swiney, and kept frictions at a minimum, not a simple matter given the divergent temperaments of his two colleagues. Aside from the general principles of management, Wilks and Dogget agreed on almost nothing.

Wilks was generous and openhanded and had a mercurial temperament which could flash instantaneously into a towering rage that would be as quickly forgotten a moment later. He hired actors because they were needy or Irish or he liked them, and he hated to economize on productions, especially on the costumes he wore so well. He sometimes tried to camouflage his own extravagance by ordering clothes for others at the same time, but it was a transparent ruse that deceived neither Cibber nor Dogget. Yet Cibber's evaluation of him a decade earlier was still true, and his merits far outweighed his flaws. He willingly shouldered many of the backstage responsibilities, and if he demanded perfection, he was untiring in his efforts to reach it, conducting long, intense rehearsals that shaped the players into a company of unprecedented quality. Onstage, he was a polished, skillful performer of exceeding charm and talent, and no actor in England could match him as a romantic leading man in either comedy or tragedy.

Dogget was the diametric opposite. He hardly came up to Wilks's handsome chin, and he was certainly no beauty. In contrast to the flamboyant apolitical Irishman, he was conservative in business and a fervent outspoken Whig. He stubbornly insisted that actors should be hired on the basis of their own merit and the theater's need, that scenery and costumes should not be replaced until they were worn out. He was as hotheaded as Wilks, but his anger smouldered instead of exploding, going deeper and lasting longer. Yet he, too, was of inestimable value to the partnership, for he was as industrious as Wilks and a fine businessman who kept the accounts in perfect order. He had a comprehensive understanding of management, and it was he who drew up the agreement that formed the basis of their working relationship.[2] As an actor, he was more limited than either Cibber or Wilks but unrivaled in his kind of comedy. Modest and unassuming in his private life, he dressed plainly and seemed the antithesis of the fashion-conscious Colley, yet they were closer to each other than either was to Wilks, and they often shared a bottle after the play, baiting each other with good-humored raillery that drew laughing crowds.

At the Saturday morning business meetings, Cibber was the balance wheel. A natural mediator, he was uniquely qualified to sympathize with each partner, and his unruffled geniality often brought about concessions without incurring rancor. Like Wilks, he enjoyed a touch of elegance and knew the value of impressive staging; like Dogget, he knew the practical need to keep costs down. He admired Wilks's generosity even as he respected Dogget's integrity, and in disputes he cast his deciding vote as often for one as the other. Of the three, he was, perhaps, the least expendable, for his diplomacy made the triumvirate work.

His tact was essential in other ways as well. He understood Rich better than his partners and realized the need for a united front against him; while he had no vindictive desire to ruin the man, neither did he intend to fall into his clutches again. Rich would not stop until every avenue was closed to him. That summer, his public defense, ostensibly written by the Drury Lane treasurer, Zachary Baggs, claimed the "renegades" had been liberally treated and listed their salaries down to the penny, and in September, he ignored the lord chamberlain's commands by announcing a production of *The Recruiting Officer*.[3] Clearly, the actor-managers needed to maintain unity in the face of such persistence.

This time, Rich had gone too far. Already sympathetic to the actors, Kent would not brook open defiance, and as the curtain was about to rise on Drury Lane's first night, he invoked the silencing order and dismissed the audience. Two months later, he gave one William Collier a license to reopen Drury Lane with its small complement of actors. Collier (no relation to Jeremy) was Rich's brother under the skin. A lawyer and an opportunist, his interest in the theater was limited to the profits returned by his Drury Lane shares, and he had neither the knowledge nor the desire to manage a theater. To protect his investment, he used his considerable influence at court and was ready to proceed by November. When he arrived at the playhouse, however, he found Rich had played his last card the night before, stripping the stage of costumes, properties, and everything portable. Collier immediately turned the management over to the stagestruck but inexperienced young Aaron Hill, who, in a matter of months, was able to bring about the same kind of actors' rebellion Rich had faced.[4]

With the favor of the town behind them, Queens should have had an excellent season. Steele gave them a successful *Tender Husband*, and Cibber's neighbor in Spring Gardens, Susannah Centlivre, a somewhat less popular *The Man's Bewitched*, for which he acted as play doctor. *The Female Tatler* attacked him for it, but Susannah published a stout defense in her preface, claiming she "willingly submitted to Mr. *Cibber's* Superior Judgment."[5] His assistance was not always so well received, but his reputation as a playwright could not be denied. Five of his plays were now in the permanent repertory, and others were frequently revived.[6]

Yet the season was not as profitable as they had hoped. Dr. Henry Sacheverell's trial for "malicious, scandalous and seditious libels" against the Whigs came in February, at the beginning of the benefit season, and Londoners, more interested in the real-life drama of the fiery preacher than in stage fictions, flocked to Westminster instead of Queens. Sacheverell's sermons against toleration and occasional conformity had angered the Whigs, but they committed a tactical blunder in bringing him to court, for the Tories took up his cause. His trial became a struggle for political superiority, and when the dust settled, the Tories had won.[7] The effect on the theater was more than the temporary loss of revenue. On 14 April 1710, the earl of Shrewsbury, distinctly less favorable to the Whig actor-managers, once more became lord chamberlain, replacing Kent.

The political maneuvering did not directly affect Cibber in any material way, for he had dealt with Shrewsbury before. What did touch him closely and deeply was the death of Thomas Betterton. The old actor had been ailing for some time, but for his benefit this year, he chose the energetic role of Melanthius in *The Maid's Tragedy*. In agony from gout, he refused to disappoint a crowded house and, against all advice, plunged his foot into cold water to reduce the swelling. Forced to don slippers instead of boots, he was still a regal figure in his rich tragedy robes, and his performance stirred the audience to a standing ovation. He died two weeks later. For Cibber it was the death of a second father. His tears were unfeigned when he joined the long train of mourners following the coffin to the East Cloister of Westminster Abbey.[8] He had lost the most cherished divinity of his youth.

The disappointing season drew toward its close when the opera finished at the end of May. Perhaps alone among the members of the theatrical company, Cibber felt a tinge of regret, for he loved music, and he admired the brilliant castrato, Nicolini, enormously. Still, he was not sorry the singers went on holiday; their endless squabbles with each other and with the actors were tiring, and the competition had been costly. Swiney left for Ireland almost at once, and the three managers considered their resources. They were so insolvent they decided on a series of benefits, which extended their season into July, the longest any of them had acted since they were young players. Even then they were short of cash, and, reasoning that they were working overtime, so to speak, they helped themselves out of the Queens' general treasury.

When Swiney returned, he was outraged to discover Wilks had appropriated £150, and Cibber and Doggett, £100 each. He complained to Shrewsbury, demanding they return their loot and be held as responsible as himself for the still-outstanding opera debts. The three managers pacified him with a new arrangement they had worked out during his absence. After Aaron Hill's debacle, they persuaded Collier to take over Queens, which left them and Swiney to manage Drury Lane. The advantages were obvious: the actors would be home again and free of operatic problems; Collier, who was receiving nothing from the silenced stage, would have at least a chance to collect a profit. Somehow, they persuaded Swiney to overlook their peculations enough to bring them a stock of scenery and costumes from Queens. Collier, who was noticeably cannier about money than about management, accepted an annual rent of six hundred pounds for Drury Lane, another yearly two hundred pounds toward opera expenses, and the triumvirate's promise not to give musical performances or even to play on Wednesdays or Saturdays, "to give the Opera a fairer Chance for a full House" (II, 103). Then he put Aaron Hill in charge of Queens.

The agreement went through all the official channels, and on Cibber's thirty-ninth birthday the new managers of Drury Lane received their license from the lord chamberlain's office.[9] They had opened the 1710-11 season at Queens, but after sixteen performances, they moved swiftly and without fanfare to Drury Lane. They immediately broke their agreement with Collier by playing on Saturdays and infuriated Swiney by refusing to accept responsibility for any part of the previous year's opera deficits. Worse, they even reduced his share of Drury Lane's profits, making it clear they wanted nothing from him but his name on the license. Swiney responded with a lawsuit, and a long battle was under way.[10]

It must be confessed that the triumvirate used Swiney rather disgracefully—perhaps no worse than Rich had done, but certainly no better. They looked upon him as an outsider, not because he was Irish (even Wilks didn't defend him on that ground) or because he had worked for Rich or because he had made a hash of the opera, but because as far as theater went, he spoke a different language. Swiney loved the theater, had worked in it for years, but he would never share the three men's intimate understanding of its inner workings. They were actors, and their management rested on that foundation. As far as they were concerned, all other theatrical activities existed solely and simply for the sake of the action on the stage. They were well aware of the practical aspects; they advertised, balanced their books, and kept the doors of the theater open; they mounted their productions well and took care to see the finish was smooth. Playwrights might provide the bones on which they modeled the flesh of their characters, but in the end, only the performance itself counted, that brief flow of time between the raising and lowering of the curtain when the actor created a world more intensely real than life itself. That and that alone was their raison d'être, and that alone shaped their decisions. Swiney would never be one of them.

Sometimes the three appeared temperamental, irresponsible, or even childish to outsiders like Swiney, and sometimes they were, but they were also artists with a profound knowledge of their intricate and complex art. If their concentration was necessarily focused on *how* rather than *what* they spoke, it did not follow that they disregarded the quality of a play, and Cibber once defended their judgment with a tart: "How should they have been able to act, or rise to any Excellence, if you supposed them not to feel or understand what you offer'd them? Would you have reduc'd them to the meer Mimickry of Parrots and Monkies, that can only prate, and play a great many pretty Tricks, without Reflection?" (II, 250-51). Because Cibber and Wilks and Dogget were actors themselves, they knew intuitively that an actor needs applause as he needs bread, and they governed accordingly. Cibber chose plays for their "theatrical" effectiveness; Wilks would sometimes play a supporting role and give the leading part to a second-rate workhorse like John Mills; and Dogget was not averse to rewarding an outstanding performer with a bonus. They felt deeply that no theatrical company could succeed unless the actors were its first consideration, and they did not think their point of view was at all unusual. To the uninitiated who, like Swiney, regarded the stage as a business venture or to the writers and critics who thought of it as a mode of literature, such supreme concern for actors was incomprehensible.

Despite the many problems they faced, Cibber looked back upon this season as the beginning of the halcyon years. Drury Lane had little competition from the opera, and although they opened only three new plays, none of which was especially successful, they managed very well with the repertory as it stood.[11] They had to make some changes to accommodate their expanded company, which now included those who had not gone to Queens, but the freedom to operate as they pleased, unfettered by either a hostile master or temperamental singers, was almost reward enough in itself.

Their monetary rewards were substantial enough that they did not need to extend the season, and as soon as they were finished in June, Wilks rushed off to play nineteen straight performances of Sir Harry Wildair in Dublin. Over at Queens, now faltering under an immense weight of debts, Collier cast a jealous eye at his prosperous rivals and began to exert his influence again, greater than ever now, for he was a strong Tory and so was most of the court. In the space of a few weeks, Hill was dismissed and Swiney moved back to the opera, with Collier replacing him as a nominal member of the Drury Lane management. The triumvirate did not welcome him, but he offered two distinct advantages: he had no intention of participating in the daily operations, and his Tory sympathies would enlist the kind of support their own Whiggism could not. They offered him a full share, but he refused, preferring an assured annual £700 instead.[12]

Cibber's own summer was darkened by the death of his brother, Lewis, from "too great a disregard for his Health" (I, 57), as Colley tactfully put it, for despite the lofty title of Fellow, Lewis had a reputation as one of the most disreputable members of the Oxford community.[13] Colley took his family to the country as usual, but this year he wrote nothing.

The managers' unity against outsiders did not prevent discord among themselves. Besides the Wilks-Dogget duels over finances, there were other disagreements. Wilks liked Charles Johnson, who presented them with a new play almost every season. Although neither Cibber nor Dogget had much regard for his work, Wilks waged an annual battle on his behalf, which he nearly always won. Cibber, on the other hand, preferred Susannah Centlivre's comedies and fought just as strenuously against Wilks's contention that her plays "had a great deal of Business, but not laughing Business."[14]

A more serious conflict arose over two Irish actors whom Wilks, perhaps prompted equally by generosity and egotism, hired without consulting either Cibber or Dogget. After a battle, his partners grudgingly consented to let them stay. Much later they learned he had also promised them a benefit. This time Dogget was "almost as intractable as Wilks himself," (II, 122) and Cibber was hard put to be a peacemaker. Taking Dogget aside, he argued that while he, too, was hurt by Wilks's "vain and over-bearing Behaviour," (II, 123) the Irishmen had done nothing more than show their inferiority to the regular actors. When Dogget nodded, Cibber reminded him how much they had all profited from Wilks's diligence, how he willingly took on long parts and performed far more often than anyone else, adding, lest Dogget take offense, that it was probably only because of a "fondness for Applause." It would be foolish, he argued, to "tempt the Rashness" of a man who could destroy them all, though the possibility Wilks would be angry enough to leave was remote. When he ended his argument, Dogget had only one question: how much would the benefit cost them? Cibber, seeing he had won his point, simply said, "I myself shall be answerable for the Charge" (II, 124).

It could be expensive, but he could afford it. Drury Lane cost forty pounds a night to open, a sum that Dogget knew as well as he had been established several years earlier. The actor whose benefit it was received anything over that figure; if the receipts for the night were less than forty pounds, the house took the loss and the actor got nothing, so beginners and minor players who could not command a large following, usually clubbed together in twos and threes to assure a profitable night.

The Irishmen had their benefit, but Dogget's concern had been well founded, for the accounts showed their receipts were ten pounds short. Cibber immediately directed Castelman, the treasurer, "to charge it received from me in the deficient Receipt of the Benefit-Day," knowing Wilks would see the notation on Saturday morning.

The moment came, and Wilks drew Cibber into the little stone passage outside the office. "What do you mean by pretending to pay in this ten pounds?" he asked angrily. "I do not understand such treatment."

Cibber's answer was blunt, "I gave Dogget my word that the Charge of the benefit should be fully paid. Since your friends neglected it, I felt I was bound to make it good."

"You and Dogget are always trying to make trouble for me," Wilks blustered, "but I can stand on my own legs, and you'll soon find I won't be used so!" Cibber said nothing, as Wilks raged predictably that he had been insulted and threatened to "tear the whole business to pieces!" If he couldn't even help a friend without causing a "senseless rout," he would go back to Ireland. "If I were gone, Dogget and you would not be able to keep the doors open a week," he warned.

It was an old and empty threat, but the time had come to answer it. Cibber spoke mildly and with too much truth to be denied. "We all have it in our power to do one another a mischief, but I believe none of us much care to hurt ourselves. You may do whatever you like. London will always have a Play-house and I shall always have a chance to play in it, even though it might not be as good as it has been. If I had thought my paying in the ten pounds could have caused such trouble, I would have been glad to have saved it" (II, 121-26).

It was now up to Wilks, who muttered ominously and stalked off. Cibber returned to the office and calmly continued to go over the accounts with Dogget. In a little while, Wilks came in looking like a storm cloud and sat down silently to work. The matter was finished, the bluff called, and never again did Wilks hire actors without consultation.

Such scenes were wearing and unnecessary in Cibber's view, but he accepted them as part of the effort needed to keep the appearance of harmony among the partners. Their position was not absolutely secure, and they were under constant stress. In January, Owen Swiney's complaints reached the courts, and they were forced to pay him his due.[15] Swiney used it to try and stave off the threat of bankruptcy a little longer, and Cibber, who liked him personally, signed a quitclaim on all the money Swiney owed him.[16]

But it was not only outside pressures that strained at the management, for the high-strung temperaments within the company demanded careful attention as well. In March, a riot erupted in the audience when one of the internal quarrels entered the public domain. It had begun when the managers accepted Ambrose Philips's tragedy *The Distrest Mother* and gave the title role to Jane Rogers, one of their better tragediennes. "Namby Pamby," as Pope dubbed Philips, insisted that Anne Oldfield have the part. Ordinarily, authors were disregarded, but Philips was a member of Joseph Addison's "little Senate." The group, mostly writers, included Richard Steele, Henry Brett, and Henry Carey, and, at this time, Swift and Pope.[17] They met frequently at Button's Coffee House, which had replaced Will's as the literary center of London after Dryden's death, and their support could guarantee success. The managers, unwilling to offend Philips, gave the role to Oldfield, who was not even grateful for the honor. She much preferred the comedies she played to such perfection and had been heard to say firmly, if inelegantly, "I hate to have a page dragging my tail about the stage."[18] Neither Anne's preference nor Jane's fury altered the decision, and while Richard Steele puffed the new "masterpiece" in the *Spectator*, Jane regaled her friends with loud complaints about her treatment. When *The Distrest Mother* opened on 17 March 1712, her claque became so violent that the guards had to be called. Jane was eventually pacified and her friends quieted, but the rivalry remained, especially after *The Distrest Mother* proved to be so popular that it went into the repertory.

The quarrels and disruptions had little effect on the audience, and the 1711-12 season was the best any of them had known. Cibber might have treated himself and his family to a comfortable holiday had not trouble of a different kind arisen at the beginning of summer. On 22 June, he was arrested and taken before Thomas Medlicott "to answer the overseers of St. Paul Covent-Garden for getting Mary Osbourne, spinster, with a bastard child."[19] This time, Drury Lane was not protected by a royal patent, and he was ordered to appear at the next Westminster Sessions. Henry Brett arranged for his release by paying the bail of forty pounds, and the charges were dropped before the matter came to court. Whether or not they were true, the story must have been known, and it may have been Mary Osbourne that Pope referred to many years later when he wrote, "And has not Colley too his lord and whore?"[20] Curiously enough, another legal confrontation occurred the day after Cibber's arrest, when Katharine had to call the police because David Seale, a "Yeoman of St. Martins in the Fields" made a "rout and tumult about her door."[21] Seale was brought to trial in August, but neither the reason for his crime nor the sentence upon him is known. The two events may have been connected or merely the kind of harassment that comes with fame, but whatever the cause, it was particularly unpleasant for Katharine, who was expecting their last child.

She was forty-five now, and her pregnancy was a matter of some concern. The births and rearing of Catherine (now seventeen), Anne (thirteen), Elizabeth (eleven), Theophilus (nine) and James (six) had taken their toll of her slender strength. The house in Spring Gardens was too crowded for the quiet she needed, and Colley began looking about for a more spacious residence. He found one in Southampton Street West, not far from Anne Oldfield's house and conveniently near the theater. They made their preparations during the summer, and before Christmas they were well prepared for the new member of the family.[22]

The advent of another child seemed to inspire Cibber's authorial pretensions, and he exaggerated very little when he said, "my Muse and my Spouse were equally prolifick . . . the one was seldom the Mother of a Child, but in the same Year the other made me the Father of a Play" (I, 264). This time he again mended "old Linnen," with a free adaptation of Corneille's *Le Cid* into *Ximena; or, The Heroick Daughter*. Seven years later he would write a preface for it, defining his approach and his concept of that elusive word, "theatrical," but at present he was concerned with practice, not theory. No more in awe of Corneille than of Shakespeare, he did what any good play doctor does, he adapted the material to his company. He exchanged the formal exposition of the first act for an "unborrow'd" set of events that eliminated the need for narration, removed the Infanta "who is always dropping in, like cold Water upon the Heat of the main Action," and gave Chimène's confidante a viable function within the plot. He cut the elaborately embroidered speeches, omitted entirely Roderigue's famous "stances" (still ravishing to French audiences today), and let a swift progression of scenes tell the story.

The most significant change is in the moral tone. Corneille's theme, love versus honor, invests both his protagonists. Honor demands that Roderigue kill Chimène's father even though the duel is forced upon him, and honor will not allow Chimène to marry her father's murderer. Divine intervention resolves the impasse when the king commands a second duel and orders Chimène to marry the victor. That it happens to be Roderigue is the sign of divine mercy, logical and proper in an absolute monarchy where the throne is believed to be occupied by God's vicegerent on earth. Cibber, however, had lived all his life in a constitutional monarchy, where royalty was not above morality. No king could alter the fact that Chimène was still to marry the man who killed her father, and he concluded: "If therefore without offending Nature or Probability, we can make the Father of *Ximena* [Chimène] recover of his Wounds, I see no Reason, why every Auditor might not in Honour congratulate their Happiness: By this Expedient their Story is instructive, and these Heroick Lovers stand at last Two fair Examples of rewarded Virtue."[23] He resurrected Ximena's father, Don Alvarez, in the last act with an entrance worthy of *Woman's Wit* or *The Lady's Last Stake*. The story became moral and instructive with love and virtue equated and rewarded, but the tragic sense of inevitability and the grandeur of the supranatural vanished completely.

The 1712-13 season began on 20 September, and the Drury Lane company played for two months with no competition, for Queens did not present an opera until 20 November. Drury Lane's houses were full, and, aside from Cibber's concern for Katharine, he was in the midst of the most "pleasing Prospect of Life" he had ever known. Steele came to a rehearsal of *Ximena* and puffed it in the *Spectator*:

I found the House so partial to one of their own Fraternity, that they gave every thing which was said such Grace, Emphasis, and Force in their Action, that it was no easy Matter to make any Judgment of the Performance. . . . Cibber himself took the Liberty to tell me that he expected I would do him Justice, and allow the Play well prepared for his Spectators, whatever it was for his Readers. He added very many Particulars not uncurious concerning the Manner of taking an Audience, and laying wait not only for their superficial Applause, but also for insinuating into their Affections and Passions by the artful Management of the Look, Voice, and Gesture of the Speaker. I could not but consent that the heroick Daughter appeared in the Rehearsal a moving Entertainment wrought out of a great and exemplary Virtue.[24]

Anne Oldfield played Ximena, and with Wilks as her leading man, the piece had every indication of success, although Anne was working under considerable strain. Her lover of more than a decade, Arthur Maynwaring, was dying of tuberculosis. She had nursed him faithfully through several attacks, but now that he was on his deathbed, his family took over. Anne, lacking the benefit of clergy, was not even allowed to see him. She was distraught at his death on 13 November and took refuge in the long rehearsals.

The play, which opened two weeks later, was not a remarkable success, but it ran for an acceptable six nights, giving Cibber one author's benefit and a lesson he never forgot. He played Don Alvarez for the opening, but relinquished it to Mills and, as was his custom, went out front to watch the play from the side boxes, concealing his identity with a wide-brimmed hat pulled low over his eyes. Although pleased with the "silent, fix'd Attention" of the majority, he could not help noticing "a Set of well dress'd merry making Criticks" who disrupted the performance with their "waggish Endeavours to Burlesque every Thing that seem'd to have a serious Effect on their Neighbours." Among them were several he counted as friends.

Ordinarily he was amused by cleverness, even at his own expense, and he enjoyed repartee unbridled by an overnice sense of propriety. It was the gentleman's form of humor, and Cibber, like his fellow actors, often indulged in it on and off the stage. But with a difference. Among his colleagues, insults were governed by an overriding respect for accomplishment, and they knew how far they could go without inflicting permanent injury. Outside the theater, no such governance obtained, and he was suddenly and painfully aware that the remarks he was overhearing were not the kind of teasing he understood and practiced but expressions of naked contempt for him and for his work.

Cibber, who could be as cutting as the sharpest wit, might sometimes be insensitive to others' feelings, but he was seldom deliberately cruel and never hypocritical. Shocked by their remarks, he recovered himself under the shelter of his hat brim, and when the same group came backstage later to offer their good wishes for success, he was able to greet them with his usual smiles. He had been badly hurt, however; he did not publish *Ximena* that year, and soon after, he announced he was "resolv'd never to trouble the Town" with another play.[25]

That resolution may not have included *Cinna's Conspiracy*, a translation of Corneille's tragedy that played three nights in February before disappearing forever. Colley took no credit for it, but Lintot's records show that he bought it from Cibber for thirteen pounds and printed it with no author listed. Colley was quite able to make the translation, but it is conceivable that, having received no applause for the performance, he wanted no more attacks either.[26]

His private worry about Katharine was eased when she was safely delivered of a daughter on 13 January 1713, the "last, tho' not least in love."[27] They named her Charlotte, and Colley spoiled her from the beginning, to the outrage of his oldest child, Catherine, who would always resent this late-comer into their lives.

The palmy days continued—for Cibber and his partners, at least. Owen Swiney was less fortunate, for, having inherited a mountain of debts with the opera, he was at last crushed beneath them. The settlement with the Drury Lane management had only postponed the inevitable crash, and in the middle of January, with debtor's prison looming ominously, he broke and ran for the safety of Holland, leaving the mountain behind him.[28] The opera staggered on, hampered by the lack of management and a ceaseless flow of creditors, and their productions matched Drury Lane neither in elegance nor in size of audience.

A tangible mark of the eminence of the Drury Lane theater was evident when Joseph Addison offered it his tragedy, *Cato*, finished at last after many years.[29] The managers were delighted and asked him to read it for the company, but the diffident author appealed to Cibber, whose expert and enthusiastic reading was so impressive that Addison requested him to play the title role. By now, Cibber knew his own limitations well enough to refuse, and they agreed young Barton Booth should play Cato; Wilks, the tempestuous Jubal; and Anne Oldfield, carrying Maynwaring's posthumous child, would play Marcia as long as she could. Cibber took the part of the villain, Syphax, a grotesque like Richard III.

They opened to a crowded house on 14 April, as an extremely nervous Addison sat in a box drinking more burgundy and champagne than was good for him. It was soon clear they had a success unmatched in Drury Lane's history. Londoners, already celebrating the Treaty of Utrecht, which had officially ended the War of the Spanish Succession on 29 March, were excited by the political sentiments. Whigs and Tories cheered alike, and the *Flying Post* commented, "The Author has taken the most effectual Method to make his Audience in Love with Liberty, Virtue, and the Country. . . . For what is represented on the Stage, if artfully manag'd, and nicely perform'd, makes a deeper Impression on the Mind, and affects one more, than any other Art or Method possibly can."[30]

Booth was a magnificent Cato. Not quite as tall as Wilks, he was nonetheless an impressive figure, athletic but graceful, with every muscle under command, and his "attitudes" were striking. His ruddy, expressive features were attractive, and his sonorous baritone gave depth to his sensitive characterizations. Distantly related to the earl of Warrington, he had been intended for religious orders and educated at Westminster (where Colley's son, Theo, was now enrolled), but at the age of seventeen, he ran away to Ireland and trained for the stage under John Ashbury. After some years, he returned to London and joined Betterton, who recognized his promise. The merger of the two companies in 1706 had been no advantage to him, for the Drury Lane management regarded him as a "young player," and gave him little encouragement. When that company went back to Queens after the silencing order, Booth stayed with Rich and began to play leading roles.

The triumvirate had, of course, kept him when they returned to Drury Lane and had grudgingly offered him better parts, finally giving him Pyrrhus in *The Distrest Mother*, the role that established him as a star. He consolidated that position with *Cato* and the help of aristocratic friends. Every night after the performance, coroneted coaches whisked him away to noble houses where he was feted as if he were the real Roman hero.

One night, early in the run, the Tories severely wounded Dogget's Whig loyalties by giving Booth fifty pounds for Cato's "honest Opposition to a perpetual Dictator, and his dying so bravely in the Cause of Liberty."[31] The Tories, Dogget said, had no right to such claims and proposed that the managers make their own gift of fifty guineas to show the "Equality and liberal Spirit" of Whigs and "to secure *Booth* more firmly" to their own interest. Wilks, seeing the dramatic effect, agreed wholeheartedly, but Cibber objected. He knew very well that Booth was intensely ambitious to enter the management, that he had complained bitterly and unveraciously to his friend, Lord Lansdowne, of being slighted and of working "for a bare subsistence only" while the triumvirate enjoyed inordinate rewards from his labors.[32]

Colley warned that such generosity would only encourage Booth's pretensions, but his partners refused to listen. Wilks claimed Cibber's objection was a "pitiful Evasion of a noble impulse," and Dogget was certain he could handle Booth. "Nobody can think his Merit slighted by so handsome a Present as fifty Guineas," he said, adding with crushing finality, that the "House, Scenes, and Cloaths are our own, and not in the power of the Crown to dispose of" (II, 133). That night, they gave Booth the prize, which he took "with a Thankfulness that made *Wilks* and *Dogget* perfectly easy," and for some time after, they twitted Cibber for his jealousy.

Cato ran for twenty performances and would have run longer, had Anne Oldfield's condition not closed it.[33] Almost simultaneously, Wilks and Dogget realized that Cibber had been right, that Booth was not only determined to become a full partner in the management but had enlisted the aid of Bolingbroke, the powerful Tory lord favored by the queen. They tried to curtail Booth's politicking by keeping him busy, giving plays in which he had a substantial role almost every night, but no sooner did the curtain fall, than Bolingbroke's carriage appeared and carried Booth off to Windsor, returning him the next day more secure in favor than ever.

Booth was a happy man. He fell in love with Susannah Mountfort and asked her to marry him, but she had been left an inheritance of three hundred pounds a year on condition that she *not* marry, and they settled for a liaison. Intoxicated by his sudden success, Booth began to make his presence felt in a way he had not been able to do previously. He could no longer complain of neglect, for he was given almost any part he wanted. Almost. He demanded Pierre in *Venice Preserv'd*, a plum long ago given John Mills, the workhorse of the company. Mills lacked fire, but he was capable, versatile, and, above all, diligent. He actually appeared more often than the stars, usually in secondary roles, and he could always be depended on to substitute in an emergency. The managers occasionally gave him a leading role, more as a reward for effort than a tribute to his talent. Booth's capricious demand was tactless at best; acceding to it would set a dangerous precedent, yet Cibber and Dogget hesitated to offend him. Wilks had no such reservations, and his Irish temper flared. If Booth took Pierre, he said angrily, he would not play Jaffeir; in fact, Booth could *have* Jaffeir, but he could not deprive Mills of one of his few prizes. Booth accepted the reproof—along with Jaffeir, which he played from this time forth.

The success of *Cato* prompted the idea of a summer season at Oxford. Addison had studied at Magdalen, and his play was bound to be warmly welcomed; Drury Lane's composer-conductor, Johann Pepusch, was to receive his doctorate there this year, and Oxford was far enough from Windsor to keep Booth from politicking so fervently. They negotiated with the academic powers and played from 14 July until 2 August. It was a triumph for all sides, for the managers had elected to give only one performance a day, which assured full houses, and they were so delighted with their net profit of £150 each that they donated £50 to St. Mary's, the University Church.[34] The actors were happy because they were paid as if they performed the usual two plays a day, and they were so discreet in their offstage behavior that Vice Chancellor Gardiner thanked them and commended them publicly for their "Decency and Order."[35] Pepusch received his doctorate in spite of a severe censure by the Oxford dons for having his doctoral composition performed by Drury Lane musicians instead of their own dignified amateurs.

A jubilant Cibber returned to London to find a household shrouded in sorrow for his sister-in-law, Rose Shore. She had been ill for some time and had made her will just after Colley left for Oxford. She died on 17 August, shortly after his return. Along with their grief, the Cibbers were soon involved in litigation over her will, which had so confused her husband's legacy that Katharine had to go to court to straighten it out.[36] Various depositions in the affair reveal that Rose had been a very prosperous widow and that the Cibbers' concern was primarily for Elizabeth's share of the inheritance. Colley's own statement pointed out that his handsome income was uncertain, that he possessed no real estate, and that his large family included three other daughters who would also need dowries. John Shore, who acted with him in this matter, added that Cibber took good care of his family, "according to his means." After months of legal maneuvering, the will was administered according to Rose's wishes. Colley said little about these problems, for any comment would be used by his enemies, whose number increased with his status, but he settled his Foppington mask more firmly in place. It was now more than personal armor, it was a wall against the world, a bulwark that protected his family.

He needed the mask in both its private and public manifestations when the 1713-14 season began. Booth had used the month's holiday to persuade Shrewsbury that he should be admitted to the license, and the word came down from the lord chamberlain's office early in October. Dogget's conviction that their holdings in the theater's stock could not be touched by the Crown was quickly proved a misconception, as Cibber had realized. Their license, held only "at Pleasure," could be revoked at any time, and Shrewsbury exercised his power by ordering them to set a value on their stock and let Booth buy into it. Profits would be divided among four instead of three, and the reluctant managers' reactions were characteristic: Wilks naively proposed they make the amount outrageously high; Dogget "had no mind to dispose of any of his Property" and refused to set a price at all; Cibber bowed to overwhelming power.

The weekly business meetings became harrowing confrontations as Wilks and Dogget, apprehensive and testy, lashed out at each other while Cibber vainly urged peaceful submission. This time, Wilks proved more tractable than Dogget, who denounced Booth as an upstart opportunist, undeserving, unqualified, and a Tory to boot. His partners held just as firm and offered him any conditions he liked, but he refused to listen. Finally, after one such session, he rose to his feet, "You may both do as you please, but nothing except the Law will make me part with my property!" Dogget was no Wilks to bluster and forget, and Cibber knew he would not retract. "You had best get a lawyer, then," he answered coldly, "for you will have to sue for it" (II, 144). Dogget stared, then without a word turned and stomped out of the office. It was his last act as a manager.

On 11 November, the old license became invalid, and a new one, adding Booth's name, took effect. Matters immediately worsened, complicated by the fact that Dogget controlled much of the theater's cash. Wilks and Cibber asked him to return the moneys to the general fund; Castelman, the treasurer, needed his signature to pay the bills; and Booth requested a statement of the accounts. Dogget refused them all, stayed away from the theater, and spent his days trying for redress from an unsympathetic lord chamberlain.

Wilks and Cibber drafted a new proposal for equitable sharing, but Dogget would neither listen nor speak to them and demanded his share of the current profits. At last, on 16 January 1714, they wrote the first of several "Humble Remonstrances" to Shrewsbury.[37] In it they described Dogget's actions, complained that they were left liable to lawsuits, and requested a ruling on whether Dogget was entitled to share in any of the present income, since he was fulfilling none of his duties as manager or as actor. Booth added an attestation of its truth, and Collier appended a note: "I hope you will Imediatly Informe her Majesty of Mr Dogget's Disobedience and signe an Order for his being struck out of the Lycence: that the business of the House may goe on which will allways be under Difficulty's

while he is in."[38] Dogget riposted with a series of his own "Humble Remonstrances," and the struggle continued through the spring. Even John
Mills entered the lists briefly with his own letter to the chamberlain's office
requesting that *he* be allowed to replace Dogget, but the request was probably not taken seriously.[39] In March, Wilks was prostrated by the death of
his wife, Elizabeth, and Cibber and Booth carried on while he slowly recovered.[40] The end of the season saw no end to the impasse, and every
summer day brought new crises. The acrimonious discussions were silenced when, with shocking suddenness, Queen Anne died of an apoplectic
stroke on 1 August 1714.[41]

The theatrical quarrel receded into limbo as the political temperature
soared to fever pitch. The Hanoverian succession had been a settled fact
since 1707, according to the Whigs who had fostered it, but a significant
number of Tories preferred a Stuart on the throne, even if it meant bringing
the Catholic Prince James Francis Edward over from France. In the turmoil
following the queen's death, the Jacobites wavered, the Whigs moved
swiftly, and on 18 September, George I arrived to ascend the English
throne. His coronation on 23 October was to have a marked effect on Drury
Lane's future. Political loyalties divided its audiences, sometimes in the
middle of a performance. Riots drove away the less aggressive for days at a
stretch, and the triumvirate had to hire guards to maintain the peace, a
precaution that added £170 to the annual expenses.

The managers could afford it, since the houses were generally full, but
they began to worry when the specter of Christopher Rich rose again. He
had not dared to use his patent during Anne's reign, but under the new
sovereign he prepared to open the theater he had rebuilt in Lincoln's Inn
Fields. Rich's death on 4 November offered only a brief reprieve, for his
son, John, completed the work and opened on 14 December with a company that included Jane Rogers (still simmering from *The Distrest Mother*)
and several other excellent actors from the old Drury Lane theater.[42]

Colley, hurt by their defection, was somewhat relieved when they told
him they had not left because of unfair treatment but because of Wilks's
ungovernable temper. What they did *not* say (and Cibber probably would
not have believed) was that they had more opportunity at Lincoln's Inn
Fields. The repertory system provided fine training for beginners and was
splendid for those with clearly defined "lines" (types) or for stars that audiences wanted to see nightly. For those in between, it was less satisfying.
Advancement was possible but difficult, and the kind of rapid rise that
Cibber, Wilks, and Booth had made was exceedingly rare. John Rich's new
theater offered a chance for quick and permanent reputation. They were
proven right. Young Rich began his rule with a series of excellent productions that caught the fancy of the town and made stars of the defectors.

Drury Lane lost another good actor when George Powell died on 14

December. He was still with the company, although the arrogant leading man who had made Cibber's life so miserable when he first entered the theater had undergone a sad metamorphosis. Dissipation had developed into an alcoholism so severe that Booth, who once had similar leanings, had been shocked into abstemiousness.[43] For the last few years Powell had been a secondary player at Drury Lane, sinking gradually into a mire of debt until at the end there was not enough money for burial. Cibber and Booth (Wilks abstaining) signed the bills for a splendid funeral, and Powell was buried, with more dignity than he had lived, at St. Clement Danes.[44]

Underlying all else was the continuing problem of Dogget. Claims and counterclaims flew back and forth via the lord chamberlain's office without either side's moving an inch from its fixed position. Dogget demanded recompense for his ill-treatment, and the managers asked that Shrewsbury "compel" him to act in plays. Both requests might have fallen into a bottomless well for all the answer they received. Apart from the unfamiliar luster of royal patronage at performances,[45] almost the only light in that dark winter was a slowly maturing plan that, ironically, had originated with Dogget but that now alienated him still further as it reached fruition.

It had arisen between that fateful month in 1712, when Queen Anne appointed twelve Tory peers to ensure their party's majority in the House and shortly before *Cato* worked its magic on Booth's career. Dogget and Cibber felt that Collier, whose Tory affiliations they disliked almost as much as having to pay him the seven hundred pounds a year he now demanded, should be replaced as their fellow licensee, and they agreed on Richard Steele as the ideal choice. Steele's association with the theater had been long and friendly. Drury Lane had produced his plays, and he in turn had given the theater accolades and puffs in the *Tatler* and the *Spectator*. About to enter Parliament, he was a Whig of considerable influence, and they had begun to sound him out on the subject. Steele was amenable, but the time was not yet ripe, and negotiations continued in a desultory fashion without coming to a conclusive agreement.

In the fall of 1714, with the Whigs back in power and the pressure from Dogget becoming unbearable, Cibber approached Steele again. This time he gave more than a nodding assent.[46] In October, with the assistance of his friend the duke of Newcastle, a new license was activated in the names of Steele, Cibber, Wilks, and Booth. Collier and Dogget at once appealed to the courts. Collier had no legal foundation for his suit and soon dropped it, but Dogget, infuriated at what he considered total betrayal, pursued it until he won a fair settlement.

Dogget's anger was icily evident wherever he went. It did not disturb Wilks or Booth, who had never been fond of him, but it was painful to Cibber, who really liked him and who never failed to salute him warmly when their paths crossed. Dogget studiously ignored Colley, and the coffeehouse patrons who had so often enjoyed their mock differences now watched the real one with malicious glee. Cibber appeared untouched by Dogget's behavior, but he was deeply sorry to lose an old friend. Often ridiculed for his claim that he did not harbor grudges, he proved it again and again in his behavior toward Dogget now and toward others later on.

The new license solved some of the company's difficulties, but it did not offer anything like the benefits of Rich's patent, and Steele, again under the aegis of Newcastle, pressed for the privilege of once more making the Drury Lane company "Gentlemen of the Great Chamber." The climate was right, and George I was agreeable. On 19 January 1715, the four managers were awarded a royal patent that invalidated the previous license and was to last for Steele's lifetime plus three years.[47]

It was an immense victory, gratifying Cibber, perhaps, even more than his partners. Beginning with none of their physical and vocal advantages, he had developed into a superior theatrical artist, easily their equal as an actor-manager and well beyond them as a playwright. More of his plays were in the repertory than any other living writer's, and for the past five years (as they would for the next eighteen), his partners had deferred to him in the selection of new works.[48] With his actor's sense and his playwright's judgment, he had already begun the change in English drama that would become part of its permanent heritage. The unpromising youngster of 1690 had become the most powerful man in the English theater.

The position drew an ever-widening circle of friends and enemies. His friends, from the great Whig lords to the most obscure artist, enjoyed the company of the man who was always "on," ever ready to amuse, and who more often laughed at himself than at others. His enemies, political and professional, found him less amusing, looked for dark motives behind his actions, and circulated gossip to show him as a vicious, insensitive clod. The story of the actor Benjamin Johnson is a good example of how such gossip worked. Davies relates that the Drury Lane managers, anxious to prevent Johnson from going over to Rich, gave him Dogget's roles, among which was Justice Shallow in *Henry IV (Part 2)*, but that when Johnson was ill, Cibber appropriated the part and did not give it back until he retired.[49] Actually, Johnson was given none of Dogget's roles, and *Henry IV (Part 2)* was not performed until 17 December 1720 with the note "Not acted these Sixteen Years." Cibber played Shallow in that performance, as he did until he retired, but Johnson never played it at all.[50]

The strength of the new patent was tested almost at once when Vanbrugh requested payment for the Queens theater stock Swiney had taken to Drury Lane years before. Shrewsbury ordered the managers to pay him an annual one hundred pounds "rent." Cibber responded with a firm letter stating that only their first license, issued when they were the "Sole Acting Company," had required such payment. After Booth's name was added, no money had been asked for or paid. Now there were two acting companies, one of which, he reminded Shrewsbury, was "made up of our Actors, whom we cannot get an Order to oblige them to return to us," and he concluded sharply that "neither the late License nor his Majesty's Letters Patents (by virtue of which we now Act) . . . obliges us to continue such payments."[51]

No more was heard of the matter, and Cibber celebrated with another test of the ban on music at Drury Lane: *Venus and Adonis*, a slight afterpiece hardly enough to break his vow of no more plays. He had put it together some time earlier but had not been able to stage it because of the restriction on using music at Drury Lane. Now the way was opened to them to add music if and when they felt it was needed. *Venus and Adonis* is a simple retelling of the legend with moral overtones, and it was set to music by Cibber's friend, Pepusch, whose future wife, Marguerite de l'Epine, made a charming Adonis. Venus falls in love with Adonis and Mars is jealous. She pacifies him with false promises and then, in a scene reminiscent of *Woman's Wit*, confesses her true feelings to Adonis. Mars emerges and threatens to kill Adonis, but when Venus interposes, rationalizes, "'Twere poor, myself to give the Blow," and leaves the boy to be killed by a boar. The verses fit the music well, although in print they are pure Cibberian bathos, as the innocent young Adonis sings:

> I've heard Men talk of Sighs and Kisses,
> But can't imagine where the Bliss is.[52]

Yet the text was not attacked, even when he published it. In twenty years he would not escape so lightly.

The preface to the printed edition gave Cibber the chance to attack Italian opera on the same moral and aesthetic grounds that Addison and Steele had laid out earlier. Morally, it was deplorable, "for no theatrical performance can be absolutely good that is not proper; and how can we judge of its propriety, when we know not one word?" Cibber asked reasonably. As a theater man, he complained of a structure in which "the songs are so often turn'd out of their places to introduce some absurd favourite of the singer, that in a few days the first book you have bought is reduc'd to little more than the title-page of what it pretends to." He joined his friends in pleading the cause of opera in English, pointing out reasonably that it was "an easier matter to instruct two or three performers in tolerable *English*, than to teach a whole nation *Italian*." More important, his mockery dimly foreshadowed *The Beggar's Opera*, although his genuine love for music led him to give praise where he felt it was due, and he concluded that "after having said so much of its absurdities, it will be but just to allow the excellencies of the *Italian* composition; the manner of being indisputably superior to all nations for a theatre."

Venus and Adonis brought no reprimand from the lord chancellor's office. It was a valuable attraction this spring when the competition from Lincoln's Inn Fields reduced the Drury Lane boxoffice by two-thirds,[53] and when the company's only successful premiere was *Lady Jane Gray*, Rowe's poignant, if nonhistorical, tragedy. The patent had given them prestige but not the enormous profits they had been making before John Rich entered the scene. Still, they were comfortable enough not to extend the season, and in June the three managers went on their separate holidays—Booth with his Susannah, Wilks with his new wife and family, and Cibber to Twickenham with Katharine and the children.[54] Cibber must have felt the need for a rest; in addition to the battle with Dogget, the struggle for the patent, and the new competition from Rich, Drury Lane had opened its doors on 188 performances this season, and Cibber had played in 100 of them.

Strawberry Hill was a quiet place twelve miles from the heat and dust of London. Here Cibber relaxed with his family: Catherine and Anne, already young ladies, Elizabeth, the "heiress," nearly so, and the willful Theo, wise beyond his eleven years. Their late child, Charlotte, was now a toddler of two and a half, spoiled by her father, who continued to leave the unpleasant task of discipline to the frail Katharine.[55]

Constitutionally incapable of the idleness he professed, Cibber set to work on another afterpiece to be produced in the fall. Like his first one, *Myrtillo* is a pastoral interlude with a simple plot set to music "in the Italian style." Laura teases her lover, Myrtillo, in a charmingly comic scene until he vows to leave her forever, at which point shepherds and shepherdesses appear and unite the two. It is a piece of froth designed as the icing on the cake of the evening and probably did not cost him a week's work, but it served to fill some of the time away from London.[56]

He probably returned to the City earlier than usual this year, for the theater was undergoing a major renovation. The elder Rich had decorated the Lincoln's Inn Fields house lavishly. He had also added special stage machinery that the younger Rich used for magic effects in pantomime afterpieces like *Harlequin Dr. Faustus*, in which disembodied legs danced about the stage and then vanished. Such "spectacles" alone drew full houses. By contrast, Drury Lane looked positively shabby, and the necessary redecoration was an expensive investment that delayed the opening of the 1715-16 season a full two weeks. For such alterations the company did not need permission from the new lord chamberlain, the duke of Bolton, a gallant who loved the theater as a spectator but had no inclination to govern it.[57]

The managers plunged at once into their rigorous schedule. Each morning one or more of the triumvirate rehearsed the next new play, each afternoon they ran through the evening's offering, and each night they were all either on the stage or in the audience. On Saturday mornings they met to decide on the next week's schedule, settle disputes among the company and review the accounts, paid with regularity every Monday. They were careful of their money; ten shillings worth of starching was as nearly documented as ten pounds worth of candles. They regularly discounted bills the odd shilling or so for cash settlement, and if the tradesman objected, they noted with some asperity, "This Bill is extravagantly dear." Advertising in the *Daily Courant* was important, but they did not hesitate to stop a five-shilling payment if a name was misspelled. On the other hand, they willingly disbursed funds to keep the productions fresh and bright. Oldfield's splendid gowns were costly, Cibber himself cheerfully spent seventeen shillings for Foppington's silver buttons and often required a special dresser, and neither Booth nor Wilks demurred at ordering yards of costly materials—especially when their partner was absent.[58]

The division of labor among the new patentees was somewhat different from that of the previous triumvirate. Their duties were equally shared, but the separate areas were less clearly defined and no one person controlled the money as Dogget had. The most marked change was in the relative tranquillity of their relationship. Booth's opinions, strong as Dogget's, were tempered by a flexibility that allowed for compromise, and, although he once confessed he disliked Wilks's outbursts of temper as much as Cibber did, he did not allow them to provoke him into the kind of ferocious scene that had so marred the earlier years.

At least part of Booth's composure came from indolence. Lacking Cibber's robust health or Wilks's endurance, he was conscientious in his duties, but he did little more. He was anything but lazy in preparing his roles (he read *Cato* through every time he played the part) and he was an excellent director of the plays in which he acted so splendidly, but he refused to spend energy without good cause. He needed a reason for passion—halfway through a languid performance, he could come backstage, call for a glass of wine and water, and reenter to electrify the audience, merely because he had caught sight of a former schoolmate whose opinion he valued.[59]

The fourth partner, the recently knighted Sir Richard Steele, had aligned himself with the powerful Whigs and, with Newcastle's patronage, had been elected to represent Boroughbridge in Parliament. He was now too involved with politics to offer more than support and encouragement from afar, and he rarely came near Drury Lane. The arrangement suited the triumvirate perfectly. The three would welcome the new play he had promised them, but his advice on daily operations was not needed, and his financial counsel was suspect. Steele was permanently in debt and had already mortgaged his share of the patent to Edward Minshull, who was to become Susannah Mountfort's lover after she broke with Booth.[60]

However skilled the three managers were in dealing with company matters, events outside the theater walls sometimes swept them up in circumstances quite beyond their control. One of these was the Jacobite uprising. In September 1715, the Scots had started an abortive rebellion to place Prince James on the throne. The back of the revolt was broken at the Battle of Sheriffmuir in November, but the emotional climate remained intense, and when the prince landed in Scotland in January 1716, crowds celebrated his "restoration" with riots all over London. The sight must have recalled to Colley his childhood memories of mobs streaming past his home during the Popish Plot fever, and the cheers for the Pretender could only have reminded him of the Glorious Revolution. The demonstrations were soon put down and the leaders imprisoned or hanged at Tyburn, but the strong feelings were slow to subside.

Cibber's Whig loyalties put him firmly on the side of the Hanovers, a political stance that would have overwhelming significance for him and for Drury Lane in the years to come. As with most men of his time, his politics carried over into every corner of his life. His aristocratic friends were Whig lords; he frequented Button's Coffee House, center of the literary Whigs; and Drury Lane itself became known as the "Whig house." Whenever he had time, he was part of the circle around Addison, soon to join the ministry, and it was as a member of this group that he met the man who was to become his archenemy, Alexander Pope.

Cibber admired the brilliant young poet who had already made a name for himself with *Essay on Criticism* and *Rape of the Lock*, and he gladly subscribed for Pope's translation of the *Iliad*, but they had little in common. Politically, professionally, and personally they were at opposite poles. Pope sympathized with the Tories and would one day reflect their views in his satires. He conceived of drama as literature and actors as the playwright's parrots. Frail, already bearing the marks of physical pain, he found in Cibber's Foppington mask a repellent image of all the values he most disliked.

They were polite enough to each other and, if Cibber is to be believed, occasionally socialized together. According to the story he told later, he, Pope, and Addison's stepson, Lord Warwick, visited a bawdy house one evening;

where his lordship's frolic proposed was to slip his little Homer, as he called him, at a girl of the game, that he might see what sort of figure a man of his size, sobriety, and vigor (in verse) would make when the frail fit of love had got into him; in which he so far succeeded that the smirking damsel who served us with tea happened to have charms sufficient to tempt the little-tiny manhood of Mr Pope into the next room with her: at which you may imagine his lordship was in as much joy as what might happen within as our small friend could probably be in possession of it. But I (forgive me all ye mortified mortals whom his fell satire has since fallen upon) observing he had stayed as long as without hazard of his health he might, I, "Prick'd to it by foolish honesty and love" as Shakespeare says, without ceremony threw open the door upon him, where I found this little hasty hero, like a terrible tomtit, pertly perching upon the mount of love! But such was my surprise that I fairly laid hold of his heels and actually drew him down safe and sound from his danger. My lord, who stayed tittering without in hopes the sweet mischief he came for would have been completed, upon my giving an account of the action within, began to curse and call me an hundred silly puppies for my impertinently spoiling the sport; to which with great gravity I replied, "Pray, my lord, consider what I have done was in regard to the honor of our nation! For would you have had so glorious a work as that of making Homer speak elegant English cut short by laying up our little gentleman of a malady which his thin body might never have been cured of? No, my lord! Homer would have been too serious a sacrifice to our evening merriment."[61]

Cibber's story may not be true—it was published at the time he was trying to ward off the *Dunciad*, and could well be the kind of sharp raillery so frequently practiced by eighteenth-century gentlemen and so shocking to the sensibilities of their Victorian descendants. Pope denied it (but without the vehemence one might expect), although he later used it as an excuse for his terrible retribution. The story may not be entirely false, and some variation of the incident may well have embarrassed Pope so painfully that it left a lasting mark.[62] Cibber said nothing about it for more than twenty-five years, and then only after severe provocation, but there is little evidence of friendly relations between them after 1716.

If Cibber amused himself with jokes, practical and otherwise, outside the theater, matters within Drury Lane were sober enough this season. The heavy expenses of redecoration, and Rich's inroads on the box office had set the company back financially. Aside from Cibber's little afterpiece, the theater presented only one new work, Addison's *The Drummer* (in which Cibber played "Tinsel"), for a wretched three performances, and times were so lean the managers gave themselves benefits at the end of the year. The political scene was still unstable, and during the summer, mobs rioted in London, brandishing the Stuart white rose and oak leaf with furious abandon until the soldiers appeared.

Cibber and his family were out of the city, but not so far away that he was out of touch. The country was fine for women and children, but London was the center of his life, and he maintained a copious correspondence. Not all the news was cheerful. Halfway through the summer he received a letter containing a detailed account of Dogget's "death." Cibber claimed later he knew it was a practical joke designed to provoke him into an expression of his "true" feelings about his former partner. Whether he was serious or not, his answer would undoubtedly have been the same, and he obliged with genuine warmth, praising Dogget's merit and imputing their quarrel "to his having naturally deceived himself in the Justice of his Cause." His only complaint, he said, was Dogget's "irreconcilable Disaffection to me upon it, whom he could not reasonably blame for standing in my own

Defence; that not to endure me after it was a Reflection upon his Sense, when all our Acquaintance had been Witnesses of our former Intimacy, which my Behaviour in his Lifetime had plainly shewn him I had a mind to renew" (II, 152). Back in London, Cibber quickly learned that not only was Dogget very much alive but that very summer had established a race for the Thames watermen, the prize being a new coat and a silver badge.[63]

Not long after, Cibber met his old friend in a coffeehouse. Although they were at the same table, Dogget ignored Cibber's salutation as coldly as ever, but when Colley opened his snuffbox, Dogget reached out his hand for a taste. After a few moments, Colley "took Courage" and asked how he liked it, and Dogget responded with the first words he had spoken to Cibber in almost three years, "Umh—the best—umh!—I have tasted in a great while!" The ice did not thaw at once, but eventually the temperature grew warm enough for Cibber to ask what had prompted Dogget to leave Drury Lane. Was it, he wanted to know, anything he had done? If so, he was eager to make amends. Dogget was reluctant to talk about his leaving, and it was difficult for him to put his feelings into words, but at last they came out in "half Sentences and *Innuendoes*."

No, it was nothing Cibber had done, it was not even the admission of Booth to the license, although "if you had stood it out as I did, Booth might have paid a better price for it.—You were too much afraid of the Court—but that's all over.—There were other things in the playhouse—no man of spirit—to be always pester'd and provok'd by a trifling wasp—a—vain—shallow!—A man will sooner beg his bread than bear it!" What had Dogget to bear, Cibber asked reasonably, that he had not?

It was not the same problem. "You can play with a Bear, or let him alone to do what he will, but I could not let him lay his Paws upon me without being hurt. You did not feel him as I did.—And for a man to be cutting of throats upon every trifle at my time of day!—If I had been as covetous as he thought me, maybe I might have borne it as well as you" (II, 154-55).

The secret was out. Crusty old Dogget, who had always seemed pre-occupied with business and his own roles, was as thin-skinned as a girl before Wilks's Irish bluster. He had never realized that Wilks did not mean half what he said or that the flamboyant personality warmed as quickly to affection as to anger. But Dogget was wrong about Cibber. He, too, had felt Wilks's temper, and he had put it into perspective long ago when he realized the caliber of the man. Cibber would never be able to change Dogget's opinion of Wilks, and things between himself and Dogget would never again be the same, but his gift of friendship had allowed the old actor to vent his feelings, and the bitterness between them gradually dissolved.[64]

Foppington's imperviousness to hostility had served a positive purpose. By this time it was indistinguishable from the puppeteer behind it, probably because some of the threads that held it in place were part of Cibber's own character. He enjoyed his public image, the richly embroidered waist-coat, the snowy linen, the silken hose; he was equally grand at home in his brocaded dressing gown, the elegantly curled wig set aside for a turban perched on his shorn pate with careful carelessness. The years of good living had thickened his figure slightly, and he had not been called "Hatchet Face" for many years, but he displayed a youthful grace as he puffed the finest tobacco in his long curved pipe or dipped with fastidious fingers into his gilded snuffbox.

At the same time, the man was separate from the mask. Like all actors, he was quite aware that the first step toward real prosperity was a prosper-ous facade, and even when he was poor he had kept up appearances. Yet his values were not those of a fop. He liked to seem indolent, but he worked as hard as Wilks; he liked to gamble, but he was never arrested for debt, nor did his family want for its needs. He was not a thrifty man, but he had put some of his earnings from the profitable 1712-13 season into the South Sea Company sponsored by the earl of Oxford and no doubt thought that for once he had been exceedingly prudent.

Cibber probably needed the returns from his investment, for the profits at Drury Lane were no larger than the previous year. A revival of Rowe's *Tamerlane* was popular enough to put it back into the repertory, although it provoked an ominous comment from Dudley Ryder: "I observed in general that the manner of speaking in our theatres in tragedy is not natural. There is something that would be very shocking and disagreeable and very unnat-ural in real life. Persons would call it theatrical, meaning by that something stiff and affected."[65] The thought echoed Aaron Hill's complaint about the actors' "affected, vicious and unnatural tone of voice" in the preface to his tragedy, *The Fatal Vision*, a grievance that would be heard more often in the next decade.

On the recommendation of Pope and his friend Dr. Arbuthnot, the managers of Drury Lane accepted *Three Hours after Marriage*, a new farce by plump, gentle John Gay, whose fund of good humor included a quality of helplessness that made a large number of people feel personally respon-sible for him. Pope had taken him into the exclusive "Scriblerian" group which boasted Swift, Oxford, Bolingbroke, Arbuthnot, and the brilliant, unstable Thomas Parnell. Gay had been less successful than the others until Drury Lane produced his satiric afterpiece *The What D'ye Call It* in 1715. Cibber suspected Pope's hand in it, and on an afternoon when both writers were in the theater, he let his feelings be known. Gay had left his pocketknife on the table, and Colley picked it up and examined the handle with elaborate care. Gay's name was engraved on it.

"What!" Colley said with mock surprise, handing it back. "Does Mr.

Pope make knives as well?"[66] It was not a remark calculated to endear him to the poet.

Pope and Arbuthnot had also helped write *Three Hours after Marriage*, but the Drury Lane managers were not optimistic about it. Wilks and Booth had no roles, the plot was negligible, and the satire would probably amuse only the Scriblerians. On the other hand, they desperately needed a new play, and Pope's recommendation assured them a sizable audience. Pope may even have offered to revise Cibber's still unpublished *Ximena* as an added inducement, although this is extremely doubtful.[67]

The plot concerns two rakes attempting to seduce a young woman the day she is married. It is merely a frame for the satire, and the audience had no difficulty in recognizing Fossile, the husband, as Dr. Woodward, a well-known and rather pompous antiquarian. His bride, played by Anne Oldfield, was a satirized conglomerate of several eminent ladies, and the character of Sir Tremendous was a merciless sketch of the critic John Dennis, who was deeply offended by it. Cibber played the leader of the two rakes, Plotwell, and some have assumed he did not know it was a caricature of himself.[68] It is inconceivable that Colley, nearing fifty and with more than a quarter of a century on the stage, should have missed the point, but by playing the role himself, he blunted the sharpness of the satire and showed such good sportsmanship that he earned the critics' admiration.

Three Hours after Marriage had a tumultuous reception in January. The Scriblerians had as many enemies as friends, and both sides were vociferous. At times the uproar was so great that the actors could not be heard and they lost some of the most telling points. On the fourth night, Pinkethman became wedged in the crocodile case where he was supposed to hide and, in trying to get out, bumped into Mrs. Garnet, knocking her unconscious. Pinkethman ad libbed his way through the emergency, but at the cost of the carefully planned lines. The literati were amused; not so the general public. The play lasted only seven nights—not a total failure but not a marked success, and it was sharply attacked by the Scriblerians' enemies.[69]

Cibber, who seemed so untroubled by the satire, was more galled than he could—or would—admit. In his own fashion he prepared a reply more devastating than any pamphlet, a revival of Buckingham's *The Rehearsal*, and it was under way even before Gay's work opened.[70] A satire originally aimed at Dryden's heroic tragedy, it had been periodically updated and continued to delight audiences. Cibber starred as Bayes, the playwright whose monstrosity is being rehearsed, and ad libbed a flippant reference to *Three Hours after Marriage*. Bayes says he had intended to bring in a conjuror, but "some of your sharp Wits, I found, had made use of it before me; otherwise I intended to have stolen one of them in, in the Shape of a

Mummy, and t'other, in that of a *Crocodile*.[71] The allusion to the disguises used in Gay's work brought roars of laughter on opening night, a glittering command performance with the Prince and Princess of Wales present. Pope was also there and, trembling with fury, rushed backstage to heap abuse on Colley.

Cibber, on his own ground, remained maddeningly cool. "Mr. Pope— you are so particular a Man, that I must be asham'd to return your Language as I ought to do: but since you have attacked me in so monstrous a Manner, This you may depend upon, that as long as the Play continues to be acted, I will never fail to repeat the same Words over and over again."[72]

The next night, Gay came backstage and challenged Cibber, who gave him a fillip on the nose. An incipient scuffle was stopped by the guards,[73] and Cibber continued to repeat the offending lines for the rest of the season. In fact, it was not much of a revenge, since only three more performances were given that year. The incident was closed for Cibber, but others kept the subject fresh. Rich presented a travesty on *Three Hours after Marriage* as an afterpiece, with a "monster" played by a "crocodile."

In April, a new lord chamberlain was appointed, Thomas Pelham-Holles, the young duke of Newcastle.[74] A dedicated Whig and friend of Steele, he seemed to promise better days for Drury Lane. The managers devoutly hoped so; after another thin year they had to extend the season until the end of June. Cibber and Booth took benefits for themselves, and Wilks, who could repair his losses in Ireland, gave one for Farquhar's children.

Cibber's resolution to write no more had undergone a sea change in the troubled economic waters of the past year, and he had searched for an idea he could work into a new play. He wanted a good role, of course, but he was no longer a young actor hungry for a part. Now he was an actor-manager who saw quite objectively that Drury Lane, which had not had an outstanding success since the younger Rich had appeared on the horizon, needed a fresh impetus and needed it soon. When he came upon Molière's *Tartuffe*, he must have regarded it as a lifesaver, and during his abbreviated holiday he set to work shaping it for the English stage.

But as he was more than an actor, so he was also more than a theater man, and as he matured, his interests had widened. He was a family man, an indulgent father who laughed heartily at four-year-old Charlotte wielding his silver-hilted sword and clad only in Theo's waistcoat as she gravely paraded before the house.[75] He was a music-lover with a sensitive ear and fine judgment, a social being who made a charming dinner companion, a gambler at White's, a wit in the coffeehouse, a brainless fop in public, and a lover of good literature in private. He was also a political animal, bred in the Protestant, conservative Whig ethic of his mother's family, a loyal Hanoverian who could still remember the autocratic Catholicism that had led to the downfall of James II, and he regarded the Jacobite uprising of 1715 as nothing short of treason.

Tartuffe appealed to Cibber; the sanctity of the family, the love story, the comic turns of plot, were just the kind of thing he liked best. For his specific purpose, however, it needed to be adapted to the company and the times, and he approached the task with workmanlike thoroughness. He wove the plot lines into a coherent whole, eliminated six characters and avoided Molière's deus ex machina conclusion. The falsely proud Orgon became a more likable dupe, the ingenue, Mariane, was transformed into a witty coquette, and the seventeenth-century hypocrite became an eighteenth-century nonjuror of the kind most feared by the Whig establishment, a Jesuit priest. In the process, Cibber lost Molière's universality, but he gained a contemporaneity perfectly suited to the times.

On Friday, 16 December 1717, *The Non-Juror* opened with Drury Lane's four top stars in the major roles. Wilks played the romantic Heartly, in love with the coquettish Maria (Oldfield); Booth was the wise and sympathetic Colonel Woodvil; and Cibber the nonjuror himself, Dr. Wolf. It was a festive night. The poet laureate, Nicholas Rowe, had written the prologue, and the audience glittered with aristocratic titles and "Persons of Quality." Even Pope set aside his anger long enough to subscribe for four tickets, but before the evening was over, the anger had flared again, and he had become one of Cibber's bitterest enemies.[76]

It was immediately clear *The Non-Juror* was exactly the kind of success they needed. Cibber had daringly played on political sentiments, but "the very Subject was its Protection; a few Smiles of silent Contempt were the utmost Disgrace that on the first Day of its Appearance it was thought safe to throw upon it" (II, 186-87). The company gave sixteen consecutive performances. Not since *Cato* had Drury Land held such audiences. Cibber had two benefits and cleared a thousand pounds.[77] The king attended, unable to understand the language but so pleased with the effects that he gave Colley permission to dedicate it to him. The royal copy, with the dedication translated into elegant French, was delivered on 1 January, and Cibber received the Crown's gratitude along with another two hundred pounds. The book went into three editions in a week, six before the end of the year, and it was the first selection in *The English Theatre for 1718*.

The performance had aroused the anger of the Tories, and Cibber's dedication was not calculated to soothe their feelings. He had written it, he said, to show "what Honest and Laudable Uses may be made of the *Theatre*" by opening the eyes "of our few Non-juring Clergy" through ridicule. He pointed to its success, modestly suggesting that it might have had three times the effect if it had not been written by a comedian. "I am sensible it may be justly urg'd against me, That even *Truth* and *Loyalty* might have lost their Lustre, by appearing to want the Defence of so inconsiderable a

Champion." He could only hope that the extraordinary reception indicated that the "Strength and Number of the *Misguided* had been exaggerated."[78] He might have added that it could also serve as a final and definitive answer to that old nonjuring adversary of his youth, Jeremy Collier.

Critical opinion split along party lines. The day after the opening, the Whig organ, *Read's Original Weekly Journal* (7 December 1717), noted that the play, "very naturally displaying the Villainy of that most wicked and abominable Crew, . . . gave great Satisfaction to all the Spectators." Another enthusiastically advised everyone to buy a copy, concluding, "and I hope to see it as common in every House as a Prayer-Book, or Duty of Man."[79] An anonymous letter urged everyone to see it, for "there never has appear'd, since the Stage of *Athens* . . . any Work of Wit so immediately and justly calculated for the Service of the Publick" but warned Cibber he had also provoked enemies who would "exert their Malice against him in a Place where he *earns his Bread*."[80]

The warning was accurate. On 28 December, the *Original Weekly Journal*, published by the Tory Nathaniel Mist, fired the first salvo with an anonymous "letter" charging that such plays "pervert the very end of Things, and turn that to Excrement which was design'd for Nourishment."[81] Three months later, Mist printed a more personal attack in a letter purportedly written by Charles Johnson, dated 1 March 1719. Referring to Cibber's profit of a thousand pounds, the letter claimed, "I hear he has been stript of it at the Groom-Porter's," and added that "the other Masters of the Play-House, seeing his Daughter very bare in Cloaths, kindly offered him a private Benefit for her; and I am credibly informed, that it amounted to fourscore Pounds, which this inhuman Father, rather than let his Child have Necessaries, made away with it also." It was a savage slur, twisting Cibber's well-known propensity for gambling into neglect of a child. He did have a benefit on 16 January, but if the proceeds went for a daughter's clothing, it was probably for Elizabeth—not because she had none, but as a trousseau gift for her approaching marriage.[82]

Attacks came from every quarter hostile to Cibber or the government. Lincoln's Inn Fields produced *The Per-juror*, an attempt to capitalize on the title of Cibber's play. John Breval's *The Compleat Key to the Non-juror*, accused Cibber of obscenity and plagiarism. Pope's anonymous *The Plot Discover'd; or A Clue to the Non-juror*, pretended the play actually poked fun at the Whigs. The anonymous author of *The Theatre-Royal Turn'd into a Mountebank's Stage* cursed Cibber as a "Cur, half Dane, half *English*," a "Mongrel of *Parnassus*," and quoted his ironic phrase in the epilogue, "'Sblood! we'll Stand it all!" as proof of his impenetrable brashness—an accusation appearing for the first time.[83]

Others connected with the play suffered as well. Rowe was chastised for writing the prologue and made the subject of the scurrilous *A Lash for the Laureat.*[84] Anne Oldfield was condemned for acting in it, and Read, for his favorable reviews, was called a "Presbyterian" [nonjuror], and "not only a Presbyterian, but a Scotch Presbyterian; not only a Scotch Presbyterian, but a Scotch Covenanting Presbyterian; and not only a Scotch Covenanting Presbyterian, but a Cameronian Scotch Covenanting Presbyterian!"[85]

Even illness elicited no sympathy. In late January, when Cibber was struck with fever and could not act for a few days, Mist published a notice, "Yesterday died Mr. Colley Cibber, late Comedian of the *Theatre-Royal*, notorious for writing the *Nonjuror*." Cibber refuted the statement on the first day he was able to go about, playing the Chaplain, his old role in *The Orphan*, and so surprising the audience with his unannounced appearance and his pallor that they "seem'd to make it a Doubt whether I was not the Ghost of my real Self departed: But when I spoke, their Wonder eas'd itself by an Applause" (II, 188). The last layer of the mask had slipped into place.

Cibber needed its protection as never before. For the first time, he was not attacked for the quality of his writing but for the content. If he understood the depth of the response, he gave no sign, and possibly he thought it would pass, but it was a turning point in his life. Never again would he have an unqualified success on the stage. He had enraged some who would never forgive him, men who took their politics, as they took their religion, with deadly seriousness. Cibber's name had become a symbol of the Whig regime as surely as Robert Walpole's would be, and the Tories found him a convenient scapegoat. Their revenge would follow him to the grave—and beyond.

FOUR

Under Attack

IN THE BEGINNING, the depth of the animosity was not noticeable. Paper battles were fairly common, usually serving to raise a few hackles, provoke a sharp riposte or two, and earn a few shillings for poverty-stricken hacks before being swept aside by the next one. With success had come attacks that a man of Cibber's prominence could expect from disappointed playwrights and jealous rivals. He had no reason to think the present assault was any different, and his opinion was buttressed by friends in and out of the theater. The disaffected were clearly in the minority, their voices drowned in the thunderous applause for *The Non-Juror*.

Yet from a distance it is obvious that this time the hostility was more than professional jealousy, that it was rooted deep in political soil. Drury Lane, with Cibber as its spokesman, had come to stand for the ministry, a symbol to Whigs and Tories alike of irreconcilable differences that went beyond politics to encompass religion, art, and philosophy in profoundly emotional terms. The anonymous satiric broadside, *An Address to the Hundreds of Drury* (supposedly delivered by Cibber to the king), portrayed him as a plagiarist, a dictator to church and state, and ridiculed his dedication to George I:

> For me, poor Dog, to offer't you, Sir,
> May seem too bold,—that's very true, Sir,
> But since a Party Play I've made it,
> You'll patronize, tho' you can't read it.[1]

Performance is a public art, and fresh opportunities for attack were provided every time Drury Lane opened its doors. Mist's *Weekly Journal* became the voice of the enemy, and scarcely an issue was without some kind of sneer at the theater, its management, or its star comedian.

In February, John Breval's slight comedy, *The Play Is the Plot* offered more ammunition. It was not outstandingly successful, but Breval had his third night. On the fourth, however, *Cato* was announced. Through some misunderstanding, deliberate or otherwise, some of Breval's friends had taken boxes for that night, and Mist printed the rumor that "a certain ruler" of the theater, "remarkable for Ill-Nature and Immorality" had insisted on the substitution, that although urged otherwise, "he obstinately persisted in his Resolution."² This was probably a hit at Cibber, but Booth would have been the more proper target, for he had a strong stubborn streak when he wanted something, and Cato was his best role. Unfortunately, Wilks, Oldfield, and Porter gave their own parts to lesser players that evening, a practice they had begun in order to give younger actors experience and exposure as well as to answer charges that the stars took all the best roles. Usually one or two major actors would play to strengthen the performance and to satisfy the audience, and on this occasion Booth and Cibber did so. Breval and his friends chose to regard the choice of both play and cast as insulting. Mist described the hissing, catcalling, and pelting of players with orange peels: "nor wou'd the Audience suffer them to capitulate or receive any Offers of Submission, but calling for a Dance, put an End to the Play in the middle of the 4th Act."³ It was a foretaste of what was to come.

Other than Mist's constant sniping, the rest of the 1717-18 season went fairly smoothly, although Drury Lane lost one of its best character actors when William Bowen was killed in a duel.⁴ Cibber passed the spring with no visible concern beyond his grief for the loss of a friend. The unremitting attacks, in fact, seemed to act as a spur, for he appeared 117 times—more than in any previous season. Foppington would not be outfaced.

The company was invited to perform at Hampton Court, and that summer Cibber established his family near the palace, where he could make the complicated arrangements while Katharine inhaled the pure country air and sipped the milk of a pet ass in a vain attempt to alleviate her asthma. Her affliction was not eased by the antics of the obstreperous Charlotte, who insisted on riding the little animal, attracting the attention of amused neighbors and embarrassing her parents greatly.⁵

The royal performances were postponed several times, and not until the 1718-19 season actually began did the company pack up its scenery and costumes to make the trek upriver. It was a sorrowful troupe, for the first performance of the season had been darkened by an unusual calamity. The play was *Hamlet* with Wilks playing the title role as usual, but the part of Ophelia had been given to Hester Santlow. It may have been at Booth's request (he was now her lover) or because Susannah Mountfort, who had formerly played it, had become increasingly unstable. When the play was well under way, a completely deranged Susannah suddenly materialized in the shadows backstage, and, after watching in silence for a time, pushed Hester out of the way and went on to play the mad scene in earnest as the rest of the cast watched in horror. It was her last performance.[6] Hampton Court was a mixed blessing. The prestige was enormous and paid the company well, but most actors found it unnerving to play in the muted atmosphere where applause was restrained and even laughter was suppressed until it was certain the king approved. Cibber observed perceptively that players tended to sink "into a Flatness in their Performance for want of that Applause" (II, 214-15). Yet they were well received, and Colley himself had signal recognition from the king for his portrayal of Wolsey in *Henry VIII*. He has been criticized for adding the pantomime of snuffing a candle between thumb and forefinger to the speech,

> This candle burns not clear; 'tis I must snuff it,
> And out it goes . . .

Such action, however, clarified the lines for the German-speaking king, who ordered the company to be given a bonus of two hundred pounds and commanded the play three times that year.[7]

Nevertheless, it was an uneven season. A revival of *Ximena* lasted four nights, but a lavish production of Dryden's *All for Love* was hailed as "perfect," and Cibber's Alexas was praised as much as Booth's Antony, Wilks's Dolabella, and Oldfield's graceful Cleopatra. Several new plays did well, particularly Charles Johnson's *The Masquerade* in which Cibber gave a virtuoso performance in two comic cameo scenes. It opened on the same night as George Sewell's *Sir Walter Raleigh* at Lincoln's Inn Fields, and the occasion brought a sharp thrust in Sewell's preface: "*Drury-Lane* is the Favourite Theatre of the Town, and I am not so vain as to oppose a single Judgment to the Publick; Yet I hope a young Author may be excused if upon hearing their *shocking Treatment* of the best Writers, he trembled to think how a new unexperienced one was to be used."[8] Johnson's preface to *The Masquerade* spoke for the successful playwright in a paraphrase of Sewell's words: "*Lincolns-Inn-Fields* is *not* the Favourite Theatre of the Town. To say otherwise would be to oppose my single Judgment to the Publick. I never heard of any Author of Merit who was rejected or ill-treated in Drury Lane; I believe that Assertion therefore to be a *shocking Calumny!*"[9] In the end, Sewell had the best of it; Johnson's comedy played seven times, but Sewell's tragedy stayed in the repertory for three years. Only Cibber suffered any lasting damage, for the printed statements remained long after the performances were forgotten.

The tides of fortune ebbed and flowed erratically throughout the spring of 1719. Wilks fell ill, seriously disrupting the schedule, and the managers had to substitute plays in which he had no role. He recovered in time for the annual benefit season (March-May) but his absence forcibly brought home the need for trained replacements, and they assigned Mills the task of directing the summer productions, when the beginners would be allowed to play roles they could never touch during the regular season.

That summer, Cibber took Katharine, still mourning the death of Elizabeth's first child,[10] to Richmond and spent the holiday writing a preface to *Ximena* in preparation for its publication. It was a considerable statement, setting forth his dramatic theory more thoroughly than anything he had ever written, and it reveals him as a thoughtful playwright with an intuitive perception and professional judgment honed by experience.

It also sets forth the actor's approach to a play, clearly defining in the process his term "theatrical," for which he was so much criticized. As he points out Corneille's "flaws" and how he has dealt with them, it is obvious he wants a tight structure with a line of action that moves swiftly from exposition to climax, each scene and character contributing to that line, with no digressions for poetic passages or specialty scenes for players. As an actor, Cibber considers the effect of the play on the audience to be paramount, and he aims for a strong impact by using the stage's resources: visual and audio effects, variety in scene and costume, unusual characterizations. Surprise is essential, although "we do not love to be startled into a pleasure; as an audience ought never to be wholly let into the secret design of a play, so they ought not to be intirely kept out of it, you may safely leave room for the imagination to guess at the nature of the thing you intend, and are only to surprise them with your manner of bringing it about."[11] He is fully aware of the constant forward press of time that disallows reflection during a performance, and he argues for clarity in dialogue and plot line, for "your imagination is not at leisure to look so far back for the propriety of what's past; you are then to be intent upon what is to come, or else what you have seen is but an interruption in what you are to see."[12] The principles Cibber preached and practiced might have come from a modern manual for playwrights. His is not a systematic and comprehensive philosophy developed by a scholar steeped in dramatic tradition but the intuitive perceptions of an actor.

Of all artists, only the performer creates under the judges' eyes. The work is the most fragile and ephemeral of creations, for a second's lapse destroys it as surely as if a painter slashed the canvas. It is just as irreparable; once destroyed, the illusion cannot be restored. Forever at the mercy of time, actors must simultaneously convince their audiences they are what they pretend to be, move the story forward, and provide an experience that engages the heart as well as the mind. There is no time to investigate philosophical ramifications or dally over poetic beauties. They must capture the fleeting moment and invest it with vitality before the inexorable sweep catapults them onward. The "substance" or intellectual content of a play is more the concern of the playwright than of the actor, who must constantly seek for ways to vivify that substance, and the art of the theater is the art of demonstration. Cibber, with his actor's imagination, wrote plays to allow performers their fullest scope, and he looked for the same thing in others' work. During more than thirty years of writing and choosing plays for the foremost theater in England, he steered its course away from the elegant literature of the Restoration and back to the earlier tradition that had produced Shakespeare. That course has determined the pattern of English drama to the present day, and his part in it gave him a major place in theatrical history.

Although Cibber's commentary in the preface seems light and reveals a professional assurance, the failure of *Ximena*, added to the harassment after *The Non-Juror*, had taken its toll. Some bitterness tinged the laughing mask in a rare admission of sensitivity:

> There is in human nature a certain low latent malice to all laudable undertakings, which never dares break out upon any thing with so much licence, as on the fame of a dramatick writer: for even the lavish applause that is usually heaped upon his first labours, is not perhaps so entirely owing to their real admiration of the work itself as to the mean pleasure they take in swelling him up to rival the reputation of others, that have writ well before him: if he succeeds in a first play, let him look well to the next, for then he is enter'd the herd as a common enemy.[13]

He knew whereof he spoke. He had become one of the "common enemy" with *Woman's Wit*, and the last season had forcibly reminded him that no amount of success could alter that status.

The preface to *Ximena* was finished by the start of the 1719-20 season. Cibber dedicated the play to Richard Steele and sent it off to the publisher, probably without realizing he had just sparked another altercation. Newcastle and Steele had come to a parting of the political ways, for Steele was a wholehearted supporter of Robert Walpole, now just emerging as the leader of the "new Whigs."[14] The party itself was divided, and Newcastle was one of Walpole's most vocal adversaries; his antagonism included his former protégé, Steele, whom he now regarded as a turncoat. Cibber could hardly have chosen a more inauspicious moment to offer Steele a public tribute.

Cibber had had a taste of Newcastle's coolness the year before. When he thanked the lord chamberlain for the two hundred pounds at the end of the Hampton Court series, Newcastle replied frostily it was not from him but the king, "who had given it from no other Motive than his own Bounty" (II, 219). The chill had increased since that time. Newcastle had demanded that Booth's role of Torrismond in *The Spanish Fryar* be given to Thomas Elrington, an Irish actor. The managers refused, and Cibber spoke for all of them when he asserted that Drury Lane was "a sort of separate Ministry," adding flippantly: "My lord, it is not with us as with you; your lordship is sensible that there is no difficulty in filling places at court; you cannot be at a loss for persons to act their parts there. But I assure you, it is quite otherwise in our theatrical world; if we should invest people with characters who are incapable of supporting them, we should be undone."[15] The reply, equating aristocrats with actors infuriated the proud nobleman, who now looked upon Cibber's effulgent praise of Steele as a public insult and grew testy enough to inquire privately of the solicitor general if the Drury Lane patent could not be revoked.

The dedication outraged others as well when Cibber referred to Steele's former association with the recently deceased Addison in a quotation from *All for Love*:

> Fool that I was! upon my Eagle's Wings
> I bore this Wren, 'till I was tir'd with soaring,
> And now, he mounts above me—

It was a thoughtless compliment, but Cibber probably intended no disrespect; he had remained friends with both men after their own relationship had cooled. It was like him, however, to use language carelessly; accustomed to showing precise nuances of meaning with voice and body, he was not always mindful of the implications to be drawn from the printed word. In this case, the penalty for his carelessness was to be a lifetime of charges that he had callously dishonored the dead.

Although the solicitor general had determined that a Crown patent could not be revoked, Newcastle was determined to remove Steele from Drury Lane's management. He demanded to see the theater's account books. Steele angrily replied they would show him only the gross charges but that it would be "impracticable" to "lay open the Several particulars of the Sallaries"—and indeed, public knowledge of their dealings with individual actors was the surest way to create dissension within the company.[16] Newcastle was not deterred; after reviewing the possibilities, he discovered a way to demonstrate unequivocally the power of his office by using Cibber as a means to punish Steele. That Cibber might be hurt in the process did not disturb him at all—the *Ximena* dedication still rankled. On 19 December 1719, he sent a sudden and unexpected order: "These are to require you immediately to Dismiss Mr. Colley Cibber from Acting at the Theatre in Drury Lane, and from being in any ways concern'd in the management of the said Playhouse: And you Colley Cibber One of the Managers and Players at the said Theatre are hereby requir'd to cease and forbear Acting, or any ways concerning your self in the Management of the said Theatre, as you will Answer the Contrary at your Peril."[17] It was a strategic masterstroke, and Cibber was out as surely as Rich had been a decade earlier. For

Drury Lane it was a disaster. They had just opened Southerne's extraordinarily successful *Spartan Dame* in which Cibber spoke the prologue and played the villain, Crites. Since he was acting four or five times a week, the repertory as well as the management was seriously crippled by his absence. Newcastle was not content with merely removing Cibber from the scene; the next step was to have him arrested. The charge is not specified, but Davies tells of Wilks and Booth desperately trying to raise the bail for his release and King, one of the boxkeepers, offering to put up the cash.

"Why, you blockhead," Wilks is supposed to have said, "it is for ten thousand pounds."

"I should be very sorry, sir," returned King, "if I could not be answerable for twice that sum."

The two managers gaped, and Booth spoke with some emotion, "What have you and I been doing, Bob, all this time? A boxkeeper can buy us both!"[18]

Whoever provided the bail, Cibber was not in prison long, but he was still not permitted to act. Steele protested to Newcastle: "Mr Cibber is a Principal Actor, and many Familyes (as well as my Property) are concern'd in his Appearance on the Stage. I hope your Grace, in the determination of this proceeding, will give way to your own Temper, which, I know, must be diverted from its natural Bent when you offer an Injury."[19] He did more; 2 January 1720 saw the first edition of *The Theatre*, in which Steele, as "Sir John Edgar," defended Cibber as an actor who had acquitted himself "with great Applause both in comedy and Tragedy;" Cibber's detractors, he added, "seem'd to attribute his Success to a Malice in his Nature, and not a Skill in his Art." He denounced the "Propensity of the Town to receive with Pleasure any thing that tends to the Personal Mortification of Mr. *Cibber*," and, fully aware of the political implications, pointed directly to *The Non-Juror* as the cause of this ill will.[20]

Neither the private letter nor the public statement had any effect on the lord chamberlain, who wanted Drury Lane under his absolute control. He informed the managers that "the mortification put upon Mr. *Cibber* was intended only as a remote beginning of evils," and that unless they accepted a license from his office, "the force of the Patent itself should very soon be made ineffectual by a Sign Manual," an order of closure signed by the lord chamberlain.[21] Steele, gambling on the favor of the Crown, refused and on 22 January petitioned the king for redress. The next day, without a mention of patent or petition, Drury Lane was silenced.[22]

Newcastle was too powerful. The managers submitted, signed a license that not only excluded Steele's name but all mention of the patent, and were allowed to reopen on 28 January. They gave *The Careless Husband* with Cibber as Foppington, in spite of Steele's anguished command that they "desist from acting" until they received orders from him, their "Affectionate Governour."[23] The signing of the license had undoubtedly been a ploy on their part to gain time and give Steele a chance to regroup his forces, but they had to ignore his request if they wanted the company to survive.

The affair roused Cibber's friends and enemies to a new pamphlet war; attacks and defenses flew thick and fast. Mist filled his columns with abuse, and John Dennis pounded away with *The Character and Conduct of Sir John Edgar* in which he scourged Steele and his "Viceroy," Cibber, in four anonymous letters. Dennis had been furious with the whole Drury Lane management since he had offered them his tragedy, *The Invader of his Country*, an adaptation of *Coriolanus*. They accepted it but had postponed the premiere for almost a year, and then presented it under what Dennis considered inopportune circumstances.[24] Most of Dennis's anger was directed against Cibber, who did not act in the play but who had probably been responsible for cutting parts of it, and who wrote the satiric epilogue for Oldfield. Irascible at best, Dennis now gave full rein to his spleen, calling actors "the worst Judges in the world" of plays and insisting: "Their sordid Love and Greediness of Gain, contributes not a little to the corrupting their Understandings. For when a foolish Play happens to have a Run, as they call it, their sordid Temper inclines them to believe it good. . . . ev'n the best Actors, with the most unblameable Conduct, are never to be trusted with Power."[25]

Such charges could have been disregarded as the ravings of a failed author, but Dennis caught the attention of the town by pouring out personal vituperation, anonymously, in terms that would be cherished by Cibber's enemies: "'Tis credibly reported, that he spit on the Face of our Saviour's Picture at the Bath, with Words too execrable and too horrible to be repeated. . . . He has neither Tenderness for his Wife, or natural Affection for his Children, nor any sympathizing Regard for the rest of Men. He has, in the Compass of two Years, squander'd away Six Thousand Pounds at the *Groom Porter's*, without making the least Provision for either his Wife or his Children."[26] Cibber was nettled enough to offer a reward of ten pounds for the author's name.[27] The notice was more in the nature of a public warning than a serious reward, for any knowledgeable Londoner would have recognized Dennis's unique style at once. Colley did not pursue the matter further, but an anonymous friend defended him in an address to Dennis: "You fall foul of Mr Cibber, the deputy governour, as you call him, and tell a notorious lie in saying he lost £6000 one season without providing for his family, when everyone that knows him can tell you he settled £300 that very year upon his children. Again you tax him with blasphemy, hardness of heart, etc., and I have inquired of everybody that has the least acquaintance—nay, even some that hate him without any reason—and all affirm they never heard of the story of the Bath. Therefore it must be concluded that thou has minted it thyself."[28] Such attacks and defenses flashed by without causing serious damage. Newcastle's actions, on the other hand, had a direct and palpable impact when he ordered the triumvirate to take an oath of obedience to him. This time it was Wilks who protested. In a remarkably tactful letter he explained his reluctance to sign "an Act that subjects me to the Office and those who shall occasionally execute it in your Grace's absence," because he had "some fears of feeling again from some of your Grace's inferior officers, what I formerly suffer'd."[29] He was not specific about what those sufferings were, but if he took the oath, he wanted to reserve the right to resign if trouble arose. Booth and Cibber stood with him, but again they had no real choice, and on 4 March they took the oath. It was a complete victory for the lord chamberlain.

Drury Lane was at Newcastle's mercy, but as long as they stayed within its walls, the three managers were relatively free to act as they pleased. They chose to present John Hughes's tragedy, *The Siege of Damascus*, in which the hero adopts Islam in order to save his mistress and his city. Cibber objected that "the audience will never tolerate a hero who changes his religion," and rewrote certain scenes.[30] Hughes, like Dennis, strongly resented the interference, but, unlike Dennis, Hughes was ill and could only fume helplessly from afar. He died on opening night, unaware that Cibber's alterations had made his play an immense success.

In spite of the difficulties, Cibber enjoyed both professional and domestic harmony in the spring of 1720. His daughter Elizabeth gave birth to a healthy daughter, and Theophilus, completing his last term at Westminster, was now pleading to enter the company.[31] Colley wrote some verses for his friend, Johann Pepusch, who set them to music and published *Six English Cantatas for one Voice.*[32] Cibber probably did not profit much from them, but it did not matter, for he was secure in his financial affairs. The government-approved South Sea Company had astonished everyone with its huge profits, and he had a good deal invested. Shares bought for £100 in April were worth £890 in June, and even if they dropped back to £750 almost at once, he had still made a handsome profit. Like many of his countrymen, he dreamed of overnight riches, and during the long vacation he moved next door to the Booths at 3 Charles Street, a prosperous neighborhood populated mainly by theater people and minor gentry.[33] He may even have had his portrait painted.[34]

The years of experience stood the triumvirate in good stead when the 1720-21 season started and Anne Oldfield, pregnant with Charles Churchill's child, was unable to perform.[35] Rumors flew about: she was ill, dead; she had become so wealthy from her South Sea investments that she was retiring. The truth was that Anne, like her employers, was beginning to age. She still bloomed brightly on the stage, but this pregnancy was not so easy as the first; she could not stand the strain of daily rehearsals and performances. The managers sighed and rescheduled the repertory to allow for her absence.

Theophilus was duly admitted to the company that fall, the latest of many young men and women to follow in a father's footsteps. Already the Millses, Pinkethmans, Norrises, and Bullocks were represented by second and even third generations; they showed varying degrees of talent but all were so well trained that Drury Lane's ensemble had become one of the best in history. Theo seemed promising and eager to learn; he worshipped Booth and followed Wilks about like a puppy, listening and asking questions that revealed a quick intelligence. Too short and unattractive to play romantic heroes, he had a fair comic imagination which, if controlled, would give him a line not too different from Colley's. Discipline was not Theo's forte on or off the stage, but he made a creditable debut as Clarence in *Henry IV (Part 2)* when it was revived on 17 December, "for the first time in sixteen years."

The play was well received; Booth as the King and Wilks as Prince Hal revealed a "dignity and grace of action and deportment, with all the tender passions of the heart, in a superior degree," and Cibber's Justice Shallow very nearly stole the show:

His manner was so perfectly simple, his look so vacant, when he questioned his Cousin Silence about the price of ewes, and lamented, in the same breath, with silly surprise, the death of Old Double, that it will be impossible for any surviving spectator not to smile at the remembrance of it. . . . Cibber's transition from asking the price of bullocks, to trite, but grave reflections on mortality, was so natural and attended with such an unmeaning roll of his small pigs-eyes, accompanied with an important utterance of tick! tick! tick! not much louder than the balance of a watch's pendulum, that I question if any actor was ever superior in the conception of expression of such solemn insignificance.[36]

Henry IV (Part 2) went directly into the repertory, and the season rolled on smoothly until the South Sea Bubble exploded. The value of the shares dropped, the directors were discovered to be scoundrels, brokers absconded, and the Bank of England watched helplessly as the economy tumbled into chaos. Like many others, Cibber faced ruin; Booth and Wilks also lost, but they had not gambled so much, and Booth, at least, was independently wealthy. For thriftless Cibber with an ailing wife and three unmarried daughters, the crash was a calamity.

His reaction was characteristic. Putting aside failure, along with his resolution to write no more, he set to work adapting Thomas Wright's *The Female Vertuosos* (borrowed from Molière's *Les Femmes Savantes*) into a satiric comedy, *The Refusal*, centered on the late bubble. It was, in essence, his revenge, which he invited other losers to share, as he concluded the epilogue:

> Let all, whose Wrongs the Face of Mirth can bear,
> Enjoy the Muses Vengeance on them here.[37]

The Refusal is a charming play in the mode of *Love's Last Shift*. Cibber changed Molière's elegant couplets into colloquial English prose and discarded the satire of "les précieuses" and their devotion to the platonic ideal in favor of a more topical attack on the mercantile cheats who had created the bubble, a topic that should have guaranteed a favorable hearing. The plot line is simple: two girls adored by two young gallants cannot marry because their father has given first refusal rights to a fop, and the story develops as they circumvent this obstacle. Sophronia (created for Anne Oldfield) faintly echoes Molière's Armande; she is "half mad with her Learning and Philosophy" (p. 3), and Cibber gives her several delightful scenes with Granger (Booth) as he woos her in high heroics. Unlike her French counterpart, Sophronia sees the error of "Pride in her Imaginary Knowledge" and falls into Granger's arms at the end.

The second couple, Frankly and Charlotte, are nicely contrasted to the first pair and act as a norm; they are young, attractive, unaffected, and in love—the ideal ingredients for a satisfactory comic ending. The obstacles arise from a set of ridiculous parents and the fop, Witling (Cibber), whose foolishness is underscored by the fact that in age he is closer to the parents than the girls. The scene in which he is cozened into returning his "first refusal" bond is a delicious piece of comic writing, while the sharp satire is softened into comedy by his good sportsmanship, as he wishes the lovers joy with a comment Cibber might have spoken in his own person, "he that has not wit enough to find himself sometimes a Fool, is in danger of being Fool enough, to have nobody think him a Wit but himself" (p. 84). The pace is rapid, the situations comic, and the denouement well prepared. In spite of the topical references, the dialogue still amuses and the work is eminently playable.

Word of the production had leaked out, and in an attempt to preempt the novelty, Rich gave his own adaptation of *The Female Vertuosos* before Drury Lane could present Cibber's. It was not the subject, however, but the author that concerned the opening night house. Five years earlier, he might have succeeded, but his enemies had been waiting for him since *The Non-Juror*, and they began to hiss the moment he stepped out to speak the prologue. Before the first scene ended, the uproar drowned out the actors' voices; as they continued, the hoots, shouts, and catcalls stopped the play several times. It was a new and unexpected experience for Cibber. He had faced noisy houses before, but never had one of his own plays met with such concerted hostility. For the first time he began to understand the nature of the dragon he had aroused. *The Refusal* had five more performances, respectable—even remarkable—in view of the situation, but it ended there. It was not revived until after Cibber's death in 1758, when it became a part of the repertory until the end of the century.

The virulence of the attacks in the playhouse and in print may have stemmed as much from Cibber's treatment of the South Sea Bubble as from personal animosity. Those who had lost their fortunes were understandably not amused, but the crash also had strong political repercussions. The scandal that accompanied it toppled the Stanhope ministry; Stanhope himself died in February, and his right-hand minister, James Craggs, was seriously ill.[38] The Tories, who might have hoped to gain from the fallen Whig ministry, had been frustrated again as Walpole moved forcefully to turn the situation to the advantage of the "progressive Whigs" he now dominated as chancellor of the exchequer. *The Refusal* merged these antagonisms and made Cibber appear, to the opposition at least, as the spokesman for Walpole's policies.

Cibber understood professional and political hostility. The former was the price of success; the latter, the common experience of public life and, as he saw it, much like the adversary relationship in court. Gentlemen slashed at each other in the arena, then sat down amiably to share a glass of wine in a civilized manner. This was Cibber's own pattern, and it is doubtful that he really comprehended the personal element at this time. He was certainly capable of anger, but on the rare occasions when he actually lost his temper, the storm was soon over. Ordinarily, he waited for his opponent's fury to abate, as with Dogget, or roused a laugh to charm away anger.

Typical of the latter approach is the story of Cibber and his friends who met at the Globe Tavern "for the enjoyment of wit and wine." Although he did not eat before a performance, he always paid his share of the bill, which was divided equally among them. After a time, however, he noticed that certain members always added expensive extra dishes for themselves. He said nothing about it, but one night he took the waiter aside, placed his order privately, and when the bill arrived, the first item was "To Mr. Cibber's supper, one pair of white silk stockings." As the group puzzled over this, Cibber smiled, "I see no reason why I should not go to as much expense about my legs as you gentlemen do about your stomachs." They laughed heartily, and the extra dishes were ordered no more.[39]

Cibber seems to have indulged in this kind of light banter often, but holding a long-term grudge was so alien to his nature that it seemed absurd. It was difficult for him to believe the harsh attacks were more than a passage in a play that would soon end. His confidence was not mere optimism. His friends outnumbered his enemies, and if they were less publicly vocal, their feelings were solidly demonstrated. His colleagues trusted his judgment, the court and its ministers applauded his performances, and his private life was serene. The smiling mask caught the arrows; the real man was constantly assured they were meaningless.

Walpole became lord chancellor of the Treasury on 3 April 1722, and Steele immediately petitioned to have his patent rights reinstated. A month later it was done, solid evidence of Drury Lane's favor with the ministry.[40] Steele had no real quarrel with his partners, but they had some reservations about him. With the patent back in force, they were less subject to the captious power of the lord chamberlain, but again they had to cut profits four ways. Steele eased some of the pain by promising them a new comedy for the next season and promptly borrowed fifteen hundred pounds to invest in the Fish Pool,[41] an insubstantial project for bringing live salmon from Ireland in ships with open wells in their keels.

During the long vacation, Cibber resolved some of his financial problems by collecting ten of his plays—including *The Refusal*—into a handsome two-volume quarto and publishing it by subscription.[42] The list swelled to 130 names, reflecting a wide circle of friends and a sizable representation of the aristocracy: ten dukes, among whom were Newcastle, Dorset, Grafton, and Wharton (who took eight sets); twelve earls; and several lords. Pope's name is missing, but his friends Bathurst and Cobham subscribed, as did a number of theater people, including Wilks, Booth, Steele, Oldfield, and Vanbrugh. By autumn, he was secure enough to send young Charlotte to Mrs. Draper's fashionable school for girls, where she would be educated in a manner suitable for a young lady "destined" for the stage. Theo had proved himself good enough to be rehired for a second season, and for some reason Elizabeth Cibber Brett entered the company. Unlike Charlotte and Theo, she had never shown any desire for the stage, but apparently her inheritance had either been spent or was insufficient for her needs.[43]

The 1721-22 season began in sorrow. Thomas Dogget died in September, and Drury Lane closed its doors on the day of his funeral. Cibber, along with Wilks and Booth, joined the mourners, and for Cibber, at least, the ceremony put the seal on the memory of those happy days when he, Dogget, and Wilks had been the official managers of the only theater in London.[44] In contrast, this year was fairly pedestrian. The company gave no new plays, and revivals of Ben Jonson's *The Alchemist* and Dryden's *Aureng-Zebe* by royal command roused little interest. Drury Lane's houses were full enough for it to withstand most of Mist's sniping until he encouraged (or began) a rumor that the theater was unsafe. The rumor was believed, and the managers were forced to hire Sir Thomas Hewitt, the royal architect, to inspect the premises and give public reassurance that Drury Lane was sound.[45]

It is clear the managers were not exerting themselves unduly to present new works, but revivals were a good way to introduce promising youngsters. Such productions were not always feasible, as they had learned from their experience with Breval, but in January they tried again with Cibber's *The Rival Fools*, not acted for a decade. Colley directed and played Samuel Simple as before, but Wilks, Booth, and Oldfield handed over their parts to minor actors. It was a special occasion for Cibber's family, for Elizabeth made her debut in a brief role.

The opening was a dismal repetition of *The Refusal*. The hisses began as the curtain rose and continued until the players could not be heard. Cibber stopped the action and stepped forth. "Gentlemen," he began, placating them with a smile, "we do not offer this play as one of our most polite entertainments, but the Town has cast reflections on us for not pushing forward our young actors. This play was revived for no other purpose . . . and therefore, I beg you to be silent and give those who are desirous the liberty of hearing."[46]

A great burst of applause answered him, and the play continued for another act. The hissing recurred and grew; the end was chaos. Hoping to salvage something from the wreckage, Wilks acted the next night, but he was subjected to the same treatment and pelted with oranges as well. One troublemaker it was said, armed himself with wooden balls painted orange, and at the end of the third act, Cibber, pale with rage, stopped the play, offered two guineas for the apprehension of the culprit, and refused to return the ticket money.[47] *The Rival Fools* was not played again.

The actors suffered the brunt of the attack, but the target was the author. It was clear even to Cibber that he was to be allowed no further success as a playwright. His enemies could do nothing about his continued popularity as an actor or about his plays already long established as repertory favorites, but they could prevent his new works and revivals from being heard.[48] Never again would he have an opening night free of disruption.

Mist gleefully gave tongue. After *The Rival Fools*, he called on Steele to depose his "fat headed Triumvirate," concluding sourly with the admission that "The Encouragement which has been given this Theatre by the Court, has made it the Fashion to go there.[49] He exploited every possibility for ridicule, and while Cibber was his favorite target, Wilks and Booth were not spared. They were less tolerant than he and wanted to answer, but Colley discouraged them. It was not advantageous, he argued, to meet Mist on his own grounds; their proper field was the stage, where they could make the terms. Moreover, Mist's attacks gave them a good deal of free publicity. He might speak for the Tories, but the Whigs were in power, and Cibber steadfastly refused to take the *Weekly Journal* seriously, even when it began referring to him as "Keyber" with irritating frequency.[50]

Mist's attacks, preserved in print, give a distorted picture of the situation, making it appear as if Cibber had no friends and Drury Lane no audiences. Yet in 1722, large numbers of Londoners demanded to see Cibber, Wilks, Booth, and Oldfield in almost every play, requested special performances of favorite roles, applauded their entrances heartily and followed their offstage lives with the same avid interest their descendants would have for cinema stars. Their very popularity was in part a handicap, for on economic grounds alone it was tempting to stay with proven favorites instead of experimenting with untried plays. Cibber usually bears the blame for rejecting new works, but he was not alone; Booth himself "often declared in public company, that he and his partners lost money by new plays; and that, if he were not obliged to it, he would seldom give his consent to perform one of them."[51]

A constant stream of manuscripts flowed to the theater—from university undergraduates heavily influenced by the classics, from gentlemen who amused themselves by writing dialogue, from hacks desperate for a few pounds, from would-be wits eager to make a name. Cibber once told Vanbrugh, "'tis not to be conceiv'd how many and how bad Plays" were submitted, but he read them all.[52] He was not always diplomatic, although he probably thought he was being kind when he rejected Elijah Fenton's *Mariamne* with, "Sir, will you take the advice of a friend? Apply yourself to some honest and laborious calling; the belles lettres and you will never agree; you have no manner of genius for poetry."[53]

Mariamne was one of Cibber's few mistakes. The offended Fenton took it to Lincoln's Inn Fields where it became a dazzling success the following February. For the most part, however, Cibber's judgment was accurate, and his partners trusted it. Drury Lane could not survive without new plays, but they were costly, and before the managers risked an untried work, they needed assurance that the money and effort would not be wasted.

The three managers thought they had that assurance when Steele announced he had at last finished his long-promised comedy, but their enthusiasm was quickly dampened when he read it to them. It seemed hopelessly dull to Booth and Wilks, who wanted to reject it out of hand as "too moral and serious" and "having in it no one laughing line."[54] Cibber, however, thought it might have possibilities if revised, and Steele, sorely in need of cash, had fallen ill—too ill for such an extended effort—agreed to let him work on it. That summer in his quiet retreat at Twickenham he settled down to the task.[55] Keeping Steele's basic structure, he mitigated the seriousness with a comic subplot that provided an excellent role for himself. He trimmed, polished, and heightened the theatrical effects, following the dramatic principles he had propounded in the preface to *Ximena*.

Cibber's part in *The Conscious Lovers* was kept a secret. The publicity giving Steele sole credit kept Mist at bay, and they opened on 7 November to a crowded and friendly house. It was at once apparent they had exactly touched the taste of the time. Along with the rest of the audience, Brigadier Charles Churchill wept openly for Oldfield's unfortunate Indiana (at which Wilks is said to have remarked, "I warrant he'll fight never the worse for that!"),[56] and any doubts Steele may have had about the revisions evaporated after he realized a profit of six hundred pounds. Cibber consoled himself for the anonymity with his share as a manager and the appreciative comments of friends: "The Character of *Tom* is a good Satyr enough upon our modern fine Gentlemen . . . and 'tis to be discern'd, that this Character receives its greatest force from Mr. *Cibber's* admirable Representation."[57] The first run lasted eighteen nights and attracted wide notice. Abbé Leblanc recommended it to Nivelle de la Chaussée, later the prime exponent of sentimental drama in France, and even enemies as bitter as Aaron Hill praised it.[58] *The Conscious Lovers* became known as the best example of sentimental comedy—the kind of drama that touched the emotions more than the intellect, that depended on situations more than dialogue, and that was immensely effective in the theater.

With the success of *The Conscious Lovers*, Cibber knew Drury Lane would have a profitable season. His family, too, was doing well. In February, his oldest daughter, Catherine, married Captain James Brown, and his two theatrical offspring were holding their own on the stage.[59] Elizabeth would never be much of an actress, but she was still in the company, or at least would be until September, when she would go over to Rich, while Theo showed real promise, and the triumvirate had enough confidence to put him in charge of the summer season.[60] Theo, whose ambitions outstripped his experience, overwhelmed the young players with a series of new works until they were too exhausted to do justice to them, but his efforts were not a complete failure, and the managers were impressed enough to give him increasingly important parts.[61]

Colley had no hand in Theo's summer activities. Katharine's asthma grew worse, and he found a quiet house in Hillingdon near Uxbridge, which he leased for several years. This year, he concentrated on adapting Shakespeare's *King John*, but by the time it was ready, Mist was already printing an ominous note: "We are advised from the Theatre in Drury-Lane, that Shakespear's Tragedy of KING JOHN, is getting up there with Alterations."[62] It was obvious that a welcome comparable to that of *The Refusal* was in the making. Cibber quietly shelved the script and said no more about it.

The company could not afford expensive failures these days. It was by no means near bankruptcy, but the group did feel the strain of Rich's competition. A master pantomimist with a Barnum-like sense of showmanship, he had built Lincoln's Inn Fields into a thriving business. Drury Lane was still the favored house, but thin nights occurred more frequently than the managers liked, especially when Rich produced one of his spectacles. Cibber called them "raree shows" and claimed they were only a cut above ropedancing, but he had to admit an empty house was hard to bear.

Drury Lane's own afterpieces were generally short plays, but in November 1723, the managers tried a pantomime created by their chief dancer, John Thurmond. *Harlequin Dr. Faustus*, with a fire-spitting dragon and magic transformation scenes, astonished and delighted the audiences, and on 14 December 1723, the *British Gazetteer* exclaimed with puzzled wonderment, "whether proper or not we shan't pretend to determine, but certainly [it was] the most magnificent that ever appear'd upon the English Stage." Their success paled when Rich countered with *The Necromancer* a month later. He had the advantage over Drury Lane in this genre, for his stage was specially fitted for magical effects, and his scenes were even more spectacular. Sold out every night, his pantomime was performed forty-nine times before the end of the season.

The managers of Drury Lane felt the pinch of such competition, but they were more comfortable in the kind of repertory they did best, and this season they decided to present Aaron Hill's adaptation of *Henry V*. It is unlikely that Cibber approved; he had little faith in Hill and disagreed entirely with his notions of acting. Hill disliked the Betterton style in which the triumvirate had been trained, and he particularly loathed Cibber's performance in tragedy. In this he was a harbinger of the future; already younger members of the audiences were starting to denounce the cadenced rhythms of tragic actors as hopelessly old-fashioned. Their protests were only a murmur at present, but they were growing louder.[63] Hill had found no real support for his ideas as yet, and after several unsuccessful efforts to produce *Henry V* by himself, he approached Drury Lane, offering costumes and scenery worth two hundred pounds as an inducement. It was a bargain, and the management accepted. Cibber did not act in the play, but even Wilks and Booth together could give it no more than five nights; Hill, bitterly disappointed, blamed everyone but himself. The triumvirate shrugged off his newfangled ideas and kept the scenery.

In the spring, the duke of Grafton replaced Newcastle as lord chamberlain. Cibber must have been pleased, for Grafton was an old friend whom he often met at White's gaming tables. The handsome duke was very different from the previous chamberlain, but his jolly Squire Western manner concealed an exceedingly clever politician. He took no interest in theater operations and never dreamed of interfering in its business; the only kind of order he would send was a royal command that the company not stray far from London during the forthcoming visit of Prussian royalty.[64]

However welcome Grafton's appointment, Drury Lane's immediate need was for a good new play. Steele was now too ill to keep his promise of another comedy. Moreover, a certain coolness had developed in the relationship after the managers stopped loaning him money. Steele, head over ears in debt, suspected they were not paying him his full share of the profits. In truth, their profits had fallen alarmingly, and his suspicions were unfounded, but his own problems blinded him to theirs, and he persisted in his demands. Drury Lane's precarious financial balance was threatened when Steele's creditors wanted to collect his debts from the box office, and a four-part indenture was hurriedly drawn up to protect the management from prosecution.[65] Baffled and angry, Steele went off to Wales, hoping to regain his health and stability in a retirement no one realized would be permanent.

Cibber returned to Hillingdon that summer to find that illness had struck his own family. The lively Charlotte was a shadow of her usual self, and for a time it was questionable that she would survive the summer. At last she was sent off to Katharine's cousin, Dr. John Hales, in the hope that his medical skill and the fresh air of Hertfordshire would effect a cure. Colley's concern for the child did not change Drury Lane's desperate need for a new work, however, and he spent the quiet weeks after her departure adapting Corneille's tragedy, *La Mort de Pompée*, into *Caesar in Egypt*.

Only genuine need could have prompted Cibber to write again after the reception of his last two plays. Yet *The Conscious Lovers* had proven that his words, if not his name, could still please an audience, and perhaps he assumed that time had softened his enemies, that like himself they held no long-term grudges. He may have thought the serious treatment of a heroic subject would be taken seriously by the town, or perhaps he did not even consider how it would be received—only that Drury Lane needed a new show. He was wrong on every count except the last. Before anyone had even seen it, Aaron Hill announced: "This evening we are to have a new Tragedy, called *Caesar in Egypt*; I am of the Opinion we shall find *Cibber* in *Egypt*, and not *Caesar*."[66]

Cibber took an eclectic approach, using Corneille's work as a foundation for incorporating bits from his own reading of Plutarch and Fletcher's *The False One*. The plot centers on Caesar's visit to Egypt after the battle of Pharsalia, his victory over Ptolemy (played by Theo), and his affair with Cleopatra. Cibber complicates the plot with the nefarious activities of Achoreus, Achillas, and Pothinus and a wholly unhistoric subplot, the mutual attraction of Antony (Wilks) and Cleopatra (Oldfield). Taking a rather unusual stance for the time, he treats Caesar (Booth) in an almost Shavian manner.

The structure of the play is sound, the sequences logical, the tempo varied, and it is perfectly theatrical, but the realistic quality so integral to Cibber's comedy is not to be found. His concept of tragedy had not changed since *Xerxes*: a classical setting, blank verse, exaggerated moral confrontations, and moments of high passion. The first element he could manage, but the verse is lamentably pedestrian, and his tragic characters are, as always, two-dimensional.[67]

Drury Lane staked a sizable amount of its dwindling resources on a sumptuous production featuring new costumes, exotic scenery, and imaginative stage effects that included elegantly painted swans floating by and saluting Cleopatra in her bower. The opening, with all four stars, should have been an occasion, but no sooner was the curtain raised than the familiar hisses and catcalls began, continuing without cease until the end of the last act. Part of the effusion came from the political partisanship Cibber had come to expect, but a new element, which none of them seemed to discern, had also crept in, an element first noted in a revealing passage by Benjamin Victor, who was there: "But alas! I can remember being of the merry Party in the Pit, the first Night of *Cibber's Caesar in Aegypt*, in which he performed the Part of *Achoreus*: and we then laught at his *quavering Tragedy Tones*, as much as we did at his Pasteboard Swans which the Carpenters pulled along the *Nile*."[68] Theatrical tastes were changing. Restoration heroic tragedy, the mode in which he had written the play, had been losing popularity for years, and the new generation was now moving away from the old acting style. Both in the writing and in the acting, Cibber's comedy changed over the years and remained freshly attuned to the times, but the same was not true of his tragedy; as Achoreus, he used the heavy cadence and deliberate gestures he had learned from Betterton. It would be sixteen years before David Garrick would burst upon the London stage to demolish the old mode once and for all, but already the formal declamation struck some as false. Aaron Hill had been harping on this very point for years, and in the laughter that greeted this Caesar, he suddenly found he had many allies.

Cibber was at last forced to realize his days as a playwright were over. He might revise or even rewrite others' work anonymously, but any play listing his name as author would be hooted off the stage. If he had been as thick-skinned as his enemies claimed, he might have shrugged the matter away and tried again, but what they chose to view as callousness might more accurately be termed pragmatism. What could he do? He was in no position to retire. Although he was not a wastrel, he was no miser either, and he liked the good life. He had provided well for himself and his family, but he would no longer be able to do so if he stopped working. Most important, he was an actor, and theater was his life. He was still the most popular comedian in London, but it was bitter to know he could no longer be anything more.

Booth and Wilks were equally dismayed when *Caesar in Egypt* did not pay its costs. A popular success was urgently needed; they could afford no more failures. Only one hope offered itself, and on the third night of the play the three managers wrote an anguished plea to Steele:

We have long wish'd for your coming to Town; but are now oblig'd to desire you to make all possible speed to us. Our audiences decrease daily, and those low Entertainments, which you and we so heartily despise, draw the Numbers, while we act only to the Few, who are blest with common sense. . . . While there are three playhouses exhibiting nonsense of different kinds against us 'tis impossible we should subsist much longer. Both the Courts have forsaken us. All we can do is to make the best of a losing Game, and part from the whole as best we can. No person living, but ourselves, is sensible of the low state we are reduc'd to. Therefore, we need not observe to you, how very needful it is to keep the secret.[69]

The managers told Steele of an offer to buy them out, hinting they might be tempted because their profits had been halved this year, and they were "very far from any hopes of their growing better." It was no use. Steele was too ill and too angry to write again.

The company retreated into repertory, but even that brought no surcease from Mist's waspishness. A few weeks later, he was complaining about the "tiresome, dull Round of the same Plays over and over again."[70] Between such grumblings and the harsh treatment of *Caesar in Egypt*, it is small wonder that Cibber sometimes seemed bemused or that for the first time in his life his remarkable memory was unreliable. Davies says that after gambling at Tom's, he would arrive at the theater "carelessly humming over an opera tune," walk on the stage and suddenly forget lines he had said a hundred times over. He was too experienced to lose stage presence; prolonging a ceremonious bow, he would drawl, "Your humble sa-a-arvant, madam," take a pinch of snuff, and strut deliberately across the stage to the prompter asking, "What is next?"[71] The Foppington mask was intact, but such lapses, the cost of his apparent imperturbability, were as unfailing an indication of stress as Wilks's tantrums.

The spring was brightened by the marriage of Theo to one of Drury Lane's best young actresses, Jane Johnson.[72] It was not a sudden match— Theo had met her in the summer of 1723, when her guardian, Richard Savage, brought her to Drury Lane.[73] This year, as a member of the regular company, she had proved herself adept in both comedy and tragedy. Cibber approved of the courtship; he knew Theo was wild (though he did not suspect how wild), and marriage should help to settle him down a bit.

With three children married, their daughter Anne working in a Leadenhall Street shop, and Charlotte still with their relatives, the senior Cibbers spent a quiet summer at Hillingdon. Colley wrote nothing, but he occasionally met with Booth, whose summer place was nearby, to plan the next year. As usual, there were changes in the company. Cibber's daughter, Elizabeth, came back to Drury Lane, and Elizabeth Younger, one of their most talented leading ladies, went over to Rich. Younger's roles went to Jane Cibber, and before the 1725-26 season was well under way, it was clear that Miss Younger's departure had been a blessing in disguise.

The promise Jane had shown in her first year was fulfilled when she took over the role of Margery in *The Country Wife*. On the night it opened, Rich presented the same play with Younger as Margery, echoing the rivalry of Oldfield and Bracegirdle twenty years earlier. The outcome was doubtful at first, but when royalty cast its vote for Jane, her Margery was "allow'd by the most judicious Criticks to be as well play'd as it ever has been since its first Representation."[74] Drury Lane needed such youngsters as the four stars grew older. Although most of his own roles were ageless, Cibber, too, felt the breath of the inevitable and this year gave his part of Young Wouldbe in *The Twin Rivals* to Bridgwater, taking the more sedate Trueman for himself.

Death was all about him. In the last few years he had lost some of his oldest and best friends: Tom Durfey, Susannah Centlivre, and his old crony, Henry Brett. Pinkethman was gone; in September a granddaughter lived only a few days[75] and in December, Wilks's son-in-law, Shaw, a dancer in the company, died suddenly. It was a sad and serious time, the grimness compounded by the lawsuit Steele had filed after learning that although the triumvirate had shared the regular profits with him, they had been paying themselves an extra "managers' salary" since 1721. Desperately poor and suspecting he had not had his fair share, Steele demanded to see Drury Lane's books and asked for his quarter of the "managers' salary" retroactive to 1721.[76] In January the triumvirate countersued with charges that Steele had neglected his duties, had mortgaged his share without their written consent, and had given them only one new play. Another litigation began its slow painful journey to the courtroom.

With neither Cibber nor Steele able to supply new plays, Drury Lane had lost two of its most important writers, and in the first half of the season the theater offered no premieres. Mist scoffed, and Dennis assailed the managers as "vipers" for their "insolent treatment" of playwrights, but the fact was that good new plays were still a rarity. Cibber's refusal of *Marianne* was often cited as evidence of his poor judgment, but his critics sedulously ignored the number of times he had been proven accurate. This year, Southerne brought the theater a new comedy, *Money the Mistress*, but when Cibber refused it, he took it to Lincoln's Inn Fields as Fenton had done. It lasted three nights, and Southerne was fortunate in being too deaf to hear the hisses drowning out his words.

The depressing season shortened tempers, particularly Wilks's, and he complained of overwork so constantly that even Cibber lost patience and decided he needed a lesson. The occasion for it arose with a revival of Vanbrugh's *The Provok'd Wife*. Cibber, who was to play Sir John Brute, handed out the parts, giving Lady Brute to Anne Oldfield; Heartfree to Booth; Lady Fanciful to his daughter-in-law, Jane; and the small role of Mademoiselle to his daughter Elizabeth. When he came to Wilks, he pretended to hesitate, "Since Constant has less to do than your usual parts, we thought you might like to ease yourself and give it to someone else."

Wilks stared at him, puzzled.

"The love scenes are rather serious and might suit Booth very well." Constant was a better role than Heartfree.

Wilks scowled but said nothing.

"If we can never revive a play without you, what would happen if you were ill?"

Wilks, who was as healthy as Cibber, turned away and poked the fire.

Cibber pushed further, "After all, you're at the top of your profession. Acting in this play would just give you unprofitable labor—and neither Booth nor I wish to impose that on you."

At that the Irish temper exploded. "So that's your plan! You're all in this together! Making yourselves look good at my expense! Putting me into disfavor with the nobility by letting them think I refused to act in a play so particularly asked for! But I can stand against all your cabals! You will not gain your ends, sir!"

Assuming an offended air, Cibber was ready. Wilks, he said, wanted to act in every play. As proof, he cited the complaints about overwork, pointing out that "the first time we offer to ease you, you fly into a passion." As the tall Irishman stared, Cibber continued: the part was in Wilks's hand; he could take it or leave it.

Wilks flung down the pages and leaned on the edge of the table, drumming his heels threateningly. Anne Oldfield tittered behind her fan, and he glowered, "If Mrs. Oldfield will choose someone else, I shall be very glad to be excused."

"It's a poor compliment to the company," Cibber muttered, referring to Wilks's attitude when others rose too fast, "to suppose only one man in it is fit to play an ordinary part with her."

Dead silence. He had gone too far, and they were on the brink of a serious rupture. At last Oldfield broke the tension. Rising gracefully and taking Cibber's arm, she moved away. "Pooh," she tossed back at the others, "you are all a pack of fools to make such a rout about nothing!" She stopped and gave Wilks a dazzling smile, "I hope Mr. Wilks will not so far mind what has passed as to refuse acting the part with me. It might not be so good as those you are used to, but I believe those who bespoke the play would expect to have it done to the best advantage." The last words were the company's standard claim to excellence, and Wilks began to thaw. "Besides, it would not be good for us to have it known there were difficulties among ourselves" (II, 233-37).

At the hint of Mist, the matter ended. Wilks had his role as well as the message, and there were no more complaints for some time. *The Provok'd Wife* was a triumph, Cibber's Sir John Brute was enthusiastically applauded as "inimitable acting,"[77] and an elated Vanbrugh promised another play for the next season.

It was not to be. Death struck again in March, when Vanbrugh, who had been staying at Whitehall, long noted for its unhealthy air, succumbed to a "quinsey in his throat," in the *London Journal*'s (2 April) terms. It was a devastating blow to Cibber; their friendship had been uninterrupted since *The Relapse*. Vanbrugh left the incomplete *Journey to London* for him to finish, but Cibber had no heart to take it up in spite of the theater's need. He may have been tempted, but a notice in the *London Journal* (2 April) that Vanbrugh had planned "a new Comedy, entitled, The Provoked Husband" must have discouraged him, for it notified his enemies that the play was in his hands. Vanbrugh had called it *A Journey to London*; Cibber renamed it *The Provok'd Husband*.

The spring of 1726 was further saddened when, shortly after the death of Vanbrugh, Theo and Jane's first-born son lived only a few days.[78] At the end of the season, however, the atmosphere lightened with the return home of a healthy Charlotte. Now thirteen, she was not the demure young lady her mother had hoped she would be but Cibber was charmed—until he discovered that, in imitation of Dr. Hales, she had been doctoring his Twickenham neighbors with quantities of expensive medications ordered from the local apothecary and charged to him.[79] He was angry but, strangely enough, he did not recognize in her behavior the same kind of role-playing he himself had done at her age. Of all his children, Charlotte was the most like Colley and the one he understood the least.

Drury Lane's 1726-27 season struck a rock when Booth came down with a fever that kept him off the stage for three months, depressing to the company and disrupting to the schedule. For a time, Cibber and Wilks chose comedies in which Booth did not play; later they added those works in which he played supporting parts that could be given to young actors like John Mills's son. The opportunity pleased the youngsters more than the managers, for some of them had exalted ideas of their own worth. Rehearsing Scandal in *Love for Love*, Mills, Jr., observed smugly that Booth always forgot the line, "Death and hell! Where is Valentine?" Cibber stepped out of his own character, Tattle, long enough to give him a withering smile. "There is more beauty in Booth's forgetfulness than in everything you remember!" he said sharply and stalked off.[80] He might privately consider Booth less gifted than Betterton, but no young player could insult him. It is a trait overlooked by those eager to portray a Cibber disloyal to his partners.

In January, a still weakened Booth returned to a great ovation in *The Distrest Mother*, and Cibber's sense of humor returned. He should have been feeling rather pleased at this time; Elizabeth Cibber Brett had found her niche as a dancer in the company, Jane was highly touted for her "lively and agreeable" Miss Prue in *Love for Love*, and Theo for his Ancient Pistol in *Henry IV (Part 2)*. Carefully coached by Colley (who had played it), Theo developed a character so extravagant that it was "impossible not to laugh" and became identified with the role.[81] He had a sure touch for comedy, but no one except perhaps Jane and the doxies of Drury Lane yet realized that the "false spirit" and "uncommon blustering" which he brought to the part of Pistol were less an act than an integral part of his own character.

Mist continued his campaign of increasingly personal attacks against Cibber with such gems as: "*Promotions*: some time ago the ingenious Mr. Cibber was made constable of Covent-Garden Parish, and for his great Genius in Poetry, 'tis thought he will be chosen Bellman next Christmas."[82] He would have done better not to mention Cibber's poetry, for the backlash from such reminders was to have an effect he did not intend. Colley's refusal to answer eventually brought others to champion him, and an anonymous "Philander" called Mist "Rich's Toad-Eater," who used Cibber as his "standing Jest." He praised Drury Lane's company, calling it "the best Britain may ever boast of," and commented that "whatever the New House does, tho' never so silly, shall be cry'd up to the Skies, and on the contrary, whatever the Old House undertakes is sure to meet with Opposition and Derision, tho' in its self ne'er so good."[83] Toward the end of spring, Mist's attention was distracted from Cibber by the spectacular feud between the rival divas, Faustina and Cuzzoni, each of whom drew crowds of enthusiastic followers from both houses. The season crawled on, closing drearily with the death of George I on 17 June 1727.

Dedicated Walpole foes took heart. The animosity between the old king and the new was common knowledge, and they hoped the new regime would sweep the Whigs from power. They reckoned without Walpole's unmatched political skills; he had managed, somehow, to remain on good terms both with the old king and the new one, and the death of George I did not create even a ripple in the ministry. Walpole was more firmly ensconced than ever, and the Tories, frustrated and furious, lashed out at Walpole, his ministry, and his spokesman.

For that public symbol of Whiggism, Drury Lane, the six-week mourning period was like a reprieve. The benefit season was never very profitable for management, and the thin houses of the spring had brought little into their pockets. It was also evident that Booth's strength was much diminished and that he needed the rest he could afford only during the long vacation. He and Hester retired to Hillingdon, along with the Cibbers, where Colley applied himself to finish Vanbrugh's play. Whether he wanted to or not, he had to brave the critics—Drury Lane *must* have something new for the next season.

The Provok'd Husband is a smooth rich comedy, polished by a master hand. Cibber cut and revised Vanbrugh's two disparate plots into a single, unified action and softened the Restoration earthiness into the genteel comedy more palatable to his age. Vanbrugh's Lady Loverule was a flagrant sinner deserving to be cast out by her husband, but Cibber thought this "too severe for Comedy," and his Lady Townley, merely "immoderate in her pursuit of pleasure," is more frivolous than vicious. This was an important change in view of Cibber's conclusion, for Vanbrugh had planned for her husband to turn her out in the end. Cibber's Lord Townley is more forgiving; when Lady Townley sees her errors and reforms, he forgives her. Against the Townleys, Cibber sets Manly and Lady Grace, "of exemplary virtue," and this pair not only serves as an example of the ideal but presents the overt moral statement so pleasing to the times.[84]

The subplot is tightly locked into the main line, and most of the city/country satire remains intact. Vanbrugh's Headpiece family become Cibber's Wrongheads, and the more raffish lines have been excised, but the low comedy scenes are relatively untouched. Lord Wronghead's ambition to enter Parliament and Lady Wronghead's eagerness to enter society draw them into the Townley circle and offer a comic parallel to the central action. Through their obstreperous daughter, their simple-minded son, and an involvement with a grasping landlady and an unscrupulous card shark, they nearly lose everything, but here, too, Cibber softened the satire. For all their foolishness, the Wrongheads are not so vile that they cannot be rescued from the worst consequences of their actions, and a rough justice at the end sends them home only slightly poorer and a great deal wiser.

The two sets of characters intermingle freely, and the two plots come together at the end. The secondary character of Manly unites them closely; he is not only Lord Townley's best friend but in love with Townley's sister, Lady Grace. Their romance is intimately bound up with the family problems, which include the Townley relatives, the Wrongheads. As Manley's own pursuit ends successfully, he helps the Townleys resolve their differences and straightens out the Wrongheads' knotted lives.

It seems fairly obvious why Cibber's tinkering focused on the Townley line. Here he was on familiar ground. The main story is a reprise of a favorite theme, the achievement of a happy marriage through the reformation of a partner—as in *Love's Last Shift*, *The Careless Husband*, and *The Lady's Last Stake*. The friendship of Manly and Lord Townley was a common pattern in contemporary plays, but Cibber's version also recalls Lovemore and Longville in *Woman's Wit*. Less comfortable with low comedy and harsh satire, he wisely trusted Vanbrugh in the treatment of the Wrongheads, changing their story only to meet the needs of his restructured main plot. The result is a perfect example of a Restoration comedy of wit adapted to the taste of the sentimental theater, and the eighteenth-century theater historian Samuel Derrick commented: "Cibber never shewed more judgment than in his happily blending of the characters of the Provoked Husband;

a Journey to London; a Play that will live as long as the Stage itself. . . . characters of low life are thrown into genteel Comedy to make it go down the better: the amusement palliates the instruction; gives force to the moral and the serious."[85]

Ironically, one of Cibber's funniest comedies was begun and concluded in an atmosphere of mourning. He started the work just after the death of the king, and before it was finished, his daughter-in-law, Jane, had given birth to a second child, who did not live.[86] As always, no hint of his private sorrow was permitted to show in his work or his image. He dedicated the play to the new queen and sold the copyright to the printer, John Watts, with the proviso that Watts not publish until after *The Provok'd Husband* opened.

By October, a festive spirit was climaxed by the coronation of George II. In his honor, the Drury Lane company revived *Henry VIII*, adding a lavish spectacle with a coronation scene of their own that included "the Ceremony of the Champion in Westminster Hall," with the actors splendidly dressed in armor borrowed, it was said, from the Tower.[87] Neither Wilks nor Oldfield played in this production, but Booth made an impressive Henry, and Mary Porter, a regal Queen Katharine. Cibber took his old role of Wolsey, still gesticulating and pinching out the mythical candle in his old-fashioned manner.

In spite of a near disaster on opening night when a false alarm of fire panicked the audience, the company had a splendid success, and audiences crowded the house. The coronation scene was the talk of the town, and many who could not attend the real coronation in Westminster Abbey took a vicarious pleasure in the theatrical show at Drury Lane. Yet the company seemed dogged by misfortune; the play had hardly opened before Booth's deteriorating health made it clear the run would have to be cut short. It was disheartening, particularly after the lean years the group had suffered, but, however much he wanted to, Booth was unable to carry the weight of the heavy role.

Afterward, Theo claimed, possibly with some honesty, that it was he who solved the problem by suggesting the company alternate *Henry VIII* with a revival of John Banks's *Anna Bullen*. Banks's Henry was less demanding for Booth than Shakespeare's. He would be supported by Wilks's brilliant Percy and Oldfield's Anna, an audience favorite, while Colley would merely trade one Wolsey for another. Furthermore, the coronation scene was as appropriate for one play as the other. It was agreed, and *Anna Bullen* proved as profitable as *Henry VIII*. In late November, however, as Booth began to rehearse Lewis Theobald's tragedy *The Double Falshood*, he no longer had strength for nightly performances. Cibber and Wilks took over in their own specialties—with the coronation scene still attached as an afterpiece to such light fare as *The Careless Husband* and *The Relapse*.

Booth collapsed before the opening, and young Charles Williams, his understudy, played the first five nights. In response to urgent pleas from Theobald, Booth tried for a week, but fever struck him down again, and he was out until after Christmas. The doctors advised complete rest. He resisted stubbornly, but after a performance of *The Double Falshood* on 9 January, he could no longer continue. Even Cibber, whose own robust health made him rather insensitive to others' weaknesses, could see that Booth's condition was serious, although he had no idea that his old friend had acted for the last time.

Fortunately unable to foresee the future, Cibber had the grace of hope to sustain him through the first half of the 1727-28 season. In November, *The Provok'd Wife* gave the Cibbers a historic family occasion when three generations appeared together: Colley as Sir John Brute, Elizabeth as Mademoiselle, and Elizabeth's seven-year-old daughter, Anne Brett, making her debut as a dancer in the aftershow.[88] At almost the same time, Cibber's daughter Anne opened her own shop in Charles Street, establishing herself firmly as an independent woman.[89] Professionally, his days were equally bright; the coronation scene attached to the various plays ran for more than forty nights and made more money than any play the company had ever produced,[90] while *The Provok'd Husband*, now in rehearsal, looked promising enough to sustain the second half of the year.

Cibber had carefully concealed the nature of his alterations, but the announcement of the play told his enemies that he had completed Vanbrugh's manuscript. The premiere came the day after Booth's last appearance, and Cibber's antagonists came in force, determined to damn this play as thoroughly as they had *The Refusal* and *Caesar in Egypt*. Certain they could distinguish Cibber's maladroit dramaturgy from Vanbrugh's, they arrived prepared to hiss the one and applaud the other; Cibber encouraged their certainty by taking the part of Lord Wronghead. The harrassment began with the first low comedy scene and, interrupted only by applause for the more serious Townley segments, continued throughout the evening. During the fourth act, the demonstration was so long that Benjamin Victor, sitting in the pit, wondered if the play would be allowed to finish at all.[91]

The curtain came down to thunderous applause, although the enemy party did not give up without a struggle. As Anne Oldfield delivered the first line of the epilogue, a loud and prolonged hiss came from the pit. Oldfield, superbly unmoved, stared down at the origin of the disruption until everyone followed the direction of her glance. Then, with a magnificent combination of scorn, contempt, and pity, she uttered the words, "Poor creature!" in tones that reached the top of the gallery. Her persecutor, embarrassed by the unexpected notice, "sunk down in fear and trembling and was heard no more."[92]

For the first time in a decade, Cibber had a success, but not without difficulty, and the demonstrations continued to be a part of each succeeding night. Mist's *Weekly Journal*, as always, provided ample space to Cibber's enemies. Mist himself, now in trouble with the law, was in France, but his assistant, Bingley, carried on the feud with gusto. On 13 January, his *Weekly Journal* printed a blistering attack on the "horrid, barbarous and cruel Murder" Cibber had committed "upon a posthumous Child of the late Sir *John Vanbroog*," and followed it with a distorted history of Cibber's stage career that created a foundation for further distortions.

Wilks was outraged, but Cibber appeared so unmoved that it is said he slept between his scenes. After the sixth performance his serenity was explained when Watts published *The Provok'd Husband* and Vanbrugh's *Journey to London* simultaneously, revealing to one and all that the hisses had been directed against Vanbrugh's scenes, the applause unwittingly given to Cibber. That night, Colley stepped forth after Oldfield's epilogue and "politely thanked" the audience for their approval, "observing that he was quite careless of the fate of his own addition, but was indeed concerned to find, that any fragment of his departed friend had incurred their censure. Such poignant satire upon the depravity of public judgment, couched in terms of such apparent zeal for a departed friend, and respect for his audience, had an effect scarcely to be conceived. The audience testified their feelings by the warmest applause, which they carried so far as to *huzza* Cibber, and put an effectual stop to the malice of the party against him.[93]

The publication of the two plays caught Cibber's enemies fairly. There was a sudden silence, and when the attacks resumed, they focused on the preface to the printed edition. Without acknowledging the previous error, Bingley now led the pack against Colley's language. Cibber was indeed guilty of at least one and perhaps two of the charges, but they were hardly unusual, and one may even have been a printer's error, for he had no more patience with the dull drudgery of editing than did his enemy Pope. The first error was the remark that Oldfield's costumes and ornaments "seemed in all respects the *paraphonalia* of a woman of quality." His enemies seized on the misspelling, and Bingley gleefully proclaimed it was thought to be "some arch Stroke of C——r's which was not fit to be spoke in *English*."[94]

The second error was egregious. Overwhelmed by the victory after so many defeats, Cibber lauded the cast generously, especially Anne Oldfield. He praised her face, her figure, her voice, and her technique and then, finding words inadequate, used a phrase that sounded better than it looked on the page, "'Tis not enough to say she here *outdid* her usual *outdoing*."[95] Said with a smile and an emphasis on "usual," it is a gracious and amusing compliment, but in print it is ridiculous. His enemies took it out of context and made so much of it that it became a catchword trotted out whenever they wanted ammunition. Cibber made no response, but in the second edition of the play, "paraphernalia" was correctly spelled, and the phrase silently corrected to "outdid her usual Excellence." His enemies ignored the change.

Halfway through a prosperous season and with an undisputed success on the boards, Drury Lane seemed to have regained some of the dominance lost over the last few years, but the company's afflictions were not yet ended. Less than three weeks after *The Provok'd Husband* was established as the hit of the season, Rich opened John Gay's *The Beggar's Opera*, a theater classic. Playing for thirty-two successive nights, it completely eclipsed *The Provok'd Husband* and went on to a phenomenal sixty-two performances by the end of the season.

It was a new kind of work, a "ballad opera" satirizing Italian opera with new lyrics set to familiar English tunes in place of elaborate arias and choruses. Gay had first offered it to Drury Lane, but Cibber turned it down; now it made "Rich gay and Gay rich," while Drury Lane's enemies hooted gleefully. Actually, Colley might have accepted it had he been a bit more obtuse, for it was not ignorance but a perception of its political satire that made him refuse it. Given his loyalty to the king and his personal friendship with Walpole, he could not have found humor in the picture of England's prime minister as a highwayman and his ministry as a den of thieves. Even Rich had had doubts and would have dropped it after the first rehearsal if Gay's friends had not pressured him into continuing. Cibber could no more have accepted such a "treasonous" work than he could have spat on the British flag.

Along with the managers' other troubles, the matter of Steele now surfaced again, and on 16 February 1728, they went before Sir Joseph Jekyll, master of the Rolls, to try their case. Cibber made the presentation and prepared his notes with care; knowing his weakness under stress, he no longer trusted his memory. When he came to deliver his speech, he was so stricken with stage fright that he wept, but his argument was clear and cogent. He held to two main points: whether Steele was obligated to share in the full duties of management and, if he was not, whether he was entitled to the extra five pounds "salary" the other managers shared among themselves each day of performance.

On the first point, Cibber maintained that Steele had never assumed the responsibility for day-to-day business. He had taken advantage of his partners, borrowing money he was unable to repay, and when they refused further loans, he had angrily withdrawn all support. Since his main value to them had been in his presence at court and his plays, this withdrawal had been costly for the theater, and Cibber turned the argument back on Steele by coolly asking, "And will Sir *Richard*, then, make us no Compensation for so valuable a Loss in our Interests?"

The second point began with a fairly detailed explanation of their management that could stand as a model for any theater. The company, Cibber said, consisted of 140 people who had to be "led, or driven, watch'd, and restrain'd by the continual Skill, Care and Patience" of the managers, who rehearsed every morning and attended every performance whether or not they were acting. They not only dealt with the actors but with all the backstage workers, as well as the "Door-keepers, Under-Servants, and Officers that, without such Care, are too often apt to defraud us, or neglect their Duty." He reminded the judge that Steele had profited well from *The Conscious Lovers*, concluding, "Sure, Sir, while we do such extraordinary Duty as Menagers, and while he neglects his Share of that Duty, he cannot grudge us the moderate Demand we make for our separate Labour?" (II, 199-208). It was a passionate, logical plea, and the judgment went in his favor.[96]

Whatever pleasure he may have had in the victory was clouded by the death of another grandchild and by fatigue.[97] He had played 129 performances this season, the most of any in his long career. When the long vacation came, he settled Katharine and the rambunctious Charlotte at Hillingdon and set out for France.[98] That country was undoubtedly more restful than home, for at fifteen, Charlotte was in the midst of a rebellious adolescence. Longing for approval, she tried hard to please her parents, but somehow her efforts invariably went amiss. Colley said he wanted to buy a new horse when he returned; she "tested" one by riding wildly about the countryside and running down a child in the process. A groom, dismissed for drunkenness, threatened Katharine with retaliation; Charlotte protected the household by shooting at imaginary shadows all night long, annoying the neighbors and giving Katharine an asthma attack.[99]

But however heinous her misdeeds, they paled beside those of her brother, Theo. Cibber's youngest daughter and his only living son had certain traits in common: both were headstrong, both had a sense of the dramatic, and both had a propensity for trouble. There the resemblance stopped. Charlotte's errors sprang from an eagerness to please others, and she had her father's charm. Theo was invincibly selfish and had only his father's ambition. The difference marked the pattern of their lives.

During the last few years, Theo's less attractive qualities had become evident. Since leaving Westminster, he had been a familiar figure in the brothels and taverns of Covent Garden, and Colley's hope that marriage would settle him had been as fruitless as Jane's valiant efforts to conceal his infidelities. Everyone in the company and, by the summer of 1728, most of London as well knew Theo was a rake and a wastrel. To Colley, who took marriage seriously, Theo's behavior meant real unhappiness.

As the 1728-29 season began, Theo's behavior was only one of many problems. Booth was still unable to act; the doctors called his illness an "inveterate jaundice" and could not cure it. With no immediate prospect of his return, the managers replaced him with Thomas Elrington, whom

Wilks had persuaded to come over from Ireland. Tall and handsome Elrington had a magnificent voice and a commanding presence: he had played
most of Booth's repertory in Dublin, and he was a splendid actor. But he
was not Barton Booth.

Working Elrington into the company took time away from rehearsing
new plays, and the managers stayed with the repertory during the first half
of the season. Novelty was needed to fill the house, however, and Cibber
had already devised something new and different. Stunned by the success
of *The Beggar's Opera* and intrigued by its form, he put together a similar
piece, although, as he was careful to note, its purpose was not at all the
same.

Love in a Riddle is a pastoral romance "recommending Virtue and Innocence" and set in Arcadia. As the play opens, the young lovers of the title
are separated, because the boy, Iphis, once tricked Ianthe into kissing him,
and she has been angry with him ever since. Under paternal pressure to
accept him as a husband, she has visited Diana's oracle and received word
that she should not marry Iphis until he solves a riddle:

> That which He cannot have, shall Iphis give;
> That which Thou canst not give, or He desire:
> That which He must not have, must Thou receive,
> That! that's the Right thy present Wrongs require.[100]

The answer is, of course, a husband, but neither Iphis nor the audience
learns it until the last moment.

The second pair of lovers find their path roughened by Philautus, "a
conceited Corinthian Courtier" (Cibber), whose desire for the girl, Pastora,
does not prevent him from pursuing Ianthe as well. His defeat brings both
pairs together. The whole play is a piece of romantic froth to which Cibber
added a little substance through a low comedy subplot in which Damon, a
young shepherd who frankly says he is not the marrying kind, is finally
matched with the shepherdess, Phillida. The two parts are not structurally
of a piece, but they are linked through the interpolation of popular tunes
with new lyrics—a direct borrowing from Gay.

The play was finished by the time the season began, and this time Cibber did not keep it secret. Eternally optimistic, he may have assumed *The
Provok'd Husband* had ended the years of concerted hostility and that this
time he would have a fair hearing. On 22 October, the *Daily Journal* huffed
that Drury Lane would present a new play "written by a celebrated Hand,
noted for his malignancy to his Brethren of the Quill, and for his ill Success
in Dramatical Performances," and on 9 November the *British Gazetteer*
puffed its disappointment that Drury Lane would imitate *The Beggar's Opera*
with a work "by one of the Managers himself."

Such notices allerted friends as well as enemies and should have balanced the house fairly evenly. This time, however, Cibber's foes found an added stimulus when Gay's next satire, *Polly*, was prohibited by the lord chamberlain. Grafton's friendship with Cibber was well known, and the Tories concluded that Colley had influenced the decision. It was illogical, for he had never done such a thing, and Grafton neither needed the satire pointed out nor was given to obeying actors.

On the opening night, the Tories were ready. Wilks had no sooner stepped forth for the prologue than a great hiss rose from the pit, and as the scene opened, a long and monstrous roar terrified the actors. Somehow they managed to continue, and the bright new actress, Catherine Raftor, even caused a brief lull in the noise. Captivated by her beauty and voice, the audience listened until a determined male voice called out, "Zounds, Tom! take care, or this charming little Devil will save all!"[101] The owner of the voice need not have worried. When Cibber entered, the clamor drowned his words; when he sang, they mocked his reedy tones with a discordant chorus, and when young Mrs. Thurmond had to point a spear at him, the pit cried out, "Kill him! Kill him!"[102] The night was a complete and utter disaster.

After it was over, Wilks and Cibber held a hasty consultation. Ordinarily *Love in a Riddle* would never have been seen again, but the next night was to be a command performance for the Prince of Wales. Hoping royalty might prove a restraining influence, they tried once more. That night, the cacophony was even worse, and at length Cibber stopped the show, walked to the footlights, and held up both hands. When the audience was silent, he reminded them of the prince's presence and promised that if they let the play proceed, it would never again be seen on a London stage. The noise-makers smelled victory and agreed to the terms. Except for a little sporadic hissing, they remained quiet to the end.[103] The next evening, the house was again full, many there to see if Cibber would keep his word. He did, and *The Orphan* played to great applause.

It was as thorough a failure as Cibber had ever known, much worse, in some ways, than *The Refusal* or *Caesar in Egypt* had been. He was fifty-seven years old, and he would not write another play. The management duties were heavier and less profitable each year, one partner was out and not likely to return soon, Anne Oldfield was often ill, weakening before their eyes, and his family problems—Theo's disgraceful behavior, Katharine's health, and young Charlotte's future—were with him always. It was a time for despair, and perhaps he felt it, but the actor could not ask for sympathy. Donning Foppington's full-bottomed wig, his frothy laces, his rich brocades, and his impervious smile, he sallied forth like an untouched youth.

The newspapers and pamphleteers had a glorious time ridiculing *Love in a Riddle* and its author, but in the end, Cibber's optimism was not entirely groundless. When the uproar had died down, he excised the subplot, as he had done with *Woman's Wit* long ago, and made it into the delightful afterpiece, *Damon and Phillida*. No one had been able to hear a word of it during the performances of *Love in a Riddle*, and without his name attached, it was well received when a group of young actors performed it at the Haymarket in the summer of 1729. Later, it became one of the most popular afterpieces of the next two generations.

He was not the only one to have a play cried down so violently. Soon after *Love in a Riddle*, Charles Johnson's *Village Opera* suffered an even worse fate, receiving not only catcalls, whistles, and threats to boycott the actors' benefits, but volleys of oranges as well. Afterward, the curious hastened to the Bedford Coffee House, eager to hear the reactions of Wilks and Cibber. The crowd was disappointed. Unwilling to give their enemies further ammunition, neither manager said a word about it.[104]

Considering the problems they faced, the season did not go badly. Oldfield's benefit in March was a glittering affair, and shortly after, Cibber's granddaughter, Anne Brett, now eleven, made her acting debut. Elrington had performed so well that Wilks and Cibber offered him his own terms if he would stay on for another season, but he refused. Homesick for Smock Alley, he sailed for Dublin as soon as the benefit season ended. Cibber and Wilks could only hope that Booth's current visit to the Amsterdam doctors would prove more beneficial than his recent sojourn at Bath.

Colley retired to Hillingdon for the last time. Without Booth the village seemed dull, and he had no desire to spend time writing another play, although he may have written a libretto for the Italian composer, Nicolai Porpora.[105] Theo, left in charge of the summer company, and Jane, expecting another child,[106] stayed in London, and this summer, Theo became acquainted with a gifted young violinist ambitious to be an actor, Richard Charke. Not only did he hire Charke, but the two became fast friends and roamed the town nightly, drinking, gambling, and whoring as if they were fine gentlemen. At length, Theo brought him to the Cibber home where Charlotte saw him and promptly fell in love.

Colley probably did not pay attention, for the beginning of the 1729-30 season was difficult. Sir Richard Steele, partially paralyzed and unable to speak, died in Wales. The status of the patent, which was to remain in force only for three years after Steele's death, was suddenly altered. The triumvirate paid off the heirs and applied for a new one. Cibber's friendship with Grafton put the three in a favorable position, but it would be a long process and further complicated the season in which Henry Giffard's new theater in Goodman's Fields brought the most serious competition they had faced since John Rich took over the theater at Lincoln's Inn Fields.

Booth returned from Amsterdam in no better health and with no prospect of joining the company. He and Hester stayed in Hampstead, where the air was supposed to be invigorating; on the rare occasions when he was well enough, he visited the theater like a ghost haunting the scenes of his life. He watched Wilks perform superlatively as Jaffeir in *Venice Preserv'd* (the role Wilks had angrily given him fifteen years before), and in his anguish could not even bring himself to join in the ovation.[107]

Had Cibber been less preoccupied with stage matters, he might have been apprehensive about Charlotte's infatuation for Richard Charke. She was only sixteen, had spent most of her life out of London, and her seeming sophistication, made up of a sketchy education and maternal indulgence, was only a thin veneer; beneath it she was as ignorant and naive as any country girl. Now being groomed for her debut on the stage, she announced she loved Charke, could not live without him, and would die if she could not marry him. Colley believed that his headstrong daughter would benefit from the discipline of the stage, and probably, like any father of the time, that marriage would be even better for her. There was no reason she should not have both, and with a husband as ideal as Charke appeared to be, she would be well established for life. He gave his consent, and two weeks after Charlotte's seventeenth birthday, she and Charke were married at St. Martins-in-the-Fields.[108]

Her nuptials came in the midst of preparations for James Thomson's tragedy, *Sophonisba*. Oldfield was magnificent in the title role, and it was a complete success—or very nearly, for Cibber's enemies were still present. The perfect iambic pentameter of "O Sophonisba, Sophonisba, O" brought snickers, and Cibber, playing the villainous Scipio, was so roundly hissed that Wilks suggested that Charles Williams, who had substituted for Booth in the early days of his illness, take over the part. Cibber agreed. The next night Williams, dressed in the same costume, was also hissed at first, but when he was recognized, the audience burst into applause. It was a painful experience for Colley, the first time such animosity had been aimed at him as an actor.

Cibber's enemies seemed to increase in strength and numbers. The *Weekly Journal* had been replaced by the *Grub Street Journal*, with Alexander Pope, master of the memorable phrase, a frequent contributor. A new antagonist now appeared in young Henry Fielding. During the previous season, Cibber had accepted Fielding's maiden effort, *Love in Several Masques*, which had four performances, but he refused Fielding's second play, and the young man revenged himself with *The Author's Farce*, a popular satire with a recognizable caricature of Colley as "Marplay."

Meanwhile, the original of the caricature prepared Charlotte for her debut in *The Provok'd Wife*, taking pains to ensure a good beginning for her career. The play was a favorite, with Anne Oldfield as Lady Brute, Wilks as Constant, and Colley as Sir John. Charlotte would be surrounded by friends and family; her husband, brother, and sister-in-law would act in the afterpiece. She was to play Elizabeth's former role, Mademoiselle, and her father tutored her carefully. She had an intuitive sense of dramatic values and a real gift for comedy, but she lacked the necessary discipline. Elizabeth had been docile, listening carefully, and struggling to follow directions, but Charlotte, who showed much greater promise, was unpredictable. She would be either excellent or very bad indeed.

Cibber tried to protect her from his enemies as much as he could, and the bills read, "Madamoiselle—a young Gentlewoman, being her first Attempt upon any Stage," but Charlotte resented the protection and thought that the anonymity showed a lack of faith. Two weeks later, billed as "Mrs. Charke, being the second Time of her Appearance on the Stage," she was so enchanted with the publicity that she rode all over London distributing handbills announcing her identity. Miraculously, she escaped the notice of her father's foes.

Anne Oldfield's performance in *The Provok'd Wife* was her last. She had been ill for some time but had insisted on playing until she was in pain so severe she could no longer withstand it. The doctors diagnosed incurable cancer. She accepted their verdict with more composure than Wilks and Cibber, made her will, and, with equal serenity, informed them that as she could no longer earn her salary she should not be paid. They gallantly refused and continued it to the end of the season. She would accept no more.[109]

The summer passed with little to recommend it. Thieves broke into Drury Lane and stole a quantity of silver lace; Booth's condition varied without improvement; Oldfield was in constant pain and her condition worsened daily. At home, Katharine was a near-invalid, and Charlotte was pregnant and miserable, unable to tell her parents of Charke's neglect and infidelities. Only Theo and Jane appeared to thrive. They had been separated but had recently reconciled, and Jane was pathetically grateful for Theo's "peace offering," a new play that he wrote for the two of them.

Colley's first role of the 1730-31 season was Fondlewife, but he took no joy in it, and Winifred Thurmond's Laetitia had little of Oldfield's elegant charm. Ironically, the next day, the papers noted that Oldfield was "in a fair way of recovery,"[110] but Cibber and Wilks knew better as they sorrowfully divided her roles among the lesser actresses.

Anne Oldfield died on the morning of Friday, 23 October 1730, and Drury Lane was dark that night. It was dark again on 27 October, when the entire company assembled for her funeral in Westminster Abbey.[111] None of the managers was able to serve as a pallbearer. Booth was too ill; Wilks, who had been her leading man for so many years, and Cibber, who put aside his flippant mask, were overcome with grief. All London mourned with a great flood of elegies, tributes, and epitaphs, but the theater played a command performance the next night, and the season continued. The pall that hung over the company did not lift for many months, however, and for Cibber and Wilks, neither the theater nor the world was ever again quite the same.

Another death that autumn was to have a more obvious effect on Cibber's life when Laurence Eusden, poet laureate, died in September. A well-publicized search began for his replacement, although the most obvious choice was not even considered: Alexander Pope might be recognized as a great poet, but as a Roman Catholic, he could not hold public office. In any case, his political sympathies would have eliminated him. The laureateship, with its annual stipend of one hundred pounds and a butt of sack, was an honor, but it was primarily a political post and had not been held by a major poet since Dryden. The occupant was expected to be a gentleman of letters and a member of the Church of England; beyond that the choice depended on the party in power.

The most prominent candidates were Lewis Theobald and the young "thresher poet," Stephen Duck. Theobald was best known for answering Pope's edition of Shakespeare with his own *Shakespeare Restored*, which had pointed out Pope's errors and earned him the position of "Prince of Dunces" in Pope's recent *Dunciad*.[112] Duck, a self-educated farm laborer, was only twenty-five, but his poems had been circulated among the cognoscenti. He gained a good deal of sympathy when his wife died in childbirth at the end of October, and he seemed to be the favorite. Cibber, along with James Ralph and John Dennis, was mockingly proposed, but beset by personal and professional ills, he did nothing to promote himself. Throughout the fall and into the winter, a paper battle raged between the various factions as journalists vied with each other in name-calling. Cibber, as might be expected, was a prime target, and the *Grub Street Journal* led a savage campaign against him; on 12 November, one of its milder attacks asked:

> Shall royal praise be ruined by such a ribald,
> As fopling C——r or attorney T——d?
> Let's rather wait one year for better luck;
> One year can make a singing swan of Duck.

But Cibber, too, had highly placed friends. Lord Macclesfield might read Duck's verses to the queen, but Lord Hervey had her confidence. The dukes of Dorset, Kent, Devonshire, and Grafton admired his plays, as did the earl of Chesterfield, and Robert Walpole had the most powerful voice in England. All of them knew and liked Cibber. He had dined, wined, and gambled with them; they sought him out when they wanted cheering. He listened to their troubles, never burdened them with his own, and his good humor was contagious.

They were more than good friends. They were powerful men with long memories. They recalled Cibber's unwavering loyalty to the House of Hanover, his long years as a Whig partisan, and his public support of their causes. They remembered *The Non-Juror* and the price of its success in the reception of *The Refusal* and *Caesar in Egypt*, his rejection of *The Beggar's Opera*, and the subsequent treatment of *Love in a Riddle*. As an author, he was surely one of the most distinguished, with more plays still in the repertory than any other living writer.[113] He had been published and pirated in Dublin, Edinburgh, and Paris, and it was commonly accepted that he had "moralized" a stage notorious for its indecency. Nor were they blind to the abuse heaped on him for the last twelve years. Even in a time when personal slurs were the common form of attack, Cibber had suffered more than most, yet he had borne those ferocious assaults with equanimity, never stooping to answer slander with slander, libel with libel. As they saw it, he deserved recognition, and their decision should have surprised no one. They named Colley Cibber poet laureate of England.

It is impossible to conceive what was in Cibber's mind that Thursday afternoon in December when he went to court to be "graciously received" by the king and hear the official announcement,[114] but as he knelt to kiss the royal hand, it must have given him some satisfaction to realize that the stage-struck youngster who had trembled in the wings at Drury Lane forty years ago, who had faced imposing obstacles, uncertain fortune, and concerted hostility to become the foremost comedian and playwright of his time and patentee of Theatre Royal, Drury Lane, had reached at last a pinnacle higher than even he had envisioned.

FIVE

Misfortunes

FOPPINGTON wore his new honor gracefully. On the night of his appointment, he visited White's coffeehouse as usual, chatting inconsequentially until the duke of Argyle asked his opinion on a current political question. Then, as Charles Macklin tells it, he made his dramatic announcement. Cibber "facetiously asked his Grace in what character he should treat, whether in the character of political critick or that of Poet Laureat; for he had the honour of informing them he had received his Fiat that very day from his puissant Patron upon his Grace's left hand, bowing very low to his Grace of Grafton, the Lord Chamberlain. . . . He then bowed gravely and gracefully round the Table, for the Fellow was handsome, a good Figure, and always elegantly dress'd."[1] He then proceeded to give a witty extempore speech on the art of persuasion. The next week, he made the laureateship valid by taking the sacrament, and with that act became a part of the nation's historical fabric.[2]

To all appearances, his cup was full. He was roundly applauded at Drury Lane, Charlotte had given birth to a healthy daughter, and friends publicly welcomed his appointment.[3] The appearance was deceptive. Ironically, the highest honor his country could bestow merely opened a new area for attacks. The post required him to write two poems a year, one for the king's birthday, one for New Year's Day, and each would be an open invitation to his enemies. As if in anticipation of the onslaught, an anonymous pen defended him: "The Town very well knows Mr. C——r has wrote well, acted better, and at this Hour understands the Laws of the Stage the best of any man in England. Who therefore has the least spark of Gratitude or good Nature in him can read the repeated pitiful Invectives of the Grubs against him with any tolerable Patience?"[4] As the beginning of 1731 approached, Cibber wrote his first ode and gave it to John Eccles, master of the King's Band, who set it to music with choruses for the royal singers. On 1 January, the *Gentleman's Magazine* announced that "Their Majesties received the Compliments of the Nobility for the New-Year" and heard it at St. James's, where it was enthusiastically praised.

So much has been written about Cibber's wretched odes that one might believe not only the author but the entire court blind and deaf to any sort of good poetry. Admittedly, his verse is bad, but neither Eusden, who preceded him, nor Whitehead, who followed, wrote better, though neither was ridiculed. Much of the concentration on Cibber was, of course, political; as the laureate, Colley was a gentleman of the court, representing a government the Tories abhorred. They could not directly attack Walpole without severe reprisals, but they could strike at his spokesman.

Another reason for such animosity was Cibber's pragmatic approach to the task. Eloquence of expression was lost on a king who spoke little English and whose courtiers were so busy seeing and being seen that they heard little more than phrases like "glorious peace," "happy Britons," and "George and Caroline." He therefore approached the writing of an ode as he would a play, using language merely as raw material. Facile if not profound, he treated lyrics as dialogue carried along by rhythmic patterns and melody. His odes were effectively performed by court musicians, and the traditional flattering hyperbole sounded grand. In print they looked ridiculous, and his enemies leaped at them.

Cibber had the choice of whining for sympathy or facing his antagonists out. As in his schooldays, he chose the latter and published his first effort. It was a tactical error; the Tories were waiting for him. Duck proved himself a sore loser with a parody; anonymous critics wrote satiric verses, epigrams, and mock "analyses" of his language; and scarcely an issue of the *Grub Street Journal* appeared without some acidulous commentary. The storm lasted five years, fueled anew each time an ode was sung.

Coincidentally, the half-decade of concerted attacks marked the bleakest period in Cibber's life, a time when he needed his genial mask as never before. "Friends" brought him attacks and asked him to read them aloud; he acquiesced, pointing the satire with comic intonations and joining in the laughter. That he seemed oblivious of the insults was no indication he was untouched. Behind the mask, he smarted enough to write at least one riposte that eventually, he felt, gave him the last laugh when he published it a decade later. It was a poem, listed as by "Francis Fairplay," burlesquing the attacks and concluding:

Thunder, 'tis said, the Laurel spares,
    Naught but thy brow could blast it,
And yet! O curst provoking Stars!
    Thy comfort is, thou hast it. [I, 47-50]

Other actions indicate more distress than his smile revealed; he gave several of his roles to younger players and appeared only seventy-two times in the

1730-31 season. Those close to him must have guessed something of his feelings. Certainly Wilks did and reacted characteristically. When Henry Carey wrote a malicious epigram about Cibber after Colley had played a benefit for him, Wilks denounced Carey's impertinence "to a man of great merit" and forbade him to come backstage.[5]

Anyone close to Cibber was liable to attack, as Theo learned. Just as *The Lover* (his "peace offering" to Jane) was about to open, rumors began to circulate that Colley was the true author. Theo, fearing the worst, sent the papers a vehement statement that his father *"never saw* the *Play,* is wholly *unacquainted* with the *Subject* and entirely *unaccountable* (whether good, bad, or indifferent) for any *one Line* in it."[6] He was not believed, and on opening night a near-riot occurred. Had it not been for Jane, *The Lover* would have closed at once, but such was her charm that it had eight performances and gave Theo two benefits.

Drury Lane's problems were added to Cibber's own. The new patent had not yet emerged from the labyrinthine governmental processes, and their license put them entirely in the power of the lord chamberlain's office. The latter part of the season was marred by the deaths of two members of the Drury Lane company: Charles Williams and the comedian, Henry Norris. Williams's death cut short a brilliant career, and Wilks found *The Constant Couple* so painful without Norris playing "Jubilee Dicky" that he announced he would not act it again except for a command performance.[7] After Mary Porter, the company's best tragedienne, was badly injured in a carriage accident, the managers cut the season short.[8]

Only an invitation to perform at Hampton Court relieved the bleakness of the year's end. It was the first since the accession of George II, and, leaving Theo in charge of the summer company, the managers began preparations. Again they were dogged by frustration, as their plans were altered over and over by a capricious court. The original proposal was to build a theater on Hampton Green; weather made this impractical, and the company was moved into the palace proper. Rehearsals had just begun when the doctors claimed the lights would be bad for the king's eyes and canceled the whole project. At last Cibber was told to bring a list of plays for the royal perusal, but only *The Recruiting Officer* was chosen, to be performed for the duke of Lorraine's visit that fall.[9]

Cibber's summer was not only frustrating, it was downright unpleasant when thieves stripped the lead roof from his house.[10] Much worse was the revelation that Charlotte's marriage had been a terrible mistake. Charke was a thoroughgoing rake who freely confessed he had married Charlotte only because she was a manager's daughter, that he had nothing but contempt for Colley, and that he intended to pursue his bachelor's life, living off her earnings and her prospects of inheritance. While still a bride, Charlotte discovered a world she had never known as she searched for him through the byways and brothels of Drury. Before she was eighteen, she had changed from a pampered young girl into a neglected wife and mother. For a time, she had concealed her agony from her parents, salving her need for affection with intense devotion to the baby, but Charke's extravagance and constant appropriation of her salary (to which he had a legal right) meant that she and Catherine Maria were often in real want. What Charlotte could not do for herself, she could for her daughter—she asked her father for help.

He gave it generously, but he never spoke of it outside the family and calmly went through his usual routine while he worked on the Birthday Ode.[11] Again it was a full performance with soloists and choristers from the King's Chapel. On 30 October, "a great Number of Wax Candles were lighted in the Windows of Mr Cibber's, Mr Booth's, and Mr Wilks's Houses . . . on account of his Majesty's Birthday," as the ode was performed.[12]

This time Cibber did not publish it, but the *Grub Street Journal* printed a purloined copy along with a merciless critique. Such attacks have been given more importance than they deserve, for they obviously do not reflect general critical opinion as much as Tory political sentiment.[13] Each January and November issue of the *Gentleman's Magazine* put Cibber's verses beside reprints from the *Grub Street Journal* and others: "The Ode for New Year's Day translated into English," "Imitation of the Keyberian Stile and Manner," or "The Laureat's Pretensions Canvass'd." Unfortunately for Cibber, the best satirists of the age were Tories, and their wit was far more effective than his own well-bred silence. Their quips, congealed in print, remained to tarnish his reputation.

At the time it did not seem serious. He was sixty years old, a popular player, and a respected manager. His sure sense of the stage was admitted even by Aaron Hill, who was grateful enough for Cibber's assistance on his tragedy *Athelwold* (produced in December) to write Wilks: "but I cannot allow myself the merit of this improvement without confessing that I owe it to a hint that Mr Cibber gave me, for which I desire you to thank him in my name. . . . I now no longer remember with a parent's animosity the murder he committed on my epilogue to *Eurydice*. . . . his service was of so much more importance than his offence."[14] *Athelwold* survived only three nights, and Hill went back to blaming Drury Lane for his own failures.

Another one-time foe also appealed to Cibber's good nature when Henry Fielding offered Drury Lane his comedy *The Modern Husband*. Again Cibber proved he did not nurture a grudge; he forgave Fielding for *The Author's Farce*, accepted his play, and even wrote an epilogue for it. In spite of a disrupted opening night, it was a success for which the Cibber family was largely responsible; Colley, Theo, Jane, and Charlotte played in it. They gave one performance as a benefit for Mary Porter and four author's nights for Fielding.

In May, Grafton signed the warrant for the new patent to go into effect in September, and for the first time in history actors were official patentees without a representative at court. Once the patent was in order, the managers seemed to feel a need to put the rest of their lives straight. At least Wilks and Booth did. Wilks might still play Valentine "with all the fire and spirit of youth," but this spring he made his will.[15] The ailing Booth asked his neighbor, Benjamin Victor, to arrange the sale of half his shares. Victor brought him John Highmore, a gentleman amateur who once paid Drury Lane £100 to let him act Lothario in *The Fair Penitent*, and Highmore gladly paid £2,500 for Booth's property. Cibber did nothing.

On 10 May 1732, Cibber and Wilks performed in *The Relapse*, the last time they would play together. At the end of the season, Wilks went off to Isleworth, and Cibber took Katharine to Scarborough spa, famed for its soft water and sea bathing. Victor also went to Scarborough and wrote disapprovingly to a friend, "Cibber is here. He goes constantly to prayers; and the curate, to return the compliment, goes, when prayers are over, constantly to—the gaming table."[16]

Again the managers left Theo to oversee the summer company, secure in the knowledge it was in good hands. Within his limited range, he had become quite a good actor as well as a capable manager. The previous summer he had produced *The London Merchant*, which had proved a popular addition to the regular repertory. He was not very likable; overbearing, egocentric, and extravagant, he took advantage of his place as a manager's son, had an exaggerated opinion of his own worth, and was openly unfaithful to his wife—but he made the summer of 1732 profitable.

On 8 September, Colley opened the season with a command performance of *The Rehearsal*, but his heart was not in it. For the first time in thirty years, Drury Lane was without the services of Robert Wilks. He had been suddenly taken ill, and the best doctors in London were unable to help him. For three weeks the company limped along, giving the few plays in which he had no role and pretending that in spite of all he would recover, but from the outset there had been no hope. On Wednesday, 27 September, exactly one month after he was stricken, Wilks succumbed.[17]

Drury Lane was closed that night and again on 4 October, the day of the funeral. Cibber, Theo, and old Mills were among the pallbearers who carried Wilks's body from his house in Bow Street to the parish church of St. Paul's Covent Garden, where he was buried beside his first wife. Although Wilks had said he wanted only a simple private ceremony, the whole company was present, and the choir of the Chapel Royal voluntarily performed an anthem "to shew their Regard for his Memory."[18]

He was mourned by everyone, but by none more than Colley. Their lives had been so intertwined that part of himself seemed gone, and Drury Lane, bereft of Bob Wilks's vibrant energy, was a tomb. There was no avoiding plays in which he had acted—he had been the mainstay of the repertory, and during the rest of October, the theater opened only two or three times a week as five of the better young actors divided and hurriedly memorized his roles. The grief-stricken Cibber scarcely acted at all.

Willy-nilly, Cibber was plunged into the multitudinous problems of management, and the inexperienced Highmore was of no help. A new complication arose when Mary Wilks sold her shares of the patent to John Ellys, an artist who only a few months earlier had painted Robert's last portrait. Gentlemen (as opposed to actors), Highmore and Ellys assumed a wholly unwarranted knowledge of theater management and insisted on having a voice in every decision. It was a new state of affairs for Cibber. In his experience, gentlemen involved in theatrical matters—men like Henry Brett, William Collier, and even Richard Steele—remained in the background, content to make an occasional policy decision but leaving the daily business to those more qualified. If, like Owen Swiney, they attempted more, they had been easily overruled by the triumvirate.

Now the balance had shifted, and the manager who knew most about the theater was in the minority. Highmore and Ellys determined the schedule, the choice of plays, the discipline of actors, and the expenditures. Within weeks, actors and bill collectors alike were unhappy, and the business meetings were nightmares. Adding to their troubles, an epidemic, probably influenza, raged in the city. Audiences were thin, many of the company were ill, and receipts were down. Highmore began to complain that Booth had deliberately deceived him on the worth of the patent.

Suddenly it was all too much for Cibber. The joy of the theater vanished; he was surrounded by hostile strangers, and the brotherhood that he, Wilks, and Booth had shared was incomprehensible to the new partners. His old roles lost their charm when he had to adapt to different interpretations, new parts were tedious chores, and it was pointless to write another play that would only be hissed off the boards. Before when adversity struck, he had always found solace in his work, but now, for the first time, he turned away from it.

He did not speak of his private anguish nor did he quarrel openly with Highmore and Ellys, but his actions spoke clearly. Without warning, he announced that "to avoid the Importance of One, and the Ignorance of the Other," he, like Mary Wilks, would have his deputy, and he farmed his own patent shares to his son for the rest of the season, in return for Theo's promise to pay him £442.[19] In fairness to the company, he continued acting until the end of the year, with a weekly salary of twelve guineas.

Theo assumed the responsibility eagerly, and by November Drury Lane seemed almost back to normal. The company needed a new play, and he chose Charles Johnson's *Caelia* with Jane, ill and far advanced in her fourth pregnancy, in the title role. The strain was too much for her, and the play had only a single performance. Business continued to be so poor that Booth was tempted to act again, but he could not even manage rehearsals. Theo himself fell victim to the epidemic. Once he dragged himself out of bed to replace an even sicker actor, but for most of the Christmas season neither he nor Jane was able to perform. Colley, untouched by illness, acted almost every night. On 18 January, Theo's daughter, Elizabeth, was born, and one week later, Jane, not yet thirty, died from complications.[20] Theo was distraught. Weeping, he followed her coffin to St. Paul's Covent Garden, vowing he would never look at another woman. His grief was no doubt genuine at the time and perhaps more than a little tinged with guilt, but it did not prevent his playing the comic Osric in *Hamlet* the next day.

The New Year's Ode, again set to music by Eccles and performed to "a very great Appearance at Court," was received "with great applause." It, too, was pirated and ridiculed. Cibber did not respond, but his actions indicate a less willing victim than his foes liked to believe. When Benjamin Victor (at Aaron Hill's suggestion) brought his *Altamira* to Drury Lane with the request that Cibber act in in it, he refused. Victor reported to Hill, who answered, "I am sorry Mr. *Cibber* Sen. is so indifferent to the Concerns of the Company, as to think it not worth his while to be in your Tragedy. The best Excuse I can make for him is, that he took it for a Banter, when you ask'd his Judgment in a Way of writing, wherein his Ignorance has so often been celebrated. Yet he would certainly have acted *Belfort* beyond all Comparison."[21] Cibber may well have suspected he was meant to be the butt of a joke. Victor had been prominent in the hooting mob at the opening of *Caesar in Egypt*.

Cibber was not indifferent to Drury Lane's problems, but he was in no position to solve them nor did he have much heart to try. He fulfilled his obligations as an actor and more. Besides his regular roles, he played a benefit performance for Wilks's widow, wrote an epilogue for Fielding's adaptation of *The Miser*, and, for the first time in many years, took a benefit for himself.[22] Immediately afterward he contracted a cold so severe that he could not act for a command performance, and he began to speak openly about retirement. Word reached Highmore, and that ambitious gentleman immediately offered to buy Colley's share of the patent. Cibber, watching the work of a lifetime disintegrate, accepted.[23]

Theo later claimed that the agreement to farm his father's shares had included the option to buy into the patent and that he felt betrayed by the sale to Highmore, but his statement is neither supported nor reliable. He may have paid all or part of the £442 as agreed, but he could not keep his promise to pay an additional £300 before the season ended, and he obviously could no more afford to buy out his father than Colley could afford to give Theo his main source of income.

Undoubtedly Highmore saw the move as a way to rid himself of the troublesome Theo. The young man had worked well under the leadership of men he respected, but he lacked the discipline for power in his own right. Once his father was out of the way, Theo made no secret of his contempt for Highmore and Ellys, and, constantly parading his thirteen years of experience, became as overbearing to them as they were to the actors. His contempt was returned; the moment the sale was complete, Highmore barred Theo from any part of the management.

Highmore now owned the majority of the patent, but he governed a rebellious company. He did not, as Christopher Rich had, finagle or cheat, but his lack of practical experience had the same effect on the actors. They grew more and more restive as he refused to listen to their ideas and complaints, disdained their traditions, and cut salaries in half.[24] Theo was their spokesman, but his abrasive personality antagonized Highmore and made him determined to have his own way. At the end of the season, the atmosphere thickened with hostility.

For Colley, the days were further darkened by the death of Barton Booth. In April, after a recurrence of the fever and jaundice, Booth turned to Thomas Dover, better known as "Dr. Quicksilver," who claimed wondrous cures with crude mercury.[25] After five days of treatment, during which Booth consumed almost two pounds of mercury, he developed a high fever. Dr. Hans Sloan replaced Dover and prescribed a series of plasters, blooding, purges, and clysters, which brought the end with merciful speed, and Booth's agony ended on 10 May 1733.[26]

Cibber grieved for him. They had been partners, friends, and neighbors for twenty years and had spent summers together at Hillingdon; and, not least, Cibber had shared the long ordeal of Booth's illness. Hester Booth evidently did not share the relationship, for she asked Highmore, not Cibber, to serve as a pallbearer. The day after the funeral, she sold her remaining share of the patent to Henry Giffard and retired from the stage.[27]

On 25 May 1733, Cibber concluded his last regular season at Drury Lane with a performance of Sir Francis Wronghead in *The Provok'd Husband*. The scratch of a pen had removed the responsibilities of management from his shoulders, and now, his final obligation to the company finished, the curtain fell at last. For more than forty years, his life and destiny had been inextricable from that of Drury Lane, and there must have been some trace of sadness behind the twinkling eyes and broad smile as he took his last bow. Yet as he strutted off the stage that night, he appeared as light-hearted as ever, and his state of mind can only be guessed. The day after this performance, Theo led most of Drury Lane's company in revolt against Highmore, who retaliated by locking the actors out and dismissing them in toto. Colley took no part in either action. He left London almost at once, taking Katharine to Scarborough where she could drink the waters, and he could be divorced from theatrical matters. However the quarrel ended, he would have no part in it.

When he returned to London, he learned that the dissidents, unable to come to terms with Highmore, had obtained a license to perform at the theater in the Haymarket and had moved there. It was rumored that Colley had tried to help Theo get a patent but that the lord chamberlain refused. The rumor has never been questioned and has been reported as fact, although it rests only on the unsupported statement of Benjamin Victor.[28]

It was easy enough to assume Cibber had access to the power centers, and he never bothered to deny the rumors. His closeness to the aristocracy was well known. He dined and gambled with them, he was seen at all their social gatherings, and the duke of Devonshire, at least, was familiar enough to have Cibber as an official witness at a property settlement.[29] It does not seem probable, however, that Colley, having twice undergone the lengthy Byzantine machinations needed to obtain a patent, would have believed his sole influence sufficient to gain one for his son.[30] Had he wished to give Theo practical support, he could have acted in the Haymarket company, but he did not appear on the stage at all this season.

Actually, Theo did not particularly need his father's help. Both Drury Lane and the Haymarket opened in September, and Londoners quickly made their preference known. Highmore's gentlemanly amateurism was no competition for the professionals, and he was soon losing between fifty and sixty pounds a week—far more than he could afford. In desperation, he charged the dissidents with vagrancy, using the excuse that they were playing in an unlicensed theater, and had them summoned before the master of Revels, but the case was dismissed.[31] He wrote to Theo asking for a reconciliation; Theo published the letter along with a strong refusal. Highmore had one of the Haymarket stars, John Harper, arrested and committed to Bridewell as a "vagabond and rogue" the day he was scheduled to play in *Henry IV (Part 1)*.[32] That night, Theo "explained" to the audience, read the part himself, and was "very kindly accepted."[33]

Highmore had made a grievous error in having such a respected player jailed, and he lost whatever public sympathy he may have had. The charges that Harper was a "wandering and begging" vagrant were obviously ludicrous, since he leased a house in fashionable Westminster and owned a freehold in Surrey. Cibber attended the trial and no doubt was greatly cheered by the actor's acquittal, although he later reflected with a tinge of irony that the triumvirate, "in twenty Years before had paid upon an Averidge at least Twenty Thousand Pounds to be protected (as Actors) from a Law that has not since appeared against us" (I, 284). He, Wilks, and Booth, quite as respectable as Harper, had never dared perform without the legal (and costly) protection of a license or patent.

The visit to Scarborough had not brought the hoped-for improvement in Katharine's health. Through the fall and winter, she grew gradually weaker, and in January she died as she had lived, quietly at home.[34] Characteristically, Cibber did not parade his grief, but his absence from the stage and the social scene is significant. Like any good gentleman, he kept his sorrow private. The nearest he came to revealing emotion was in a poem published during the year of Katharine's death, a poignant lyric entitled "The Blind Boy," which may have referred to their son James:

> O say! what is that Thing call'd Light,
>   Which I can ne'er enjoy;
> What is the Blessing of the Sight,
>   O tell your poor Blind Boy?
>
> You talk of wond'rous things you see,
>   You say the Sun shines bright:
> I feel him warm, but how can he
>   Then make it Day, or Night.
>
> My Day, or Night my self I make,
>   When'er I wake, or play;
> And cou'd I ever keep awake,
>   It wou'd be always Day.
>
> With heavy sighs, I often hear,
>   You mourn my helpless woe;
> But sure with patience I may bear,
>   A loss I ne'er can know.
>
> Then let not what I cannot have,
>   My cheer of Mind destroy,
> Whilst thus I sing, I am a King,
>   Altho' a poor Blind Boy![35]

His enemies seem to have respected his feelings, at least in part. The bad verse of the Birthday Ode of 1733 and the New Year's Ode of 1734 were ridiculed as usual, but not a single attack appeared on "The Blind Boy." The last verse of the poem may have reflected his dead son's philosophy; more likely it is Cibber's. Katharine was gone, but he would not let what he could not have destroy him. Before long, he filled his days with activity; he was seen at the mall, at concerts and coffeehouses, and he gambled incessantly. Yet he did not return to the stage, even when a bankrupt Highmore sold out to Charles Fleetwood, and Theo's actors went home to Drury Lane.[36]

The return of the company coincided with a distinct change in Cibber's life. Katharine's death was the last of the long succession that had begun with Anne Oldfield. The anguish Highmore had caused was over, and

Drury Lane was back on a steady course again. However loudly Cibber proclaimed his disengagement from the theater, he could not be wholly unaffected by it. As things worked out so often in his life, his decision to retire had been fortunate, and now, relieved of all responsibility, he was free to do as he pleased. During the spring of 1734, restless and still mourning Katharine, he chose to go back to Scarborough.

He may have wanted no more than an escape from his empty London house, but it is not inconceivable that he also wanted to avoid Theo's approaching marriage. Theo, forgetting his protestations of eternal fidelity to Jane, was courting Susannah Arne, a lovely young singer. She had been introduced to the London public in 1732 by her brother, Thomas, when she sang the title role in his opera *Amelia* at the Haymarket. Both brother and sister had worked in Theo's rebel company, and she had returned to Drury Lane with them. Theo proposed to her in March, and they were married on 21 April 1734 with all the Cibbers except Colley in attendance.[37]

Colley's disapproval of the match has been attributed to greed, and it is true that Susannah had little to offer Theo in the way of material wealth. The charge, however, does not agree with Colley's character; even his bitterest enemies did not call him grasping. His objection was most probably to Susannah's Roman Catholicism, for his antipathy to her church never wavered. Apart from his personal feelings, it would have been most impolitic for the poet laureate to participate in a Catholic service, and it was very like him to shun such unpleasantness by leaving the city.

At Scarborough, the mask was firmly in place as he basked in the smiles of the ladies to whom he paid outrageous compliments in verse:

> Too much, *Sybilla*, we endure,
>   While you with double Forces arm'd,
>   With your enchanting Voice secure
> The hopeless Heart your Eyes have warm'd.[38]

In the fashion of the times, he sometimes scratched such froth on windows, prompting Pope to rite later, "Mr Cibber . . . writes his Verses now in such a manner that nobody can use them as they were wont to do, for nobody will wipe his breech with a pane of Glass."[39] The verses, obviously no more than passing gallantry, were printed in London, where they were subjected to the same merciless criticism as his official odes.[40] Grub Street had done its work well, and any would-be wit was certain of a laugh if he pointed his jests at the poet laureate.

The smile never faltered, but again Cibber's actions contradict it. After a long and happy marriage, he was lonely without Katharine, and he stayed in Scarborough only a short while. He did not go there again, nor did he revisit Twickenham, Richmond, or Hillingdon, where he and Katharine had spent their holidays together. Instead, early in the summer he went to Bath, which his old friend, Richard "Beau" Nash, had transformed from the dusty village where Colley had played for Queen Anne into the most elegant and popular spa in England.

Cibber had known the "King of Bath," as Beau was called, since the turn of the century, when Nash had been one of London's penniless young adventurers, known for his charm and his luck at gambling. The luck seems to have been genuine—he was never considered a cheat—and it followed him in 1705, when he was lured to Bath by its reputation for gaming. He found it a dreary, uncomfortable, and occasionally dangerous spot, where ladies spent their days playing cards in a canvas tent, and booted gentlemen swaggered about, smoking, drinking, and dueling with abandon. Nash, putting himself in charge, provided an assembly house where visitors could be properly introduced, and he engaged a good band of musicians for dancing. He drew up a code for behavior, posted it in the Pump Room, and enforced it. Promiscuous smoking and dueling and even the wearing of swords were prohibited; ladies and gentlemen must dress and behave with propriety. By 1734, Bath had become a place of comfort, charm, and gracious entertainment.

The place was well suited to the gregarious actor. For an important visitor like Cibber, church bells were rung from the moment he entered the city until he reached his lodgings. Nash, the accepted dictator of all social matters, arranged his schedule on the principle of relaxation without boredom. Morning bathing in the hot sulfurous waters was obligatory (according to Beau's "rules"), but attendance at church afterward was not, and Cibber usually preferred to stroll on the Grand Parade or read his London papers at the coffeehouse. In the afternoon, he could go to the Pump Room and drink the abominable water or to the Assembly Rooms and have tea with the ladies. His passion for gambling could always be satisfied; Nash shared it, and games were available except on Tuesdays and Fridays, when the famous balls, considered the most glittering outside the court, were the order of the evening.

Cibber stayed long enough to greet the Princess Amelia and her new husband before returning to London, refreshed and ready with the new Birthday Ode. At Drury Lane, Fleetwood welcomed him warmly and, knowing the value of his name, offered any terms he liked if he would act there. Colley accepted and at the end of October acted Bayes in *The Rehearsal* to a full house.[41] He still savored the warmth of applause, but he had neither the need nor the desire to be in the regular company again. He played a benefit for his sometime friend, Owen Swiney, now returned from the Continent, and five more performances in the spring.[42]

If Cibber valued his peace of mind, he had good cause not to become involved in Drury Lane. Fleetwood's management was a great improvement; he turned over the daily business to Theo and Charles Macklin, who had kept Highmore's company from complete disintegration, but the friction between the two left its mark on the rest.[43] Theo's officiousness grated on the passionate Macklin, and Macklin's rising popularity offended Theo; sooner or later, Fleetwood would have to choose between them.

When some of his actors went over to Rich, Fleetwood lured James Quin back to Drury Lane. Quin was a major acquisition; his Richard III was considered better than Cibber's, and his Falstaff was universally acclaimed a masterpiece. Like Colley, he had been trained in the Betterton school of acting, and the two of them were old friends. Before long, they were comrades in arms as well; Aaron Hill attacked them both in his newly established theatrical journal, *The Prompter*. Hill, calling for the "naturalism" he had been promoting for ten years, mocked Quin's "hoarse monotony" and Cibber's "unseasonable grimaces."[44] Quin was so enraged that he came to blows with Hill, but Cibber ignored him.[45]

While Colley seemed as little disconcerted by Hill as by the rash of attacks on his odes, his serenity masked a number of private troubles. His daughter Catherine bore a short-lived son, and soon afterward was widowed.[46] Theo's wife, Susannah, had a still-born child and was in a precarious state of health,[47] while the temperamental, tempestuous Charlotte waged constant war with Fleetwood. Her mother's death had removed the only stabilizing influence in her life, and now, barely twenty-one, she was as demanding as a veteran diva. Nicknamed "Mrs. Haughty" by the rest of the players, she refused all advice, including her father's.

He had better relations with Susannah. Cibber had come to like his fragile daughter-in-law, whose delicacy and sweet singing reminded him of Katharine. He knew her voice was not of the finest quality and he firmly believed, "if not best, 'tis nothing," but when Theo told him she read a part "very prettily," he began to teach her the elements of acting. His affection was shared by Owen Swiney and cemented a bond already firm now that thirty years had smoothed over their differences. The two old men attended her comings and goings so often that one wit was moved to remark, "There go Susannah and the elders," but Cibber could easily shrug off such barbs when she proved an unusually able pupil.[48] Later he was to remark he "never knew a woman so capable of the business or improve so fast."[49]

Charlotte was a different matter, and before the end of the season, one of her battles with Fleetwood ended with her stalking out and refusing to return. Cibber did not approve of her actions and must have found her flamboyance wearing, but he had a soft spot for his wayward youngest child, and he was concerned for her future. She showed no desire for his assistance, but in a furious display of independence, possibly brought on by her husband's departure for Jamaica, she gathered together a company of her own and began producing plays during the summer.[50]

Cibber escaped his children's troubles by leaving the city. In the late spring, he went down to Kent to try the chalybeate waters of Tunbridge Wells, more palatable than those of Bath, although not quite as fashionable. Under the tutelage of Beau Nash, the city fathers were trying to change that image by adding amusements and comforts to attract visitors, and as Cibber strolled along the Pantiles, he often saw Beau's famous white hat among other familiar chapeaux.

The Wells were no real competition for Bath, and Cibber was soon off to the western spa where he stayed until the middle of October. He made a great pretense of being a leisured gentleman, claiming he was happy to be "justly excused" from the hard work of the stage and sought only "Ease and Chearfulness" these days (I, 248), but his actions do not confirm his words. By the time he returned to London, he had finished the Birthday Ode, prepared a new edition of *Richard III*, written a prologue for Theo, and agreed to make four more guest appearances for Fleetwood.

He soon learned that Charlotte's venture had, as might be expected, landed her in difficulties. As the summer came to an end, so did her company, mostly young actors contracted to the patent theaters. Undaunted, Charlotte gathered a few untrained players, rented the small York Buildings theater, and presented a work of her own. *The Art of Management*, mocking Fleetwood as "Brainless" and Macklin as "Bloodbolt," was an ill-considered attempt to put her grievances before the public. It destroyed any hope of reconciliation, but Charlotte, as impulsive as a child, did not think of consequences. She flung herself into the enterprise with such energy that she fell ill after the first night and had to close, losing everything. At the end of her resources, she and Kitty were nearly starving when Colley learned of her plight and brought her home.[51]

It was not an ideal plan. Catherine, Cibber's oldest daughter, had already moved in to keep house for him. She had brought her own daughter with her, and she did not relish the idea of two more responsibilities. Charlotte said Catherine had always hated her, probably an exaggeration, but it is obvious the two sisters were temperamental opposites. Catherine may always have felt deprived; her sister Elizabeth had been their uncle's favorite and the first married, and her sister Anne had been an independent businesswoman before her marriage.[52] Catherine, who had never shown any bent for the stage, was far more the granddaughter of Jane Colley and the gentry than any of the others; she had married properly and lived quietly, yet now she was widowed and dependent on her father. Born during the lean years, she had been seventeen when Charlotte appeared, a late child of prosperity, spoiled by parents who could afford to grant her every wish. In Catherine's eyes, the favored Charlotte had been given everything and had thrown it all away. She needed stern discipline, not coddling. Charlotte, passionate, volatile, and adventurous, could not understand her sister's sense of decorum and discipline, and in her memoirs she frequently refers to Catherine's disapproval. Their quarrels were sharp and repeated, keeping the house in a constant turmoil, the very thing Colley most disliked.

He found a way to ease some of the tension by making his acting at Drury Lane conditional upon Charlotte's being readmitted to the company. Fleetwood was reluctant, but it was the only way to obtain Cibber's services, and he finally agreed to overlook *The Art of Management* and take her back. Charlotte, not at all grateful for his forbearance, promptly reverted to her former ways and fought with him incessantly. At last, after a particularly violent dispute, she once more "took French leave."[53]

She went directly to Fielding, who was preparing to open his "Grand Mogul's Company" at the Haymarket. The first play was *Pasquin*, and when Charlotte took the part of Lord Place, a virulent satire on Colley, Catherine decided it was time to discipline her troublesome sister.[54] Convening a family council, she had Charlotte summoned from the Haymarket and led the family in berating her until at last, "baited like a Bull at a Stake," their "enraged and obstinate" victim refused to answer.[55] Cibber was infuriated and finally stomped out, vowing not to return until Charlotte was gone. With no more ceremony than if she were sweeping the floor, Catherine turned the young woman into the street. The break was complete. Charlotte never again saw her sister or spoke with her father.

During this siege, Cibber found surcease at Drury Lane, where he fulfilled his acting commitments and observed his protégée, Susannah, rehearsing her first major part in Aaron Hill's translation of Voltaire's *Zaire*. Anglicized into *Zara*, it opened on 12 January 1736, played thirteen nights, and made Susannah a star, with a bonus of fifty pounds and an immediate raise in salary. Hill had insisted on coaching her and took full credit for her success, but Cibber's influence is evident in the many comments on her "sing-song" delivery of lines, a sure sign of the Betterton school and a techniue she practiced to the end of her career.[56]

Cibber must have relished Susannah's success, but he wisely kept silent about his own contribution. Although the Grubs had overlooked his odes this year, he may have felt that any identification with Susannah could only jeopardize her present favor. He grieved for the death of her second child, but he removed himself from closer association at this time.[57] He filled his days with visits to coffeehouses, dinners at aristocratic tables, and, of course, gambling at White's. The old chocolate house, always known as the haunt of gamblers, had burned in 1733 and was now reestablished as a gentleman's club with a glittering membership that included Walpole,

Chesterfield, Newcastle, Marlborough, and a host of other Whig nobility. A single blackball excluded; Cibber, elected unanimously, was the first actor to become a member.

When the social season ended, he visited the country estates of friends like Chesterfield or Giles Earle or Newcastle's brother, Henry Pelham. Quite probably Catherine and her daughter went with him, as they made their leisurely way to Bath, their summer mecca for the decade. Each autumn, they returned to London in time to have the new ode rehearsed for the royal birthday.

The 1737-38 season found Drury Lane in the midst of a new crisis. Theo, delighted with Susannah's success and her increased earnings, which he pocketed, was determined to make her a major star. Zara had been followed by other leading dramatic roles, but now, he thought, she should show her versatility and play Polly in *The Beggar's Opera*. The role belonged to Kitty Clive, who refused to give it up, but Theo was adamant.[58] The "Polly War" reached the newspapers, fomenting such partisanship among admirers that neither actress could appear without being attacked by the rival faction. It was good for the box office but disastrous for company morale, and Colley, with his dislike of unpleasantness, could only shake his head and stay away.

Cibber was not aloof, however, when Fleetwood, in need of a new play, asked for his still unproduced *Papal Tyranny in the Reign of King John*. Colley hesitated, concerned about its reception. The play would have been performed ten years ago but for the "disagreeable Apprehensions of a First Day," he said, but Fleetwood was confident it would succeed with Quin as the King and Cibber as the Cardinal. He could name his own price. Colley, perhaps thinking the circumstances had indeed changed over the years, gave him the script.

As soon as the news was out, the anti-Cibber forces united. At their head were the young Templars, law students as notorious for their self-proclaimed critical judgment as for their lack of inhibition. Their combined voices could drown out any actor, and Cibber, who had never begged favors for himself, now asked for one on Fleetwood's behalf with a letter to the *Daily Advertiser*: "I think myself obliged, in Conscience and Honour, to do all in my Power, to incline the Town to favour it: By Favour I do not mean a Partiality in their Applause; which is indeed but a sort of Defiance, to other true Judges, who have an equal Right, where they think it faulty, to condemn it; the Extent of my Hopes are, for a fair and candid Hearing."[59] Nothing he could have said would have softened them, and his letter provoked a flurry of hostile replies in verse and prose. It was good publicity, and Fleetwood, with the profits from the "Polly War" fresh in mind, continued rehearsals. But when Rich presented Shakespeare's *King John*, and Fielding did the same, with a satirical prologue attached, it was obvious to

Cibber that *Papal Tyranny* was doomed. One morning early in March, he arrived at the theater in an unusual state of perturbation, snatched the script from the prompter's desk and departed without a word.[60] Fleetood gave up the idea, and Cibber did not act at all this season.

Part of his perturbation may have been caused by Charlotte. After spending the summer in Fielding's theater, she had been hired by Lincoln's Inn Fields at the beginning of the 1736-37 season and seemed to be settling down. She and Kitty moved in with her sister Elizabeth,[61] and the breach in the family might have been healed had she not, after a few weeks, gone back to the Haymarket to appear in Fielding's knife-edged satire of Walpole, *The Historical Register for the Year 1736*. Charlotte was not in the scenes directly ridiculing Walpole or Colley, but she had a prominent role, and she chose the play for her own benefit.[62]

She knew her father's tolerance for ridicule and probably did not realize how much she had hurt him with her grotesque parody in *Pasquin*. After the terrible last scene at home, she may even have been too angry to care, but Fielding and Cibber certainly saw the implications of her performance. Foppington had laughed heartily at *Pasquin*, but Cibber, who had overlooked so much, did not forgive this time.

Notoriety did not bring prosperity to Fielding. Salaries at the Haymarket were minimal, and Charlotte, as thriftless as her father, was soon in financial difficulties. Not understanding the enormity of her recent actions, she again appealed to him for assistance. His answer was cold:

Dear Charlotte,
I am sorry I am not in a position to assist you further. You have made your own bed, and therein you must lie. Why do you not dissociate yourself from that worthless scoundrel, and then your relatives might try and aid you. You will never be any good while you adhere to him, and you most certainly will not receive what otherwise you might from your father.

Colley Cibber[63]

He has been censured for the iciness of this reply, but it is clear that although he closed the door, he did not lock it. Charlotte might knock again if she left Fielding. This, however, was no longer possible, since neither patent theater would have her, and he was her only means of livelihood.

The problem was soon exacerbated, for Fielding's satires had roused powerful forces. The Whigs were outraged, and Walpole, who a decade earlier had laughed at *The Beggar's Opera*, was no longer amused. Aging, gouty, and faced with growing opposition in his own party, he had become personally less tolerant and politically less secure. He had not supported Sir John Barnard's bill for controlling the theaters in 1735, but now he was ready to act. His opportunity came when Henry Giffard brought him *The Golden Rump*, an anonymous satire supposedly deposited on the doorstep of

Goodman's Fields.[64] It was so offensive that within the shortest possible time a Licensing Act, giving the government absolute control of the theater, had passed the Commons.[65]

The question was debated in the public journals and coffeehouses long before it came to a vote in the House of Lords. Aside from Cibber's personal anger over Fielding's exploitation of Charlotte, his feelings were ambivalent. On the one hand, he felt the man had gone too far and that his attacks on the government were dangerous rabble-rousing; on the other, Cibber himself detested the idea of censorship, and he applauded Chesterfield's brilliant speech opposing it.[66] His ambivalence was resolved on 5 June 1737 when the bill passed and the independence that Cibber, Wilks, and Booth had achieved back in 1715 was erased as cleanly as if it had never existed.

Fielding did not forgive Cibber either. His grudge against Colley had now lasted several years, and while he may not have seriously believed that Cibber influenced the passage of the Licensing Act, he knew Walpole had; in his eyes, the two were inseparable and equally guilty of taking away his livelihood.[67] In May, when it was clear the Licensing Act would mean the end of the Haymarket company, Fielding disbanded it and turned to the study of law—but one day he would have his revenge.

Charlotte, cast into a world for which she was completely unprepared and desperate to keep herself and Kitty alive, embarked on a series of disastrous business ventures that would in time earn her a reputation as a demented eccentric. She became in turn a grocer, a puppeteer, a valet, an innkeeper, and a strolling player, beginning each new career with an optimism that always seemed well founded to her—until her lack of stability and practical business sense inevitably brought failure. Yet she was not quite the madwoman observers claimed; somehow, in spite of all obstacles, she supported herself and her daughter without help from her family and without, like many women, engaging in prostitution.

Cibber turned his back on her. As soon as the vote was taken, he left for Bath to immerse himself in a project he had often talked about but had never really begun, a history of his years in the theater. Now, perhaps seeing the end of that era, he was in a unique position to share his extensive knowledge and he felt impelled to record it. He wrote sporadically as the spirit moved him, and when he brought the Birthday Ode to London in the autumn, he had only a few finished pages. Recalling *Papal Tyranny* and similar experiences, he would keep his history a secret until it was in print.

Possibly he was too cautious. *The British Theatre* this year included more of his plays, six, than of any other author; the Birthday Ode was only mildly attacked; and the January issue of the *Gentleman's Magazine* contained John Stanley's musical setting for "The Blind Boy" without remark.[68] At Drury Lane, Theo and Susannah shone brightly, and before Colley left

London this year, he saw his granddaughter, Anne Brett, married to the prompter William Rufus Chetwood.[69]

Yet there was some reason for caution. Cibber was still a public figure and no matter what honors he had received or how respectably he lived, in the eyes of many he still represented a disreputable profession. At Tunbridge Wells, which he now visited regularly before going to Bath, he was publicly snubbed by the Reverend Mr. Whiston because that exemplar of Christian virtue heard he was an actor, "and, as I have heard, a pimp."[70] And there was the matter of Theo.

If anyone should have made Cibber concerned about his good name it was Theophilus. Cibber's only son was no longer the bright young rebel who had led the company to victory over a despotic management. In the last few years he had become an arrogant, tiresome braggart trading on his father's name and his wife's talent. His extravagances had increased with Susannah's success, for her subsequent raises in salary had brought him a new and badly needed source of income. He spent her money as freely as his own, occasionally salving his conscience by presenting her with lavish gifts he could not afford.

His own expenses far outstripped Susannah's, and the debts mounted. He lived like a lord, kept a carriage, gambled for high stakes, and dressed in the latest fashion. Colley repeatedly warned him about his wastefulness, but Theo had no more use for advice than did Charlotte. It is said that Colley once met Theo wearing an unusually grand suit. The father gazed at him sorrowfully, shook his head and said, "'The', I pity you."

"Don't pity me," Theo replied flippantly. "Pity my tailor."[71]

He was living far beyond his means, and when the specter of debtors' prison began to rise, he looked about for another source of income. He found it in William Sloper, a wealthy young gentleman who had championed Susannah in the "Polly War." All through the spring of 1737, Theo courted his favor, inviting him to his home, and deftly extracting cash from him in return. "Cousin Thompson," as Theo called him before the servants ("Mr. Benefit," behind his back), genuinely admired Susannah and apparently did not mind that Theo's frequent absences "on business" left them alone together.[72] Susannah must have welcomed Sloper's company; her feelings for Theo had cooled swiftly after he not only collected her salary but also stole all her costumes and jewels. When the season ended, Theo persuaded Sloper to rent a house for the three of them at Kingston. The next step was clear, at least to Theo: Sloper would have Susannah in return.

Theo miscalculated badly, for although he supposedly forced Susannah into Sloper's bed at gun point, they really did fall in love.[73] When they returned to London for the 1737-38 season, Sloper arranged for lodgings in Leicester Fields where he and Susannah could meet privately. Here matters stood until the spring of 1738, an intolerable situation for all three. Neither

Sloper nor Susannah could be divorced, and Theo, head over ears in debt, could not survive without "Mr. Benefit's" assistance. By April, his creditors had become so insistent that his only safety lay in flight.[74]

He went to France, where he stayed two months, writing effusive letters to Susannah, calling her "my Angel" and "the best of Wives," telling her how much he loved her and begging her to be true to him. It is not clear whether he was preparing the extraordinary plan he finally put into effect or whether he was merely covering himself in case she charged him with desertion. It is clear, however, that Susannah wanted nothing more to do with him, and on his return to London in June, she left the city with Sloper. They went to Buckinghamshire, where Susannah, pregnant with Sloper's child, could rest and regain her strength. As soon as Theo discovered their whereabouts, he sent men to bring her back to London and sequestered her.[75] Sloper informed her family, the Arnes, and her brother, Thomas, gathered a group of friends to rescue her one evening while Theo was at the theater. Theo replied with a lawsuit demanding five thousand pounds from Sloper for "Assaulting, Ravishing and Carnally Knowing" his wife.

Colley must have been hard put to retain a semblance of good humor when he brought the Birthday Ode to London that fall. The town gossiped about Theo and Susannah while the family mourned the death of Elizabeth's husband, Dawson Brett.[76] Yet when Fleetwood asked Cibber to play Shallow in *Henry IV (Part 2)*, he calmly agreed. It was a triumph, as Tom Davies, who was in the house that night, reported: "Whether it was owing to the pleasure the spectators felt on seeing their old friend return to them again, *though for that night only*, after an absence of some years, I know not; but surely, no actor or audience were better pleased with each other."[77]

The pleasure was a contrast to offstage matters, for both Cibber and Elizabeth were called as witnesses in Theo's court case. Elizabeth had little to say except that Susannah was currently living with the Arnes and not with Sloper, as Theo's lawyers charged. Colley's testimony was carefully neutral. He admitted his initial disapproval of the match but said they had been "much happier" than he had expected; he told of Theo's lavish gifts to Susannah, but he also praised Susannah's acting in glowing terms. His words did not affect the verdict. The court recognized Theo's legal rights but deplored his behavior; he won his case, but he was awarded only ten pounds in damages—not enough to cover his lawyer's fees.[78]

The trial provided wonderfully lurid gossip, and the scandal was long-lived. Susannah, publicly disgraced, disappeared from view, but Theo, although thoroughly hissed the next time he played, continued to act at Drury Lane and compounded his effrontery by publishing his letters to Susannah.[79] Beset with debt, he was so often in a foul temper or hiding from the bailiffs that Fleetwood sacked him at the end of the season. He was promptly jailed for debt, and his two daughters, Jane and Betty, went to live with their Aunt Elizabeth.

The unpleasantness of this winter was compounded by Charlotte, whose unshakable confidence in her own abilities had led her from one failure to another and finally into debtors' prison. The horror of it shocked her into writing desperate letters to everyone she knew, one of which was almost certainly to her father.[80] She does not mention his response in her *Narrative*, but a letter often cited as proof of his unforgiving nature may have been the answer:

Madam,
    The strange career which you have run for some years (a career not always unmarked by evil) debars my affording you that succor which otherwise would naturally have been extended to you as my Daughter. I must refuse therefore—with this advice—try Theophilus.

Yours in sorrow, Colley Cibber[81]

The original of the letter, however, is not in Cibber's handwriting. If Charlotte's view of Catherine is correct, the answer came from her, and Colley never saw Charlotte's plea.

Colley had contracted one more role for Drury Lane, a farewell performance, for which he chose *Richard III*. The selection was odd in view of his preference for comedy, but it fitted his mood more closely than the inane Foppington mask he wore so constantly these days. On 31 January 1739, he braved a wintry night to play Richard for the last time. If his audience found it a museum piece, it forgave him and applauded politely, but he was not deceived. He was an anachronism, his grimaces and gestures out of place in this new era, and he knew it. When Benjamin Victor, noticing an unfamiliar weakness in his performance, hastened backstage to see if he were ill, Cibber told him he was well enough, but, "would give fifty guineas to be sitting in my easy chair by my own fireside just now."[82]

Outside of the theater, Foppington amused himself as usual, worked on his nearly finished memoirs, and sat with his granddaughter, Jenny, for a portrait by Vanloo.[83] He looked and behaved like a man in his forties, and he kept pace with men many years his junior.[84] Wherever he went, he was treated with cordial respect, and his entrance at White's was invariably greeted with cries of "Old King Coll! Welcome, welcome, King Colley!"[85]

Cibber's regular attendance at Tunbridge Wells and Bath was often interrupted these days by invitations to the country houses of Dorset, Chesterfield, and other friends. He was an excellent guest, frankly enjoying their hospitality and considerate of his hosts. At the duke of Richmond's, he flattered the daughter of the house by listening two mornings in a row to her detailed recital of a novel she was reading.[86] In August, he received the same favor from Henry Pelham, when, as a guest at Pelham's estate,

Esher Place, he spent three days reading the finished pages of the *Apology* to his host.

Pelham's insistence on hearing the entire manuscript was undoubtedly from genuine interest, for it is not an autobiography but a fascinating history of the theater, written with grace and good humor. Cibber disarms his critics by admitting his faults and asking, "But why make my Follies publick? Why not? I have passed my Time very pleasantly with them, and I don't recollect that they have ever been hurtful to any other Man living. . . . To me the Fatigue of being upon continual Guard to hide them is more than the Reputation of being without them can repay" (I, 2-3). He gave his enemies little ammunition from his private life, sketching in the early years only lightly, saying nothing of his personal sorrows, and keeping his family entirely out of the narrative.

It is, perhaps, the most honest portrait of an actor ever drawn. Cibber's joy in his profession and his respect for its practitioners had not decreased a millimeter since he first set foot in Drury Lane, and he looked upon acting as the highest of the arts: "The most that a *Vandyke* can arrive at, is to make his Portraits of great Persons seem to *think*; a *Shakespear* goes farther yet, and tells you *what* his Pictures thought; a *Betterton* steps beyond 'em both, and calls them from the Grave to breathe and be themselves again in Feature, Speech and Motion" (I, 104-5). He practiced what he preached by setting forth in his own voice the character he had so painstakingly drawn over the years, the character that later critics and scholars would accept at face value. Yet the image of a vain, empty-headed Foppington, concerned only with himself, inordinately proud of small success and impervious to insult, lacks substance. It is an actor posturing before an audience, and he indicates as much in his dedication: "If this *Apology* for my past life discourages you not from holding me in your usual Favour, let me quit this greater Stage, the World, whenever I may, I shall think This the best-acted Part of any I have undertaken" (I, lxx-lxxii).

The substance appears when Cibber speaks of the theater, for, try as he would to play the clown, his feelings were too deep to conceal. His pictures of players are vivid and memorable, his perception of what makes a play work on the stage has never been surpassed, and his insight on management is a primer for successful theater. Here, his tone becomes sober, at times passionate: "What equal Method can be found to lead or stimulate the Mind to a quicker Sense of Truth and Virtue, or warm a People into the Love and Practice of such Principles as might be at once a Defence and Honour to their Country? In what Shape could we listen to Virtue with equal Delight or Appetite of Instruction?" (II, 28)

As in Cibber's life, the Foppington character played him false, and critics have been quick to pounce on the *Apology*'s flaws. Cibber's casual attitude toward dates has frequently been pointed out, along with his misquo-

Colley Cibber with his granddaughter, Jenny, 1740. Engraved by Edward Fisher from a painting by J.B. Vanloo. Courtesy Henry E. Huntington Library

Caius Gabriel Cibber, engraving by A. Bannerman. Courtesy Henry E. Huntington Library

Charlotte Charke. Courtesy
Henry E. Huntington Library

Theophilus Cibber in the
character of a fine gentleman
"from an Original Drawing by
Worlidge." Courtesy Henry E.
Huntington Library

Anne Oldfield, from a painting attributed to Jonathan Richardson. Courtesy
Henry E. Huntington Library

Barton Booth. Engraved by
Evans, from an original
painting. Courtesy Henry E.
Huntington Library

Below, Robert Wilks.
Engraving by I. Faber from a
painting by I. Ellys, 1732.
Courtesy Henry E.
Huntington Library

Colley Cibber in the character of Lord Foppington. Engraved by J.H. Robinson from the portrait by J. Grisoni. Courtesy Henry E. Huntington Library

The Drury Lane stage, ca. 1740. Courtesy Henry E. Huntington Library

The Non-Juror. Courtesy Henry E. Huntington Library

tation of Shakespeare, and he is charged with denigrating the characters of Wilks and Booth. It is true that after forty years he was hazy about time, but his memory for plays and people is surprisingly accurate, and his misquotations are probably exactly what he said on the stage, since most of Shakespeare's plays were radically "improved" for eighteenth-century audiences. He remembered speeches he had not heard for almost half a century, and his detailed decription of Betterton's Hamlet is unforgettable.[87]

Cibber idolized the old actors, and his memories of them were those of the star-struck young player worshipping his gods. Wilks, Booth, and Dogget, however, were his brother-managers. He had worked with them, accommodated to their idiosyncrasies, admired their talents, and suffered from their flaws, and his evaluation was not blinded by idolatry.

Considering Cibber's reputation for vanity, the most surprising quality in the *Apology* is his modesty. He tells much of Wilks's astonishing capacity for work but little of his own. He cites Booth's triumph in tragedy but notes only his own incapacity for it. He is proud of his position as a patentee but almost gives the impression that it happened by chance, and, while he credits Drury Lane's success to the triumvirate's hard work and discipline, he does not make the egoist's claim to sole credit. He never tries to gain vicarious prestige by larding his pages with aristocratic names and tales of the glittering circles in which he moved. He was a complex man, and a proud one, but he was not vain.

Actorlike, Cibber avoided the unpleasant. He said nothing about the savage attacks that had marked his life since *The Non-Juror*, although his laughing, semiapology to Pope suggests that some of the arrows had reached home. Only once did he give way to anger, and that was in speaking of the "Herculean Satyrist," Fielding, whom he called a "broken Wit" and administered the actor's ultimate reproof by refusing to name him (I, 285-87). It was a mild rebuke for which Fielding would exact a heavy price.

Cibber brought the manuscript back to London and, still euphoric from Pelham's compliments, dedicated it to him. The dedication, dated 6 November 1739 (Cibber's sixty-eighth birthday) is more than the graceful compliment it appears. Pelham's two young sons died that month, and although as a well-bred gentleman Cibber makes no reference to the bereavement, the warmth of his words is an expression of consolation and friendship.

The smooth words give no suggestion of the rough road Cibber himself was traveling. Scarcely had he come home than the scandal of the previous year was reopened when Theo, still desperate for money, brought a second lawsuit against Sloper. This time he demanded ten thousand pounds on the grounds that his income had been reduced by Sloper's interference.[88] That is, Susannah had not been able to act during her pregnancy, and thus Theo had been deprived of her salary. He was awarded five hundred pounds—

nowhere near enough to pay his creditors and certainly not worth the renewed stigma. The matter furnished Cibber's enemies with fresh material, but Theo, who had been hired by Rich this year, appeared regularly at Covent Garden, insensible of shame.

Cibber did not testify at the second trial nor did he refer to it in public. He attended rehearsals for the royal odes, saw his daughter Anne Boultby make her debut at Drury Lane,[89] and prepared the *Apology* for publication. His son's shame was not his, and he refused to wear sackcloth. His full-bottomed wig was as carefully brushed, his lace as immaculate, and his conversation as sparkling as ever. But he did not act this year, and he avoided Theo.

By spring, the imminent publication of the *Apology* could no longer be kept secret, and he braced himself for attack, especially after Fielding's new journal, the *Champion*, which had replaced the *Grub Street Journal* as his principal critic, commented a week before the publication, "However that illustrious Person may wind up as a Man he will certainly end as an Author with a very bad Life."[90] Yet when the book appeared on 7 April 1740, the general response was favorable, and it went into its second edition within a month.

Only Fielding made any real effort to decry it, and from the beginning of April to the end of May, the pages of the *Champion* were filled with mocking references. Fielding could not challenge the theatrical knowledge, so he attacked the language and style. It was ample return for the two-page reference Colley had made to him, but it was to be only a part of his final revenge.

Cibber did not reply. He could afford to ignore the playwright-turned-law-student, whose only reputation at this time came from plays that, in Cibber's opinion at least, had brought a terrible calamity to the theater. He had no need for defense; the *Apology* earned him fifteen hundred pounds, which, with unusual foresight, he put into an annuity. He took his family to Tunbridge Wells and, basking in the adulation his book brought him, paid court to the ladies in light verse. His life seemed to have entered a peaceful stage that continued through the autumn, when, back in London, he found no new scandals from Theo and the Birthday Ode was all but ignored by the press.

Cibber enjoyed the busy London season immensely. His claim of preference for his easy chair was about as valid as the Foppington image, and his social life was as active as he could make it. This fall he renewed his acquaintance with the notorious Laetitia Pilkington, whom he had met the year before, in 1739, a few months after she had arrived from Ireland. She was pert, pretty, and utterly charming, but her reputation had been destroyed when her husband divorced her for adultery.[91] With Dublin society closed to her, she moved to London, took rooms opposite White's and set about making her living as a writer. She sent Cibber a copy of her first published poem, *The Trial of Constancy*, and, to her amazement, he appeared one day quite without warning, running up her stairs "with the vivacity of a youth of fifteen," introduced himself with a courtly bow, and asked to see her other writing. He was impressed with it, wept unashamedly over a poem called "Sorrow," and invited her to breakfast the next day.

The next morning Cibber listened to her history for three hours, so charmed that his servant had to remind him of a dinner engagement with the duke of Grafton. Laetitia returned the next day at his invitation, and when she ended her story he engaged himself to sell it if she would write it just as she had told it.[92]

Cibber told her to write some new poems and send them to him at White's. She obliged with a paean of praise, "To Mr. Cibber," which he showed to all the members, insisting they subscribe to it. He was persuasive, they were generous, and Laetitia received a comfortable sum. She wrote others which Cibber touted, bringing her a steady stream of golden guineas. The members of White's called on her frequently when Cibber was in town, but when he left, their visits—and the stream of guineas—dwindled. He was always assured of a warm welcome from her when he returned.

Another friendship began this year when Samuel Richardson published his novel *Pamela*. Cibber applauded its virtuous heroine and its sentiments that echoed his own plays, and the two men became fast friends in spite of the differences between them. Richardson's sentiment was part of his own character, and his behavior was circumscribed by propriety; Cibber's sentiment was professional—the actor seeking to affect his audience. His delight in making outrageous statements for laughs often shocked Richardson's conservative sensibilities, yet they were fundamentally compatible and developed a close relationship, strengthened a few months later when Fielding's merciless parody, *Shamela* was published as by "Conny Keyber."

Before that, however, Fielding had a final blow to deal the *Apology*, one that Cibber had no reason to anticipate and for which he could not have been prepared. Insulated by friends old and new, he had dismissed the attacks in the now deceased *Champion* along with those in *An Apology for the Life of Mr. T . . . C . . .* , which had come out while he was away, and which paired Colley and Theo as two versions of the same fool. Fielding may not have written all of it, but he certainly had a hand in it, for the style is unmistakable.[93]

If Cibber believed that Fielding's burning resentment had been satisfied, he misunderstood the man. On 29 November, *The Laureat; or, The Right Side of Colley Cibber* appeared with a supplement, *The History of the Life, Manners and Writings of Aesopus, the Tragedian*, a specious biography. Although the works are anonymous, from the evidence it is difficult to conclude that anyone but Fielding could have written them. In the words of classic mystery tales, he had the means, the opportunity, and the motive, and it was published by J. Roberts, who had printed much of Fielding's previous work. In the first place, Fielding was certainly the most skillful prose satirist of the day, and his rapidity of writing was legendary. Second, he had been called to the bar on 20 June and during the summer was assigned to the western counties where, far from London, he had plenty of idle time. Finally, his professional and political antipathy to Cibber had never cooled, and his friendship with Charlotte formed an even more personal cause. Twice he hired her for his company, the second time after she flouted her father's wishes and broke with Fleetwood. Something about Cibber grated on Fielding; he must have been sympathetic to Charlotte after the family quarrel which she, never in the least reticent, undoubtedly revealed. It is significant that in all his savaging of Colley and Theo, there is not one slur against her, when her career provided abundant opportunity for ridicule.

Internal evidence also points to Fielding. The writer of *The Laureat* was a Tory who came on the London theatrical scene in the late twenties. Vague gossip and outright errors in the early part suggest that the information is derived from theatrical gossip: he errs in naming Wilks's first performance in 1698 and, evidently unaware of *Woman's Wit*, says Cibber's second play was *Perolla and Izadora*;[94] his anecdotes of later years are much more specific and his description of a new playwright's tribulations hints at personal experience. He also says he did not know Vanbrugh, who died in 1725, but did see *Love in a Riddle* (7 January 1729)—Fielding came to London in 1728. The burlesque form is a Fielding favorite; he had used it previously in *The Author's Farce* and *Tom Thumb*, and would use it again in *Shamela* and *Joseph Andrews*.[95] The attacks on Cibber's language mght have come straight from the pages of the *Champion*: "To unravel the Meaning of an Author who is obscure, unconnected, and wrapt up and conceal'd in the clinquant Tinsel of Metaphor, and unnecessary Figures; who leads you continually out of the Way, by long, tedious and unnecessary Digressions; is not only groping in the Dark, but it is an unpleasant and a tedious Labour."[96] The tone is unexceptionally malicious. When convenient, he misquotes, misunderstands, and misinterprets, all with the barbed wit that became a Fielding trademark.[97]

One of *The Laureat*'s most frequently quoted charges is that Cibber behaved insolently to new playwrights, that he enjoyed "choaking singing birds," as he called them. Cibber, of course, did select most of the new works during the time of the triumvirate, and the three produced many over the years. Writers whose plays were accepted usually took the credit for themselves; rejected authors blamed Cibber. He had rejected Fielding's *The Temple Beau*, possibly with a harsh, "Sir, there is nothing in it to coerce my passions," as he sometimes said, but no one in the history of the theater has solved the problem of rejecting a play without injury to the author's feelings.

Aesopus is more personal, more biting, and more slanderous than the *Laureat* proper. It begins with a contemptuous reference to Cibber's parents and reviews his life by citing every known scrap of gossip available, even to repeating two stories from *Joe Miller's Jest Book* (1738) with the punch lines attributed to Cibber.[98] It points to his gambling, to his reputed lack of religion, and suggests that he not only had backstage amours but acted as a pimp for aristocratic friends and paints a picture of a man universally hated without explaining how he had reached and maintained his position of eminence.

The superior satire presented the gravest danger to Cibber's reputation, since it was used as a primary source by scholars. Searching for material to discover what was behind the mask of the *Apology*, they turned to the *Laureat*.[99] Oddly enough, while refusing to believe Cibber on almost any point, many chose to overlook the patent bias of his enemy and accepted the amusing and spiteful anecdotes as truth. But in his zeal to attack, the author of the *Laureat* passed over the major part of Cibber's long career to concentrate on the part he knew, the last five years of active management. It was a great disservice, for the rage of a Tory satirist painted as grotesque a caricature as Lord Place in *Pasquin* or Ground-Ivy in *The Author's Farce*—the image that for two hundred years would be called Colley Cibber. Fielding had taken his full measure of vengeance.

SIX

Retirement

IN 1740, Cibber's reputation seemed indestructible. Although he was no longer an integral part of theatrical management, his influence was still strong. On 6 December, each of London's three theaters was showing one of his plays, and each company contained a member of his family: the Chetwoods at Drury Lane, Anne Boultby at Goodman's Fields, and Theo at Covent Garden.[1] The year of 1741 began auspiciously enough with "a great Number of the nobility, Foreign Ministers and other Persons of Distinction" listening to Cibber's ode, set to music by Dr. Greene, at St. James's.[2] Let the Tories howl as they would, those in the seats of power enjoyed and applauded him.

The smooth surface concealed rocks, however, for the Chetwoods were having financial troubles, and William was soon languishing in the King's Bench Prison. To help them, Cibber played *The Old Batchelor* for their benefit at Covent Garden on 12 January 1741. Rich must have seen the advantages of Cibber's name, for he persuaded the old actor to repeat the performance twice more. Colley was happy to play opposite Peg Woffington,[3] and even wrote an "Epilogue upon Himself" for that occasion which concluded audaciously,

> If for my Folly's larger List you call,
> My Life has lump'd 'em! There you'll read 'em all.
> There you'll find Vanity, wild Hopes pursuing;
> A wide Attempt, to save the Stage from Ruin!
> There I confess, I have *outdone* my *own outdoing!*
> As for what's left of Life, if still 'twill do;
> 'Tis at your Service, pleas'd while pleasing you.[4]

Three performances brought freedom to Chetwood and six hundred pounds to Rich.

The Chetwoods left for Ireland at the end of the season, followed by

154

Quin, who, in turn, invited Susannah to be his leading lady in Dublin. Quin returned to England at the end of the summer, but Susannah stayed on, enjoying a success that had not been hers for three years. Her debut as Indiana in *The Conscious Lovers* made her a favorite with Irish audiences, and they were demonstrative in their affection. Her alto solo in the premiere of Handel's *Messiah* brought even the formidable Dr. Patrick Delany, Chancellor of St. Patrick's Cathedral, to his feet crying, "Woman, for this may all your sins be forgiven you!"[5] The Chetwoods' fortune was less impressive. William worked as prompter for the theater; Anne played only small parts, for she was, he said, only "an agreeable *Actress*, when the part suited her Voice."[6] But they managed to stay out of debtors' prison.

Cibber's life was unruffled either by his family's troubles or the political battles that spilled over from Parliament to the drawing rooms of London. In the spring of 1741, England had just embarked on the War of the Austrian Succession, a war that would eventually topple Walpole. Colley's sympathies remained with the Whigs—he dined and gambled with Devonshire and Grafton in their homes, in the coffeehouses, and at White's. His days were not all politics, and he spent almost as much time with artists, musicians, and writers removed from the political realm; he took tea with Richardson and called on Laetitia Pilkington, whom he vainly tried to help out of her incessant financial tangles.[7] In the summer he visited Henry Pelham or the earl of Chesterfield at their country houses, returning home in time to hear the Birthday Ode sung at court, to glitter among the mighty at Sir Thomas Robinson's ball that night,[8] and to see the new young actor who had taken London by storm.

If David Garrick had been trained in the Betterton school, he would never have produced such a startling effect, and had he made his debut a decade earlier, it is doubtful if even the avant garde would have applauded him. Now, however, circumstances, time, and player concurred. With his own intuitive knowledge and extraordinary sense of theater, Garrick introduced a new concept, the kind of "natural" acting Hill had been demanding since the twenties. Perhaps "spontaneous" would be more accurate, for even Betterton had insisted actors must "follow nature," the raw material which the actor had to formalize into art. Betterton's precepts had guided the brilliant Drury Lane quartet that dominated the stage from 1710-30, and there had been no real challenge to their style until Garrick's appearance in *Richard III*. His hunchback, now blazing, now smouldering, did not speak in the cadenced tones of traditional tragedy but in a fashion that seemed close to ordinary speech. His gestures were not stylized or his movements stately; his manner was quick and nervous (but with the ease of complete control), riveting the attention and producing an electrifying response in his audience. It was revolutionary and seemed to Londoners of 1741 the ultimate in realism.[9]

Actors trained in the old school disagreed, and Quin reflected their feelings when he claimed that if Garrick were right, then all of them had been wrong. Cibber's own schooling put him on Quin's side, and he said so. After seeing two versions of *The Rehearsal*, he announced, "Garrick is well enough, but not superior to Theophilus,"[10] and once, at tea with his boyhood idol, Anne Bracegirdle, he decried Garrick's acting until she exclaimed, "Come, come, Cibber, tell me if there is not something like envy in your character of this young gentleman! The actor who pleases everybody must have some merit."

He felt the force of the reproof, paused a moment to take a pinch of snuff, and replied, "Why, faith, Bracey, I believe you are right; the young fellow is clever."[11]

In fact, he even praised Garrick to his face, and the young actor proudly wrote his brother that "old Cibber has spoke with the greatest Commendation of my Acting."[12] Cibber may not have been wholehearted in his approval, but he never played Richard again.

Cibber had his choice of roles in the season of 1741-42, and at the earnest request of a nearly bankrupt Fleetwood, he played Sir John Brute in *The Provok'd Wife* on 3 December. Only his name was on the bill, and Horace Walpole's note, "Old Cibber plays tonight, and all the world will be there," suggests he was probably the one actor in London who could draw a crowd away from Garrick's Lothario.[13] Rich also wanted Cibber's services, and for him Colley not only played Sir John but recreated Lord Foppington, Justice Shallow, and Sir Novelty Fashion "at the Particular Desire of Persons of Quality" or by royal command.[14]

At seventy, Cibber must have found the effort fatiguing, for he went to Bath early this year and almost immediately developed a fever. The illness was serious enough for the April issue of the *Gentleman's Magazine* to list his death. It was premature. Catherine called in Beau Nash's friend, Dr. Oliver, a leading Bath physician, and under his ministrations Cibber recovered completely. Nevertheless, the fever had weakened him, and he lingered in Bath until May, missing the debut of his granddaughter, Jenny, at Drury Lane. Theo, in and out of debtors' prison and suddenly realizing what his two daughters might be to him, had introduced Jenny speaking the epilogue at his benefit on 20 March. A month later, he claimed another benefit for the two girls, *The Orphan*, in which Jenny played Cordelio.[15] She received seventy-eight pounds, which Theo appropriated, and then he began making arrangements for her to enter the regular company in the fall.

After Cibber's slow recuperation, he was eager to return home when the weather improved. He left Bath the moment he felt able and reported back to Dr. Oliver with a true Londoner's passion that in spite of the difficult journey, "it prov'd to be the best Physick I could possibly have taken.

I had no sooner got to Kingston than I began to breath new life, which every Hill wee climb'd but the more invigorated: I felt no fatigue, my Spirits and appetite encreas'd, to the last mile, till I danc'd into my own Door."[16] The revitalization was more than physical. He gave up the house in Charles Street and moved Catherine, her daughter, and himself into an elegant new house on Berkeley Row (later Berkeley Square), the heart of the most fashionable district in London. His neighbors were no longer theatrical people but those he met at White's and visited in the country, men like Chesterfield, Jersey, the lords Halifax and Salisbury and the duke of Beaufort.

He needed all the strength he could muster, for he was about to undergo the last and most crucial phase of the public calumny he had endured since *The Non-Juror*. His adversary this time was not a Grub Street hack or the relatively unknown Henry Fielding, but the most famous and brilliant poet of the century, Alexander Pope, a man so feared that his satires had brought him threats of bodily harm and so renowned that Alderman Barber once offered him five thousand pounds just to mention his name in a poem. As chief of the Tory satirists, he was a formidable opponent.

Pope's anomisity toward Cibber appears to have been not only political but also personal and professional. Politically, they had been on opposite sides since 1716, when Pope forsook Addison's circle of Whigs, and Cibber's subsequent *Non-Juror* had made the breach permanent. Their personal lives contrasted as sharply as their politics. Pope spent most of his days in pain, his social life limited by his physical frailty. Cibber seemed to sail through life on a wave of exuberant good health (his recent illness had been the first of any consequence), and the easy laughter of the amiable mask gave him an enviable popularity. Finally, there was the unbridgeable difference in professional views. Pope was quite aware of his position as the foremost poet of his time—he had devoted his life to the creation of lasting poetry, and he revered language as the highest expression of the human spirit. Cibber was the quintessential actor, and his attitude toward the written word can only be described as cavalier. Words were merely the foundation for a character brought to life by the actor, and the occasional forgotten or misplaced speech was unimportant as long as he maintained the illusion. This attitude, carried over in Cibber's plays and verse, was anathema to Pope; yet over the years it had brought applause and glory to Colley, still the most popular living playwright and the officially designated poet of England.

These three elements provide the basis but not the immediate cause for Pope's last devastating attack. Actually, there may have been two causes. The first was the *Apology*. Cibber had paid Pope a handsome tribute, "Not our great Imitator of *Horace* himself can have more Pleasure in writing his Verses than I have in reading them" (I, 21) but immediately vitiated the effect by suggesting that Pope attacked him for self-serving reasons: "One of his Points must be, to have many Readers: He considers that my Face and Name are more known than those of many thousands of more consequence in the kingdom: That therefore, right or wrong, a Lick at the *Laureat* will always be a sure Bait, *ad captandum vulgus*, to catch him little Readers" (I, 35-36). Nothing could have exasperated Pope more, and, like Fielding, he was determined to have his revenge.[17] Unlike his fellow satirist, however, Pope worked slowly, editing and polishing his work until each couplet gleamed with perfection.

For the poet, in poor health and easily fatigued, to undertake a major attack, the anger must have gone deep. Even so, he might not have gone ahead had not the political climate of 1742 brought him to the boiling point. At the beginning of February came Walpole's long-expected fall, but not the equally long-awaited end of Whig administration. Walpole was out as prime minister, the king created him earl of Orford, putting him into the House of Lords, and in the brief power struggle that accompanied this crisis, the Whigs banded together and retained their supremacy. The Tories, out since 1715, were frustrated and bitter, and in Pope's eyes, the Whig symbol was Colley Cibber, whose smiling face was everywhere he turned.

In March, Pope published his *New Dunciad*, the fourth and final chapter of his epic catalog of fools. The original *Dunciad*, published in 1728, had pilloried all those he considered second-rate, focusing on Lewis Theobald, who had roused Pope's fury by pointing out the errors in his edition of Shakespeare.[18] The fourth part transformed the final lines of the original into a full-length poem and took on a more serious tone, but, except for a line referring to the Goddess of Dullness, "Soft on her lap her Laureat son reclines," there was no special emphasis on Cibber. In the summer, however, rumors began to circulate that Pope was revising the entire poem, deposing Theobald and making Cibber the Prince of Dunces.

As the rumors grew, Cibber's friends urged him to speak out in his own defense, warning him that "a Disgrace, from such a Pen, might stick upon me to Posterity."[19] He had to admit the point. Even at the time of the *Apology* he had dimly perceived a need to set the record straight and, although he had maintained his protective persona, he could assume his words on theater had revealed the keen mentality behind it. He still wore the Foppington mask in society, and now, barely emerged from the shadow of death, he could see the danger that if it were accepted as the reality, his name, his reputation, the *Apology*, and all that had gone into their making would be destroyed.

He could not ignore the danger this time, but Pope's past behavior precluded any attempt to approach him privately, even if that had been Cibber's style.[20] The only alternative was a public statement, either an outright plea for mercy or a warning to stop. Cibber chose the latter and spent the month of June writing his answer not only to Pope but to all his critics, cautioning them that he, too, owned a sharp pen.

In July, he published his *Letter from Mr. Cibber to Mr. Pope*, a 66-page pamphlet. It briefly removed the Foppington mask, and his words were no longer toned by bland indifference. Likening himself to the famous boxer "Rugged and Tough," who would bear a drubbing until his opponent was exhausted, he promised to "have the last Word," and began by repeating his favorite dictum: a man's work stands or falls by its own merit, not by others' opinions. He himself laid no claim to literary eminence, for he had written "more to be Fed than Famous," but Pope's "ruling Passion," he charged, turning the poet's own words against him, was a "lust of Praise" that led him to demolish the reputations of men too insignificant to inflict real injury. "A Man might as well triumph for his having kill'd so many silly Flies that offended him" (p. 12), he wrote, echoing Swift's view that Pope's enemies would have been "peaceably buried in Oblivion" had they not been immortalized in the *Dunciad*.

Having opened with a backhanded compliment, he came directly to the point. Pope had claimed he never attacked anyone who had not previously attacked him, but Cibber had always been an open admirer of the poet. "How comes it then," he asked reasonably, "that in your works you have so often treated him as a Dunce or an Enemy?" His pretended search for an answer, however, was in itself an attack. Could it be, he asked, because his comedies had been so successful? Because he could act as well as write? Or because his "inferior Talents" had made him Pope's social equal? "It could not be," he protested with calm irony, "simple ill-nature" (p. 16). He gave his own "explanation," reaching into the past for *The Rehearsal*'s ridicule of *Three Hours after Marriage*, citing the extraordinary success of *The Non-Juror*, "not so much to commemorate the Applause . . . as to shew the World one of your best Reasons for having so often publish'd your Contempt of the Author" (p. 29).

For the first time, he replied to the charges leveled against him. To the accusation of plagiarism, he answered truthfully that his revisions of old plays had given new and extended life to many "that had been dead to the Stage out of all Memory." His original works had been successful—*Love's Last Shift* had been played every season for the last forty-seven years—and he asked, "Is a Tailor, that can make a new Coat well, the worse Workman, because he can mend an old one?" (pp. 31-33). He admitted tragedy was not his forte, adding that neither could he "dance upon the Rope, or make a Saddle, nor play upon the Organ," before asking with sudden fervor, "But if I have made so many crowded Theatres laugh, and in the right places too, for above forty Years together, am I to make up the Number of your Dunces, because I have not the equal Talent of making them cry too?" (pp. 32-34).

Cibber laughed at his tormentors and at himself, but the undertone was serious, and when he came to Pope's *Epistle to Dr. Arbuthnot* (1734), he stopped laughing entirely at the line, "And has not Colley too his Lord and Whore?" If he had changed it to read "And has not *Sawney* too his Lord and Whore," he asked, "Would not the Satyr have been equally just? Or would any sober Reader have seen more in the Line than a wide mouthful of Ill-Manners? Or would my professing myself a Satyrist give me a Title to wipe my foul Pen upon the Face of every Man I did not like?" (pp. 44-45). Whether Cibber merely resented the slur upon his marital fidelity, or whether it was the fact that it had been published the very month of Katharine's death, it was the one area in which his defense became an outright attack on Pope. How deeply he felt is obvious in the bawdy-house story he now recounted (see chapter 3). It occupied only a small proportion of the *Letter*, but it would be, Cibber knew, fully exploited by Pope's enemies. Having delivered this blow, he made a rapid-fire attack on the rest of Pope's insults, concluding with unaccustomed severity: "For if a Man, from his being admitted the best Poet, imagines himself so much lifted above the World, that he has a Right to run a muck, and make sport with the Characters of all Ranks of People, to soil and begrime every Face that is obnoxious to his ungovernable Spleen or Envy: Can so vain, so inconsiderate, so elated an Insolence, amongst all the Follies he has lash'd, and laugh'd at, find a Subject fitter for Satyr than himself?" (pp. 61-62). He sent a copy to Dr. Oliver in Bath with a note, "I will not ask your Opinion, because if you like it, you will have no very good one of Him. But I hope you will find I have done him no injustice; for I like his Poetry, tho' that does not like me."[21] Then he sat back to watch the reaction.

It was not long in coming. *A Blast upon Blast; or a New Lick at the Laureat*, a hasty attack on Cibber, appeared two days after the *Letter* and was soon followed by an avalanche of others. Pope had as many enemies as Colley, and the bookshops were soon filled with engravings, pamphlets, and broadsides ridiculing the bawdy-house adventure.[22] Newspapers and magazines kept the battle going, and even the nobility entered the fray when Lord Hervey published *The Difference between Verbal and Practical Virtue*, a poetic contrast between Pope and Cibber far more savage than the *Letter* had been. Colley was given the credit for the book, but his contribution seems to have been limited to the acidulous preface: "I own, I am greatly elate on the Laurels the Town has bestow'd upon me for my Victory over you in my Prose Combat; and, encouraged by that Triumph, I now resolve to fight you on your own Dunghil of Poetry, and with your own jingling Weapons of Rhyme and Metre. I confess I have had some Help; but what then? since the greatest Princes are rather proud than asham'd of Allies and Auxiliaries when they make War in the Field, why should I decline such Assistance when I make War in the Press?"[23] Hervey had his own grievance against Pope. The *Epistle to Dr. Arbuthnot* contained a portrait of him that became a classic of vilification.

It has been suggested that Pope provoked Cibber with rumors in order to generate interest in his new version of the *Dunciad*. It seems more probable, however, that his aim had not been, in Cibber's words, "ad captandum vulgus" (to capture the crowd) but to provoke a public attack in order to say honestly he ridiculed only those who had mocked him in print. In either case, he had succeeded beyond his wildest hopes, but he paid a high price. Jonathan Richardson, Jr., happened to be in Twickenham when Cibber's *Letter* arrived and watched Pope read it, his face writhing in anguish even as he assured Richardson, "These things are my diversion."[24] Later, in better control, Pope wrote Hugh Bethel, "It [the *New Dunciad*] provoked Cibber to write a very foolish & impudent Letter, which I have no cause to be sorry for, & perhaps next Winter I shall be thought to be glad of: But I lay in my Claim to you, to Testify for me, that if he should chance to die before a New & Improved Edition of the Dunciad comes out, I have ready, actually written (before & not after his death) all I shall ever say about him."[25] During the autumn, as Pope eased his pain by restructuring his epic, the controversy continued. With the impact of his *Letter* proven beyond all doubt, Cibber began to see the advantages of direct statement and drafted another. This time it was not an overt attack but an amusing discourse that obliquely both mocked and complimented Pope. *The Egoist; or, Colley upon Cibber* is written in one of Pope's favorite modes, the Horatian epistle, a dialogue between a *persona* and an *adversarius*, stating, developing, and concluding a premise. Cibber was wise enough not to attempt verse, but he follows almost exactly the structure of Pope's own *apologia* for satire, *An Epistle to Dr. Arbuthnot*. There are, of course, differences. Cibber does not claim Pope's position as a satirist and his argument rests on a different base, but the similarities are too great to be ignored.

That Cibber had Pope in mind is evident from the first, when Frankly, the *adversarius*, tries to persuade the Author to publish some discarded scraps of writing. The Author refuses, and Frankly suggests he print them anonymously "with a flim-flam Story of an accident." He could then pretend to be angry that his work had been "stolen" and publish the "correct" version under his own name—exactly as Pope had done with his own correspondence. The passage on critics paraphrases Pope's own words in *Arbuthnot* and turns them against him; if a critic is unjust, says Cibber, "Every honest Man will think him a Slanderer" (as his own friends called Pope), but if he is just, then, like Pope, Cibber will heed his words, adding that he "will take care not to be more ridiculous by being out of Humour" (p. 27) with the censurer, a gibe at the poet's sensitivity.

Cibber also adopts Pope's stance on praise. Frankly asks why Cibber does not print the compliments paid him by "men of Merit," adding, "You would not find fault with a Present of Value?" Cibber's answer sounds like *Arbuthnot*: "Yes, but I would, if I did not like the Terms I am to receive it upon; and I should think publishing my own Praise, would be buying the favour too dear" (p. 65).

The nearest Cibber ever came to defending any of his work is in his comment on the annual odes: "If *Horace* himself had been obliged, like me, to have wrote four and twenty times upon the same Subject, might it not be a fair Question whether he would have been always able to come up to his Carmen Saeculare?" (p. 50). He denies flatly that he publishes them. They are printed without his "Consent or Knowledge," he says, with probable accuracy, filched from rehearsals by "some poor Spy of the Press."

The subject of morality permeates the whole work as Cibber applies Pope's principles to himself. Pope claimed he never attacked simple ignorance and stupidity except when accompanied by pretentiousness and arrogance. Cibber admits the possibility of the first but denies the latter and points to the hypocrite's fear of being found out, concluding, "as there is no Guilt in Stupidity, I can't see why a Blockhead is to blame if he goes to bed with a quiet Conscience." At that, Frankly asks reasonably why the Author is so fond of being "an avowed Blockhead?" The answer is forthright: "Pardon me, I don't insist upon the Title! I am full as willing to pass for a Man of Sense; but when People won't let me, what have I to do but (like other Blockheads) think well of myself?" (p. 36). It was the kind of statement most offensive to Pope. Only the insistence that Cibber's wealth of good humor was actually unrelieved depravity could give Pope's wit the necessary edge, and this humble but unrepentant admission of ignorance disarmed the "sacred lance" of satire.

A new baiting campaign began, when Cibber was sent an "unauthorized" leaf of the *Dunciad*.[26] He riposted with a second pamphlet, a terse and sharp *Letter* asking Pope directly, "are you so sure, that any Man's calling me stupid is a Proof of my being so? Or, if a saucy Satyrist were to stile you an *Adonis* or a *Thyrsites*, would that either make you a handsome Creature, or an ill-natur'd one?"[27] Clearly he had been hurt, and even Pope was momentarily affected, writing to Warburton, "I begin to be more scrupulous of hurting him & wish him more Conscientiously impudent."[28]

Cibber did not oblige, and since he did not appear on the stage either, the quarrel faded from the public press. Through his family, however, his name was as constantly before the public as ever. Susannah had returned from her Irish triumphs and, having obtained a legal writ to prevent Theo from collecting her salary, was acting at Covent Garden. Theo, forbidden to play in the same theater as his wife and persona non grata at Drury Lane, was working for Henry Giffard at Goodmans Fields. The Chetwoods, too, were back from Ireland after a brief sojourn in Liverpool, and Theo had hired Anne at the beginning of the 1742-43 season.[29] He also lured his daughter Jenny, who had begun the season at Drury Lane, over to Giffard. She and her sister lived with Elizabeth (now married to Joseph Marples, a merchant) and were being coached in acting by their Aunt Charlotte, with whom Elizabeth was still close. Charlotte's checkered career was raising eyebrows, especially since, to protect herself from the bailiffs, she had taken to wearing men's clothes and calling herself "Charles Brown."[30] She was quite out of her father's life, but he undoubtedly heard about her. All London did.

Not by word or deed did Colley give the slightest indication that he was breathlessly awaiting Pope's epic, and his life followed precisely the pattern it had for the last decade. He saw the same people, attended the same places and, as always, seemed to enjoy himself immensely. To most of the world he was the self-centered, carefree laureate, and only a few saw him otherwise. One of these was Laetitia Pilkington, who spent several months in debtors' prison until her fervent appeals brought Cibber to the rescue. Robbed the very day she was released, she again went to him and, to her surprise, was welcomed "like a fine lady." He listened courteously as she explained her predicament, then remarked casually, "I told your melancholy story to the Duke of Richmond, and he gave me five guineas for you—there they are." The grateful Laetitia thanked him with an effusive paean in the *Gazette*, and Cibber was touched, although he told her the lines "were more proper to be addressed to an Archbishop than to him, who had nothing to boast of more than a little common humanity."[31] She was not the only recipient of his generosity, but, as if he were embarrassed to reveal an aspect so alien to his public image, he never spoke of such deeds, and not many of those he helped were as openly grateful as Laetitia. Spring passed into summer and summer into fall without event. Cibber traveled to Bath and came back refreshed and ready with the Birthday Ode.

At the end of October, the *Dunciad* appeared, finally and absolutely seating a grotesque caricature of Foppington on the throne of Dullness. That image, labeled "Cibber" and immortalized by Pope's glittering lines, would send his name echoing down the ages as a synonym for vice and folly. Generations of readers would laugh and dismiss Cibber without troubling to discover whether or not the image had any substance. What Fielding had provided for scholars in *The Laureat*, Pope gave to the common reader in his poem. Cibber's reputation was thoroughly and irrevocably tarnished.

It seemed less important in 1743, for Cibber's contemporaries felt his

Letter had removed the worst of the sting. Pope and his friends might chortle with glee, but the *Dunciad* was not received with unqualified praise. In November, the *London Magazine* printed an epigram on the bawdy-house episode:

> Colley made P—— a poetical *Tom Tit*,
> P—— him a *hero* quite devoid of wit:
> Colley unmov'd cries out, Well done, good brother!
> For one shrewd turn richly deserves another.
> But yet a diff'rence manifest is shewn,
> You set me up, whereas I pluck'd you down.

Yet the injury was real, and Cibber knew it. He had promised to have the last word, and he would have it.

Cibber's third pamphlet *Letter* to Pope reveals that he might be un-bowed but he was not indifferent. This time he included a second adversary, Pope's friend William Warburton, who had written a preface for the last *Dunciad* under the name "Richard Aristarchus" and had, in Cibber's opinion, influenced the change of hero.[32] Warburton was a clergyman, Cibber noted, and asked, "How can you hope that so idle a Frolick, as your standing *Stickler* in a Battle between a peevish Poet, and a laughing Comedian, would not soil your Character?"[33] His comments to Warburton demonstrate a surprising familiarity with the cleric's work, but noticeably lack humor, as, indeed, does the *Letter* itself. He was weary, he said, of Pope's "Oyster-mouth'd Muse" and the epithets "Brazen, Brainless, Coxcomb, Blockhead, Impudent, with that Burthen of your Song, Dull upon Dull," and for once he openly defended himself: "I neither wrote, nor spoke against you or your Writings; the worst I did, even when they endeavour'd to ridicule me, was to laugh with the rest of your Readers: Was it then so mortal an Offence never to have been uneasy at whatever you had said of me?" (pp. 13-14). It was a long letter, and it was final; he had kept his promise. Unfortunately for Cibber's reputation, his "last word" expired with the quarrel, while Pope's penultimate statement survives more than two hundred years later.

Nothing more was heard from Twickenham. In truth, Pope's frail body was nearing the end of its strength, and the revision of the *Dunciad* was his last major work. Whether Cibber knew this or had simply grown tired of the game is unknown, but despite the pleas of friends, he refused to pursue it. The decision was to his credit. Pope died 30 May 1744, leaving behind a brilliant and devastating vision of a corrupt world. His lines would be quoted, the vision accepted, and Cibber would be held up to the ages as the Prince of Dunces.

Out of context, the heat of the controversy and the longevity of the poem have made it seem as if Cibber's entire life was centered about this one event. Yet even as the last battle was joined, his days continued in the same unbroken pattern with only the slight variation of performances at Drury Lane. Fleetwood begged Cibber to appear again, and four days before the third *Letter* was published, he played Fondlewife in *The Old Batchelor*.[34] He acted three more times to crowded houses and tumultuous applause, his popularity undiminished by the caricature that was to outlive him.

Cibber was seen in White's, at the coffeehouses, and in the mall. He visited Chesterfield and persuaded him to assist Laetitia Pilkington, penniless as usual.[35] He called on Richardson and Peg Woffington and Owen Swiney and a host of other friends, and finally, when the weather permitted, he took his two Catherines to Bath, returning, as was his habit, in the autumn.

Although Cibber had not been a prime mover in the theater for more than a decade, he was still associated with it by preference and by family. The beginning of the 1744-45 season held more interest than usual, for several changes had taken place during his absence. Fleetwood, trying desperately to keep from losing Drury Lane, had hired Susannah Cibber as Garrick's leading lady, effectively preventing Theo from entering the company. Theo had been at Drury Lane part of the previous season until his dislike of Garrick and his disruptive behavior made Fleetwood send him packing. He had gone over to Rich at half his usual salary, but by the end of the year Rich didn't want him either. Threatened as always with debtors' prison, he decided to start a company at the Haymarket with himself and his daughter, Jenny, as the stars. He invited Charlotte with her daughter, Kitty, to join and collected a motley crew of unemployed actors that included his niece, Anne Chetwood.

By the time Colley arrived in London, Theo had opened his version of *Romeo and Juliet* with himself and fourteen-year-old Jenny in the title roles and Charlotte as the Nurse.[36] He even wrote a prologue for himself, and Garrick, who attended a performance, commented: "I never heard so vile and scandalous a performance in my life; and, excepting the speaking of it, and the speaker, nothing could be more contemptible. The play was tolerable enough, considering Theophilus was the hero. . . . Mrs Charke played the Nurse to his daughter, Juliet; but she was so miserable throughout, and so abounded in airs, affectation, and *Cibberisms*, that I was quite shocked at her: the girl, I believe, may have genius; but unless she changes her preceptor, she must be entirely ruined."[37] Despite Garrick's opinion, Jenny's performance was viewed favorably in the papers, but anything Theo touched was doomed.[38] The lord chamberlain withdrew the permission to perform, and after one or two abortive attempts to ignore the ruling, Theo gave up and disbanded the company.[39]

Somehow, Theo talked Rich into taking him and Jenny into Covent

Garden, possibly because he also promised Colley would act in a premiere of *Papal Tyranny in the Reign of King John*. The play was twenty years old and had been shelved twice before, but now the time seemed ripe. Prince Charles Edward, supported by the French, was about to attempt the return of the Stuart monarchy. Catholic and Protestant hatreds flared once more, and the play should, Rich thought, be as topical as *The Non-Juror* had been so long ago.

Cibber said he had "endeavour'd to make it more like a play than what I found it in Shakespeare,"[40] and for him that meant a narrower focus of action, a more tightly constructed plot, and an emphasis on emotional elements. He eliminated ten characters and added three, concentrated on the conflict between John and the Cardinal, and sweetened the religio-political statement with generous infusions of pathos and romance.

The play begins with England and France at war because King Philip of France has promised to place King John's nephew, Arthur, on the English throne. When Rome interferes in the person of Cardinal Pandulph, John defies the church and is excommunicated. Arthur is captured by the English, and John orders him killed, but in an emotionally charged scene, Hubert, the man assigned to the murder, cannot bring himself to do it. His care is wasted, however, for Arthur commits suicide by leaping from the battlements.

Meanwhile, the Dauphin invades England, collecting disaffected English nobles to his cause. By now John is dying; he repents of his attack on Arthur and is received into the church by the Cardinal, who then tries to persuade the Dauphin to make peace. The Dauphin refuses to listen until Blanche, the Spanish princess whom he loves, persuades him, and the story ends with the war over and history back on its course. The characters are as artificial and the verse as poor as anything Cibber ever wrote, but with Quin as King John and Cibber as Pandulph, Rich was assured of an audience.

In view of Cibber's last few premieres and with the *Dunciad* feud still smouldering, rehearsals were kept secret, and Rich put out no advance puffs. The policy held speculation to a minimum, and when, on 15 February, Cibber stepped forth as Cardinal Pandulph, he was greeted warmly.[41] In all fairness, the applause was probably a show of affection for the actor, but despite the appreciation of his "great spirit and vigour," many found his tragic style sadly outmoded. Victor was unexpectedly gentle in his discussion of the performance: "He acted the Part of Cardinal *Pandolph* himself; led to it, I presume, by his long Performance of Cardinal Wolsey, which he had acted many Years with Success; but in 1744 [*sic*], besides his just having lost all his Teeth, he was attempting to speak in a Theatre much larger than he had been so long used to; therefore my Readers will conclude, his Auditors could only be entertained with his Attitudes and Conduct, which were truly graceful."[42] But Thomas Davies, who was also present that night, probably reflected the majority opinion: "The unnatural swelling of his words displeased all who preferred natural elocution to artificial cadence. . . . He affected a stately magnificent tread, a supercilious aspect, with lofty and extravagant action, which he displayed by waving up and down a role of parchment in his right hand; in short, his whole behaviour was so starchly studied that it appeared eminently insignificant, and more resembling his own Lord Foppington than a great and dignified churchman."[43] Theo's Dauphin was also disliked, but young Jenny's Arthur was wholeheartedly approved, especially the scene where the young duke pleads for his life. The play ran for ten consecutive performances to excellent houses in spite of the competition from Garrick's superior production of Shakespeare's *King John* with Susannah Cibber as Constance.

Garrick had generously postponed the opening, but he had been perfectly right when he told Cibber the old style would no longer be accepted by an audience. Colley had replied tartly, "How do you know? You never tried it," but now Garrick's *King John* far outshone Quin's, and his production was a tremendous success.[44]

On 26 February 1745, the curtain fell at last, and three generations of Cibbers stood before the audience as Colley took his last bow on an English stage. Neither the play nor the performance had shown him at his best, but he had no regrets. It had been a profitable venture for Rich and it had brought Colley four hundred pounds, which he at once put into an annuity. Theo, concerned with his own problems, seemed to forget about Jenny, and she and her sister came to live in Berkeley Square.

When Colley returned from Bath this year, the rumors of a Scottish uprising had become a reality. Prince Charles Edward landed in May, and the clans gathered about the handsome young Stuart. London spent an uneasy summer, its worst fears realized in September with the shocking defeat at Prestonpans, and as the Scots marched southward, the English hastened to mobilize their forces. The theaters roused war sentiment with benefit performances for injured veterans and the production of anti-Catholic plays like *The Non-Juror*. On "Black Friday" (6 December) came the news that the prince and his army were in Devon, an easy march to London. The city was panic-stricken until the Scots, outnumbered, quarreling among themselves, and realizing that the promised support from France would not come, began the long retreat to Culloden.

The war fever did not touch Cibber directly, but he could scarcely avoid it when it permeated the very air. As customary, he took refuge from unpleasantness in gambling at White's, whose members would bet on anything. The club kept a betting book, and the first recorded entry—in the members' own writing—is a bet on Cibber's life.[45] He laughed heartily at such bets, and his only evidence of stress during this period was an occasional touch of absentmindedness, which he invariably passed off with a jest. Charged with failing to follow suit in a game of whist, he disarmed his partner with a smiling, "Don't be angry, sir. I can play ten times worse if I like."[46]

He also saw a good deal of Laetitia Pilkington. He had introduced her to Samuel Richardson, and now they shared the progress of Richardson's new novel, *Clarissa Harlowe*, as the author sent them new installments. Cibber was fascinated with the heroine, but when he first learned her fate, he threw down the manuscript and refused to read further. "I would no longer believe in Providence, or eternal Wisdom, or Goodness governs the world, if merit, innocence, and beauty are to be so destroyed. Nay!" he exclaimed, with tears in his eyes, "my mind is so hurt with the thought of her being violated, that were I to see her in Heaven, sitting on the knees of the blessed Virgin and crowned with glory, her sufferings would still make me feel horror, horror distilled."[47]

He wrote to Richardson, and eventually the novelist sent him the entire manuscript, asking for suggestions and hoping "he would not spare it."[48] Cibber's response was lyrical: "I have got through 210 pages, with a continual resolution to give every occasional beauty its laudable remark, but they grow too thick and strong upon me, to give me that agreeable leisure. I read a course of full five hours and a half, without drawing bit (as the jockeys call it); in which time my attention has got the better of my approbation, which all the while longed to tell you how I liked it. . . . O Lord! Lord! can there be any thing yet to come that will trouble this smooth stream of pleasure I am bathing in?"[49] By the time he finished, he became more objective. With a playwright's sense of audience, he urged cutting away "whole branches" of secondary characters and pleaded for a happy ending, but Richardson, worried that his moral instruction might be subverted, refused. Cibber's age, he said, made his "half tired Mind" look for "little more than Amusement."[50]

Cibber's claim to prefer amusement to moral instruction horrified Richardson as much as it had Cibber's friends in his youth, but the claim was not borne out by his actions. He continued to help Laetitia Pilkington long after it was clear her troubles were chronic and of her own making; as star-crossed as Charlotte, she would surely have spent most of her time in debtors' prison without his aid. In a way, she *was* another Charlotte, with the same vivacious personality, the same lack of foresight, and the same capacity for making the wrong choice. Unlike Charlotte, however, Laetitia always listened respectfully (though she seldom followed his precepts) and was pathetically grateful for all favors.

Cibber also helped Benjamin Victor begin his career of theater management in Dublin. In spite of Victor's professed hostility earlier, Cibber recommended him to Chesterfield, then lord lieutenant of Ireland, and wrote lengthy letters filled with excellent advice on how to manage a theatrical company. Victor followed the advice, prospered, and sent back rapturous descriptions of his successes.[51] Their friendship was closer in their correspondence than it had ever been while Victor was in London.

Only his family neither asked nor received advice from Colley. Theo, unable to agree with any of the managers, went from theater to theater, often out of work and always in trouble, until his father shrugged, "your dramatic Heroes are never contented, so e'en let them fight their own Battles."[52] Charlotte moved from crisis to crisis, married again, and left London to join a troupe of strolling players.[53] It must have been a relief, if not to Colley at least to Catherine, to have her removed from the reach of gossip for nine years.

The spring of 1746 brought news of the duke of Cumberland's victory at Culloden, and the house of Hanover breathed easier. Cibber celebrated with his countrymen and took the waters of Bath in carefree ease, or at least with such ease as a man unaccustomed to idleness could take. Once again he turned to writing, and this time chose a mode entirely new to him, a serious book on a subject unrelated to the theater.

Five years earlier, Cibber had been one of the three thousand subscribers to Conyers Middleton's thick, two-volume *History of the Life of Marcus Tullius Cicero*. He and Middleton had a common friend in Lord Hervey and a common enemy in Warburton, with whom Middleton had been involved in a furious theological quarrel. Cibber read and made copious notes on Middleton's book and now amused himself by putting them into order. Before long, he had a thick volume of his own words, and when he came back to London in the autumn, *The Character and Conduct of Cicero* was ready for a publisher.

Laetitia Pilkington called on him (for once not asking for money), and he read portions of it to her. She was so impressed that she wrote a poem for it, which Cibber offered to have printed after a little "correction," and she gladly handed it over to him. When he returned it to her the next day, she discovered that his emendations consisted of eliminating the effulgent praise of himself, and she remonstrated with him.

"Well, madam," he said with a smile, "there are two guineas for your flattery, and one more for the liberty I took." As she began to thank him, he interrupted her. "I have more good news for you. Mr. Stanhope altered a line, for which he desires you will accept a guinea, and Mr. Hervey also pays you the same compliment for changing one monosyllable for another." He filled her hands with gold.[54] She claimed her poem was to have been in the first edition, but for some reason it was not. Possibly Cibber, as he so often said, preferred not to publish his own praises.

He dedicated *Cicero* to George Bubb Dodington on New Year's Day, 1747, and sent the manuscript to his printer, John Watts. It is a curious work with no pretense to profound scholarship, a compilation of thoughtful, amusing, often unconventional opinions. He had, for example, no respect for Pompey's expansion of the Roman empire, holding that the same amount of energy spent in defending Rome would have been "the only true, compleat and real Glory," an astonishing statement in an age that thought highly of military exploits.[55] His admiration for Cicero's rhetoric led him to compare orators and actors with what at first appears to be unexpected humility, distinguishing between the orator's "Eloquence" which comes from sincerity, and the actor's art of "Elocution": "And tho' the Actor may, in proper Places, be allow'd, even to a Commendation, to imitate the Orator, yet the Orator's Imitation of the Actor—will but lower him to a Meanness unprofitable" (p. 24). It was not humility, however, for he quickly added his own opinion that excellence in acting is more difficult to achieve than excellence in public speaking; that, in fact, history proves "a *Complete Actor* has been a much greater Rarity than an *Accomplish'd Orator*" (p. 25), a position certain to antagonize all politicians, preachers, and tub-thumpers.

The response to the book was mixed. Horace Walpole sent a copy to Thomas Gray, who did not appreciate the humor and replied loftily that it was "as pert and as dull as usual," and wondered if "reason and truth" would know their own faces if they "saw themselves so bedizened in tattered fringe and tarnished lace, in French jewels and dirty furbelows, the frippery of a stroller's wardrobe?"[56] To which Thomas Davies retorted sharply, "I hope the distressed writer called for his lavender drops, to relieve him in his exquisite feelings," and noted that the Rev. John Horne (better known as Horne Tooke) had quoted Cibber's "cogent and unanswerable" remarks on the murder of Julius Caesar.[57]

Cibber received all comments with equanimity and without varying his routine in the slightest; *Cicero* had been a work of leisure, not ambition. He played the social game in London during the season and in Tunbridge Wells during the summer. Here, in July of 1747, he met Garrick, who had just concluded negotiations to share in the management of Drury Lane and was casting about for new plays. As Fleetwood had, he approached Cibber for a new comedy, saying respectfully, "I should be glad to have the honor of bringing it into the world."

"Who have you to act in it?" Cibber asked.

"Why, there are Clive and Pritchard, myself, and some others."

Cibber let Garrick wait as he nonchalantly took a pinch of snuff. "No," he said at last, "it won't do."[58] He may have been flattered, but he neither had any comedies stored away nor did Garrick inspire him to write a new one.

He was not indifferent to the theater, and he maintained his many friendships. He and Owen Swiney transferred their affection from Susannah to Peg Woffington, of whom Cibber once said that if she "were to stand a Quarter of an Hour's Conversation with any Male Creature under forty, I am afraid the Flesh, or the Devil, would be apt to be very busy about her."[59] Fortunately for Peg, neither he nor Swiney was eligible, but he often called at her lodgings where he was assured of a warm welcome and a reminder of his own stage days. The playwright Arthur Murphy recalled an evening when, after many earnest requests to perform, Cibber turned to Woffington and said, "Well, you jade, if you will assist my memory, I will give you the first speech of Sir John Brute." He then delivered the speech "with little assistance from the lady, in the most masterly manner . . . and when he had praised the good qualities of Lady Brute, closing with 'But here she comes,' his expression of disgust was more strikingly characteristic of a surfeited husband than anything of a similar nature he [Murphy] had ever witnessed on the stage."[60]

In the summer of 1747, Laetitia Pilkington went home to Ireland and finished her *Memoirs*, and subscriptions poured in "from all quarters." With some security at last, she wrote Cibber happily, "I do assure you, Sir, the honour you have shewn me makes me looked upon as a person of consequence here," and said she had "made every body as much in love with your humanity, as they are charmed with your Cicero." Her copy was constantly borrowed by "persons of taste and eminence," and she begged for a picture of him to put in it.[61]

He responded warmly with a long letter congratulating her on her good fortune and referring to her past trials with some frank avuncular advice. "Common sense might have prevented as many misfortunes as your high and mightiness has run through, and don't suppose it possible you can have a grain of wit till you have twenty pounds in your pocket. With half that sum, a greater sinner than you may look the devil in the face." He was aware of her flattery, but if, he said, she was telling the truth about *Cicero*, he would send her ten copies to give to friends, and, pleased that the use of his name had helped her, concluded, "If the value I have for you gives you any credit in your own country, pray stretch it as far as you think it can be serviceable to you." She could repay him fully "by sometimes letting me hear of your well-doing."[62] It was such a letter as he might have written Charlotte had they been on similar terms.

Laetitia's absence ended the drain on his purse, but he missed her lively conversation. Not that he lacked companionship—he was welcome everywhere, although the more conservative were sometimes shocked at his levity. He was not insensible to serious matters, but he was constitutionally incapable of remaining solemn for very long, and only those who knew him well saw the heart beneath Foppington's mask. Richardson, often horrified by Cibber's words, eventually understood what they concealed, but less intimate acquaintances took comments like, "I am for the church, though I don't go," at face value, and shook their heads.[63]

Aristocratic friends, less bound by convention, understood the assumption of morality beneath the mask, for they operated on the same premise and often made even more outrageous comments. Men like Chesterfield, now back from Ireland, spent hours laughing and joking with him. Gossip has it that young Samuel Johnson first approached the earl as a patron for his projected dictionary, but he was told Chesterfield was "occupied" and was kept waiting for an unconscionably long time. When the door finally opened on a laughing Cibber taking his leave, Johnson was outraged and never forgave either man.

In the spring of 1748, Cibber went to Tunbridge bearing the news of Lord Lovat's trial for treason. He may have been one of the fashionable who bought tickets and crowded into Westminster to see the old laird condemned for his part in the Scottish rebellion, but the man who so earnestly sought the cheerful aspects of life would hardly have cared to witness a public execution.[64] At Tunbridge, he could drink the pleasant, iron-flavored water with Beau Nash, chat with Richardson and pay court to the beautiful adventuress Elizabeth Chudleigh. She had captured all hearts and was soon to extend her domain to Bath, where she reigned until she went too far and appeared at a masquerade ball as a naked Venus.

Colley immediately fell victim to her charms and paid her his usual gallantries; Richardson (perhaps jealous of the attention Cibber drew) translated them as "over head and ears in love" and gossiped about seeing Cibber sitting on a bench, his face "more wrinkled than ordinary with disappointment."

"I thought you were of the party," Richardson commented, "Miss Chudleigh is gone into the tea-room."

"Pshaw!" replied Colley. "There is no coming at her, she is so surrounded by the toupets!" In a few moments, however, he was called for and, Richardson said, "in he flew, and his face shone again, and looked smooth."[65]

Cibber was so enchanted with her that he dedicated a little dialogue to her. Ironically, *The Lady's Lecture* is about choosing a husband, a subject on which Miss Chudleigh, secretly married to Augustus Hervey, had no need of advice.[66] Reaching back to *The Careless Husband*, he revived the elegant and experienced Sir Charles Easy and gave him a clever nineteen-year-old daughter. If, as seems likely, it reflects Cibber's views on the rearing of daughters, he was indeed a most unorthodox parent, for Miss has evidently been given a good deal of freedom and banters with her father as an equal.

Unlike similar characters in Cibber's plays, the father-daughter relationship is warm, and they agree perfectly on the qualities that make a desirable husband. Modesty, they decide, is important, and virtue essential, although not too grave, for "no body has a right to be chearful *but* the Innocent."[67] They differ when Miss says she is not interested in marrying for fortune or social position but will wait for a man she can respect and love. Sir Charles teases her, calling her old-fashioned and counseling her pragmatically not to despise affluence. "I don't desire you make it your Master, but I hope you will allow Fortune may be a very good Servant" (p. 36).

Two remarkable points are quite apart from the usual attitude of the time: the first is Miss's liberated refusal to be disturbed at the prospect of remaining unmarried; the second is more significant and is very likely Cibber's own. The question of choosing a husband, he says, is better left to a well-brought-up child than to a parent, however experienced and well meaning, for marriage is "a mere State-Lottery, where the chance of a Prize will be just as equal, whether the Ticket be of your choosing or mine" (p. 24). Such liberality shocked people, and when Cibber added that the blessing of a happy marriage "might be as well brought about by the Man *you* like as by the Man *I* like," Richardson wrote waspishly, "The piece is calculated, as it stands at present, to throw down all distinction between parents and children."[68]

Had Cibber really been thinking of Elizabeth Chudleigh? Or of Jenny, now old enough to marry? Or even, perhaps, of Charlotte? Certainly his daughter had been dear to him before the break, and he may have harbored some guilt for permitting and indeed encouraging her disastrous marriage. If so, *The Lady's Lecture* seems a kind of attempt to justify his lack of strict governance over his own children.

Although such questions may have crossed Cibber's mind occasionally, he did not dwell on them, and, in fact, would scarcely have had the opportunity, for there were many calls on his time. There were the annual odes to write, balls to attend, and a voluminous correspondence to maintain. Victor wrote often for advice on theater management and was grateful for Cibber's long, thoughtful answers, supplementing them with the *Apology*. "I esteem your History of your own times in the Theatre, as one of the most valuable of my Books," he wrote, "and find myself under frequent Occasions to consult you there."[69] Cibber sent him a copy of Edward Moore's *The Foundling*, which he considered "immoderately good," the best play he had seen in fifteen years.[70] Victor was not as enthusiastic, but he was charmed with Cibber's "readiness to be pleased with a dawning Genius."[71]

Victor and Cibber bantered back and forth, informing each other about theatrical matters in their respective cities, and in the summer of 1749, Victor invited Theo to come and work in Dublin. Without Theo's running from bailiffs or quarreling publicly with theater managers, Cibber's life went smoothly through the season. His odes were performed and printed without comment, he sold the copyright for the *Apology*, now in its third edition, and set off for his summer visit to the waters.[72] He met Richardson again and heard the outline of *Sir Charles Grandison*, shocking the author by laughing merrily at the idea of a male virgin and by defending openly the idea of a "moderate rake." Richardson could not understand the point and would not take such a view seriously. Cibber, he wrote later, was "as gay and lively at seventy-nine as he was at twenty-nine," in spite of the fact that he was "a sober man who has seen a great deal and always dressed well."[73] Richardson apparently considered the two aspects incompatible.

When the family returned to London in the fall of 1750, Jenny entered the Drury Lane company. Garrick had quarreled with Susannah, who had gone over to Rich, and either he thought Jenny could replace her or he wanted to show Colley that even a Cibber would have to learn the new style. Garrick had been listening to rumors and, as he angrily wrote to the countess of Burlington: "I have been told by some Gentlemen of the White's Club, that any Praises they bestow'd upon Me, were Death to him [Cibber], & he always Endeavour'd as much as in him lay, to hurt me in their Opinions, & to criticise Me in my Characters; his Behaviour to Me was always the reverse, which is so certain an indication of a mean contemptible Mind, that I have never cultivated his Acquaintance, & I believe I have disappointed him by not offering that incense to his vanity, which he has so often receiv'd & which he expects from every young Actor."[74] It is a pity he never checked the accuracy of the stories, for they are not supported elsewhere, and it is the only time Cibber stands accused of hypocrisy.

Whatever Garrick's private reasons, he cast Jenny as Alicia in *Jane Shore*, taking the part of Hastings himself and using the rehearsals to instruct her in his manner of performance. Colley's training had been too thorough, however, and halfway through, Garrick wrote that whatever "Genius" she might have was "so eclips'd by the Manner of Speaking the Laureat has taught her, that I am afraid it will not do."[75] His doubts were proven right when they opened, and Cross noted in his prompter's book that she was "not lik'd at all, tho' not hiss'd." The announcement that *Jane Shore* would be acted again *was* greeted with hisses, the play was canceled, and Jenny gave up the stage.[76]

At the beginning of December, Cibber was taken with a severe fever. For ten days he was delirious, and when he regained his senses he was so weak that he doubted he could recover. Just before Christmas, he wrote sadly to the lord chamberlain: "I know no nearer way of repaying your favours for these last twenty years, than by recommending to the bearer Mr Henry Jones for the vacant laurel: Lord Chesterfield will tell you more of him."[77]

Jones, an Irish bricklayer-cum-poet, had written a panegyric on Chesterfield while the earl was lord lieutenant. Mistaking Chesterfield's graceful acceptance for patronage, he followed him to England in 1748, where he became a member of the literary circle that included Cibber. Colley admired his work enough to nominate him for the laureatship, but Chesterfield coolly told Horace Walpole that "a better poet would not take the post, and a worse ought not to have it." The question became immaterial when Cibber recovered. On Christmas day he was well enough to write Richardson that, "tho' Death has been cooling his heels at my door these three weeks, I have not had time to see him," and if Richardson would only visit him, he would "order Death to come another day."[78]

By February, Cibber was back to normal and so pleased about the remedy that he wrote a testimonial about "Dr. James's Fever Powder."[79] White's continued to lay bets on how long he would live, but he resumed his social life where it had left off. Warburton's nine-volume edition of Pope's collected *Works* appeared in March 1751, and the reminder of the old feud stimulated Cibber to write a last reply, a poem, published in a quarto edition. This time it was no longer a matter of personal vindication but a laughing rejoinder for the amusement of friends.

The *Rhapsody upon the Marvellous* draws its inspiration from the odes of Horace and Pindar and claims to be "a Scrutiny into Ancient Poetical Fame, Demanded by Modern Common Sense."[80] It is a slight piece, ridiculing the use of the supernatural (the "marvellous") in the classics, but Cibber also attacks other matters: the worship of ancients qua ancients, obfuscating scholarship, and Italian opera. He shows little reverence for Horace, whose ideas, he says, "swell and swell," or for Pindar's extravagant similes, and there are many references to Pope. In this, his final word at last, he places his old enemy above Horace, a tribute Pope would never have accepted during his lifetime.

Cibber read the piece to Richardson on a warm September afternoon, and his friend wrote later, "It was a hot day; and he read till he was in a breathing, and wiped and acted like any thing: and every body was pleased."[81]

Now that he was in his eightieth year, Cibber was beginning to feel his age. Last summer he had not taken the long trip to Bath, and now even Tunbridge seemed too far. He had a welcome relief from one public duty this year when the birthday celebration was postponed and probably the New Year's as well, for no ode was published. Yet he was still not ready to take root in his easy chair. He helped Henry Jones with his turgid tragedy, *The Earl of Essex*, and he wrote an epilogue for Hannah Pritchard to deliver at the opening of *Eugenia*.[82]

The death of Frederick, Prince of Wales, darkened the spring of 1752, although it carried none of the concerns that had fretted people earlier. The Hanover succession was assured, and the country already adored the handsome young man who would one day be George III. As an official of the court, Cibber observed the six-week mourning, but his private life underwent no radical change until Theo returned from Ireland, bringing with him his usual accoutrements of scandals, quarrels, and debts. It was difficult to ignore Theo when he dragged the Cibber name through every gutter in London and then pleaded loudly for help to get out of debtors' prison, but Colley managed it.

In November, Cibber's brother-in-law, John Shore, died. It had been many years since they had been close. A lasting break had occurred when John married his housekeeper, an act even Charlotte had regarded as mad, and Shore carried his anger to the grave. In his will he left to "Mr Colley Cibber, the poet Laureat and to each of his children still living," one shilling because of "their evil behavior towards me."[83] Not even Elizabeth, whose husband was bankrupt, was shown any favor.[84]

Whether because of Theo's troubles, Shore's will, or a new illness, Cibber did not exert himself for the Birthday Ode this year and used the same one he had in 1750. In truth, he could have used the same one every year for all that anyone listened to it or, this year, even bothered to read it. The beginning of 1753, however, was more auspicious, and the New Year's Ode had not only a lavish performance but a warm reception at court. As he bowed to the applause, he appeared as cheerful as ever, and if his gait was a bit slower, the gamblers at White's were still willing to bet he would live at least another two years.[85]

He saw little of distant friends during the cold winter days, but when the weather warmed, he wrote Richardson that "My female fry are all on tiptoe for their jaunt to North End, and will not let me rest, till I have settled the day and hour to your mind."[86] The visit on 3 June was a consummate success. Colley was so taken with Richardson's reading from *Sir Charles Grandison* that three days later he wrote again: "The delicious meal I made of Miss Byrom on Sunday last, has given me an Appetite for another Slice of her off from the Spit, before she is served up to the publick table; if about 5 aclock to morrow afternoon, will not be inconvenient, Mrs Brown [Catherine] & I will come, and nibble upon a bit more of her."[87] In spite of his laughter at the idea of the hero's masculine chastity, he now read and accepted the finished version completely, writing a lengthy encomium that, he said, was insufficient: "Yet since I was born I cannot say that in all my reading of ancients or moderns, I ever met with such variety of entertainment, so much goodness of heart, and so indefatigable a capacity to give proofs of it! Can any man be a good moral writer that does not take up his pen in the cause of virtue? I had rather have the fame that your amiable zeal for it deserves, than be preferred as a poet to a *Pope* or his *Homer*."[88]

He began to think of death, and he carefully wrote out his will, a simple statement, for he had no complicated holdings (see appendix 3). He thought often of the past, and this year he sent a copy of the Birthday Ode to the duke of Newcastle, with a note explaining that the memory of Pelham's many favors was fresh in his mind and that he had "only Poetical Coin to repay the Obligation." It was no better than his previous odes, but it was a gracious way to express his pleasure in the duke's friendship.

In October 1754 he lost the last of his old friends when Owen Swiney died, leaving his entire fortune to Peg Woffington. In the same month, the last of Cibber's feuds ended with the death of Henry Fielding. The shadow was creeping closer, but Colley was not yet ready to take its hand.

White's members still wagered on his longevity, and one bet came to a bizarre conclusion. On 4 November, Lord Mountfort bet Sir John Bland one hundred guineas that Beau Nash would outlive Cibber. The following summer, Bland, deeply in debt, left for France, where he died under mysterious circumstances. By the end of the year, Mountfort was also ruined by gambling, but on New Year's Eve, he was under no visible strain as he celebrated at White's. The next day he called his lawyer and made his will, then, having ascertained it was both legal and unbreakable, went into the library and shot himself.[89]

Cibber, who had been called wastrel, rake, inveterate gambler, and a hundred other less polite names, outlived them both, and as 1755 dawned, his days continued their calm succession. Theo's incessant quarrels were on the periphery of Colley's life, and the only other interruption this year, the return of Charlotte, touched him even less. As much a Londoner as her father, she came back to the city chastened by a life of poverty and failure. In dire need, she found a garret and began to write her memoirs. After the first installment appeared in print, she wrote her father a last, pleading letter, admitting her errors and begging for reconciliation.[90] It was returned to her enclosed in a blank sheet.

Only two explanations seem possible. Either Cibber held a private and unreasonable grudge against Charlotte, or the letter was rejected by Catherine before he saw it. Charlotte seemed to think the latter, for she incorporated the text into a subsequent installment of her memoirs, perhaps hoping he would read it there, but they never met again. Theo helped her for a while, but his company was soon forced to disband, and she went back to writing, producing two novels, *The History of Henry Dumont* (with an idealized father figure) and *The Lover's Treat*, in which an evil elder brother is clearly a male Catherine who meets a fate Charlotte may well have wished for her sister. Neither book has much worth, but they served to keep her alive until she could get back into the theater.

Cibber said nothing of his private feelings. He wrote his odes, saw them performed and pirated, called on friends, and visited White's with his sense of humor intact. Horace Walpole met him there one day and greeted him, "I am glad to see you look so well, sir."

"Egad, sir," the elegant old gentleman twinkled, "at eighty-four, it is well that I am able to look at all!"[91]

His eighty-fifth birthday passed and he began the last year of his life in good health. He knew he could not last forever, but he savored each day of the spring and the summer without distressing himself or others with worries about how many more he would have. If he had been so inclined, he could have reviewed his life with some smugness as autumn approached again. His belief in himself had been proved sound, and in this, the final season, he still had more plays on the London stage than any living playwright. Only Shakespeare, with plays adapted almost beyond recognition, could boast of more.

Death, when it came, on Sunday, 12 December 1757, was as gentle as the last years had been. According to Benjamin Victor, who was in London at the time, Cibber spoke to his manservant at six A.M. "in seeming good Health." Three hours later, the servant returned to find him dead, lying on his pillow exactly as he had last been seen.[92]

He was not buried in Westminster Abbey as other poets laureate have been, nor does he even have, like Shadwell, a memorial plaque there. Several versions of the actual burial site have been suggested, but according to the records of his own parish, he was buried in the churchyard of Grosvenor Chapel on South Audley Street.[93]

Colley Cibber's life stands as a paradigm of the actor's fate. While he was on the stage, his presence was vividly intense, but once he was gone, it vanished like the character when the curtain falls. As an actor he was brilliant, as a playwright he introduced a new mode of comedy, and as a manager he changed the course of the English theater. He believed his work would justify him in the eyes of posterity. He was wrong. The wickedly witty caricatures of Pope and Fielding have replaced the human being and little is left to refute them. The actor's art is ephemeral: the mask of the *Apology* became fixed in the *Dunciad*, his plays are rarely performed, and even the physical evidence of his existence is scarce. The records are meager, the house where he lived was demolished in 1938, and his very grave was destroyed during the bombings of World War II.

In an age that worshipped intellect and logic, Colley Cibber was an actor to the core, living by intuition and emotion. Playing his role, he was called a brazen, brainless coxcomb, but from behind the Foppington mask emerges a quite different person, one that was, as Dr. Johnson astutely perceived, "by no means a blockhead"[94] but a sensitive, creative artist who hated ugliness, pain, and violence, who was humble about his gifts but proud of the position he had earned. Cibber's part in moving drama from its place as a handmaiden of literature to that of an art in its own right has made him important in the history of the theater. Foppington was an impostor, but the man who created him was real, a pragmatic dreamer captivated by the illusion even as he operated the stage machinery.

Epilogue

WITHIN twenty-four hours, a new contest for the laurel had begun. Henry Jones, William Mason, John Lockman, and Samuel Boyce were mentioned, but there was no great battle as there had been at Cibber's appointment. Thomas Gray refused the honor, and in the end, William Whitehead had it. His poems were no better than Cibber's and considerably duller, but they were not attacked.

Catherine moved quickly to prove her father's will. She and Jenny had been named coexecutors along with Henry Furness (already deceased), and she undoubtedly saw that the bequests were scrupulously observed. Theo and the widowed Anne Boultby received £50 each, Elizabeth and Charlotte £5, Jenny and her sister, Betty, £1,000, and the rest went to Catherine, who presumably passed her share on to her own daughter. Cibber left no real estate, no great investments, but for all his giddiness, he had been careful, and his fortune was sizable.

On 12 January 1758, Catherine placed a notice in the *Public Advertiser*: "To be Lett, Elegantly Furnish'd, the House of the late Colley Cibber, esq.: in Berkley Square, the corner of Bruton Street." She lived to see her daughter marry "John Thomas, Esq ." on 4 June 1761[1] and died a few months after. Jenny married a William Ellis, but she died before 1762, possibly in childbirth.[2] Betty's future is not known.

In March, Theo, "in mourning for his Father," produced *The Insolvent; or Filial Piety* at the Haymarket, speaking a prologue that traded outrageously on Colley's name. Shortly after, he accepted an offer from Benjamin Victor and at the end of October left for Ireland in an old trader, the *Dublin*. A storm arose, the ship was wrecked, and all but a handful were lost. Weeks later, Theo's chest was washed up on the shores of Scotland and shipped to Victor, who was deeply affected by the sight of it. Theo's

180

life ended as it had begun, in a tempest. In marked contrast, Susannah Cibber, as every theater historian knows, remained a star at Drury Lane until her death in 1766, and she was buried in Westminster Abbey.

Nothing more is known of Anne Boultby's life, and of Elizabeth Marples only that she had started a restaurant in Fullwood's Rents. Her daughter, Anne Chetwood, appears once more. After the death of William Rufus in 1760, she wrote a pathetic letter, probably to Devonshire, then lord chamberlain, or to her grandfather's friend, Grafton. "May it please your Grace," she began:

I am an unfortunate grand daughter of the Late Colley Cibber whose unhapines was never to feell for the distress of his own family otherwise then by a Partill Judgement the flictions of his Children was greatly owing to his unfeelingnes my Mother My Lord never Commited She Could Say it on her Death Bed an Act of Disobedeince: to her and my Aunt Charke he Left but five pound Each to there Children nothing but the bulk of his fortune my Aunt Brown had and my uncle Theophilus Daughters had a thousand pound Each Worn down by Affliction and growing in years not brought up to Earn my Bread by Servile Business a wrong Judgement in Parents who flatters us with Hopes we never tast the old Nobility all dead who usd thro pity to Aleavate the Distresses of my family inforces me to plead to your pity in this hope that my Aunt Charke Shard in your Compassion I never and please your grace Intrested your Assistance before but as I am informed your Benevolence at this to be in the Number as my distress is great and all I am Capable to do is with my Needle and there is no imploy all Publick Charity, taking it in that Heaven with its Choisest Blessings may await you Shall ever be the fervent Wish and Prayer of your most Obeadent servant. Ana Cheetwood[3]

The "noble Lord's" answer is lost in time.

Charlotte's fate was less dramatic than her brother's. In March 1758, she played briefly at Canterbury but returned to London the following year for Bartholomew Fair. She requested permission from Devonshire to perform ten nights at the Haymarket before the season opened, since "an ill state of Health" prevented her from acting in the winter. This may have been the "Compassion" mentioned in Anne Chetwood's letter, for Devonshire granted the permission. Charlotte played to her last London audience on 28 September. Alone, ill, and penniless, she died 6 April 1760.

Her daughter, Kitty, had married the actor, John Harman, at Lymington in 1750.[4] After strolling for several more years, they went to America with Lewis Hallam's company in 1758 and Kitty stayed on with the company after her husband's death, which occurred about the same time as Charlotte's. Eventually she became their "comic old woman" and a much respected actress. When she died, 27 May 1773, *Rivington's Gazette* printed her obituary, the first for an actress in America.[5]

She is the last of Cibber's known descendants. The acting line stopped with Kitty, who had no children, and the other descendants have vanished into oblivion. Even in his family, Colley suffered the actor's fate—the play was over, the characters only "such stuff as dreams are made on."

Appendixes

The Genealogy of the Cibber Family

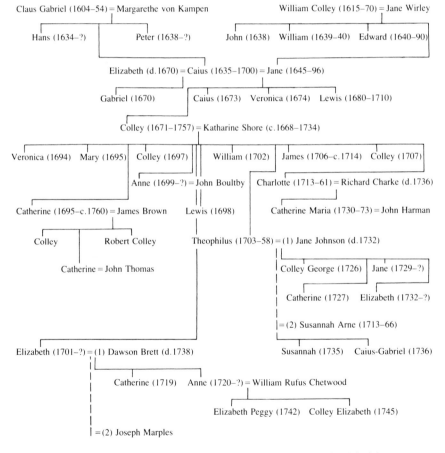

Note: Single date indicates birth and death in same year.

Colley Cibber's Second Letter
to Alexander Pope

Sir,

As our familiar Correspondence has hitherto been carried on, with very little Ceremony, I shall, without farther Preface, let you know, that there is lately come to my Hands an undoubted Copy of some new Lines, which in the next Edition of your *Dunciad*, now in the Press, you intend to Honour my name with. I take it for granted they were sent me by your own Direction, because I cannot imagine any other Person could be equally impatient to doe me that sort of Favour. Having therefore promis'd (in my late *Letter*) to have the last *Word* with you, I am willing, as fast as you place any thing to my Account, to ballance it, that our *short* Reckonings may continue us the same *long* Friends, we are like to be, for the rest of our Lives.—But to the Point? The Lines I have receiv'd are These:

"Close to those Walls, where Folly holds her Throne
"And laughs to think *Monroe* would take her down;
"Where o'er the Gates, by his fam'd Father's Hand,
"Great Cibber's brazen, brainless Brothers stand. &c.

Why, really, *Sir*, this facetious Thought of *brazen* and *brainless*, which you have been so frequently, and seem so immoderately fond of, is so little varied in the Dress, it used to appear in, that I am unwilling to be too serious upon it, lest, like yourself, I should be guilty of Repetition, and give an Instance of that Stupidity, which your *brazen Lines* have a mind to lead me with. However, to come as near your Compliment, as I can, and if possible to match it in Dulness, I will rather chuse to sport a nonsensical Pun with your intemperate Wit, than throw away my Reason upon its Frenzy. First then give me leave to observe, that these Figures, upon the Gates of *Bedlam*, do not *stand* but *lye*. Do you observe, *Sir*? I say they are

A Second Letter from Mr. Cibber to Mr. Pope. In Reply to Some Additional Verses in His Dunciad, Which He Has not yet Published. London. 1743. This letter has not previously been reprinted in its entirety.

no more *upright* than you are when you *stand*, or write; may they *lye* as flat, as you sometimes do when you *write*. Not that I insist upon this to be now the Case; for it is pretty plain that here (like Mr. *Bays*) you have chosen to write *standing*. You see, *Sir*, how low I am forced to sink, that I may be upon a Par with your Satire, by not seeming to undeserve it. Here you will, at least, allow that I do you justice. Nay I will yet do you more, and shew the World how ingeniously your learned Friend *Scriblerus* has illustrated the merry Merit of these Verses, in his Notes, viz.

"Ver. 30. *brazen—Brothers.*
"The Criticks have disputed, whether these Images were of Brass, or two Blocks; let this be decided according to the Person related to them is judg'd to have the greater share of Assurance or Stupidity."

Adod! Mr. *Pope*, I did not think your Friend had been such a Wit! why this is so very fine you might almost have wrote it yourself! What a miraculous Strength, and Power has he given to my Assurance, and Stupidity! How prettily has he insinuated, that Stone is Brass, or Brass is Stone, according as I am known to shine in either of those Qualities? What a *curiosa Felicitas* has he hit upon? But, dear Mr. *Pope*, not to be too serious with you, are you so sure, that any Man's calling me stupid is a Proof of my being so? Or, if a saucy Satyrist were to stile you an *Adonis* or a *Thyrsites*, would that either make you a handsome Creature, or an ill-natur'd one? Would not one Fact be a better Reproach than fifty bare confident Assertions? Or, to come a little closer to the Case, if in your passing the Street, an Oyster-woman, with a broad Laugh, should shew you the sign of an Owl, and a Monkey, and bawl out to you, look! look! Poet *Pope*! There's a Brace of your Brothers! Would there be any great Difference, between her Wit upon You, and yours upon Me? unless that, probably, You might be more hurt by the one, than I possibly might by the other?

And so, *Sir*, if these Verses, with the Note upon them, is a Specimen of that formidable Vengeance, I am to tremble at, for the insolent Dulness, and Stupidity of my late Letter to you, you are heartily welcome to go on with it. But unless you think it worth while to mend your Hand upon me, I am in doubt, whether I shall give you the Trouble of any farther Reply. In the mean Time, to get out of your Debt, as fast as I can, though my poetical Payments are not made in such golden Coin, as yours; yet, if you will accept of what *Brass* I am Master of, the following Sum is at your Service. *viz.*

> Still *brazen, brainless*! Still the same dull Chime!
> Is Impudence, in Prose, made Wit, by Rhime?
> No Wonder then, thou art so fam'd in Satire.
> Thou needst but rhime, and leave the Rest to Nature.
> Thy Nature be my Champion then—I have done!
> No Pen can worse betray thee, than thy own!
> On me, thy Wit's so worn, so void of Smart;
> I read, I yawn, and (by your leave) F——t.

From my easy Chair,   Colley Cibber
Feb. 13, 1742/3

APPENDIX THREE

Colley Cibber's Will

In the Name of God Amen. I Colley Cibber of the parish of Saint George Hanover Square in the County of Middlesex Esquire do make and ordain this my last Will and Testament in manner and form following (that is to say)—Imprimis I give and bequeath unto my Son Theophilus Cibber the Sum of fifty pounds and to my daughter Ann Boltby Widow the sum of fifty pounds. Now I give unto my daughter Elizabeth the Wife of Joseph Marples the Sum of five pounds and no more and to my Daughter Charlotte Chark Widow the like sum of five pounds and no more. Now I give and bequeath to my Grand-Daughter Jane Cibber the Sum of One Thousand Pounds and to my Grand-Daughter Elizabeth Cibber the like sum of One Thousand Pounds to be paid her at her age of twenty one years or Day of Marriage which shall first happen. Now all the Rest and Residue of my personal Estate whatsoever and wheresoever (having no Real Estate to dispose of) I give and bequeath unto my Daughter Catherine Brown Widow and Relict of the late Colonel James Brown deceased and I do institute and appoint my good friend Henry Furness of the parish of St. James Westminster in the County of Middlesex Esquire my said Daughter Catherine Brown and my said Grand-Daughter Jane Cibber Executor and Executrixes of this my last Will and Testament and I do hereby revoke all former and other Will and Wills by me at any time heretofore made and I declare this my last Will and Testament. In Witness whereof I the said Colly Cibber have hereunto set my Hand and Seal this twenty fourth Day of October in the twenty seventh Year of the Reign of our Sovereign Lord George the Second by the Grace of God of Great Britain France and Ireland King Defender of the Faith and so forth. And in the Year of our Lord One Thousand seven Hundred and fifty three—Colley Cibber—Signed

Colley Cibber

Signed sealed published and declared by the said Testator as and for his last Wil and Testament in the presence of us who at his Request and in his Presence of us and in the presence of each other have of our Names hereto as Witnesses.

Waldegrave—Robt. Bertie—Duncannon.

Cibber's will is in the Public Record Office, London.

Chronological List
of Cibber's Roles

(First appearances)

1690	Sir Anthony Love	Servant to Sir Gentle
	Alphonso, King of Naples	Sigismond
1691	Bussy D'Ambois	Pyorot
1692	The Marriage Hater Match'd	Splutter
	The Orphan	Chaplain
	The Rape	Albimer
	The Traytor	Pisano
1693	A Very Good Wife	Aminadab
1694	The Double Dealer	Lord Touchwood
	The Ambitious Slave	Amorin
	Don Quixote, I	Perez
	Don Quixote, II	Duke Ricardo
1695	The Old Batchelor	Fondlewife
	Agnes de Castro	Lorenzo
	Philaster	Pharamond
1696	Love's Last Shift	Sir Novelty Fashion
	The Lost Lover	Smyrna
	Pausanius	Artabazus
	The Female Wits	Praiseall
	The Relapse	Lord Foppington
	Aesop	Aesop
1697	Woman's Wit	Longville
	The Triumphs of Virtue	Antonio
	A Plot and No Plot	Bull, Jr.
	The Sham Lawyer	Careless
	Marriage a la Mode	Argaleon
	The Humourous Lieutenant	Demetrius
	The Imposture Defeated	Bonde
	The Scornful Lady	Sir Roger
1698	The Campaigners	Marqui Bertran
	Greenwich Park	Young Reveller

1699	King Lear	Gloster
	The Jovial Crew	Hilliard
	The Earl of Essex	Burleigh
	Richard III	Richard
1700	Venice Preserv'd	Renault
	The Grove	Parmenio
	The Pilgrim	Mad Englishman/Cook
	Volpone	Corvino & Volpone
	Love at a Loss	Cleon
	Love Makes a Man	Clodio
	Achilles	Ulysses & Calchas
	Epicoene	Sir John Daw
	All for Love	Alexas
1701	The Alchymist	Subtle
	The Bath	Crab
	Sir Harry Wildair	Monsieur Marquis
	The Rover	Frederick
	The Generous Conqueror	Malespine
	The Funeral	Lord Hardy
1702	The Modish Husband	Lord Promise
	Bartholomew Fair	Busy
	The Comical Rivals	Johnny
	She Wou'd and She Wou'd Not	Don Manuel
	The Twin Rivals	Young Wouldbe
	The False Friend	Don John
1703	The Old Mode and the New	Tom Pistole
	The Fair Example	Springlove
	Vertue Betray'd	Wolsey
	Sir Courtly Nice	Sir Courtly
	The Libertine Destroy'd	Antonio
1704	The Lying Lover	Latine
	Squire Trelooby	Wimble
	The Northern Lass	Howdee
	The Rehearsal	Volscius
	Henry IV, 1	Worcester
	The Careless Husband	Lord Foppington
1705	Oedipus	Tiresius/Phorbas
	Farewel Folly	Mimick
	The Quacks	Refugee
	Hampstead Heath	Lampoon
	Perolla and Izadora	Pacuvius
1706	Hamlet	Osric
	The Man of Mode	Sir Fopling Flutter
	King Arthur	Osmond
	The Recruiting Officer	Brazen
	The Gamester	Count Cogdie

	The Platonick Lady	Sharper
	The Tender Husband	Humphrey Gubbin
1707	*Marriage a la Mode*	Celadon
	Henry VIII	Surrey
	Caius Marius	Citizen
	The Beaux' Stratagem	Gibbet
	Julius Caesar	Plebeian
	The Double Gallant	Atall
	The Lady's Last Stake	Sir George Brilliant
1708	*Love for Love*	Ben
	Bury Fair	Trim
	The Fine Lady's Airs	Nick Nack
1709	*Henry IV, 1*	Glendower
	The Rival Fools	Samuel Simple
	Henry VIII	Cranmer
	Othello	Iago
	The Country Wife	Sparkish
	Love for Love	Tattle
	The Man's Bewitch'd	Manage
1710	*The Villain*	Villain
	The Rival Queans	Alexander
	Epsom Wells	Kick
1711	*Injur'd Love*	Captain Cruize
	The Wife's Relief	Riot
1712	*Ximena*	Don Alvarez
1713	*The Humours of the Army*	Major Outside
	Cato	Syphax
1714	*Jane Shore*	Gloster
1715	*Lady Jane Grey*	Bishop Gardiner
1716	*The Drummer*	Tinsel
	The Amorous Widow	Barnaby Brittle
	Henry VIII	Wolsey
1717	*Three Hours after Marriage*	Plotwell
	The Rehearsal	Bayes
	The Non-Juror	Dr. Wolf
1718	*The Way of the World*	Witwoud
	The Play Is the Plot	Peter Pirate
1719	*The Masquerade*	1st and 2d Figures
	Chit Chat	Alamode
	The Spartan Dame	Crites
1720	*The Committee*	Abel
	Love in a Tub	Dufoy
	Henry IV, 2	Shallow
	The Plain Dealer	Novel
1721	*The Refusal*	Witling
1722	*The Conscious Lovers*	Tom

1723	*Love in a Forest*	Jaques
	Humphrey, Duke of Gloucester	Beaufort
	The Fatal Constancy	Tryphon
1724	*Caesar in Aegypt*	Achoreus
1725	*The Twin Rivals*	Trueman
1726	*The Rival Modes*	Earl of Late-Airs
	The Provok'd Wife	Sir John Brute
1728	*The Provok'd Husband*	Wronghead
	Love in Several Masques	Rattle
1729	*Love in a Riddle*	Philautus
1730	*The Humours of Oxford*	Ape-all
	Sophonisba	Scipio
1732	*The Modish Couple*	Grinly
	The Modern Husband	Lord Richly
1745	*Papal Tyranny in the Reign of King John*	Cardinal Pandulph

Total number of documented performances: 2,936

Notes

Abbreviations

BL	British Library, London
C	Chancery Office, London
EAL	Early American Literature
EIC	Essays in Criticism
ECS	Eighteenth-Century Studies
HLQ	Huntington Library Quarterly
JAAC	Journal of Aesthetics and Art Criticism
JEGP	Journal of English and Germanic Philology
LC	Lord Chamberlain's Records, London
MLN	Modern Language Notes
MLR	Modern Language Review
MP	Modern Philology
MRO	Middlesex Record Office, London
NCTR	Nineteenth-Century Theatre Research
PCC	Prerogative Court of Chancery
PQ	Philological Quarterly
PRO	Public Record Office, London
RES	Review of English Studies
SAQ	South Atlantic Quarterly
SB	Studies in Bibliography
SN	Studia Neophilologica
SP	Studies in Philology
TN	Theatre Notebook
TS	Theatre Survey

CHAPTER ONE

1. Baptismal register, St. Giles-in-the-Fields, 20 November 1671. It was the custom to wait two or three weeks before baptizing a healthy child. Those not likely to live were christened immediately.

2. I am indebted to Mr. Hans-Friedrich Schütt, Archivdirektor of Flensburg, for information on the early history of the Gabriel family. For further details, see his article, "Claus Gabriel" in *Nordelbingen*, vol. 44/1975.

3. The crest was combined with that of the Colley family when Caius Gabriel handed it

on to his son. The Italian origin of the name "Cibber" seems evident in the pronunciation, for the first syllable was unquestionably a sibilant. In early records it is spelled Seber, Ceber, Sibber, and Zibbar.

4. The Stones were prominent artists. Nicholas Stone the elder studied with Hendrik de Keyser (Peter's father) and married Keyser's daughter before moving back to London. His statues of Elizabeth I, Edward VI, and Charles I are now in the Guildhall Museum, London. His oldest son, Henry, was a painter; his second, Nicholas, a sculptor. John, the youngest, took over the workshop after the deaths of his father and brothers.

5. Caius Gabriel did not get the commission, but the lord chamberlain's recommendation suggests his credentials were well established.

6. By this time, the guilds took in members from all trades but required a sizable fee, or "redemption," for admission.

7. Baptismal register, St. Giles-in-the-Fields, 29 September 1668. The burial record for Gabriel has not been found, but he is never mentioned again. The burial record for Elizabeth is in St. Giles-in-the-Fields, dated 18 July 1670. The record of Caius's marriage to Jane Colley is in St. Giles-in-the-Fields, dated 24 November 1670: "Caius Gabriel Cibber (widower), e.g. plinth of Charles I (statue, Charing Cross) married to Jane Colley at St. Giles by licence." The license gives added details: "Caius Gabriel, of St. Giles-in-the-Fields, sculptor, widower, about 33, and Mrs. Jane Colley, of Drury Lane, London, spinster, about 25, and at own disposal" (Joseph Foster, ed., *London Marriage Licenses, 1521-1869* [London, 1887]).

8. "The History of the Life, Manners and Writings of Aesopus the Tragedian," printed with *The Laureat; or, the Right Side of Colley Cibber, Esq.* (London, 1748), p. 99. "Aesopus" was supposed to be Cibber.

9. William of Wykeham (1324-1404) founded Winchester College and New College, Oxford. He was a monk, and the line was obviously the collateral one from his sister, Alice.

10. *The Victoria History of the Counties of England: Rutland*, ed. Archibald Constable (London, n.d.), II, 184.

11. Colley Cibber, *An Apology for the Life of Mr. Colley Cibber*, ed. R. W. Lowe (London, 1889), I, 9. All further references to the *Apology* are from this edition and page citations are in the text.

12. Information on both Caius Gabriel's and Jane's finances comes from the manuscript notebooks of George Vertue (1684-1756), engraver-antiquarian who collected material for a history of art and artists in England (BL, Add. ms. 23,067).

13. Ibid. Burial register, St. Giles-in-the-Fields, 11 August 1673: "Buried: Caius, son of Caius Ceber." The christening register, 14 May 1674: "Christened: Veronica, daughter of Caius Gabriel Cibber." Neither the baptism record of Caius nor the burial record of Veronica has been found, and it is possible that Caius Gabriel was in prison when these two events occurred.

14. The twenty-foot square relief on the base of the monument shows an allegory of the fire and the rebuilding of the City. For this, Caius Gabriel was paid £600, but he had an outstanding debt to Samuel Beake for that amount, which he had to settle, plus court costs (Harald Faber, *Caius Gabriel Cibber* [Oxford, 1926], p. 8).

15. In *The Life and Times of Colley Cibber* (London, 1928), p. 20, Dorothy Senior comments on Cibber's well-known slenderness at the beginning of his career, "Poor half-starved boy— no wonder he was lean! Food in the Cibber household cannot have been plentiful, with the head of the house always in debt and the eldest son not earning." In *Mr. Cibber of Drury Lane* (New York, 1939) Richard Hindry Barker suggests, "In his [Cibber's] autobiography he clearly expresses his contempt for his father—the contempt of the successful for the unsuccessful man—and this feeling may easily reflect the experiences of his early childhood" (p. 5).

16. Caius Gabriel could not have been in prison more than two or three years, and then probably not continuously. He was finally freed when Colley was about four. After 1675, he was steadily employed on commissions. The Leathersellers' agreement to accept his fountain on 6 May 1679, noting Caius Gabriel was "lately a prisoner" in King's Bench Prison (Faber, p. 21), indicates a past condition not necessarily recent.

17. Legend has it that Oliver Cromwell's porter, then an inmate of Bedlam, was the original model. Carved from Purbeck stone and painted black to preserve them from the elements, the statues quickly became admired landmarks in London. Pope and Wordsworth refer to

them, and Hogarth used them as models for Rakewell and the religious fanatic in the last scene of *The Rake's Progress*. The statues, stripped of their paint, are now at Bedlam Hospital, Eden Park.

18. In 1663, the church had been destroyed by lightning. It was rebuilt by 1672, and the fifth earl of Dorset added the Sackville Chapel, with the sculpture. The tomb is a baroque work in black and white marble with the recumbent figure of the earl's recently deceased son as the focus, his mourning parents kneeling on each side, and a relief of their other children around the pedestal. The fifth earl died before it was finished and was succeeded by his son, Lord Buckhurst, the Restoration poet and rake who introduced Nell Gwyn to Charles II and who would be lord chamberlain when Colley entered the theater.

19. Rate books, St. Margaret's, Westminster.

20. On holidays, it is said, the mermaid spouted wine, although how this was done was never explained, and the fountain itself has long since disappeared.

21. The fountain in Soho Square was later sealed off and the sculpture dismembered. The statue of Charles II stands in Soho Square today, but the river gods (Thames, Humber, Tyne, and Severn) that surrounded it went to Grimsdyke, Harrow Weald. On 7 May 1681, Cibber was paid £80 by Trinity College for carving the statues of Divinity, Law, Physics, and Mathematics, placed on the central piers at the east side of the roof (Faber, p. 40).

22. Faber, p. 20. His work here included statues of the Four Seasons, Two Senses, and Juno. Five of them still stand in the gardens at Belvoir.

23. Baptismal register, St. Margaret's, Westminster, 17 August 1680.

24. Probably Colley's holidays with his father were infrequent, for Caius Gabriel traveled so much that even Christopher Wren could not always find him. On 9 September 1682, Wren wanted "Cajus Cibber if I can find him" to carve the statues for Tom Tower at Oxford (Faber, p. 29). Evidently Wren could not locate him, for Cibber did not do them.

25. Lady Victoria Manners, "The Rutland Monuments in Bottesford Church," *Art Journal* (1903), 339. The complete letter is quoted in her article.

26. The reference to a broken leg appears in a lawsuit brought against Caius Gabriel. While working at Belvoir, he had boarded his workmen at an inn at Exton, paying their expenses by the week, as was the custom. Some time later, the innkeepers, dissatisfied with his settlement of the bill, sued him, claiming he had evaded their original charge made out to "Gabriel Cibber" by insisting his name was "Caius Gabriel." Cibber countersued and won, but the documents have been misread (see F. S. Tupper, "Colley and Caius Cibber," *MLN*, 55, 5 [1940Icb, 393-96), leading to the assumption that a son Gabriel was involved. The documents pertaining to the suit are in the Public Record Office, C 6/277/24.

27. Dorothy Senior notes, "Throughout his life it is plain that Cibber had not been dowered at birth with the gift of Friendship" (p. 4). R. H. Barker remarks, "At Grantham, as at Drury Lane in later days, Colley was generally unpopular" (p. 6). Even the more favorable biography by Leonard Ashley, *Colley Cibber* (New York, 1965) says, "Cibber almost deliberately made himself unpopular" (p. 18).

28. In the *Apology*, I, 68, Cibber refers to "being well known in Lord *Devonshire's* Family" when he was serving in the earl's regiment. Since he joined up after the regiment had left Chatsworth, he could only have become familiar through previous visits.

29. Faber, p. 49. Caius Gabriel was at Chatsworth c. 1687-90. He designed the chapel and carved the figures of Faith and Justice beside the altar, a Lucrece and an Apollo for the Grand Staircase, and for the garden, two sphinxes, a Flora, and the great Neptune Fountain, which still works.

30. The warden of New College and two Fellows, along with the master of Winchester and two of his Fellows, formed the "Chamber" of examiners. Originally, Winchester scholars were expected to go into the church, and the founder's rules required all entrants to be able to perform plainsong. Aside from this, the most important requirement was the recommendation of an influential patron. Not until the nineteenth century was a system of merit established for entrance to the college.

31. In *Dramatic Miscellanies* (London, 1784) Thomas Davies says: "Cibber and Verbruggen were two dissipated young fellows, who determined, in opposition to the advice of friends, to become great actors. Much about the same time, they were constant attendants upon Downs [*sic*], the prompter of Drury-lane, in expectation of employment" (III, 217).

32. Davies, *Miscellanies*, I, 58.

33. Charles Gildon, *The Life of Mr. Thomas Betterton* (London, 1710), pp. 43-55. Gildon says Betterton showed him a sheaf of papers in which he had written his advice to young actors. Since Gildon's biography of Betterton devotes a great amount of space to this subject, I am assuming the advice was taken from Betterton's notes.

34. Cibber played Sigismund in George Powell's *Alphonse, King of Naples*, and Pyorot in Durfey's version of *Bussy D'Amboys*. Neither is an important role.

35. Cibber says he went three-quarters of a year before he was paid. This fits the date of *King Arthur*. The opera has a large cast and probably utilized the entire company.

36. Davies, *Miscellanies*, III, 444.

37. Caius Gabriel was at Hampton Court until 1696. His main work here was the "Triumph of Hercules over Envy" on the East Pediment, with William III as Hercules and Louis XIV, Envy. He also carved the "Boy with Bagpipes" (now at the Victoria and Albert Museum), two great flower pots, and two coats of arms and created several figures in metal. See Peter Cunningham, "New Materials for the Life of Caius Gabriel Cibber," *Builder*, 22 November 1862, pp. 835-36.

38. Players were not paid when the theater was dark (e.g. Lent, summer, and royal mourning). Some had salaries large enough to extend over Lent and the long vacation of summer; others had sidelines. The young players who had neither were sometimes allowed to play two days a week (except for Passion Week) during Lent, and usually several times during the summer.

39. Betterton had invested his life savings in a shipping venture which was lost at sea in 1692. At Drury Lane, Sir William Davenant's son, Alexander, was the patentee and had taken over the management some time earlier, although his knowledge of theatrical affairs was minimal. In constant need of money, he even borrowed from his actors, attempting to recoup his losses with lavish productions that seldom showed a profit.

40. Barker states unequivocally, "In the first place it can safely be said that he [Cibber] was not the sort of person to endear himself to his immediate associates at Drury Lane. He was a snob and a social climber" (p. 121).

41. Charlotte Charke, *A Narrative of the Life of Mrs. Charlotte Charke* (London, 1755), p. 80. Charlotte was born in 1713 and says her mother was forty-five at the time. This would make Katharine about twenty-five at the time of her marriage to Colley, who was then twenty-one.

42. For details of the story of Mountfort's death, see Albert S. Borgman, *The Life and Death of William Mountfort* (Cambridge, Mass., 1935).

43. Cibber played the small part of Splutter in *The Marriage Hater Match'd*. Dogget's Solon was so popular that, for some time after, he was nicknamed "Solon." For details on Dogget's life, see *A Biographical Dictionary of Actors, Actresses, Musicians, Dancers, Managers, and Other Stage Personnel in London, 1660-1800*, ed. Philip H. Highfill, Jr., Kalman A. Burnim, and Edward A.Langhans (Carbondale, Ill., 1973-), s.v. "Doggett, Thomas" (hereafter cited as *Biographical Dictionary*). 10 vols. to date.

44. *Notes and Queries*, 11th ser. 4 (July-December, 1911), 366.

45. Shore's barge was built long before the marriage, and Narcissus Luttrell describes it as more like a business venture than a spiteful revenge on his daughter. On 2 May 1693, he writes, "The queen went lately on board of Mr Shores pleasure boat against Whitehall, and heard a consort of musick, vocall and instrumentall; it was built for entertainment, having 24 sash windows, and 4 banquetting houses on top" (Luttrell, *A Brief Historical Relation of State Affairs from September 1678 to 1714* [Oxford, 1857], II, 88; quoted in *The London Stage, 1660-1800*, ed. Van Lennep et al. [Carbondale, Ill., 1960], I, 421). Moreover, Matthias Shore paid taxes on at least three houses in St. Martin's parish, and, since the young Cibbers are not listed in the rate books, they may have lodged in one of them.

46. On 30 May 1693, by warrant of his former patron, the duke of Dorset, now lord chamberlain, Caius Gabriel Cibber was "sworn and admitted upon ye decease of Peter Bennier [Besnier] unto the place of Sculptor in Ordinary to His Majesty" (Faber, p. 12).

47. There has been some confusion of identity here. The original Sir Thomas Skipwith died on 2 June 1694, six months after Davenant absconded. His son, also Sir Thomas and also a barrister, inherited the shares and was active in the management.

48. There is a discrepancy about the date of the performance in the *Apology*, and possibly

Cibber's memory faltered. The parish record shows that he was, as he says, married "before I was Two-and-Twenty," on 6 May 1693, but the premiere of *The Double Dealer* was in October of that year, and Cibber probably did not replace Kynaston until January 1694, the month his daughter Veronica was born. He may have confused the performance, relating it to his marriage instead of the birth of a child who did not live.

49. Baptismal register, St. Martin's-in-the-Fields, "Veronica," born and christened 18 January 1694.

50. Cibber added only three relatively small roles in 1693-94: Amorin in *The Ambitious Slave*, Perez in *Don Quixote*, Part I, and Duke Ricardo in *Don Quixote*, Part II.

51. "After-money" was the half-price charged those who came to see only the latter part of the play. By 1694, it was common practice at Drury Lane and brought in £700 to £800 a year.

52. PRO, LC 7/3.ff.2-3 lists fifteen separate complaints against the management. The petition for redress was signed by all the leading actors except George Powell.

53. Baptismal register, St. Martin's-in-the-Fields, "Mary," born and christened 14 January 1695.

54. Verbruggen and Susannah Mountfort were married early in 1694, after which his roles improved noticeably. Cibber says Betterton erred in not taking them (particularly Susannah) with him to Lincoln's Inn Fields. Certainly she was one of the few skilled players left at Drury Lane.

55. Betterton wrote at least four plays as well as several adaptations and an opera, *The Prophetess*, with Dryden; Mountfort wrote at least five, including the popular *Greenwich Park*; and Powell wrote seven, most of which had leading roles for himself.

56. Colley Cibber, *Three Sentimental Comedies*, ed. Maureen Sullivan (New Haven, 1973), contains *Love's Last Shift*, *The Careless Husband*, and *The Lady's Last Stake*. Her introduction gives valuable insight on the background and concepts of the plays as well as thoughtful analyses of the texts.

57. Louis Kronenberger, in *The Thread of Laughter* (New York, 1952), reflects a common twentieth-century reaction: "We may hope that Cibber had the grace to smile, if not blush, when he wrote those words, for in their conscienceless pandering they are surely among the most indecent ever written" (p. 149). In context it is clear Cibber is teasing the debased tastes of the beaux in the pit.

58. See John Harrington Smith, *The Gay Couple in Restoration Comedy* (Cambridge, Mass., 1948), pp. 168-70, for a lucid interpretation of Loveless's reformation and the reasons for it. Other examinations of the play are Helga Drougge, "Colley Cibber's 'Genteel Comedy': *Love's Last Shift* and *The Careless Husband*," *Studia Neophilologica*, 54,1 (1982), 61-79; B. R. S. Fone, "*Love's Last Shift* and Sentimental Comedy," *Restoratione and Eighteenth-Century Theatre Research*, 9,1 (1976), 11-23; and Shirley Strum Kenny, "Humane Comedy," *Modern Philology*, 75,1 [1977], 29-43.

59. Davies, *Miscellanies*, III, 412. *Love's Last Shift* was translated into French as *La dernière ressource de l'amour*, but a thorough search of the Bibliothèque Nationale and the Bibliothèque de l'Arsenal failed to locate it under the title, as some would have it, *La dernière chemise de l'amour*.

60. Alan Roper states, "Cibber can invent an action to show that the laws of matrimony are dictated by reason. What he cannot do is invent a language which is at once entertaining and demonstrative that reason teaches the happiness of a virtuous marriage. Instead he offers two languages, one for wit, one for morality, and provides neither for their reconciliation, nor their interesting conflict" ("Language and Action in *The Way of the World*, *Love's Last Shift*, and *The Relapse*," *ELH*, 40,1 [1973], 49).

61. Critics of the eighteenth and nineteenth centuries were generally favorable. *Biographia Dramatica* ed. David Erskine Baker (London, 1812) considered the only improbability was in Loveless's failure to recognize his own wife after ten years of marriage but conceded that it was "made ample amends for by the beauty of the incident, and the admirable moral deduced from it" (p. 203). Twentieth-century critics, insisting on an interpretation that disallows any hope of reform, sound like Victorian moralists. F. W. Bateson, *English Comic Drama, 1700-1750* (Oxford, 1929): "the difficulty is not so much the wretchedness of the writing as the psychological *volte-face*. There was nothing in what preceded to prepare us for Loveless' conversion;

there is nothing in what follows to justify it" (p. 22); Allardyce Nicoll, *British Drama* (London, 1932): "Nothing shows better the hypocritical veneer which spreads over the age" (p. 281); Paul E. Parnell, "Equivocation in Cibber's 'Love's Last Shift,'" *SP*, 47 (1968), says Cibber is "the most suave and devious of literary entrepreneurs, striving continually and successfully to please two antipathetic audience groups, always seeming to commit himself to one viewpoint, while never antagonizing the other" because "a passionately defended viewpoint causes disagreement, and possibly hurts sales; and Cibber is primarily dedicated to the pursuit of success" (p. 533); Alan Roper adds that *Love's Last Shift* is "psychologically false, morally dishonest, and aesthetially whole only in the skillfulness of its plotting" (p. 69). None of these views considers the context of the times or that the twenty-four-year-old actor was honestly trying to amuse an audience in a manner consistent with both morality and theater.

62. 10 December 1695, Baptismal register, St. Clement Dane's. Since there are variant ways of spelling the name, for purposes of clarity I have consistently referred to Cibber's wife as "Katharine" and to his daughter as "Catherine."

CHAPTER TWO

1. After finishing at Hampton Court, Caius Gabriel never left London again. Besides the works mentioned in the text, he worked for Wren on St. Paul's Cathedral, carving the Phoenix on the East Pediment and the keystones for the eighty-foot central arches—after they were in place. Matthias Shore's will, dated 5 March 1695/6, left a few minor bequests to friends, the remainder of his sizable estate to his wife with the provision that after her death it would be divided equally between his three children, William, Katharine, and John (PRO [98] 1700.80; PCC, p. 372). The reference to his daughter as "Katharine Shore" was probably for legal clarity and not, as Barker has it (p. 18), evidence of Matthias's continued hostility to the marriage.

2. Goodman was implicated in the Fenwick plot to kill William III but was given £500 to disappear and not testify. He went to France and is thought to have died there.

3. "Could he, when he was an arrant Boy, draw a good Comedy, from his own raw uncultivated Head?" (John Dennis, *Critical Works*, ed. Edward Niles Hooker [Baltimore, 1939-43], I, 408).

4. Colley Cibber, *Love's Last Shift; or, the Fool in Fashion* (London, 1696). Cibber's friend Richard Norton (1666-1732) lived at Arlebury House, Hants, and was a member of Parliament from Andover in 1698. Davies, *Miscellanies*, says he was so fond of the stage that he was "accused of turning his chapel into a theater" (II, 210). He wrote one tragedy, *Pausanius*, which failed in 1696.

5. On 18 May 1696, Horden was killed in a senseless tavern brawl by a Captain Burgess, who had already been convicted of killing a man the previous year. In November, Burgess was pardoned (*The London Stage*, I, 462). The death of the handsome young actor caused great grief among the ladies, several of whom came in their coaches "to visit him in his Shrowd" (Thomas Whincop, *Scanderbeg* (London, 1747), pp. 249-50).

6. In the preface to *Woman's Wit; or, the Lady in Fashion* (London, 1696), Cibber says, "during the time of my writing the two first acts I was entertained in the New Theatre." The change of theater may have been only an experiment, for no documents indicate he had been given permission, and he appeared in none of the new company's plays.

7. Sir John Vanbrugh, *The Relapse*, ed. Curt Zimansky, Regents Restoration Drama Series (Lincoln, Nebraska, 1970), p. 39.

8. J. Woodstock offered to design it, but the elders chose Caius Gabriel, who did it for no payment. It was noteworthy for the reredos figures carved in wood. Most of the cost was paid by Christian V of Denmark, but Princess Anne's husband, Prince George, also contributed. Caius Gabriel sent the king a copper engraving of the church, signed "C. Gabriel Cibber, Flensborg, Architectus." Harald Faber, *Caius Gabriel Cibber* (Oxford, 1926), p. 53. The church was destroyed in 1896.

9. Vanbrugh's play was taken from Boursault's *Esop à la ville* but was much altered and included a contemporary gossip item about Beau Nash, whose generosity in giving up his fiancée to a rival parallels Aesop's actions. See Willard Connelly, *Beau Nash* (London, 1955), pp. 16-17.

10. Cibber was to have all the receipts of the third night (minus the house charges of £40); if the fourth night brought £55 or more, the charges would be refunded, and if the fourth and fifth nights brought more than £40 each, he would receive everything over that figure in a sixth-night benefit. If they were less, he was to make up the difference (PRO, LC 7/3). 29 October 1696.

11. Dogget had come over to Drury Lane this year, but he did not stay permanently.

12. Colley Cibber, *Woman's Wit; or, The Lady in Fashion* (London, 1697).

13. The situation foreshadows Dr. Wolf in *The Non-Juror* and indicates that Cibber's anti-Catholicism was already well developed in 1697.

14. Baptismal register, St. Martin's-in-the-Fields, "Colley," born 8 May, christened 23 May 1697. There is no burial record, but it is obvious the child did not live.

15. The marble monument bore the Cibber and Colley coats of arms, and the inscription read: "Jana uxor Caji Gabrielis Cibber olim Frederici III Regis Daniae & Norvetiae &c. postea Caroli II & nunc demum Gulielmi III Regum Magnae Britanniae &c. statuarii."

16. The gift was announced in the *Post-Boy*, 24-27 July 1697. The bronze statue, relieved with touches of gold, has a Latin inscription signed by "Caius Cibberus Statuarius Regius MDCLXXXXVII." It still presides over the courtyard and was undoubtedly the reason Lewis was admitted to the school. According to Thomas F. Kirby, *Annals of Winchester College* (London, 1892), Lewis entered the college from "St. Margaret's, London" (p. 214).

17. Undated petition, PRO, LC 7/3. A recognizance was filed on 6 October 1697 [MJ/SR(W), No. 113] registered on the calendar of recognizances [WSP/1697/Oct/1], but no indictment or record of further proceedings has been found. As one of Drury Lane's ten major actors, Cibber was now a member of the royal household, one of the "Gentlemen of the Great Chamber," and under the lord chamberlain's protection.

18. Jane Lucas came to Drury Lane in 1693, usually playing lower-class types in comedies. She never charged Cibber again, and after 1702, she disappeared from the London stage.

19. Jeremy Collier, *A Short View of the Immorality and Profaneness of the English Stage* (London, 1698), p. 214.

20. Cited in *The London Stage* I, 495. Davenant was stabbed to death on 18 May near his home in Gray's Inn Lane. Two Dutch sailors were arrested for the crime, but they were acquitted, and the real murderers were never caught (*Flying Post*, 21-23 July 1698).

21. Baptismal register, St. Martin's-in-the-Fields, "Lewis," born 28 March, christened 17 April 1698.

22. Colley Cibber, *Xerxes* (London, 1699) prologue.

23. Ibid.

24. Ibid. Act V, iii.

25. The satirical "Inventory" of Drury Lane's properties in the *Tatler*, 16 June 1709, lists "The Imperial Robes of *Xerxes*, never worn but once."

26. Like *Woman's Wit*, *Xerxes* was not included in *Plays by Mr. Cibber* (1721). Both were issued in the 1736 edition, but Cibber probably had nothing to do with it.

27. Hazelton Spencer's *Shakespeare Improved* (Cambridge, 1927), setting Cibber's version beside Shakespeare's, is a malicious attack on Cibber. A more favorable comparison given in an unpublished dissertation by William Cleveland (1911) is in the Bodleian Library, and a brief commentary is in Christopher Spencer's introduction to *Five Restoration Adaptations of Shakespeare* (Urbana, Ill., 1965).

28. Contemporary or slightly earlier redrafts of Shakespeare are *Troilus and Cressida* (Dryden); *The Tempest* (Dryden and Davenant); *King Lear* (Dryden and Nahum Tate); Davenant's *Macbeth*, *Much Ado about Nothing*, and *Measure for Measure* (also adapted by Charles Gildon); *Romeo and Juliet* (both James Howard and Otway); Thomas Shadwell's *Coriolanus* and *Timon of Athens*; *Cymbeline* (Thomas Durfey); *Midsummer Night's Dream* (Elkanah Settle's *The Fairy Queen*); *Sauny the Scot* (Charles Lacy's *Taming of the Shrew*); *Henry VI* (John Crowne); and *Henry IV* (Betterton). If Cibber needed specific precedent, Tate had already revised *Richard III* into *The Tyrant of Sicily*, set in Renaissance Italy. For other listings, see Albert E. Kalson, "Eighteenth-Century Editions of Colley Cibber's *Richard III*," *Restoration and Eighteenth-Century Theatre Research*, 7,1 (1968), 7-17.

29. Cibber's *Richard III* has been incessantly compared with Shakespeare's by later scholars. A brief list of comments includes Francis Gentleman's introduction to Bell's *British Theatre*

(London, 1773); John Genest, *Some Account of the English Stage from the Restoration in 1660 to 1830* (Bath, 1832), II, 195-219; William Jaggard, "Imitations of Shakespeare," *Notes and Queries*, 173 (20 November 1937), 370-73. R. H. Barker's view is based primarily on the hostile *Laureat*; Albert E. Kalson, "Colley Cibber Plays *Richard III*," *Theatre Survey*, 16,1 (1975), 42-55, attacks Cibber's interpretation, citing the same sources as Barker, and contains a number of errors; Leonard Ashley's analysis in *Colley Cibber* (1965), notes its weaknesses but pronounces it "brilliantly stageworthy" (p. 48).

30. Baptismal register, St. Martin's-in-the-Fields, "Anna" [sic], born 8 October, christened 15 October 1699.

31. Wilks is not listed in *The London Stage*, but Cibber (*Apology*), Victor (*The History of the Theatres of London and Dublin*, London, 1761-77), Davies (*Miscellanies*), and John Doran *Their Majesties' Servants* (New York, n.d.), 3 vols. agree that he was at Drury Lane c. 1692-93. He married Elizabeth Knapton, whom he met at dancing class, and she went with him to Ireland in 1694. His return to London in 1699 was the beginning of a long and extremely successful career.

32. See Arthur Colby Sprague, "A New Scene in Colley Cibber's *Richard III*," *Modern Language Notes*, 42,1 (1927), 29-32.

33. Cibber was an inveterate gambler but probably did not gamble to excess. He was never in debtor's prison, and there is no support for his enemies' claim that he neglected his family's welfare.

34. Anne Mason, countess of Macclesfield, was married at fifteen. The marriage was unhappy on both sides, and she was sent back home by her husband within the year. In 1698, the earl filed for a divorce, charging she was unfaithful with the Earl Rivers, by whom she had three children, but Macclesfield's behavior was considered so improper that Anne was looked upon with sympathy. She was awarded her entire dowry and became a lady-in-waiting to Princess Anne.

35. The role is listed merely as "Cook" in Fletcher's play, but Cibber probably added the stammer to differentiate between the two roles he was playing, and it was listed as "Stuttering Cook" in subsequent productions throughout the century.

36. According to a notation on Matthias Shore's will [PROB 11/455 1177], he died on 27 May 1700. His son William was immediately appointed to his place as sergeant trumpeter.

37. Vertue says Caius Gabriel was "always poor but a gentleman." There were at least two portraits of him. One, a miniature by Marcellus Laroon, shows him holding a small medallion and was owned by Colley (Vertue, BL, Add. MS 23,072.f.93 and 23,069.f.63). The other, a watercolor by Christian Richter, was eventually owned by Horace Walpole and was sold at Strawberry Hill for 30 shillings. It was engraved on copper by A. Bannerman and shows the artist holding a pair of compasses. The original seems to have disappeared.

38. 24 June 1700 (*Flying Post*, 24-27 June 1700).

39. T. F. Kirby, *Winchester Scholars* (London, 1888), p. 204. Lewis received his B.A. in 1704 and shortly afterward was ordained by Dr. Compton, bishop of London. He stayed on at Oxford, took an M.A. in 1707, and became a Fellow of New College.

40. For comment on Cibber's treatment of this type, see Richard E. Brown, "The Fops in Cibber's Comedies," *Essays in Literature*,9,1 (1982), 31-41, and Lois Brown, "Colley Cibber: The Fop as Hero," in *Augustan Worlds*, ed. J. C. Hilson, M. M. B. Jones, and J. R. Watson (New York, 1978), 153-64.

41. Pope refers to this scene in the *Dunciad*, III, *The Poems of Alexander Pope*, ed. John Butt (London, 1963) 367-68: "And idle Cibber, how he breaks the laws, / To make poor Pinky eat with vast applause."

42. For a detailed analysis of the Collier battle, see Sr. Rose Anthony, *The Collier Controversy* (Milwaukee, 1937).

43. Colley Cibber, *Love Makes a Man* (London, 1701), dedication.

44. Colley Cibber, *Ximena; or, the Heroick Daughter* (London, 1719), preface.

45. Baptismal register, St. Paul's, Covent Garden, "Elizabeth," christened 16 March 1701. The church was known as the "actors' church."

46. Abbé Jean Leblanc, *Letters on the English and French Nations* (London, 1747) says Cibber told him he "made two journies to Paris, on purpose to study their airs, and assume their character, at tables in public houses of entertainment. . . . if he did not imitate them so well,

as the English imagin'd he did, I am not surpris'd: for he ingenuously acknowledg'd to me, he did not know enough of our language to hold a conversation" (II, 41).

47. Charles Killigrew, master of the Revels, was the son of Sir William Killigrew who had held one of the two theatre patents issued by Charles II. When Killigrew's company merged with Davenant's in 1682, both patents were valid, and complicated bookkeeping was required to give the shareholders their due. Killigrew sued Alexander Davenant, and later Christopher Rich, claiming they had cheated him.

48. Baptismal register, St. Martin's-in-the-Fields, "William," born 6 August 1702, christened 1 October. The long delay suggests that he may have been born at the Bretts' home in Gloucestershire. The child did not live long.

49. Barker (p. 34) says Cibber turned to adaptation because of Collier's attacks and the failure of *Woman's Wit* and *Xerxes*, but it seems more likely that Cibber freely chose this path, since, as a working actor with limited time for writing, he would find it easier and faster to adapt works from Drury Lane's large stock of old plays than to create new ones from whole cloth.

50. The play had a long life and was still popular in the late nineteenth century when Ada Rehan played Hypolita in Dion Boucicault's version.

51. Advertised for 24 October 1702 but deferred, the first recorded performance is on 30 April 1703, after which *The School Boy* played frequently, becoming one of the most popular afterpieces of the century. Cibber did not publish it until 1707.

52. *Daily Courant*, 21 January 1703.

53. On 24 February 1703, Vice Chamberlain Stanley requested Rich to come to his office and go over the complaints, but nothing was done about them.

54. *The Rival Quaens* is not listed in *The London Stage*, but it may have had a special performance in 1703, for it is mentioned in the third dialogue of the anonymous *Visits from the Shades* (1704). It was apparently not performed again until 1710, and Cibber did not publish it. The first edition was printed in Dublin (1729).

55. Baptismal register, St. Martin's-in-the-Fields, "Theophilus," born 25 November 1703, christened 19 December.

56. Joseph Spence, *Observations, Anecdotes, and Characters of Books and Men*, ed. James Osborne, 2 vols. (Oxford, 1966), has two stories of Lewis's wildness. In one, Dr. Burton supposedly found a melancholy Lewis sitting in the Common Room, calling himself "a sad dog—guilty of every sin except murder." "'Why thou has been a very wicked fellow indeed,' said Dr. Burton. 'Why, yes,' Lewis answered, 'though there is one more I have not been guilty of, and that is covetousness. Prithee, Sim, do lend me a guinea—and I'll try to be guilty of that, too.'" (I, 901).

57. Colley Cibber, *The Careless Husband*, in *Three Sentimental Comedies*, ed. Maureen Sullivan, p. 156. Both this edition and that of William W. Appleton (Regents Restoration Drama Series, 1966) contain excellent introductions to the play. All page references are to the Sullivan edition.

58. Several twentieth-century critics, disregarding the historical framework and judging by their own contemporary standards, have been strongly skeptical of the characters' motivations. See Ernest Bernbaum, *The Drama of Sensibility* (Cambridge, Mass., 1925); Allardyce Nicoll, *A History of Early Eighteenty-Century Drama* (Cambridge, 1925); Ashley Thorndyke, *English Comedy* (New York, 1929); Paul Parnell, "The Sentimental Mask," *PMLA* 77 (December 1963), 529-35; Ben R. Schneider, *The Ethos of Restoration Comedy*, (Chicago, 1971). More recently, however, Maureen Sullivan's introduction to *Three Sentimental Comedies* points out the strong moral commitment exemplified in the scene and in the play. See also Helga Drougge, "Colley Cibber's 'Genteel Comedy': *Love's Last Shift* and *The Careless Husband*," *Studia Neophilologica*, 54,1 (1982), 61-79.

59. According to a manuscript note in Robert Bolling's *A Collection of Diverting Anecdotes, Bons Mots and other Trifling Pieces*, dated 1764 (Huntington Library, San Marino, California, BR 163, V. 9, I, i, 34-36), a story that the play was writen by the earl of Granville, Lord Orrery, and a Colonel Byrd was current in the colonies at that time, indicating the longevity of such rumors.

60. Baptismal register, St. Martin's-in-the-Fields, "James," born 25 July 1706, christened 7 August.

61. Groves, *Dictionary of Music and Musicians*, S.V. "Swiney, Owen." Groves, who once owned the letter, quotes several very friendly terms used by Swiney to Cibber.

62. *The London Stage*, II, 136.

63. See Marilyn Klawiter, "A Third Source for Cibber's *The Comical Lovers*," *Notes and Queries*, 22, 11 (1975), 488-89.

64. Cibber created the role of Gibbet in this play. Farquhar's friend Wilks undertook the care of the playwright's children.

65. A lawsuit deriving from William Shore's will names him, "James, a blind child."

66. Baptismal register, St. Martin's-in-the-Fields, "Colley," born 29 October 1707, christened 25 November. The child did not live.

67. Colley Cibber, *The Double Gallant* (London, 1707). For further remarks on the text, see John W. Bruton, "The Text of Colley Cibber's *The Double Gallant; or The Sick Lady's Cure*, *Studies in Bibliography*, 30 (1977), 186-96.

68. Susannah Centlivre's *Love at a Venture* was taken from Thomas Corneille's *Le galant double*, but while Cibber used elements of her adaptation, he took nothing more than the title from the French. The rest of the plot was filled out from Burnaby's *The Ladies' Visiting Day*. For an analysis of the sources, see F. W. Bateson, "*The Double Gallant* of Colley Cibber," *Review of English Studies*, 1,3 (1925), 343-46.

69. Colley Cibber, *The Lady's Last Stake* (London, 1708). All quotations are from this edition.

70. Davies, *Miscellanies*, III, 432.

71. Maureen Sullivan traces the traditions of this play in her introduction to *Three Sentimental Comedies* and gives a good background for reading.

72. Whincop, p. 195, says it "had very bad Success indeed. I remember there was something in it very ridiculous, of a Man's coming on the Stage with a long Angling-rod going to fish for *Miller's Thumbs*, which made the Audience afterwards, frequently, when the Author appeared, call out *Miller's Thumbs*." Cibber's character spoke the lines.

73. Sir Thomas Skipwith died this year, and some months afterward, Brett turned over his shares to his son, Charles Skipwith, who took no hand in the management at all.

74. The role of Subtle in *The Alchemist* was one of Cibber's most popular characters, and the piece of business he created for it sheds some light on his stage presence. While handling the urinal on the alchemy table, he accidentally dropped it. He did not lose character, but stood and stared at the pieces "with such an air of comic dismay" that the audience burst into laughter and applause. He tried to omit the piece of stage business afterward, but the audience insisted on its being repeated, and it became part of the tradition (Thomas Wilkes [Samuel Derrick], *A General View of the Stage* [London, 1759], pp. 257-59).

75. PRO, LC 7/3.

CHAPTER THREE

1. *Female Tatler*, 16-19 September 1709. The article was anonymous.

2. Dogget's rules called for the managers to meet weekly and settle all bills before the profits were shared and for all expenditures to be entered in the account book and kept by the treasurer. All three had to consent to hiring, firing, changes in actors' salaries, and the selection of new plays. Managers were to take turns overseeing the house (at least one to be in the audience every night), and each was to take six apprentices. All holdings (scenery, costumes, etc.) were to be appraised, and if a manager left the company he would be paid for his share; if he died, his property went to the theater (BL, Add. MS. 38,607.ff.30-31).

3. Zachary Baggs's statement lists Betterton's salary as £638.15.05, Wilks's as £299.01.05, and Cibber's as £212.10.10 (reprinted in Percy Fitzgerald, *A New History of the English Stage* [London, 1882], I, 167-69).

4. Hill put his brother, who knew nothing of the theater, in charge. After many quarrels, he locked the actors out of the theater, but they broke in and attacked him. Hill protested, and the lord chamberlain issued a second silencing order.

5. Susannah Centlivre, *The Man's Bewitch'd; or, The Devil to Pay* (London, 1710), preface.

6. Cibber's plays in the repertory this year were *Love Makes a Man*, *Love's Last Shift*, *The Comical Lover*, *The Careless Husband*, and *The School Boy*. *Richard III*, *The Double Gallant*, and *She*

Wou'd and She Wou'd Not were revived from time to time; there may have been a production of *The Rival Queans*.

7. Sacheverell was given a virtual slap on the wrist. He was suspended from preaching for three years, but he could perform other clerical duties and even accept preferments. After the expiration of his sentence, he preached his first sermon on Palm Sunday, 1713, at St. Saviour's, Southwark.

8. Betterton's last performance was on 13 April; he died on 28 April. For a eulogy and description of his funeral see the *Tatler*, no. 167 (3 May 1710).

9. The license was made out to Cibber, Wilks, Dogget, and Swiney, signed by Shrewsbury. BL, Add. MS. 38,607.ff.64-65, and PRO, LC5/155.f.41.

10. PRO, C 8 621/30. The suit dragged on until 19 May 1712.

11. The only new plays were *Marplot* (S. Centlivre, six performances), *The Generous Husband* (C. Johnson, three performances) and *Injur'd Love* (anonymous, five performances).

12. Had Collier accepted their offer, Cibber says, "he had got three hundred Pounds a Year more . . . our Shares being never less than a thousand annually to each of us, 'til the End of the Queen's Reign in 1714" (*Apology*, II, 109).

13. No date is given for Lewis's death beyond the year, but since Colley wrote no play this summer, it seems reasonable to suppose it occurred about this time.

14. Susannah Centlivre, *The Perplex'd Lovers* (London, 1717), preface.

15. Drury Lane had paid Swiney £350 for the Queens stock (PRO, LC 7/3.f.125, and Barker, p. 87). Now they were to give him £200 a year (PRO, LC 5/155.ff.99 and 126, C 11 6/44, and C 2342/26).

16. The quitclaim included "all actions, accounts, causes, bills, bonds, writings, debts, etc." It was signed and sealed by Cibber, witnessed by Charles Chambers and Richard Castelman on 10 May 1712 (Folger Library, Drury Lane MSS, W.b.486).

17. Addison and Steele's *Spectator* was a great advantage for the theater. Pope and Swift soon went over to the Tories, and by 1715, Pope was seriously alienated from Addison and the group. He named the group the "little Senate" in his portrait of Atticus, later incorporated into *Epistle to Dr. Arbuthnot*.

18. Doran, II, 9, refers to the custom of dressing all tragedy heroines in long gowns which pages carried and arranged. By convention, pages were as "invisible" as the black clad property men in the Chinese theater.

19. Cibber/Osbourne, 11 June 1712 (o.s.), MRO, WJ/SR/2192.

20. Alexander Pope, *Epistle to Dr. Arbuthnot*, line 97. This is almost the only suggestion of the kind.

21. MRO, WJ/SR/2192, ind. 24 and recog. 75.

22. St. Martin's rate books, 1712, note Cibber as "gone away before Crismus."

23. Colley Cibber, *Ximena; or, The Heroick Daughter* (London, 1719), preface, xlii-xliii.

24. *Spectator*, no. 546 (26 November 1712).

25. *Ximena*, preface, xxi.

26. *Cinna's Conspiracy* is a fairly close translation from the French, with a few changes to speed the action. Genest says, "This play has been ascribed to Cibber, but with little probability, as no reason is assigned, why he should conceal his name" (III, 511). Both Defoe (1713) and the *Biographia Dramatica*, however, credit him with it, and John Nichols, *Literary Anecdotes of the Eighteenth Century* (London, 1812-15), VIII, 204, cites a memorandum from Lintot dated 16 March 1713. The Bibliothèque de l'Arsenal in Paris lists Cibber as the "Traducteur de Corneille (Pierre), *Cinna's Conspiracy*. London, 1713" (Rf. 2007).

27. Baptismal register, St. Martin's-in-the-Fields, "Charlotte," christened 8 February 1713. The quotation is from Charlotte Charke, *A Narrative of the Life of Mrs. Charlotte Charke* (London, 1755), p. 14; a modern reprint has been edited by Leonard Ashley (Gainesville, Fla., 1969).

28. Swiney left on 14 January. He went from Holland to France and Italy. After a few years he returned briefly to England and secured a foreign customs post, but he did not make his home there until twenty years later.

29. In the *Apology*, II, 128, Cibber says he and Steele read the first three acts of *Cato* "nine years before it was acted" (1704) and that they tried unsuccessfully to talk Addison into finishing it for Betterton. When the Tories came to power, Addison changed his mind and gave it

to Drury Lane. For background on Addison and his political career, see Peter Smithers, *The Life of Joseph Addison* (Oxford, 1968).

30. *Flying Post*, 30 April–2 May 1713.

31. *Apology*, II, 130n. The Tory comment was meant as a caustic reference to Marlborough.

32. BL, Add. MS. 38,607.ff.6-8. Actually, aside from Oldfield, Booth was the highest paid actor in the company.

33. Robert Gore-Browne, *Gay Was the Pit* (London, 1957), p. 131, says Anne gave birth sometime between 9 May and the end of June 1713. The child did not live.

34. *Apology*, II, 139. The Oxford archives do not have a record of this gift, but there is no reason to doubt Cibber's word. The company probably played at the Sheldonian. It was the only logical place and fits Cibber's description; the Oxford Theatre Accounts for this year have an entry for a curtain, a rare expenditure. The known plays they presented, besides *Cato*, were *Julius Caesar*, *Othello*, *Sir Courtly Nice*, and *Hob in the Well*.

35. BL, Add. MS. 32,249.

36. Rose Shore's will is in the Public Record office, C 6/391/7, 13 June 1713. William Shore had left directions for the disposition of his estate, but she had altered them somewhat to leave the bulk to Elizabeth Cibber, her favorite niece. She named Richard Farewell and Daniel Lewin as executors, and the problem seems to have risen when someone (not John Shore or the Cibbers) charged them and Rose's servant, Elizabeth Jones, with mismanagement. After numerous depositions, a statement of accounts cleared up the matter, and there were no further difficulties (PRO C 6/392/12).

37. Most of the "Humble Remonstrances," charges, and countercharges from both sides can be found in BL, Add. MSS 32,607.ff.10-18, 32,506.ff.20-21, and 32,685.f.30; also PRO, LC 7/3.

38. There are two known copies of this letter. The original appears to be in Wilks's hand and is in the possession of Mr. Robert Eddison of London. The vice chamberlain's copy is in the British Library, Add. MS 38,607.ff.10-12.

39. BL, Add. MS 32,607.ff.15-16.

40. Elizabeth Knapton Wilks died 21 March 1714. She was buried at St. Paul's, Covent Garden, and Robert Wilks wrote an inscription for her grave (W. R. Chetwood, *The British Theatre* [Dublin, 1750], p. 236).

41. The queen's death occurred the day after her horse, Star, won £1,000 at York, a coincidence that antigambling moralists were quick to cite as a contributing factor.

42. Besides Jane Rogers, the defectors included Christopher Bullock and his son, Benjamin Griffin, Theophilus Keene, George Pack, and Frances Maria Knight.

43. *Biographical Dictionary*, s.v. "Booth, Barton."

44. The expenses, according to the bills (Folger Library, W.b.110), included an elm coffin covered with fine black silk and a large velvet pall, silver candlesticks and sconces with wax tapers, seven pounds of tallow candles, cloaks, scarves, and gloves for the pallbearers and mourners, a hearse and eight mourning coaches with eight pairs of horses, and twenty-two men to carry lighted flambeaux. The total was £11.00.00.

45. Queen Anne never visited the public theaters and had few command performances at court, but the house of Hanover offered strong support. In the 1714-15 season, Drury Lane gave twenty-six command performances. George I attended once, the Prince and/or Princess of Wales at least seven times.

46. Steele was elected to Parliament in August 1713 but was ejected in March 1714. For an account of the political maneuvers leading up to this, see Calhoun Winton, *Captain Steele* (Baltimore, 1964), pp. 176-201.

47. Drury Lane's license was granted 13 October 1714 (PRO, LC 7/3.f.133). The patent, as noted in the text, came three months later (PRO, LC 7/3.f.42).

48. Cibber had seven plays on the boards this season. Only Shakespeare had greater representation, and of the living playwrights, only Vanbrugh came close with five.

49. Davies, *Miscellanies*, I, 306. An example of rumor repeated until it was considered to be truth. Davies (1712?-85) was only a child in 1720 and still very young when Cibber retired. Much of the information in *Dramatic Miscellanies* reflects theater gossip rather than firsthand knowledge.

50. Dogget's main roles were distributed as follows: Sir Oliver (*She Wou'd if She Cou'd*) and Sir Nicholas (*Love in a Tub*) went to Henry ("Jubilee Dicky") Norris; Barnaby Brittle (*The Amorous Widow*) to William Bowen and later Norris; Ben (*Love for Love*) to Benjamin Griffin; Hob (*The Country Wake*) and Fondlewife (*The Old Batchelor*) are not listed, but probably to Cibber.

51. Cibber to Shrewsbury, 22 January, 1712/13 PRO LC 7/3. The earlier payments were to assist the struggling opera; Cibber says the managers had hoped their cooperation would "recommend us to the Court," implying it had not. Quoted in Barker, p. 103.

52. Colley Cibber, *Venus and Adonis* (London, 1736), p. 11.

53. Ashley, *Colley Cibber*, p. 187.

54. Wilks married Mary Fell, a widow with five children, on 26 April 1715. Marriage register, St. Paul's, Covent Garden. In 1723, her son Charles married William Penn's daughter—who was also Wilks's god-daughter (Doran, II, 41).

55. In her *Narrative*, Charlotte tells of several incidents demonstrating this in her own case and indicates it was his usual practice.

56. Cibber may also have written *The Bulls and Bears*, an afterpiece that had two performances at Drury Lane in December. It was never printed and no author is listed in the bills, but John Breval credits Cibber with it in *The Confederates* (London, 1717).

57. Vicary Gibbs, *The Complete Peerage* (London, 1913), s.v. "Bolton, 3rd Duke." He was the first aristocrat to marry an actress—Lavinia Fenton, the first Polly in *The Beggar's Opera*. She had been his mistress for twenty-three years.

58. In the Folger Library, DL MSS W.b. 110 holds an extensive collection of the Drury Lane bills from 1715-17.

59. Davies, *Miscellanies*, I, 224. The friend was supposed to be Temple Stanyan, at the time secretary to Viscount Townshend. *Biographical Dictionary* attributes a speech to Booth, "No, no! I will not have it said at Buttons that Barton Booth is losing his powers!" (s.v. "Booth, Barton").

60. Susannah and Booth had bought a lottery ticket together c. 1713. When it won, he offered her all, but she insisted on sharing and asked him to keep her half. He returned the money in 1718 when he was about to marry Hester Santlow, and Susannah gave the £3,200 into Minshull's keeping. He invested and lost it all, and Victor, *Memoirs of Barton Booth* (London, 1733), p. 9, says the loss contributed to her early death.

61. Colley Cibber, *A Letter from Mr. Cibber to Mr. Pope* (London, 1742), pp. 48-49.

62. In *New Light on Pope* (London, 1949), Norman Ault suggests that Cibber's story might contain some truth, at least enough for Pope to have harbored a long-festering grudge.

63. Dogget left a bequest to continue the race and it is still held each 1 August. The rowers begin "at that time of tide when the current is strongest against them," and go from the site of the Old Swan, near London Bridge, to that of the White Swan, Chelsea.

64. Somehow Cibber talked Dogget into acting in three benefits in the spring of 1717: for Mary Porter, Barnaby in *The Amorous Widow* (18 March), for Hester Santlow, Ben in *Love for Love* (25 March), and for Elizabeth Bicknell, Hob in *The Country Wake* (1 April). After this, he never set foot on the stage again.

65. Dudley Ryder, *The Diary of Dudley Ryder*, ed. William Matthews (London, 1939), 6 November 1716. The next day, Ryder quoted a Spaniard, Signor Castilio, "He thinks we have not enough of action and gesture, our players say their parts as if they were reading a book and have nothing of that expressive force of looks and voice and gesture which gives life and spirit and nature to their action." Such criticism was to become public opinion in another decade.

66. Spence, *Observations*, I, 235.

67. The idea is suggested in Breval's *A Complete Key to the New Farce Call'd Three Hours after Marriage* (London, 1717) and in *The Confederates*, pp. 24-25. These two references are the only indication that such an unlikely collaboration was considered, and since Breval was intimate with neither Pope nor Cibber, it seems more likely to be theater gossip than truth.

68. George Sherburn makes this assumption in "The Fortunes and Misfortunes of *Three Hours after Marriage*," *Modern Philology*, 24 (1926), 91-109.

69. John Dennis's *Remarks upon Mr. Pope's Translation of Homer*, printed a month later, shows his bitterness, Charles Johnson mocked *Three Hours after Marriage* in his prologue to *The Sul-*

taness, as did Breval in the works cited above. Among the most offensive to the authors was the anonymous *A Letter to Mr. John Gay, Concerning his late Farce Entituled, A Comedy* (London, 1717), which asserted that the actors had left out much of the play's "Obscenity and Prophaneness," concluding "What blessed Times do we live in, when Reformation begins at the Children of *Drury-Lane* and the Actors good manners exceed those of their Authors!" (pp. 8–9).

70. *Three Hours after Marriage* opened on 16 January, and *The Rehearsal*, on 7 February. The latter had not been presented since Estcourt's death in 1712, and since Cibber, who formerly played Volscius, now took Estcourt's role of Bayes, it was probably treated as a new production, and the planning must have begun before Gay's play opened.

71. In Gay's play, Plotwell hid himself in a mummy case, his cohort, Underplot, in a crocodile skin.

72. Cibber, *Letter . . . to Mr. Pope*, pp. 18–19.

73. George Paston [Emily Morse Symonds], *Mr Pope, His Life and Times* (London, 1909), I, 197.

74. 13 April 1717. For the duke's tumultuous relations with Richard Steele, see *The Correspondence of Richard Steele*, ed. Rae Blanchard (Oxford, 1941), p. 48; John Loftis, *Mr. Steele at Drury Lane* (Los Angeles, 1952); Calhoun Winton, *Sir Richard Steele*, (Baltimore, 1970), pp. 1–26.

75. Charke, *Narrative*, pp. 17–18.

76. William M. Peterson, "Pope and Cibber's *The Non-Juror*," *Modern Language Notes*, 70,5 (1955), 332–35, cites three specific instances that would have offended Pope: Maria, the coquette, reads his *Rape of the Lock*, she refers to "this odious Homer" (obviously Pope's translation of the *Iliad*), and the villain, Dr. Wolf, quotes "Eloisa to Abelard" when he tries to seduce Lady Woodvil. All three references would be immediately identifiable to the audience of the time.

77. *Applebee's Original Weekly Journal*, 21 December 1717. For other encomia, see Dudley Miles, "A Forgotten Hit: *The Non-Juror*," *Studies in Philology*, 16,1 (1919), 67–77.

78. Colley Cibber, *The Non-Juror* (London, 1718), dedication. For later discussions of this work, see Ronald L. Hayley, "Cibber, Collier, and the Non-Juror," *Huntington Library Quarterly*, 43,1 (1979), 61–78, and Hayley, "Pope, Cibber and A Clue to the Comedy of the Non-Juror," *Studies in Philology*, 76,2 (1978), 182–201.

79. *Some Cursory Remarks on the Play call'd The Non-Juror* (London, 1718).

80. Published with *The Theatre-Royal Turn'd into a Mountebank's Stage* (London, 1718). The letter is attacked in this pamphlet.

81. Nathaniel Mist (d. 1737) was a printer. His journal was a strong voice for the Tories and consistently attacked the Whig ministry, particularly Walpole, using Cibber as the whipping boy.

82. Elizabeth Cibber married Dawson Brett sometime during the spring. Their families had lived a few doors apart since the Cibbers moved to Southampton Street in 1712.

83. *The Theatre-Royal Turn'd into a Mountebank's Stage*, p. 17.

84. *Apology*, I, 35, has the line, "right or wrong, a Lick at the *Laureat* will always be a sure Bait." A note by Robert M. Lowe in his edition of the *Apology* (London, 1889) 2 vols., I, 35 quotes Edmund Bellchambers' remark in his edition of the *Apology* (London, 1822), p. 114, that it was the title of a pamphlet "in which some of Mr. Cibber's peculiarities have been severely handled," stating he had been unable to locate such a work. Cibber's reference was more probably to the attack on Rowe, so similar to those on himself when he became poet laureate.

85. *The Theatre-Royal Turn'd into a Mountebank's Stage*, p. 7. Cibber's epilogue, spoken by Anne Oldfield, was lightly ironic, but it also underlined his claim that only the disloyal would attack him: "Was't not enough the Criticks might pursue him! / But must he rouse a Party to undo him! / These Blows I told him on his Play would fall, / But he, unmov'd, cry'd—Blood! we'll stand it all. / When PRIESTS turn TRAITORS, where's the mighty Matter? / Since when has Treason been exempt from Satire?"

CHAPTER FOUR

1. Broadside, Bodleian Library, MS Rawl, Poet 207.f.125.
2. Mist's *Original Weekly Journal*, 1 March 1718.
3. Ibid.
4. Bowen, a hotheaded Irishman, quarreled with James Quin and forced a sword fight. He was mortally wounded, but on his deathbed generously insisted Quin should not be blamed, "The Gentleman did it fairly. If I die, I forgive him," adding with wry honesty, "but if I live, I will be revenged." His death came before his annual benefit, but the managers gave a performance of *The Old Batchelor* to help his family. s.v. "Bowen, William" in *Biographical Dictionary*.
5. Charke, *Narrative*, pp. 21-22.
6. Possibly Saturday, 20 September 1718. She was Susannah Verbruggen's daughter. The *Biographical Dictionary* (s.v. "Mountfort, Susannah") cites the story that she went mad after the birth of a child, and George Anne Bellamy said Cibber told her the story of this night, *An Apology for the Life of George Anne Bellamy*, 5 vols. (London, 1785), I, 187-88.
7. PRO, LC 5/157.f.87. Davies (*Miscellanies*, I, 397) describes Cibber's Wolsey.
8. George Sewell, *The Tragedy of Sir Walter Raleigh* (London, 1719), preface.
9. Charles Johnson, *The Masquerade* (London, 1719), preface.
10. Baptismal and burial registers, St. Paul's, Covent Garden. "Catherine," daughter of Dawson and Elizabeth Brett, born 4 April 1719, buried 8 April 1719.
11. Colley Cibber, *Ximena; or, The Heroick Daughter* (London, 1719), preface, p. xxvi.
12. Ibid., pp. xxvi-xxvii.
13. Ibid., p. xix.
14. For details of the Newcastle/Steele differences, see Calhoun Winton, *Sir Richard Steele* (Baltimore, 1974), pp. 23-31, and John Loftis, *Steele at Drury Lane* (Los Angeles, 1952), pp. 121-27.
15. Robert Hitchcock, *An Historical View of the Irish Stage* (Dublin, 1794), II, 67-68.
16. Richard Steele, *Correspondence*, ed. Rae Blanchard (London, 1941), p. 145. The objection was that lesser-paid actors would then demand higher salaries. See also Winton, *Sir Richard Steele*, pp. 165-86 and Loftis, *Steele*, pp. 127-49.
17. PRO, LC 5/157.f.138.
18. Davies, *Miscellanies*, III, 108.
19. Steele, *Correspondence*, pp. 146-47.
20. Richard Steele, *The Theatre*, ed. John Loftis (Oxford, 1962), 23 January 1720, p. 28.
21. Francis Gentleman, *The Dramatic Censor*, ed. J. M. Williams (London, 1812), p. 123.
22. PRO, LC 5/157.ff.415-16.
23. Steele, *Correspondence*, pp. 152-53.
24. Drury Lane accepted Dennis's play in the 1717-18 season, and evidently he expected the company to produce it at once. The managers postponed it; Dennis threatened to sue. Scheduled for 10 November 1719, the opening was delayed because of Charles Beckingham's benefit for his *King Henry the Fourth of France* at Lincoln's Inn Fields that night. Dennis's play opened next evening, putting his own author's benefit on Friday, 13 November, when, he said, most of the town was away celebrating the king's return from Hanover. The play lasted only three nights, and Dennis never forgave the triumvirate. For the full list of his grievances, see John Dennis, *The Invader of his Country* (London, 1719), preface.
25. Dennis, *The Critical Works of John Dennis*, ed. Edward Niles Hooker, 2 vols. (Baltimore, 1939-43) II, 184-85.
26. Dennis, II, 188-89.
27. Steele, *The Theatre*, ed. Nichols, 2 vols. (London, 1791), II, 401.
28. Steele, *The Theatre*, II, 396.
29. Robert Wilks to the Duke of Newcastle, 29 February 1719/20, BL, Add. MS 32,685.ff.51-53.
30. Thomas Davies, *Memoirs of the Life of David Garrick*, 2 vols. (London, 1780), I, 210.
31. Baptismal register, St. Paul's, Covent Garden, "Anne," daughter of Dawson and Elizabeth Brett, 8 May 1720.

32. Johann Pepusch, *Six English Cantatas for one Voice* (London, [1720]); Cibber wrote the lyrics for the last song.

33. Two letters from Steele (then in Edinburgh) dated 15 and 21 August 1720, were addressed to "Mr Cibber to Mrs Hodge under cover in Angell Court," suggesting the Cibbers were then in the process of moving (BL, Add. MS 5145.f.155). Charles Street later became Wellington Street, Strand; Cibber's neighbors included Benjamin Victor, John Mills, Wortley Montague, and George Bubb Dodington.

34. Giuseppe Grisoni (1692-1769), a Walloon painter who lived in England 1715-28, painted the portrait, now in the Garrick Club. It shows Cibber as Lord Foppington.

35. Oldfield became Churchill's mistress in 1717. See Gore-Browne, pp. 146-49.

36. Davies, *Miscellanies*, II, 319.

37. Colley Cibber, *The Refusal* (London, 1721), p. 2. All page references are to this edition. For other comments on this play, see Ashley, pp. 70-71, and Rodney L. Hayley, "The Swingeing of Cibber: The Suppression of the First Edition of *The Refusal*," *SB*, 28 (1974), 290-97.

38. Stanhope died 6 February, James Craggs, Jr., (the minister) on 15 February, and Craggs's father (possibly a suicide) on 17 March.

39. Sholto Percy and Reuben Percy, *The Percy Anecdotes* (London, 1822), p. 109.

40. PRO, LC 5/157.f.213.

41. The articles of agreement, signed 19 September 1721, provided that all the profits and losses should be divided equally among the four, that at Steele's death, the survivors should pay his heirs £1,200 for his share, and that none of them should mortgage, sell, or otherwise part with his part of the property without written consent from the other partners. For the borrowing and Fish Pool story, see Steele, *Correspondence*, pp. 34-35. See also Winton, *Sir Richard Steele*, pp. 187-214 and Loftis, *Steele at Drury Lane*, pp. 216-20.

42. Colley Cibber, *Plays Written by Mr. Cibber* (London, 1721).

43. Possibly Dawson Brett became an invalid; at any rate, Elizabeth's inheritance disappeared, and Charlotte speaks frequently of her sister's poverty and difficult life.

44. The *British Journal*, 30 September, described the funeral. Dogget was buried at Eltham, Kent, beside his wife.

45. The *Daily Courant*, 26 January 1722, printed Sir Thomas Hewitt's report to the lord chamberlain, here given in part: "We examin'd all its Parts with the greatest Exactness we could, and found the Walls, Roofing, Stage, Pit, Boxes Gallery, Machines, &c. sound, and almost as good as when first built, neither decay'd, nor in danger of falling; and when some small Repairs ae made, and an useless Stack of Chimneys (built by the late Mr. Rich) taken down, the Building may continue for a long time, being firm, the Materials and Joints good, and no Part giving way; and capable to bear much greater Weight than is put upon them." It was signed and dated "Scotland-Yard, 23 January 1722," with a note stating that the "Stack of Chimneys" had already been removed. Mist did not print Hewitt's statement.

46. *Weekly Journal*, 6 January 1722.

47. *Weekly Journal*, 13 January 1722.

48. Seven of Cibber's plays: *Love's Last Shift, Love Makes a Man, Richard III, The Careless Husband, The Double Gallant, She Wou'd and She Wou'd Not*, and *The Comical Lovers* were part of Drury Lane's standard repertory and were played annually. The first three were also standard at Lincoln's Inn Fields.

49. *Weekly Journal*, 13 January and 17 February 1722.

50. The spelling was evidently introduced to ridicule both Cibber's use of Latin and his father's foreign birth. On 3 March, Mist printed a "Letter" by "W. J.": "By KEYBER I suspect some Foreigner is intended, by the German Turn which is given to the Name, for we know well that That Nation turns *Caesar* into KEYSAR." This kind of barb led to the mistaken opinion that his name was pronounced "Kibber."

51. Davies, *Miscellanies*, I, 208.

52. *The London Stage*, II, cxlix.

53. Davies, *Life of Garrick*, p. 210.

54. Wilkes, p. 43. See also Loftis, *Steele at Drury Lane*, pp. 183-202.

55. Cibber leased a house at Strawberry Hill, Twickenham, and spent several summers there, although he never purchased it, nor, indeed, ever owned any property. Horace Walpole later bought the place and built his home on the site.

56. Doran, *Annals of the English Stage*, I, 344.

57. *St. James's Journal*, 18 November 1722.

58. Aaron Hill to Benjamin Victor, 21 February 1723, quoted in Victor's *Memoirs of the Life of Barton Booth* (London, 1733), p. 172.

59. Marriage register, St. Bene't, Paul's Wharf, 5 February 1723.

60. During the 1723-24 season, Elizabeth played small roles at Lincoln's Inn Fields, but she returned to Drury Lane in the fall of 1724.

61. Theo did several new plays: Richard Savage's *Sir Thomas Overbury*, his own alteration from Shakespeare's *Henry VI*, John Breval's revised *The Play is the Plot*, and Eliza Haywood's *A Wife to be Let* with John Thurmond's ambitious *Apollo and Daphne* as an afterpiece. At the end of summer, their production of Francis Hawling's *The Impertinent Lovers* received short shrift, and he complained bitterly that the actors had not even learned their lines for it.

62. Both the *London Journal* (28 September 1722) and Mist's *Weekly Journal* (12 October 1722) noted the planned production.

63. Hill was the first to make such harsh criticisms. General adverse commentary on Cibber's acting in tragedies did not appear until the 1720s, and it is difficult to judge how much was a result of partisanship. Even Davies, who agreed with the view, says Cibber was "much celebrated for some parts in tragedy" (*Miscellanies*, I, 19).

64. *Weekly Journal*, 16 June 1724.

65. The indenture, drawn up on 3 June 1724, was signed by Steele, Wilks, Booth, Cibber, Steele's creditors, and David Scurlock, Steele's trustee. See Steele, *Correspondence*, 171n. and Loftis, *Steele at Drury Lane*, pp. 221-25.

66. *Plain Dealer*, 9 December 1724.

67. For further commentary, see Ashley, *Colley Cibber*, pp. 71-72.

68. Victor, *History of the Theatres*, II, 164.

69. BL, Add. MSS 5145.

70. *Weekly Journal*, 23 January 1725.

71. Davies, *Miscellanies*, III, 451.

72. Marriage register, St. Ben't, Paul's Wharf, 22 May 1725.

73. Richard Savage claimed to be the illegitimate son of Mrs. Henry Brett, formerly countess of Macclesfield, and the Earl Rivers. A sometime poet-playwright-actor, Savage was a ne'er-do-well who courted the powerful and appears to have had great charm. He was Jane Johnson's guardian until her marriage.

74. *London Journal*, 20 November 1725.

75. Burial register, St. Paul's, Covent Garden, "Elizabeth," daughter of James and Catherine Brown, 23 September 1725.

76. PRO, C 11/2416/49.

77. Davies, *Miscellanies*, III, 427.

78. Christening register, St. Martin's-in-the-Fields, "Colley George Cibber" son of Theophilus and Jane Cibber, 19 April 1726.

79. Charke, pp. 37-39.

80. Davies, *Miscellanies*, III, 456-67.

81. Davies, *Miscellanies*, I, 294-95.

82. *Weekly Journal*, 5 November 1726.

83. *British Gazetteer*, 11 March 1726.

84. Colley Cibber, *The Provok'd Husband* (London, 1728), preface. For comment on this play, see Barker, pp. 142-45, Ashley, *Colley Cibber*, pp. 72-75, and Peter Dixon and Rodney Hayley, "The *Provok'd Husband* on the Nineteenth-Century Stage," *NCTR*, 8 (1980), 1-16.

85. Wilkes, pp. 43-44.

86. Baptismal register, St. Martin's-in-the-Fields, "Catherine," daughter of Theophilus and Jane Cibber, born 8 August, christened 3 September 1727.

87. Charles II is said to have loaned Betterton his own coronation robes for *Henry V* (*Biographical Dictionary*, s.v. "Betterton, Thomas"), but the 1727 production of *Henry VIII* is the first record of such elaborate staging of the coronation. The idea has sometimes been borrowed for later productions.

88. Thursday, 9 November 1727. Anne Brett was listed as "a little Girl." On 21 November, after a performance of *Sir Courtly Nice*, she was listed as "Miss Brett" in the same dance.

89. On 1 November 1727, the *Daily Post* carried the following advertisement: "ANNE CIB-
BER. From BRADSHAW's, the *Black-moor's Head* in *Leadenhall-street*, now at the *Golden Jar* in
Charles-street, *Covent-Garden*, sells all sorts of *China* and *Japan Ware*, the best TEA, as *Pecoe*,
Congou, *Sagoe*, and Chocolate: Also fine Hollands, Cambricks, &c. and most sorts of Millinar
Goods."

90. By the end of the season, it had been acted seventy-five times.

91. Victor, *History of the Theatres*, II, 105.

92. Davies, *Miscellanies*, III, 438.

93. J. T. Kirkman, *Memoirs of the Life of Charles Macklin* (London, 1799), I, 131-32.

94. *Weekly Journal*, 24 February 1728. Bingley, too, was soon in trouble with the Whig
ministry and was out. The name of the paper was changed to *Fog's Weekly Journal*. Its importance diminished, it continued until c. 1734.

95. Scholars have usually assumed that Cibber's use of the phrase derived from Dryden's
praise of Elizabeth Barry in his preface to *Cleomenes, the Spartan Hero*: "Mrs. Barry, always
Excellent, has, in this Tragedy, excell'd herself" (London, 1692). A more likely source is in
Southerne's words on her performance in *The Fatal Marriage; or, the Innocent Adultery*: "I have
been a little accessary to the great Applause, that every body in saying she outplays herself"
(London, 1694). The ridicule of Cibber's preface lived longer than he did. As late as 1771,
Horace Walpole referred to women's jewelry as "what Cibber called the *Paraphonalia of a
Woman of Quality*" (Walpole to Mary Coke, 22 August, *Correspondence*, ed. W. S. Lewis [New
Haven, 1937-83], XXXI, 157).

96. Steele, *Correspondence*, 171n.

97. There is no available parish record, but an infant, "Colley Brown," born in 1728, was
buried in the family plot at the Danish church in Wellclose Square.

98. Charlotte Charke, *Narrative*, pp. 40-41.

99. Charke, *Narrative*, pp. 47-49.

100. Colley Cibber, *Love in a Riddle* (London, 1729), p. 20.

101. Chetwood, pp. 127-28.

102. *The Laureat*, p. 46.

103. *Country Journal; or, The Craftsman*, 11 January 1729.

104. *The Private Journal and Literary Remains of John Byrom*, ed. Richard Parkinson (Manchester, 1854-57), p. 335.

105. Cibber is said to have written the English libretto for Nicolai Porpora's opera, *Mith-
ridates*. Porpora, in England this year, had the libretto translated into Italian and wrote the
music. It was produced in England in February 1736.

106. Baptismal register, St. Martin's-in-the-Fields, "Jane," daughter of Theophilus and
Jane Cibber, born 13 July, christened 1 August 1729. She was the second grandchild to live.

107. Davies, *Miscellanies*, III, 241-42.

108. Marriage register, St. Martin's-in-the-Fields, 3 February 1730.

109. Gore-Browne, p. 185.

110. *Daily Post*, 19 September 1730.

111. Gore-Browne, pp. 186-87.

112. Pope's mock epic, *The Dunciad*, had been published in 1728, revised with satiric foot-
notes into the *Dunciad Variorum* in 1729. Cibber is mentioned as one of the many writers Pope
considered bad, but he did not replace Theobald as hero for fifteen years.

113. In the 1730-31 season, nine of Cibber's plays were on the London stages: *Love Makes
a Man*, *The Provok'd Husband*, *The Lady's Last Stake*, *Love's Last Shift*, *Richard III*, *The Careless
Husband*, *The Double Gallant*, *The School Boy*, and *Damon and Phillida*. All major theaters (Drury
Lane, Lincoln's Inn Fields, Goodman's Fields, and Haymarket) performed them for a total of
fifty-one times. Oddly enough, Goodman's Fields presented more (twenty-seven) than Drury
Lane (ten).

114. On Friday, 4 December 1730, the *Daily Post* announced: "Yesterday Colley Cibber
Esq; the famous Comedian and Comic Author, was at Court, and had the Honour to kiss his
Majesty's hand (on his being appointed Poet-Laureat in the room of the Rev. Mr. Lawrence
Eusden, deceas'd) and was graciously receiv'd."

CHAPTER FIVE

1. Folger Library, ART vol. b., 19.f.72.

2. 13 December 1730, MRO. Cibber's official taking of the sacrament was a requisite public acknowledgment that he belonged to the Church of England.

3. Baptismal register, St. Clement Dane's, "Catherine Maria Charke," christened 6 December 1730.

4. *Weekly Register*, 5 December 1730. A verse defense, "A Hymn to the Laureat," by Mary Chapman, was printed in the *Whitehall Evening Post*, 9 January 1731, and concludes: "May empty Journals weekly rail. / May all dull bards repine: / If Wit unequall'd shou'd prevail, / The *Laurel*'s justly thine."

5. Davies, *Miscellanies*, III, 255.

6. *Daily Post*, 9 January 1731.

7. Wilks kept his word and played it only once more—for a royal command performance on 1 May 1731.

8. Davies, *Miscellanies*, says that on weekends Mary Porter went to her home outside of London, driving herself in a one-horse chaise. Approached by a highwayman, she threatened him with a pistol, but when he pleaded poverty as his reason for crime, gave him £10. She lashed her horse onward, the chaise overturned, and she suffered a permanently dislocated hip. While recovering, she inquired about the man, learned his story was true, and raised £60 for him (III, 464-66).

9. Negotiations began in early June and a full series was planned, but the only play acted was that given for the duke of Lorraine, 18 October 1731.

10. Presumably while Cibber was a Hampton Court; George H. Cunningham, *London* (London, 1931), p. 775.

11. Charke, *Narrative*, p. 51. Of her husband, Charlotte says, "I seldom had the Honour of his company but when Cash run low; and I as constantly supplied his Wants; and have got from my Father many an auxiliary Guinea."

12. *Daily Advertiser*, 1 November 1731.

13. Almost every contemporary attack on Cibber is quoted from *Fog's Weekly Journal*, the *Grub Street Journal*, the *Craftsman*, or, later, the *Champion*. All were instruments of Tory sentiment. For additional notes about Cibber's odes, see: Alan Downie, "Pope, Swift and An Ode for the New Year," *RES*, 32 (May 1981), 161-72 (1733 ode); John E. Sitter, "Cibber and Fielding's Quintessential Ode," *Notes and Queries*, 223 (February, 1978), p. 44 (1736 ode); Richard Frushell, "Cibber's 1743 Ode and some Advice to the Laureat," *Notes and Queries*, 217 (October 1972), 374-76 (1743 ode).

14. Aaron Hill, *Works*, 4 vols. (London, 1753), I, 87. See also Dorothy Brewster, *Aaron Hill* (New York, 1913).

15. *The Life of That Eminent Comedian Robert Wilks, Esq.* (London, 1733), p. 34.

16. George H. Cunningham, p. 836. Here, Cibber also met the dowager duchess of Marlborough, with whom he played cards, and Edward Young, who had been a schoolmate of Lewis Cibber and who later entertained Colley in his home.

17. The announcement of Wilks's death appeared in the *Daily Post* on 28 September 1732.

18. H. Barton Baker, *Our Old Actors*. 2 vols. (London, 1878), I, 119.

19. *A Letter from Theophilus Cibber to John Highmore, Esq.* (London, 1733).

20. Baptismal register, St. Paul's, Covent Garden, 24 January 1733; burial register, St. Paul's, Covent Garden, 28 January 1733.

21. 5 January 1733. On 1 January, Hill had written to Victor: "What if Mr. *Cibber* Sen. would take upon him this Part? As the walk would be new to him, it would be an Increase to his Reputation; for I am confident he could touch it in a strong and natural Perfection" (Victor, *History*, I, 179-83).

22. Cibber played Sir John Brute in *The Provok'd Wife* on 26 February 1733, the first benefit of the season.

23. On 24 March 1733, the *Weekly Journal* remarked acidly: "Colley Cibber, Esq.; one of the Patentees of Drury-Lane, being now possessed of a more commodious Post, has sold his entire Share of the Cloths, Scenes, and Patent, to John Highmore, Esq; and at the End of this Season he is, we hear, to quit the Stage."

24. Theophilus Cibber, *A Letter . . . to John Highmore.*

25. Dover had written *Encomium Argenti Vivi; A Treatise upon the Use and Properties of Quicksilver* (London, 1733) detailing numerous cures he had effected, and claiming, "It is well known what great Quantities of crude Mercury are now taken in the Mouth, about an Ounce at a Time. . . . Some have swallowed in this Manner to the weight of twenty, thirty, forty Pounds of it. In Substance it cannot possibly do the least Harm, being as innocent as any Thing in Nature taken that Way."

26. *Biographical Dictionary*, s.v. "Booth, Barton."

27. Victor, *History*, II, 19-22.

28. Victor, *History*, spoke strongly: "I must own I was heartily disgusted with the Conduct of the Family of the *Cibbers* on this Occasion, and had frequent and violent Disputes with Father and son, whenever we met! It appeared to me something shocking that the Son should immediately render void and worthless, what the Father had just received Thirty-one Hundred and Fifty Pounds for, as a valuable consideration" (I, 14).

29. On 29 September 1733, Devonshire sold property inherited from the duke of Dorset to John Morse in payment of an old debt. The document is in my possession.

30. One of the inconsistencies in the attacks against Cibber's character appears here. His enemies tried to claim that Cibber's aristocratic friends regarded him merely as an object of ridicule, a court jester, and simultaneously charged that he exerted a great deal of influence on their decisions. Neither seems to be true. In spite of Cibber's court connections, negotiations for the patent begun 10 May 1731 did not go into effect until September 1732.

31. *London Evening Post*, 3 November 1733.

32. BL, (Eg. 2320), notes that *Henry IV* was to be done, but that "This Day Mr Harper [who played Henry] was taken up as a Vagabond on the Statute 12 of Q Anne and committed by Sir E. Clarges." Harper was tried on 22 November and acquitted on 28 November on the grounds that he could not be a vagrant if he was a householder. The papers covered the arrest and trial thoroughly.

33. *London Evening Post*, 12 November 1733.

34. Burial register, St. Martin's-in-the-Fields, 20 January 1734.

35. The poem was printed in the first volume of *The British Musical Miscellany* and as a broadside in 1734; and it was also set to music twice: *The Merry Medley; or a Christmass Box* (London, n.d.), and "Set by Mr. Stanley," in Joseph Ritson's, *A Select Collection of English Songs* (London, 1783), II, which was reprinted from the *Gentleman's Magazine* of January 1740. Later translated into German by Craigher, it was also set to music by Schubert in 1825 as "Der Blinde Knabe."

36. On 24 January 1734, Charles Fleetwood bought out Highmore for £2,250 and Mary Wilks for £1,500 (*Survey of London*, vol. 16: *Charing Cross*, ed. G. H. Gater and Walter H. Godfrey (London, 1935). Fleetwood obtained the patent for little more than Highmore had paid for half (Victor, *History*, II, 26) and immediately arranged for the dissidents' return. Their first performance at Drury Lane (12 March) starred Theophilus in *The Mother-in-Law*.

37. *Daily Advertiser*, 23 April 1734. Susannah's parents must have suspected Theo's apparent reformation, for the marriage agreement included an arrangement to protect her earnings. This was to prove inadequate later. See Mary Nash, *The Provoked Wife* (Boston, 1977), p. 74.

38. *Gentleman's Magazine*, August 1734, and *The Scarborough Miscellany for the Year 1734* (London, 1734).

39. Alexander Pope, *Correspondence*, ed. George Sherburn, 5 vols. (Oxford, 1956), III, 435. Pope to Hugh Bethel, 28 September 1734.

40. The verses were ridiculed in the *Gentleman's Magazine* of August 1734 and in the *London Magazine*, August and September 1734.

41. 31 October 1734. Cibber also acted Foppington in *The Careless Husband* (14 November), Clodio in *Love Makes a Man* (20 November), and Sir John in *The Provok'd Wife* (2 December).

42. When Swiney left England in 1713, he went to Italy, possibly with help from Nicolini or other singers he had worked with at the Haymarket. He returned to England briefly in 1718, worked in the Customs House and was keeper of the King's Music, but he soon went back to Italy and in 1730 was in Bologna writing to Coleman about engaging singers for Handel's opera (12 July). When he finally came home, he was badly in need of money, and on

25 February 1735, Colley played Fondlewife in *The Old Batchelor* for his benefit. From this time on, they were fast friends.

43. Charles Macklin (1699-1797) had been a strolling player before coming to London permanently in 1730. He was a brilliant actor in the "new" style. He had stayed with Highmore when Theo's group left, held the company together, and his star was rising. He and Theo were unfriendly rivals. For an account of Macklin's career, see William W. Appleton, *Charles Macklin* (Cambridge, Mass., 1960).

44. *Prompter*, 19 November 1734.

45. On 2 November 1734, the *Grub Street Journal* attacked Cibber in an article by "Somebody"; on 14 November, an article by "Outis" (Nobody) defended him. Hill assumed this was Cibber, but it is entirely out of his character to praise himself so openly as: "his Observations on Mr *Quin* are very just; but far from being so upon Mr *Cibber*, who . . . performs every Character he represents inimitably well."

46. A Robert Colley Brown was buried with the Cibber family in the Danish Church, Wellclose Square, in 1735.

47. Burial register, St. Paul's, Covent Garden, "Susannah, daughter of Theophilus Cibber," 14 February 1735.

48. This story first appears in *A Blast upon Bays; or, a New Lick at the Laureat* (1742) and is often related to their similar attendance on Peg Woffington. At least two facts argue against this identification. The author calls the lady "Susanna-Maria," Susannah's full name, while Margaret Woffington was always known as "Peg;" he uses the past tense—by 1742, Susannah and Colley hardly saw each other, and Swiney's attachment to Woffington was just beginning to burgeon.

49. *The Tryal of a Cause for Criminal Conversation* . . . (London, 1739), pp. 28-29.

50. Charlotte says Charke went to the West Indies "about a year" after her mother's death (*Narrative*, pp. 78-79). His name is not mentioned on theater bills after the end of the 1734-35 season, and he probably left during the summer of 1735. He died in Jamaica some months later.

51. This event is, of course, speculation, but Charlotte suggests that at the time of her break with the family, which occurred at the end of the 1734-35 season, she was living at home.

52. Anne Cibber married John Boultby sometime between 1728 and 1734.

53. Charke, *Narrative*, p. 62.

54. Lord Place is a fop, and Charlotte aped her father's mannerisms with deadly accuracy. At one point, Place suggests another character should be poet laureate, and when he protests he cannot write poetry, Place exclaims, "No matter for that—you'll be able to make Odes. . . . I know you may be qualified for the Place without being a Poet."

55. Charke, *Narrative*, pp. 124-25.

56. Cibber wrote the Prologue for *Zara*, so he was at least concerned with the production. Hill's nephew acted the leading male role and was also coached by his uncle, but he failed miserably and refused to act after the second night. On 4 February 1736, he published an open letter to Hill in the *Daily Post*, charging him with bad teaching and concluding with "The Player's Epitome," mocking the "natural" style.

57. Burial register, St. Giles-in-the-Fields, "Caius-Gabriel, son of Theophilus Cibber," 5 April 1736.

58. Catherine Raftor Clive (1711-85) had been a close friend of Theo's first wife. She entered the Drury Lane company in 1728. She married a barrister, Robert Clive, in 1733, but they separated amicably in 1735. She had an excellent singing voice and was much admired for her Polly in *The Beggar's Opera*.

59. 4 February 1737. For a full review of this skirmish, see Emmet L. Avery, "Cibber, *King John*, and the Students of Law," *MLN*, 53 (April 1938), 272-75, and C. W. Nichols, "Fielding and the Cibbers," *PQ*, 14 (1922), 278-89.

60. Davies, *Miscellanies*, I, 5.

61. Charke, *Narrative*, p. 65. Until she left to enter the grocery business, Charlotte lived with Elizabeth.

62. Performed first on 3 May 1737. The main play was Fielding's *The Sailor's Opera*, in

which Charlotte played Kitty Cable; the afterpiece was *The Historical Register*, in which she burlesqued Christopher Cock, the auctioneer.

63. Howard P. Vincent, "Two Letters of Colley Cibber," *Notes and Queries*, 168 (1935), 3-4. Ashley (*Colley Cibber*, p. 157) suggests that the words "worthless scoundrel" refer to a lover, but the circumstances and timing indicate Fielding is more probable.

64. It was purportedly brought to Walpole by Henry Giffard, manager of Goodman's Fields. Rumor had it that Walpole brought pressure on Giffard, who was having financial problems, and arraanged the "discovery" of the play to give an excuse for closing down Fielding. *The Golden Rump* was never produced or printed.

65. The Licensing Act required the following: (1) All London theaters were restricted to Westminster and its liberties and must be licensed by the lord chamberlain; (2) a £50 fine would be levied for taking part in an unlicensed theater for "hire, gain or reward"; (3) every play presented to the public must bear the lord chamberlain's seal of approval. For a complete review of the background, politics, and theatrical situation of this time, see Vincent J. Liesenfeld, *The Licensing Act of 1737* (Madison, Wis., 1981).

66. Chesterfield's speech, reported in the *Gentleman's Magazine* in June 1738, pp. 409-11, pointed to the danger of placing too much power in the hands of one man, the value of satire as a social corrective, the difficulty of discerning the difference between printed and spoken libel, and the fact that suppressed plays, once printed, would reach a wider audience than the stage, as was the case with Gay's *Polly*.

67. Fielding repeatedly pairs Walpole and Cibber in the *Champion*. On Tuesday, 1 April 1740, he concludes an attack on Walpole by turning to Cibber, "As for my other Bear, I cannot much brag of his Abilities, but he is very tame, and will suffer himself to be stroked; besides which, he often diverts Company, when he is not at Stake, with his Tricks, and may be indeed not improperly called a Dancing Bear."

68. *The British Theatre* was published 14 May 1737 and included *The Provok'd Husband, She Wou'd and She Wou'd Not, The Careless Husband, Love Makes a Man, Love's Last Shift*, and *The Lady's Last Stake*, all of which were still playing in repertory.

69. Marriage register, St. Benedict and St. Peter, Paul's Wharf, "William Rufus Chetwood of St. Paul's Covent Garden and Anne Brett of same," 15 June 1738.

70. Colley Cibber, *An Apology for the Life of Mr. Colley Cibber*, ed. Edmund Bellchambers (London, 1822), p. 40n. Aside from the *Laureat*, it is the only reference of this kind.

71. W. S. Austen and John Ralph, *The Lives of the Poets Laureate* (London, 1853), p. 282.

72. *The Tryal of a Cause*, pp. 41-44.

73. *The Tryal of a Cause* . . . , pp. 28-29.

74. Nash, p. 117.

75. *The Tryal of a Cause* . . . , p. 19.

76. Burial register, St. Paul's, Covent Garden, "Dawson Brett," 23 November 1738.

77. Davies, *Miscellanies*, I, 306.

78. Nash, p. 146.

79. Susannah left her parents' home and took rooms at a Mrs. Knightley's house in Devonshire Street, calling herself "Mrs. Archer." She never went out, but Sloper occasionally visited her. The letters were published in Theophilus Cibber, *Four Original Letters* (London, 1739).

80. Enthoven Theatre Collection, Victoria and Albert Museum. Undated letter.

81. Charke, *Narrative*, pp. 89-90. The original is in the Enthoven Theatre Collection of the Victoria and Albert Museum.

82. Victor, *History*, I, 48.

83. The portrait which is in the National Gallery, London, shows a young girl in the background, probably Cibber's granddaughter, Jenny, whom he trained for the stage. She would have been the right age at this time. Jean-Baptiste Vanloo (1684-1745) was in England from 1738-42.

84. In an undated letter, Giles ("Tom") Earle wrote that Cibber "return'd from Tunbridge, where he went to drink the Waters—for a little Immortality, I suppose—Health and Spirits I am sure he does not want (for he looks but Forty, 'tho he is, I believe, Sixty-nine)." BL. Add. MS 11796.f.2.

85. Algernon Bourke, *History of White's* (London, 1892), p. 25.

86. John Carteret Pilkington, *The Real Story* (London, 1760), p. 209.
87. *Apology*, I, 101-2. Later (I, 185), Cibber tells of Mrs. Barry's delivering a new prologue for *The Double Dealer* in honor of Queen Mary, "Two Lines of it, which tho' I have not since read, I still remember. 'But never were in *Rome* nor *Athens* seen, / So fair a Circle, or so bright a Queen.'" This performance had taken place in 1693.
88. *An Account of the Life of that Celebrated Actress, Mrs. Susannah Maria Cibber, with Interesting and Amusing Anecdotes. Also the two Remarkable and Romantic Trials between Theophilus Cibber and William Sloper* (London, 1887), p. 55.
89. Anne played Amanda in *Love's Last Shift* on 5 May 1740.
90. 1 April 1740. The *Champion* attacked him again on 15, 22, 29 April and on 6, 8, 10, 17, and 24 May; soon after, Fielding left for the west country. The *Grub Street Journal* had come to an end on 29 December 1737, and most of the attacks on Cibber ceased at that time.
91. Laetitia Pilkington, *Memoirs of Mrs. Laetitia Pilkington*, ed. J. Isaacs (New York, 1928), pp. 133-34.
92. L. Pilkington, pp. 208-10.
93. *An Apology*, structured parallel to Cibber's *Apology*, purports to be Theo's memoirs, showing him to be the thoroughly corrupt son of a corrupt father. Fielding began *The Champion* with a fellow law student, James Ralph, who is often considered the author of *An Apology*. Ralph may have written part of the book, but his satire is less subtle and skillful than Fielding's.
94. The writer says Wilks's first role was Palamede in *Marriage a la Mode*, but actually Wilks played Sir Harry Wildair in *The Constant Couple* first.
95. See also Sean Shesgreen, "Cibber in Fielding's *Jonathan Wild*," *American Notes and Queries* 12 (1973), 88-90.
96. *The Laureat*, p. 1. The same charges, in the same terms, were the major theme of the *Champion* articles.
97. In his *Apology*, Cibber pays a compliment to "a truly Noble Commissioner" who had been responsible for building a bridge. The *Laureat* diminishes it to "a *certain Commissioner*, what Commissioner we know not," but almost anyone would have recognized the reference to the earl of Pembroke, who had laid the first stone of Westminster Bridge on 29 January 1739. Cibber also speaks of a "Noble Person, who . . . does me the flattering Honour to threaten my Work with a Supplement" (II, 118). The *Laureat* twists it to read "a NOBLE PERSON who does him the flattering Honour to *promise* to publish" (p. 77). Colley evaluated his partner of more than thirty years, Robert Wilks, with full awareness of both his assets and liabilities: "Though *Wilks* had more Industry and Application than any Actor I had ever known, yet we found it possible that those necessary Qualities might sometimes be so misconducted as not only to make them useless, but hurtful to our Commonwealth; for while he was impatient to be foremost in every thing, he frequently shock'd the honest Ambition of others, whose Measures might have been more serviceable, could his Jealousy have given way to them" (II, 225-26). The *Laureat*'s answer reveals a lack of knowledge about actors' behavior in a company: "*Colly, thou reason'st ill*: Why shou'd not the Industry and Ability of *Wilks* have rais'd their Emulation? Why should they not, by his Example, have been industrious? No, their Ambition was shocked, and they wou'd be nothing, since they cou'd not be equal to him" (p. 93).
98. The two stories were old in Joe Miller's time:

Pollio: My dear Aesop, I love thee better than anything in this world.
Aesop: Except a shilling.

Lentulus: I shall certainly live to see thee pox'd and hang'd.
Aesop: Yes, my Lord, if I converse with your Women or deal in your Politics.

99. Cibber's biographers, Senior and Barker, and to a lesser extent, Ashley, along with the editors of the two earlier editions of the *Apology*, Lowe and Bellchambers, have relied heavily on the *Laureat*'s words.

CHAPTER SIX

1. *Love Makes a Man* (Drury Lane), *Love's Last Shift* (Goodman's Fields), *The Double Gallant* (Covent Garden).

2. Dr. Maurice Greene had replaced John Eccles as court composer after Eccles's death in 1735.

3. On 6 December 1740, the *Dublin Evening Journal* reported on Woffington's success as Sir Harry Wildair in *The Constant Couple* and added the note, "Mr. Cibber has promis'd to do all in his Power to Improve her, which he thinks her very capable of."

4. The lines are quoted in Colley Cibber, *The Egoist; or, Colley upon Cibber* (London, 1743), p. 54.

5. Davies, *Miscellanies*, II, 110. Handel, out of favor with the court, had also retreated to Ireland.

6. William Rufus Chetwood, *A General History of the Stage, From its Origin in Greece down to the present Time* (London, 1749), p. 130.

7. In her *Memoirs*, Mrs. Pilkington gives many instances of Cibber's assistance: once he paid her debts to release her from prison, another time he redeemed furniture she had pawned, and he pressured all and sundry to loan or give her money.

8. Walpole, *Correspondence*, I, 115.

9. The *Biographical Dictionary* (s.v. "Garrick, David") quotes Thomas Davies's description of Garrick's Richard, noting the confusion of critics, "They had long been accustomed to an elevation of the voice, with a sudden mechanical depressing of its tones, calculated to excite admiration and entrap applause. To the just modulation of the words, and concurring expression of the features from the genuine workings of nature, they had been strangers for some time." Their doubts were soon "turned into surprize and astonishment, from which they relieved themselves by loud reiterated applause."

10. John Taylor, *Records of my Life* (New York, 1833), p. 151.

11. Davies, *Life of Garrick*, p. 46.

12. David Garrick, *Letters*, ed. David M. Little & George M. Kahrl, 3 vols. (Cambridge, Mass., 1963), I, 34.

13. Walpole, *Correspondence*, XXII, 222.

14. At Covent Garden, he played Sir John on 14 December, Foppington on 4, 7, and 17 January 1742, Shallow on 12 and 20 February. The last was a command performance.

15. 28 April 1742. The performance was advertised as "Benefit of Miss Cibber and her sister, daughters of Mr Cibber by the late Mrs Jane Cibber. . . . Tickets to be had of Bradshaw, &c. [where Anne Cibber worked, apparently] and of Miss Cibber and her Sister at Mrs Brett's in Berwick St., near Soho."

16. Howard P. Vincent, "Two Letters of Colley Cibber," *Notes and Queries*, 168 (5 January 1935), 3.

17. Evidence for Pope's early decision to revise the *Dunciad* is found in James Sutherland's introduction to the Twickenham edition of Pope's *Works* (New York, 1943), pp. xxxii-xxxvii.

18. When Pope decided to edit the plays of Shakespeare, he appealed for assistance from experts, among whom was Lewis Theobald. Theobald offered none, but after Pope's edition was published, he wrote a long article pointing out many errors and later compounded the offense by publishing his own edition.

19. Colley Cibber, *A Letter . . . to Mr. Pope*, pp. 6-7.

20. Pope had once invited the bookseller Edmund Curll to take tea privately with him, ostensibly to make peace after Curll had bootlegged some of Pope's poems. The tea, however, was laced with an emetic, and Curll's sufferings were graphically described by Pope in an article, "Dr. Wormwood's Stomach Powders." The incident was well known.

21. Vincent, p. 3.

22. See *Universal Spectator* (7, 14, 21 August 1742); *Gentleman's Magazine* (August); *The Scribleriad, Blast upon Blast* (19 August); *Sawney and Colley* (31 August); and Lord Hervey's *A Letter to Mr. Cibber on his Letter to Mr. Pope*. At least four engravings were also published.

23. [Lord John Hervey], *The Difference between Verbal and Practial Virtue* (London, 1742).

24. George Paston [Emily More Symonds], *Mr. Pope His Life and Times* (London, 1909), I, 687.

25. Pope, *Correspondence*, IV, 415.

26. Spence, *Observations*, I, 149, quotes a letter from Pope to Lord Marchmont (21-25 February 1743): "I won't publish the fourth *Dunciad* as 'tis new-set till Michaelmas, that we may have time to play Cibber all the while. . . . He will be stuck, like the man in the almanac, not deep, but all over. He won't know which way to turn himself to. Exhausted at the first stroke, and reduced to passion and calling names, so that he won't be able to write more, and won't be able to bear living without writing."

27. See appendix 2 for text of this letter.

28. Pope, *Correspondence*, IV, 449-50.

29. R. J. Broadbent, *Annals of the Liverpool Stage* (Liverpool, 1908), p. 19. A Dublin company came to Liverpool in August 1742, and played at the Old Ropery Theater. Anne played for Giffard most of the season, except for a month when she gave birth to a still-born child: 2 December 1742, "Elizabeth-Peggy, daughter of William Chetwood of St. Martin's." Burial register, St. Paul's, Covent Garden.

30. This is a curious choice, for "Brown" was the married name of Catherine, whom Charlotte thoroughly disliked.

31. L. Pilkington, pp. 280-82.

32. Warburton had been an ambitious young scribbler in the thirties and won Pope's gratitude with an impassioned defense of the *Essay on Man* against charges of atheism. Pope later made Warburton his editorial adviser and literary heir.

33. Colley Cibber, *Another Occasional Letter from Mr. Cibber to Mr. Pope, Wherein the New Hero's Preferment to his Throne, in the Dunciad, seems not to be Accepted* (London, 1744), p. 24. Citations in the text are from this edition.

34. He played Fondlewife on 5 January 1744, Sir John Brute in *The Provok'd Wife* on 13 and 23 January (with Peg Woffington as Lady Brute and his granddaughter Anne Chetwood as Mademoiselle), and Shallow in *Henry IV (Part I)*, on 27 January.

35. L. Pilkington, pp. 334-35. Cibber took one of her poems to Chesterfield, who gave him two shillings for her, cautioning him, "don't put them into your silver pocket, lest you should make a mistake and pay your chair with them." When Cibber repeated the conversation to Laetitia, he concluded, "So here, Madam, are the two *guineas* for you!"

36. Charlotte must have had some qualms, for when her father came to London, she left off playing the Nurse and switched to male roles, calling herself "Charles."

37. Garrick, *Letters*, II, 43-44.

38. On 2 October 1744, the *Daily Advertiser* commented that "every one allow'd Miss Jenny Cibber (who has given Proofs of an uncommon Genius) was greatly improv'd in the character of Juliet," and the October *Gentleman's Magazine* printed a poem of unqualified praise with the footnote: "The young lady . . . 'tis said, discovers as promising a genius for the stage as any of her sex, that have been esteem'd the ornament of the British theatre."

39. He tried to open an "Academy" where he would sell tickets to a concert. The tickets allowed the purchasers to see a "free" performance of a play. The practice was illegal, but he did manage a few more performances of *Romeo and Juliet* before he was closed. He also arranged a production of *The Beggar's Opera* as a benefit for Charlotte, in which she played Macheath.

40. Colley Cibber, *Papal Tyranny in the Reign of King John* (London, 1745), preface.

41. "This Play was rehearsed privately, and brought out, on a sudden, before there was Time to form a Party against it, and so met with Applause. Mr. Cibber performed the Part of Pandolph the Pope's Legate, himself with great Spirit and Vigour, notwithstanding his Age, which was considerably above 70" (Whincop, p. 198).

42. Victor, *History*, II, 163.

43. Davies, *Miscellanies*, I, 40-41.

44. Ibid., III, 471.

45. "Lord Montfort and Mr. Heath wager Sr. Wm. Stanhope One Hundred Guineas each, that Mr. Colley Cibber is alive this day five years, Jany. 31. 1745/6" (Bourke, II, 6).

46. John Taylor, p. 152.

47. Samuel Richardson, *Correspondence*, ed. Anna Laetitia Barbauld, 6 vols. (London, 1804), II, 131.

48. T. C. Duncan Eaves and Ben D. Kimpel, *Samuel Richardson* (Oxford, 1971), pp. 180-81.

49. Richardson, *Correspondence*, III, 167-70.
50. Eaves and Kimpel, p. 214.
51. In *History*, II and III, Benjamin Victor quotes at some length from both sides of the correspondence.
52. Victor, *History*, II, 203-7.
53. John Holland, *Theatre Notebook* 23 (Autumn 1968), 38. Holland's note cites the parish record from St. George's Hanover Square: "May 2. Mr. John Sacheverell of St. Andre's, Holborn, and Mrs. Charlotte Charke of Kensington." The marriage is rather mysterious, for Charlotte used his name only once at a performance in Clerkenwell, and she left London within a month. She does not mention him at all in her *Narrative*.
54. L. Pilkington, p. 381.
55. Colley Cibber, *The Character and Conduct of Cicero* (London, 1747). Quotations are from this edition.
56. Walpole, *Correspondence*, IV, 13-14.
57. Davies, *Life of Garrick*, II, 201-3.
58. Davies, *Miscellanies*, III, 471.
59. Victor, *History*, II, 207-22.
60. John Taylor, p. 151.
61. Richardson, *Correspondence*, II, 158-61.
62. Richardson, *Correspondence*, II, 161-67.
63. Spence, *Observations*, I, 357-58. He added, "Old Colley is himself a Comedy."
64. The eighty-year-old chief of the Fraser clan had been captured after Culloden and brought to London to be tried. He was immensely fat and was caricatured by Hogarth, but his behavior at the trial and in prison was so exemplary that even his adversaries respected him. The last man to be beheaded on an English block, he walked to the scaffold calmly and spoke only once, "Dulce et decorum est pro patria morior."
65. Richardson, *Correspondence*, II, 317.
66. The lovely and witty Elizabeth Chudleigh secretly married the Honorable Augustus Hervey, later the earl of Bristol, in August 1744. Later, in collusion with him, she obtained an annulment in order to marry the duke of Kingston in March 1769. After the duke's death, she was convicted of bigamy but escaped the sentence of branding by fleeing to the Continent where she remained for life.
67. Colley Cibber, *The Lady's Lecture* (London, 1748), p. 43.
68. Richardson, *Correspondence*, III, 319.
69. Victor, *History*, II, 211-19.
70. Spence, *Observations*, I, 896.
71. Victor, *History*, II, 211-19.
72. Cibber sold the copyright to Robert Dodsley for £52.10 (*Apology*, I, 4n).
73. Richardson, *Correspondence*, VI, 65-67.
74. Garrick, *Letters*, II, 10.
75. Garrick, *Letters*, II, 158.
76. She pleased some, however, for on 19 October 1750, the *Midwife* commented of her performance, "I must do her the justice to observe that she play'd the part much better than cou'd be expected from one of her years and practice; and if a proper regard is paid to her modesty and merit, I make no doubt she will become an exceeding good player."
77. Walpole, *Correspondence*, 20, 214.
78. *London Stage*, IV, 228.
79. The testimonial appeared in the *General Advertizer*, 1 February 1751, and describes his illness in detail, saying that a dose of the powder "in some Tamarinds, unknown to me" brought an overnight improvement.
80. Colley Cibber, *Rhapsody upon the Marvellous* (London, 1751). All citations in the text are from this edition.
81. Eaves and Kimpel, p. 182.
82. *The Earl of Essex* was produced at Covent Garden on 12 February 1753 and was a great success. *Eugenia*, a translation of a French tragedy, was by the Reverend Mr. Francis. It played six nights at Drury Lane.

83. Shore's will was made 1 February 1748 and proved 20 November 1752 in the prerogative court of Canterbury.

84. Elizabeth's husband, Joseph Marples, was listed in the *Gentleman's Magazine* under "Bankruptcies" in July 1753.

85. Bourke lists four bets in 1746 (II, 8-9) and one in 1749 (II, 20) as to whether Cibber would outlive Beau Nash; four that he would live two years or more (April 1751 [II, 20-22] and March 1753 [II, 30]); and two by Lord Mountfort in November 1753 (II, 33).

86. Richardson, *Correspondence*, II, 175-76.

87. Richardson, *Correspondence*, II, 176. "Miss Byrom" is a character in *Sir Charles Grandison*.

88. Richardson, *Correspondence*, II, 177-79.

89. Bourke, II, 33.

90. Charke, *Narrative*, 265-67.

91. Macqueen-Pope, p. 145.

92. George H. Cunningham cites the story that Cibber died "next to the Castle Tavern in Islington," (p. 40) but there is nothing to support this. The words of Victor, in London at the time of Cibber's death, carry more weight, especially when confirmed by the papers of 13 December 1757: *Lloyd's Evening Post*, *Public Advertizer*, *British Chronicle*, *London Chronicle*, and *London Evening Post*.

93. The burial register and sexton's books of St. George's, Hanover Square, record, 18 December 1757: "Audley, South Audley or Grosvenor Chapel, of Colley Cibber, Esq., (aged 87 years), of Berkeley Square." Grosvenor Chapel was built in 1730, and its churchyard was commonly used for burials from St. George's.

94. James Boswell, *Life of Samuel Johnson*, ed. G. B. Hill, rev. L. F. Powell, 6 vols. (Oxford, 1934), I, 402.

EPILOGUE

1. Marriage register, St. George's, Hanover Square, "John Thomas Esquire and Catharine Brown," 4 June 1761.

2. A note in the margin of Cibber's will, dated 6 November 1762, names Catherine Brown "deceased" and Jane Cibber Ellis, who "survived the said Catherine Brown Widow and died intestate." The administration of the estate was then granted to "Catherine Thomas, formerly Brown, the Daughter and sole Executrix named in the Will of the said Catharine Brown." Harvard Theatre Collection; reprinted in Ashley, *Cibber*, p. 202.

3. Kitty's marriage took place on 6 January 1749/50 (parish register, Lymington, Hampshire).

4. On 3 June 1773, the *Gazette* printed the following notice: "On Thursday last, died, in the 43rd year of her age, Mrs. Catherine Maria Harman, granddaughter to the celebrated Colley Cibber, Esq., poet laureate. She was a just actress, possessed much merit in low comedy, and dressed all her characters with infinite propriety, but her figure prevented her from succeeding in tragedy and genteel comedy. In private life she was sensible, humane and benevolent. Her little fortune she has left to Miss Cheer, and her obsequies were on Saturday night attended by a very genteel procession to the cemetery of the old English Church." The church, with all its records, was burned by the British in 1776.

Bibliography

An Account of the Life of that Celebrated Actress, Mrs. Susannah Maria Cibber, with Interesting and amusing Anecdotes. Also the Two Remarkable and Romantic Trials between Theophilus Cibber and William Sloper. London, 1887.

The Actor; or, A Treatise on the Art of Playing. 2d ed. London, 1755.

Adams, H. C. *Wykehamia.* London, 1878.

Adams, Henry Hitch, and Baxter Hathaway. *Dramatic Essays of the Neoclassic Age.* New York, 1950.

Addison, Joseph, and Richard Steele. *The Tatler.* Ed. George A. Aitken. London, 1898.

An Address from the Hundreds of Drury. London, 1718.

Agate, James, ed. *The English Dramatic Critics (1660-1932).* London, 1932.

The Age of Dullness. London, 1757.

Aitken, George. *The Life of Richard Steele.* 2 vols. London, 1889.

Animadversions on Mr. Congreve's Late Answer to Mr. Collier in a Dialogue between Mr. Smith and Mr. Johnson. London, 1698.

An Apology for the Life of Mr. T . . . C . . . , Comedian, Being a Proper Sequel to the Apology for the Life of Mr. Colley Cibber, Comedian. London, 1740.

Appleton, William W. *Charles Macklin: An Actor's Life.* Cambridge, Mass., 1960.

Armstrong, John, *Miscellanies.* 2 vols. London, 1770.

Arundel, Dennis. *The Story of Sadler's Wells, 1683-1964.* London, 1965.

Ashley, Leonard R. N. *Colley Cibber.* New York, 1965.

———. "Colley Cibber: A Bibliography." *Restoration and 18th Century Theatre Research,* 6, nos. 1, pp. 14-27, and 2, pp. 51-57 (1967).

Ashton, John. *The Fleet.* London, 1888.

Aston, Anthony. *A Brief Supplement to Colley Cibber, Esq.; His Lives of the late Famous Actors and Actresses.* Reprint ed., with Lowe's edition of Cibber's *Apology* (London, 1889).

Ault, Norman. *New Light on Pope.* London, 1949.

Austin, Wiltshire Stanton, and John Ralph. *The Lives of the Poets Laureate.* London, 1853.

Avery, Emmet. "Cibber, *King John*, and the Students at Law." *MLN*, 53 (April 1938), 272-75.

———. "The *Craftsman* of July 2, 1737, and Colley Cibber." *Research Studies of the State College of Washington*, 7,1 (1939), 90-103.

———. "Dancing and Pantomime on the English Stage, 1700-1737." *SP*, 31,3 (1934), 417-52.

———. "The Defense and Criticism of Pantomimic Entertainments in the Early Eighteenth Century." *ELH*, 5 (1938), 127-45.

———. "Fielding's Last Season with the Haymarket Theatre." *MP*, 36,3 (1939), 283-92.

———. "Some Notes on Fielding's Plays." *Research Studies of the State College of Washington*, 3,2 (1936), 48-50.

———. "The Stage Popularity of *The Rehearsal*, 1671-1777." *Research Studies of the State College of Washington*, 7,2 (1939), 201-4.

Ayre, William. *Memoirs of the Life and Writings of Alexander Pope.* 2 vols. London, 1745.

Baker, David Erskine. *Biographia Dramatica; or a Companion to the Playhouse.* 3 vols. London, 1812.

Baker, H. Barton. *History of the London Stage and Its Players, 1576-1903.* London, 1904.

———. *The London Stage: Its History and Traditions from 1576 to 1888.* 2 vols. London, 1889.

———. *Our Old Actors.* 2 vols. London, 1878.

[Baker, Henry]. *The Universal Spectator.* 4 vols. 3d ed. London, 1756.

Barbeau, A. *Life and Letters at Bath in the Eighteenth Century*, London, 1904.

Barker, Kathleen. "John Hippisley's Earliest Farce." *TN*, 26, no. 1 (Autumn 1972), 21-22.

Barker, Richard Hindry. *Mr. Cibber of Drury Lane.* New York, 1939.

Baskerville, Charles Read. "Play-Lists and Afterpieces of the Eighteenth Century." *MP*, 23,4 (1926), 445-64.

Bateson, F. W. "*The Double Gallant* of Colley Cibber." *RES*, 1,3 (1925), 343-46.

———. *English Comic Drama*, 1700-1750. Oxford, 1929.

The Battle of the Authors Lately Fought in Covent-Garden. . . . London, 1720.

The Battle of the Players. London, 1762.

The Battle of the Poets; or, the Contention for the Laurel. London, 1731.

Bedford, Arthur. *The Evil and Danger of Stage Plays. . . .* Bristol, 1706.

Beljame, A. O. *Men of Letters and the English Public in the Eighteenth Century.* Trans. E. O. Lorimer; ed. Bonamy Dobree. London, 1948.

Bell, John. *Bell's British Theatre, Consisting of the Most Esteemed English Plays.* 36 vols. London, 1791-1802.

Bell, Walter George. *The Great Fire of London in 1666.* London, 1920.

Berger, A. V. "*The Beggar's Opera*, the Burlesque and Italian Opera." *Music and Letters*, 17,2 (1936), 93-105.

Bernbaum, Ernest. *The Drama of Sensibility.* Cambridge, Mass., 1925.

A Biographical Dictionary of Actors, Actresses, Musicians, Dancers, Managers and Other Stage Personnel in London, 1660-1800. Ed. Philip H. Highfill, Jr., Kalman A. Burnim, and Edward A. Langhans. Carbondale, Ill., 1973-. 10 vols. to date.

Bibliography

Black, William Henry. *History and Antiquities of the Worshipful Company of Leathersellers of the City of London.* London, 1871.

Blair, Hugh. *Letters on Rhetoric and Belles Lettres.* New York, 1824.

A Blast upon Bays; or, A New Lick at the Laureat. London, 1742.

Boas, F. S. *An Introduction to Eighteenth-Century Drama, 1700-1780.* Oxford, 1953.

Bolling, Robert. "A Collection of Diverting Anecdotes, bon Mots and Other Trifling Pieces." 1764. Huntington Library, *MS* BR 163. San Marino, California.

Borgman, Albert S. *The Life and Death of William Mountfort.* Cambridge, Mass., 1935.

Boswell, James. *The Life of Samuel Johnson.* Ed. George Birbeck Hill; rev. L. F. Powell. 6 vols. Oxford, 1934.

Bourke, Algernon. *The History of White's.* 2 vols. London, 1892.

Bowyer, John Wilson. *The Celebrated Mrs. Centlivre.* Durham, N.C., 1952.

[Bramston, James]. *The Man of Taste.* London, 1733.

[Breval, Joseph]. *A Compleat Key to the Non-Juror.* London, 1718.

Brewster, Dorothy. *Aaron Hill, Poet, Dramatist and Projector.* New York, 1913.

The British Album. Dublin, 1780.

Broadbent, R. J. *Annals of the Liverpool Stage.* Liverpool, 1908.

Broadley, A. M. *The Age of David Garrick by Percy Fitzgerald.* 17 vols. London, 1868.

Broadus, Edmund Kemmer. *The Laureateship: A Study of the Office of the Poet Laureateship in England.* Oxford, 1921.

Brown, Jack Richard. "From Aaron Hill to Henry Fielding." *PQ,* 18,1 (1939), 85-88.

Brown, Richard E. "The Fops in Cibber's Comedies." *Essays in Literature,* 9 (Spring 1982), 31-41.

Brown, T. Alston. *History of the New York Stage, 1732-1901.* 3 vols. New York, 1903.

[Brown, Thomas]. *The Life of the Late Famous Comedian, Jo. Haynes.* London, 1701.

Bruton, John W. "The Text of Colley Cibber's *The Double Gallant; or, The Sick Lady's Cure.*" *SB,* 30 (1977), 186-96.

Burn, John Southden. *The History of Parish Registers in London.* London, 1829.

Burnaby, William. *Works.* Ed. F. E. Budd. London, 1931.

Burney, Charles. *A General History of Music.* 4 vols. London, 1782-89.

Burton, E. J. *The British Theatre: Its Repertory and Practice.* London, 1960.

The Buskin and Sock. Dublin, 1843.

Byrom, John. *The Private Journal and Literary Remains of John Byrom.* Ed. Richard Parkinson. 2 vols. N.p., 1855.

Cameron, Kenneth M. "Jo Haynes, '*Infamis.*'" *TN,* 24 (Winter 1969/70), 56-67.

Carey, Henry. *Poems.* Ed. Frederick T. Wood. London, 1930.

Carlisle, Nicholas. *A Concise Description of the Endowed Grammar Schools in England and Wales.* London, 1818.

The Case of our Present Theatrical Disputes, fairly stated. London, 1743.

Chancellor, E. Beresford. *The Annals of Covent Garden and its Neighborhood.* London, n.d.

———. *The Lives of the British Sculptors.* London, 1911.

Chandler, Knos. "Two Fielding Pamphlets." *PQ,* 16,4 (1937), 410-12.

Charke, Charlotte. *The Art of Management; or, Tragedy Expell'd.* London, 1753.

———. *The History of Henry Dumont, Esq; and Miss Charlotte Evelyn.* London, 1756.

———. *The Lover's Treat; or, Unnatural Hatred.* London, n.d.

———. *The Mercer; or, Fatal Extravagance.* London, 1758.

———. *A Narrative of the Life of Mrs. Charlotte Charke* (1755). Ed. Leonard Ashley. Gainesville, Fla., 1969.

Chesterfield, Earl of. *Characters of Eminent Personages of his own Times.* 2d ed. London, 1777.

Chetwood, William Rufus. *The British Theatre.* Dublin, 1750.

———. *Chronological Diary for the Year 1734.* London, 1735.

———. *A General History of the Stage, From its Origin in Greece down to the present Time.* London, 1749.

Churchill, Charles. *The Rosciad.* London, 1762.

Cibber, Colley. *Another Occasional Letter from Mr. Cibber to Mr. Pope.* London, 1744.

———. *An Apology for the Life of Mr. Colley Cibber, Comedian, and Late Patentee of the Theatre-Royal.* London, 1740. Ed. Edmund Bellchambers, London, 1822; ed. Robert W. Lowe, 2 vols., London, 1889; 2 vols., Waltham Saint Lawrence, 1925; ed. B. R. S. Fone, Ann Arbor, Mich., 1968.

———. *The Blind Boy.* London, 1735.

———. *Caesar in Aegypt.* London, 1725.

———. *The Careless Husband.* London, 1705. Ed. William Appleton, Regents Restoration Drama Series, Lincoln, Nebr., 1966.

———. *The Character and Conduct of Cicero.* London, 1747.

———. *The Comical Lovers.* London, 1707.

———. *Damon and Phillida.* London, 1729.

———. *The Double Gallant; or, The Sick Lady's Cure.* London, 1707.

———. *The Dramatick Works of Colley Cibber, Esq.* 5 vols. London, 1736.

———. *The Dramatic Works of Colley Cibber, Esq.* 4 vols. London, 1760.

———. *The Dramatic Works of Colley Cibber, Esq.* 5 vols. London, 1777.

———. *The Egoist; or, Colley upon Cibber.* London, 1743.

———. *The Lady's Last Stake; or The Wife's Resentment.* London, 1707.

———. *The Lady's Lecture.* London, 1748.

———. *A Letter from Mr. Cibber to Mr. Pope.* London, 1742.

———. Letters to Richardson, 20 May, 6 June 1753. Huntington Library, *MSS* 34562-34564. San Marino, California.

———. *Love in a Riddle.* London, 1729.

———. *Love Makes a Man; or, The Fop's Fortune.* London, 1701.

———. *Love's Last Shift; or, The Fool in Fashion.* London, 1696.

———. *Le mari poussé à bout.* In *Traductions du Théâtre Anglois,* vol. 5. Paris, 1784.

———. *Myrtillo.* London, 1716.

———. *The Non-Juror.* London, 1718.

———. *An Ode for His Majesty's Birth-Day.* London, 1731.

———. *An Ode to his Majesty, for the New-Year 1730/31.* London, 1731.

———. *Papal Tyranny in the Reign of King John.* London, 1745.

———. *Perolla and Izadora.* London, 1706.

———. *Plays Written by Mr. Cibber.* 2 vols. London, 1721.

———. *A Poem on the Death of Our Late Sovereign Lady Queen Mary.* London, 1695.

————. *Polypheme*. London, 1734.

————. *The Provok'd Husband* (with Sir John Vanbrugh). London, 1728. Ed. Peter Dixon, London, 1974.

————. *The Refusal; or, The Ladies Philosophy*. London, 1721.

————. *Rhapsody upon the Marvellous*. London, 1751.

————. *The Rival Fools*. London, 1709.

————. *The Rival Queans*. Ed. William Peterson. Lake Erie College Studies, vol. 5. Painesville, Ohio, 1965.

————. *The School Boy; or, The Comical Rivals*. London, 1707.

————. *She Wou'd and She Wou'd Not; or, The Kind Impostor*. London, 1702.

————. *A Second Letter from Mr. Cibber to Mr. Pope*. London, 1743.

————. *Three Sentimental Comedies*. Ed. Maureen Sullivan. New York, 1973.

————. *The Tragical History of King Richard III*. London, 1700.

————. *Venus and Adonis*. London, 1715.

————. *Xerxes*. London, 1699.

————. *Ximena; or, The Heroick Daughter*. London, 1735.

Cibber, Susannah. *The Oracle*. London, 1752.

Cibber, Theophilus. *An Epistle from Mr. Theophilus Cibber, Comedian, to Mr. Thomas Sheridan, Tragedian*. Dublin, 1742.

————. *An Epistle from Mr. Theophilus Cibber to David Garrick, Esq.* London, 1755.

————. *Four Original Letters*. London, 1739.

————. *An Historical Tragedy of the Civil Wars in the Reign of King Henry VI*. London, 1724.

————. *A Letter from Theophilus Cibber, Comedian, to John Highmore, Esq.* London, 1733.

————. *A Lick at a Liar; or, Calumny Detected*. London, 1752.

————. *The Lovers*. London, 1730.

————. *Memoirs of the Life of Barton Booth*. London, 1753.

————. *Romeo and Juliet* (revision of Shakespeare's play). London, 1748.

————. *A Serio-Comic Apology for Part of the Life of Mr. Theophilus Cibber, Comedian*. Dublin, 1748.

————. *Two Dissertations on the Theatres*. London, 1756.

Clark, William Smith. *The Early Irish Stage from the Beginnings to 1720*. Oxford, 1955.

————. *The Irish Stage in the Country Towns*. Oxford, 1955.

————. "Restoration Prompt Notes and Stage Practices," *MLN*, 51,4 (1936), 226-30.

Cleveland, Arthur. *Cibber's Revision of Shakespeare's Richard III*. Philadelphia, 1911.

A Clue to the Comedy of the Non-Juror. London, 1718.

A Collection of all the Humourous Letters in the London Journal. London, 1721.

Collier, Jeremy. *A Short View of the Immorality and Profaneness of the English Stage*. London, 1698.

The Comedian; or, Philosophical Enquirer, III. London, 1732/33.

Conder, Edward. *Records of the Whole Craft and Fellowship of Masons*. London, 1894.

Congreve, William. *The Complete Works*. Ed. Montague Summers. 4 vols. London, 1923.

Connelly, Willard. *Beau Nash*. London, 1955.

Cook. A. K. *About Winchester College*. London, 1917.

Bibliography

[Cooke, Thomas]. *The Battle of the Poets; or, The Contention for the Laurel*. London, 1731.

Cooke, William, *The Elements of Dramatic Criticism*. London, 1775.

"Corinna." *Critical Remarks on the Four Taking Plays of the Season*. London, 1719.

Corneille, Pierre. *Oeuvres*. 3 vols. Paris, 1960.

Cox, H. Bartle. *Ange-Jacque Gabriel*. London, 1926.

Craftsman, 1731-37.

Crane, R. S. "Suggestions toward a genealogy of the 'Man of Feeling.'" *ELH*, 1,3 (1934), 205-31.

Crawford, Mary Caroline. *The Romance of the American Theatre*. New York, 1940.

Crean, P. J. "The Stage Licensing Act of 1737." *MP*, 35,3 (1937-38), 239-55.

Croissant, De Witt C. "Early Sentimental Comedy." *Essays in Dramatic Literature*. The Parrot Presentation Volume. Ed. Hardin Craig. Princeton, 1935, pp. 47-71.

———. "A Note on The Egoist or Colley upon Cibber." *PQ*, 3,1 (1924), 76-77.

———. *Studies in the Work of Colley Cibber*. Bulletin of the University of Kansas Humanistic Studies, 1. Lawrence, Kans., 1912.

Cross, W. L. *The History of Henry Fielding*. 3 vols. New Haven, Conn., 1918.

Cumberland, Richard. *Memoirs*. London, 1806.

Cunningham, George H. *London*. London, 1931.

Cunningham, John E. *Restoration Drama*. London, 1966.

Cunningham, Peter. "New Materials for the Life of Caius Gabriel Cibber." *The Builder*, 22 November 1862, pp. 835-36.

Daily Advertiser. 1731-54.

Daily Courant. 1702-35.

Davies, Thomas. *Dramatic Miscellanies*. 3 vols. London, 1785.

———. *Memoirs of the Life of David Garrick*. 2 vols. London, 1780.

Davis, Rose Mary. *Stephen Duck, the Thresher Poet*. University of Maine Studies, 2d ser., 8. Orono, 1926.

Defoe, Daniel. *A Tour thro' London about the Year 1725*. Ed. Sir Mayson M. Beeton and E. Beresford Chancellor. London, 1929.

Delany, Mary Granville. *Autobiography and Correspondence*. 6 vols. London, 1861.

Dennis, John. *The Critical Works of John Dennis*. Ed. Edward Niles Hooker. 2 vols. Baltimore, 1939-43.

Denoon, D. G. "The Statue of King Charles I at Charing Cross." *Transactions of the London and Middlesex Archaeological Society*. n.s. 6 (1933) pp. 460-486.

Dent, E. S. *Foundations of English Opera*. Cambridge, Mass., 1928.

Derrick, Samuel. See Wilkes, Thomas.

Tò diabebouloumenon; or, the proceedings at the Theatre-Royal, Drury-Lane. London, 1723.

Dibdin, Charles. *A Complete History of the Stage*. 5 vols. London, 1800.

Dillon, Viscount. "Charles I at Charing Cross," *Middlesex and Hertfordshire Notes and Queries*, 4 (1898), pp. 1-4.

The Disputes between the Director of D——y and the Pit Poetentates. London, 1744.

D'Israeli, Isaac. *Calamities and Quarrels of Authors*. 3 vols. London, 1859.

Dixon, Peter, and Rodney Hayley. "*The Provok'd Husband* on the Nineteenth-Century Stage." *NCTR*, 8,1 (1980), 1-16.

225

Bibliography

Dobree, Bonamy. *Restoration Comedy*. Oxford, 1924.

———. *Restoration Tragedy*. Oxford, 1954.

Dobson, Austin. *Samuel Richardson*. London, 1902.

Dodds, John Wendell. *Thomas Southerne, Dramatist*. New Haven, Conn., 1933.

Doering, J. Frederick. "Hume and the Theory of Tragedy." *PMLA*, 52,4 (1937), 1130-34.

Dolmetsch, Carl. "William Byrd II: Comic Dramatist?" *EAL*, 6 (Spring 1971), 18-30.

Doran, J. *Their Majesties' Servants*. 3 vols. New York, n.d.

Dorman, James H. *Theater in the Antebellum South*. Chapel Hill, N.C., 1967.

Downer, Alan S. "Nature to Advantage Dressed: Eighteenth-Century Acting." *PMLA*, 58 (December, 1943), 1002-37.

Downes, John. *Roscius Anglicanus; or, an Historical Review of the Stage*. Annotated by Thos. Davies. London, 1789; ed. Montague Summers. London, 1926.

Downie, J. A. "Pope, Swift, and *An Ode for the New Year*." *RES*, 32 (May 1981), 161-72.

The Dramatic Congress. London, 1843.

Draper, John W. "The Theory of the Comic in Eighteenth-Century England." *JEGP*, 37,2 (1938), 207-33.

Drougge, Helga. "Colley Cibber's 'Genteel Comedy': *Love's Last Shift* and *The Careless Husband*." *SN*, 54,1 (1982), 61-79.

Duck, Stephen. *Poems on Several Subjects*. London, 1730.

Dudden, F. H. *Henry Fielding: his Life, Work and Times*. 2 vols. Oxford, 1952.

Duerr, Edwin. *The Length and Breadth of Acting*. New York, 1962.

Dunscombe, John. *Letters by Several Eminent Persons, Deceased*. 3 vols. London, 1773.

Eaton, Walter Pritchard. "Colley Cibber as Critic." In *The Actor's Heritage*. Boston, 1924.

Eaves, T. C. Duncan, and Ben D. Kimpel. *Samuel Richardson*. Oxford, 1971.

Egerton, William. *Faithful Memoirs of the Life, Amours and Performances of that Justly Celebrated, and most Eminent Actress of her Time, Mrs. Anne Oldfield*. London, 1731.

Egmont, Earl of. *Manuscripts*. London, 1920.

Ehrstine, J. W., John R. Ellwood, and Robert C. McLean, eds. *On Stage and Off*. Washington, D.C., 1968.

Elwin, Malcolm. *The Playgoer's Handbook to Restoration Drama*. London, 1928.

"English Stage Comedy." In *English Institute Essays*, ed. W. K. Wimsatt. New York, 1955.

Esdaile, Mrs. "Some Sussex Monuments." *Sussex Notes and Queries*, 8 (August 1941), 185-87.

An Essay on Acting. London, 1744.

An Essay on Satirical Entertainments. 3d ed. London, 1772.

An Essay on the Stage; or, The Art of Acting. Edinburgh, 1754.

An Essay on the Theatres; or, The Art of Acting. London, 1745.

Faber, Harald. *Caius Gabriel Cibber*. Oxford, 1926.

Fielding, Henry. *The Champion*. 2 vols. London, 1741.

Fisher, Dorothy Canfield. *Corneille and Racine in England*. New York, 1904.

226

Fitzgerald, Percy. *A New History of the English Stage.* 2 vols. London, 1882.

Flecknoe, Richard. *A Short Discourse on the English Stage.* London, 1664.

Flying-Post; or, the Post-Master. 1712-29.

Fog's Weekly Journal, 1728-32.

Fone, B. R. S. "*Love's Last Shift* and Sentimental Comedy." *Restoration and Eighteenth-Century Research,* 9,1 (1970), 11-23.

[Foote, Samuel]. *A Treatise on the Passions.* London, n.d.

Ford, Boris, ed. *From Dryden to Johnson.* Baltimore, 1960.

Ford, Paul Leicester. *Washington and the Theatre.* New York, 1899.

Free Briton. 1727.

Fujimura, Thomas Hikara. *The Restoration Comedy of Wit.* Princeton, 1952.

Fyvie, John. *Comedy Queens of the Georgian Era.* London, 1906.

Gagey, Edmond McAdoo. *Ballad Operas.* New York, 1965.

Galt, John. *The Lives of the Players.* 2 vols. London, 1831.

Garrick, David. *Letters.* Ed. David M. Little and George M. Kahrl. 3 vols. Cambridge, Mass., 1963.

Genest, John. *Some Account of the English Stage from the Restoration in 1660 to 1830.* 10 vols. Bath, 1832.

[Gentleman, Francis]. *The Dramatic Censor.* Ed. J. M. Williams. London, 1812.

Gentleman's Magazine. 1730-57.

Gildon, Charles. *A Comparison between the Two Stages.* Ed. Staring B. Wells. Princeton, 1942.

———. *The Life of Mr. Thomas Betterton.* London, 1710.

Gilmore, Thomas B. "Colley Cibber's Good Nature and His Reaction to Pope's Satire." *Papers on Language and Literature,* 2,4 (1966), 361-71.

Glicksman, Harry. "The Stage History of Colley Cibber's *The Careless Husband.*" *PMLA,* 36 (1921), 244-50.

Goldstein, Malcolm. *Pope and the Augustan Stage.* Stanford, Calif., 1958.

Gore-Browne, Robert. *Gay Was the Pit.* London, 1957.

Gosse, Edmund. *Life of William Congreve.* London, 1924.

Gray, Charles Harold. *Theatrical Criticism in London to 1795.* New York, 1931.

Gray, W. Forbes. *The Poets Laureate and Their History and Their Odes.* London, 1914.

Green, Frederick C. *Literary Ideas in Eighteenth-Century France and England.* New York, 1966.

Griffith, R. H. "A 'Wildfrau Story' in a Cibber Play." *PQ,* 12,3 (1933), 298-302.

Grove, Sir George. *Dictionary of Music and Musicians.* Ed. H. C. Coles. New York, 1940.

Habbema, D. M.E. *An Appreciation of Colley Cibber.* Amsterdam, 1928.

Harbage, Alfred. *Annals of English Drama, 975-1700.* Rev. and ed. S. Schoenbaum. Philadelphia, 1964.

Hawkins, Frederick. *The French Stage in the Eighteenth Century.* London, 1884.

Hayley, Rodney L. "Cibber, Collier, and *The Non-Juror.*" *HLQ,* 43,1 (1979), 61-75.

———. "Pope, Cibber, and *A Clue to the Comedy of The Non-Juror.*" *SP,* 76,2 (1979), 182-201.

———. "The Swingeing of Cibber: The Suppression of the First Edition of *The Refusal.*" *SB,* 28 (1975) 290-97.

Hédelin, Francois [Abbé d'Aubignac]. *The Whole Art of the Stage.* London, 1684.

[Hervey, John]. *The Difference between Verbal and Practical Virtue.* With a Prefatory Epistle from Mr. C——b——r to Mr. P. London, 1742.

Hill, Aaron. *The Prompter.* Ed. William W. Appleton and Kalman A. Burnim. New York, 1966.

———. *Works.* 4 vols. London, 1753.

Hill, John. *The Actor: A Treatise on the Art of Playing.* London, 1750.

Hillhouse, J. T. *The Grub-Street Journal.* Durham, N.C., 1938.

Hilson, J. C., M. M. B. Jones, and J. R. Watson, eds. *Augustan Worlds: New Essays in Eighteenth-Century Literature.* New York, 1978.

Hitchcock, Robert. *An Historical View of the Irish Stage.* 2 vols. Dublin, 1794.

Holland, Norman. *The First Modern Comedies.* Cambridge, Mass., 1959.

Holland, Peter. *The Ornament of Action: Text and Performance in Restoration Comedy.* Cambridge, Mass., 1979.

Hopkins, Kenneth. *The Poets Laureate.* Carbondale, Ill., 1966.

Horn-Monval, M. *Répertoire Bibliographique des Traductions et Adaptations Françaises du Théâtre Etranger du xv.e Siècle à nos Jours.* 5 vols. Paris, 1963.

Hotson, Leslie. *The Commonwealth and Restoration Stages.* Cambridge, Mass., 1928.

Hughes, John. *Letters.* Ed. John Duncombe. 3 vols. London, 1773.

Hume, Robert D. "The Dorset Garden Theatre: A Review of Facts and Problems." *TN*, 33,1 (1979), 4-17.

Ireland, Joseph. *Records of the New York Stage.* 2 vols. New York, 1866.

Irving, Henry Brodribb. "Colley Cibber's *Apology*," *Two Lectures.* London, 1904.

Jackson, Alfred. "Play Notices from the Burney Newspapers, 1700-1703." *PMLA*, 48,3 (1933), 815-49.

———. "The Stage and the Authorities 1700-1714 (As Revealed in the Newspapers)." *RES*, 14 (January, 1938), 53-62.

Jackson, Allan S. "Little Known Theatrical Prints of the Eighteenth Century." *TN*, 22,3 (1968), 113-16.

[Jacob, Giles]. *The Poetical Register.* 2 vols. London, 1719.

Jacobs, Arthur. *A Short History of Western Music.* Baltimore, 1972.

Jenkins, David Clay. "The James Street Theatre at the Old Tennis-Court." *TN*, 23,4 (1969), 143-50.

Johnson, Edgar. *One Mighty Torrent: The Drama of Biography.* New York, 1955.

Johnson, Wallace. "Affective Value in Later Eighteenth-Century Esthetics." *JEAC*, 24 (Winter 1965), 311-14.

Jordan, R. "Some Restoration Playgoers." *TN*, 35,2 (1981), 51-57.

A Journey from London to Scarborough. London, 1734.

Kahl, William F. "Apprenticeship and the Freedom of the London Livery Companies, 1690-1750," *Guildhall Miscellany*, 7 (August 1956), 17-20.

Kalson, Albert E. "Colley Cibber Plays *Richard III*." *TS*, 16,1 (1975), 42-55.

———. "Eighteenth-Century Editions of Colley Cibber's *Richard III*." *Restoration and 18th Century Theatre Research*, 7,1 (1968), 7-17.

Kelly, John Alexander. *German Visitors to English Theaters in the Eighteenth Century.* Princeton, 1936.

Kennet, White. *Memoirs of the Family of Cavendish.* London, 1708.

Kenny, Shirley Strum. "Humane Comedy." *MP*, 75,1 (1978), 29-43.

————. "Perennial Favorites: Congreve, Vanbrugh, Cibber, Farquhar, and Steele." *MP*, 73, (May, 1976), S4-S11.

————. "Theatrical Warfare, 1695-1718." *TN*, 27,4 (1973), 130-45.

Kirby, Thomas Frederick. *Annals of Winchester College*. London, 1892.

Kirkman, J. T. *Memoirs of the Life of Charles Macklin*. London, 1799.

Knapp, Mary E. *Prologues and Epilogues of the Eighteenth Century*. New Haven, Conn., 1961.

Kronenberger, Louis. *The Thread of Laughter*. New York, 1952.

Krutch, Joseph Wood. *Comedy and Conscience after the Restoration*. New York, 1961.

Lamson, Roy. "Henry Purcell's Dramatic Songs and the English Broadside Ballad." *PMLA*, 53,1 (1938), 148-61.

Lancaster, Henry Carrington. *A History of French Dramatic Literature in the Seventeenth Century*. 2 vols. Paris, 1932.

Langbaine, Gerard [and Charles Gildon]. *Lives and Characters of the English Dramatic Poets*. London, 1699.

Langhans, Edward A. "New Early Eighteenth-Century Performances and Casts." *TN*, 24 (Summer 1972), 145-46.

A Lash for the Laureat; or, An Address by Way of Satyre. London, 1718.

The Laureat; or, the Right Side of Colley Cibber, Esq. London, 1740.

Lawrence, W. J. "Doors and Curtains in Restoration Theatre." *MLR*, 15,4 (1920), 414-19.

Leach, Arthur F. *A History of Winchester College*. London, 1899.

Leblanc, Abbé Jean. *Letters on the English and French Nations*. 2 vols. London, 1747.

Lecky. W. E. H. *A History of England in the Eighteenth Century*. 8 vols. London, 1878-90.

Leech, C. "Shakespeare, Cibber, and the Tudor Myth." In *Tennessee Studies in Literature*, II, Ed. Alwin Thaler and Norman J. Sanders. Knoxville, 1964.

A Letter to Colley Cibber, Esq.; on his Transformation of King John. London, 1745.

A Letter to John Gay, Concerning his Late Farce, Entituled, A Comedy. London, 1717.

Lewis, D. B. W., and Charles Lee, eds. *The Stuffed Owl*. New York, 1930.

Liesenfeld, Vincent, "The 'First' Playhouse Bill: A Stage Ghost." *TN*, 22,1 (1977), 9-12.

————. *The Licensing Act of 1737*. Madison, Wis., 1984.

The Life and Times of Thomas Betterton. London, 1888.

The Life of Mr. John Dennis, the Renowned Critick. London, 1934.

The Life of That Eminent Comedian Robert Wilks, Esq. London, 1733.

The Life of the Late Famous Comedian, Jo. Haynes. London, 1701.

A List of the Nobility, Quality, and Gentry, at Scarborough During the Spaw Season, in the Year 1733. London, 1734.

Lloyd, Robert. *The Actor, A Poetical Epistle*. London, 1760.

Loftis, John. *Comedy and Society from Congreve to Fielding*. Stanford, Calif., 1959.

————. *The Politics of Drama in Augustan England*. Oxford, 1963.

————. *Steele at Drury Lane*. Los Angeles, 1952.

London Magazine, 1731-60.

London Marriage Licenses, 1521-1869. Ed. Joseph Foster. London, 1887.

The London Medley. London, 1731.

The London Stage, 1660-1800. Eds. William Van Lennep, Emmet L. Avery, Arthur

H. Scouten, George Winchester Stone, Jr., Charles Beecher Hogan. 5 vols. Carbondale, Ill., 1960-68.

Lovett, David. *Shakespeare's Characters in Eighteenth-Century Criticism*. Baltimore, 1935.

Lowe, Robert W. *Thomas Betterton*. London, 1891.

Luttrell, Narcissus. *A Brief Historical Relation of State Affairs from September 1678 to 1714*. 6 vols. Oxford, 1857.

Lynch, Kathleen. "Thomas D'Urfey's Contribution to Sentimental Comedy." *PQ*, 9,3 (1930), 249-59.

Lysons, Daniel. *The Environs of London*. 2 vols. London, 1800.

———. *An Historical Account of those Parishes in the County of Middlesex which are not Described in the Environs of London*. London, 1810.

McAleer, J. J. "Shakespeare's Adapter." *Shakespeare Newsletter*, 11 (December 1961), 42.

MacDonald, W. L. *Pope and his Critics*. London, 1951.

MacMillan, Dougald. "The Text of *Love's Last Shift*." *MLN*, 46,8 (1931), 518-19.

MacQueen-Pope, W. J. *Pillars of Drury Lane*. London, 1955.

———. *Theatre Royal Drury Lane*. London, 1945.

Mallet, Charles Edward. *A History of the University of Oxford*. 3 vols. London, 1927.

Manners, Lady Victoria. "Garden Sculpture by Caius Cibber." *Country Life*, 68 (1930), 382.

———. "The Rutland Monuments in Bottesford Church." *Art Journal* (1903), 335-39.

Markham, Algernon A. *The Story of Grantham and Its Church*. Gloucester, 1907.

Marly, Diane de. "The Architect of Dorset Garden Theatre." *TN* 29, 3 (1975), 119-24.

Melville, Lewis [Lewis Saul Benjamin]. *Bath under Beau Nash*. London, 1907.

———. *More Stage Favourites of the Eighteenth Century*. London, 1929.

———. *Stage Favourites of the Eighteenth Century*. London, 1928.

Memoirs of the Life of the Right Honourable Joseph Addison, Esq. London, 1719.

The Merry Medley; or, A Christmass Box. 2 vols. London, 1745.

Mignon, Elizabeth. *Crabbed Age and Youth*. Durham, N.C., 1947.

Miles, Dudley H. "A Forgotten Hit: *The Non-Juror*." *SP*, 16,1 (1919), 67-77.

———. *The Influence of Molière on Restoration Comedy*. Nw York, 1910.

———. "The Original of the Nonjuror." *PMLA*, 23,1 (1915), 195-214.

———. "The Political Satire of The Non-Juror." *MP*, 13,5 (1915-16) 182-304.

Miller, Frances Schouler. "Notes on Some Eighteenth-Century Dramas." *MLN*, 52,3 (1937), 203-6.

[Miller, James]. *Harlequin-Horace; or, The Art of Modern Poetry*. London, 1735.

Mist's Weekly Journal. 1718-28.

Mitchell, Louis D. "Command Performances during the Reign of Queen Anne." *TN*, 24,3 (Spring 1970), 111-17.

Moore, C. .A. "Shaftesbury and the Ethical Poets in England, 1700-1760." *PMLA*, 31,2 (1916), 264-325.

[Morris, Corbyn]. *An Essay toward Fixing True Standards*. London, 1744.

Muir, Kenneth. *The Comedy of Manners*. London, 1970.

Mullin, Donald. "Lighting on the Eighteenth-Century Stage: A Reconsideration." *TN*, 34,2 (1980), 73-85.

Muralt, Beat. L. [R. S. de]. *Lettres sur les Anglois*. 3 vols. Paris, 1726.

[Murphy, Arthur]. *The Gray's Inn Journal*. 2 vols. London, 1756.

Murray, Grace A. *Personalities of the Eighteenth Century*. London, 1927.

Murrie, Eleanor Boswell. *The Restoration Court Stage*. Cambridge, Mass., 1932.

Nash, Mary. *The Provoked Wife: The Life and Times of Susannah Cibber*. Boston, 1977.

New, Melvyn. "The Dunce Revisited: Colley Cibber and Tristram Shandy." *SAQ*, 72 (Autumn, 1973), 547-59.

Nichols, Charles W. "Fielding and the Cibbers." *PQ*, 1,4 (1922), 278-89.

———. "A Note on *The Stage Mutineers*." *MLN*, 35,4 (1920), 225-27.

Nichols, John. *Literary Anecdotes of the Eighteenth Century*. London, 1812-15.

———. *Minor Lives*. Ed. Edward L. Hart. Cambridge, Mass., 1971.

Nicholson, Watson. *The Struggle for a Free Stage in London*. London, 1906.

Nicoll, Allardyce. *British Drama*. 3d ed. London, 1932.

———. *The English Theatre*. New York, 1936.

———. *A History of Early Eighteenth-Century Drama*. Cambridge, 1925.

———. *A History of Restoration Drama, 1660-1700*. Cambridge, 1928.

Nolte, Fred O. *Early Middle Class Drama, 1696-1700*. Ottendorfer Series of Germanic Monographs, 19. Lancaster, Pa., 1935.

North, Roger. *Memoirs of Musick*. Ed. Edward F. Rimbault. London, 1846.

Noyes, Robert Gale. "Songs from Restoration Drama in contemporary and Eighteenth-Century Poetical Miscellanies." *ELH*, 3,4 (1936), 291-316.

Odell, George C. D. *Annals of the New York Stage*. 15 vols. New York, 1927.

———. *Shakespeare from Betterton to Irving*. New York, 1920.

Old England's Worthies. London, 1847.

[Oldys, William]. *The History of the English Stage, from the Restauration to the Present Time*. London, 1741.

———. *Memoirs of Mrs. Anne Oldfield*. London, 1741.

Olleson, Philip. "Vanbrugh and Opera at the Queen's Theatre, Haymarket." *TN*, 26,3 (1972), 94-101.

Overton, J. H. *The Nonjurors*. London, 1902.

Palmer, J. L. *The Comedy of Manners*. London, 1913.

Parnell, Paul E. "Equivocation in Cibber's *Love's Last Shift*." *SP*, 57,3 (1960), 519-34.

———. "The Sentimental Mask." *PMLA*, 78,5 (1963), 529-35.

Paston, George [Emily Morse Symonds]. *Mr Pope His Life and Times*. 2 vols. London, 1909.

Paul, H. G. *John Dennis, his Life and Criticism*. New York, 1911.

Pearlman, E. "The Hamlet of Robert Wilks." *TN*, 24,3 (1970), 125-33.

Peavy, Charles D. "The Chimerical Career of Charlotte Charke." *Restoration and 18th Century Theatre Research*, 8,1 (1969), 1-12.

———. "The Pope-Cibber Controversy: A Bibliography." *Restoration and 18th Century Theatre Research*, 3,2 (1964), 51-55.

Percy, Sholto, and Reuben Percy [Joseph Clinton Roberts and Thomas Byerly]. *The Percy Anecdotes*. 20 vols. London, 1822.

Perry, Henry Ten Eyck. *Masters of Dramatic Comedy and Their Social Themes.* Cambridge, Mass., 1939.

Peterson, William H. "Cibber's *She Wou'd and She Wou'd Not* and Vanbrugh's *Aesop.*" *PQ*, 35,4 (1956), 429-35.

———. "Pope and Cibber's *The Non-Juror.*" *MLN*, 70,5 (1955), 332-55.

———. "The Text of Cibber's *She Wou'd and She Wou'd Not.*" *MLN*, 71,4 (1956), 258-62.

Pilkington, John Carteret. *The Real Story.* N.p., 1760.

Pilkington, Laetitia. *Memoirs of Mrs. Laetitia Pilkington.* Ed. J. Isaacs. New York, 1928.

Poems on Several Occasions. Dublin, 1749.

Pollock, Thomas Clark. *The Philadelphia Theatre in the Eighteenth Century.* Philadelphia, 1933.

Pope, Alexander. *Correspondence.* Ed. George Sherburn. 5 vols. Oxford, 1956.

Prosser, Eleanor, "Colley Cibber at San Diego." *Shakespeare Quarterly*, 14,3 (1963), 253-61.

[Ralph, James]. *The Case of the Present Theatrical Dispute Fairly Stated.* London, 1743.

———. *The Touchstone.* London, 1729.

Rankin, Hugh F. *The Theater in Colonial America.* Chapel Hill, N.C., 1965.

Reddaway, T. F. *The Rebuilding of London after the Great Fire.* London, 1940.

Reflections on the Principal Characters in a late Comedy call'd The Provok'd Husband. London, 1728.

Rennel, Gabriel. *Tragi-Comical Reflections of a Moral and Political Tendency, occasioned by the Present State of the Two Rival Theatres in Drury-Lane and Lincolns-Inn-Fields.* London, 1723.

A Review of the Tragedy of Jane Shore. London, 1714.

Reynolds, W. Vaughan. "Goldsmith's Critical Outlook." *RES*, 14 (April, 1938), 155-72.

Richardson, Samuel. *Correspondence.* Ed. Anna Laetitia Barbauld. 6 vols. London, 1804.

Rogers, Francis. "Handel and the Five Prima Donnas." *Musical Quarterly*, 29,2 (1943), 214-24.

Roper, Alan. "Language and Action in *The Way of the World*, *Love's Last Shift*, and *The Relapse.*" *ELH*, 40 (Spring, 1973), 44-69.

Rosenfeld, Sybil. "Dramatic Advertisements in the Burney Newspapers, 1660-1700." *PMLA*, 51,1 (1936), 123-52.

———. "Some Notes on the Players at Oxford, 1661-1713." *RES*, 19 (October, 1943), 366-75.

———. *Strolling Players and Drama in the Provinces, 1660-1765.* Cambridge, 1939.

———. *The Theatre of the London Fairs in the Eighteenth Century.* Cambridge, 1960.

———. "Unpublished Stage Documents." *TN*, 11,3 (1959), 92-94.

Ross, Julian E. "Dramatist versus Audience in the Early Eighteenth Century." *PQ*, 12,1 (1933), 73-81.

Russell, Douglas A. *Theatrical Style: A Visual Approach to the Theatre.* Palo Alto, Calif., 1976.

St. George's Chapel May Fair. Ed. George J. Armytage. London, 1889.

Bibliography

St. James's Evening Post. 1715-16.

Sawney and Colley. London, 1742. Ed. William Powell Jones. Augustan Reprint Society. Los Angeles, 1960.

Sawyer, Paul. "The Popularity of Various Types of Entertainments at Lincoln's Inn Fields and Covent Garden Theatres, 1720-1733." *TN*, 24,4 (1970), 154-63.

The Scarborough Miscellany: For the Year 1734. London, 1734.

Schneider, Ben Ross. "The Coquette-Prude as an Actress's Line in the Restoration Comedy during the Time of Mrs. Oldfield." *TN*, 22,4 (1968), 143-55.

————. *The Ethos of Restoration Comedy.* Chicago, 1971.

Schultz, W. E. *Gay's Beggar's Opera.* New Haven, Conn., 1923.

Scribleriad. London, 1742.

A Seasonable Examination of the Plays and Presentations of the Proprietors of, and Subscribers to, Play-Houses erected in Defiance of the Royal Licence. London, 1735.

Seilhammer, George O. *History of the American Theatre before the Revolution.* New York, 1968.

Senior, F. Dorothy. *The Life and Times of Colley Cibber.* London, 1928.

Shadwell, Thomas. *Works.* Ed. Montague Summers. 4 vols. London, 1927.

Sheldon, Esther K. *Thomas Sheridan of Smock Alley.* Princeton, 1967.

Shelley, Henry C. *The Life and Letters of Edward Young.* Boston, 1914.

Shenstone, William. *Letters.* Ed. Duncan Mallam. Mineapolis, 1939.

Sherbo, Arthur. *English Sentimental Drama.* East Lansing, Mich., 1957.

Sherburn, George. "The Fortunes and Misfortunes of *Three Hours after Marriage.*" *MP*, 24,1 (1926), 91-109.

Sheridan, Thomas. *An Humble Appeal to the Publick, Together with some Considerations on the Present Critical and Dangerous State of the Stage in Ireland.* Dublin, 1758.

————. *Vindication.* Dublin, 1747.

Siebert, Donald T., Jr. "Cibber and Satan: *The Dunciad* and Civilization." *ECS*, 10,2 (1976/77), 203-21.

Smith, Dane Farnsworth. *The Critics in the Audience of the London Theatres from Buckingham to Sheridan.* Albuquerque, 1953.

————. *Plays about the Theatre in England, 1671-1733.* New York, 1936.

Smith, John Harrington. "French Sources for Six English Comedies, 1660-1750." *JEGP*, 47,4 (1948), 390-94.

————. *The Gay Couple in Restoration Comedy.* Cambridge, Mass., 1948.

————. "Shadwell, the Ladies, and the Change in Comedy." *MP*, 46,1 (1948), 22-33.

————. "Tony Lumpkin and the Country Booby Type in Antecedent English Comedy." *PMLA*, 58, (December, 1943), 1038-49.

Smithers, Peter. *The Life of Joseph Addison,* 2d ed. Oxford, 1968.

Some Cursory Remarks on the Play Call'd The Non-Juror. London, 1718.

Speaight, George. *The History of the English Puppet Theatre.* London, 1955.

[Spence, Joseph]. *A Full and Authentick Account of Stephen Duck, the Wiltshire Poet.* London, 1731.

————. *Observations, Anecdotes, and Characters of Books and Men.* Ed. James Osborne. 2 vols. Oxford, 1966.

Spencer, Christopher. *Five Restoration Adaptations of Shakespeare.* Urbana, Ill., 1965.

Bibliography

Spencer, Hazelton. *Shakespeare Improved.* Cambridge, Mass., 1927.

Spink, Reginald. "A Restoration Sculptor from Flensborg: The Work of Caius Gabriel Cibber." *Denmark* (1961), 9-10, 19.

Sprague, Arthur Colby. "A New Scene in Colley Cibber's *Richard III.*" *MLN*, 42,1 (1927), 29-32.

The Stage Beaux Toss'd in a Blanket. London, 1704.

Steele, Richard. *Correspondence.* Ed. Rae Blanchard. London, 1941.

———. *The Spectator.* Ed. Donald F. Bond. 5 vols. Oxford, 1965.

———. *The State of the Case Between the Lord Chamberlain of His Majesty's Household, and the Governor of the Royal Company of Comedians.* London, 1720.

———. *The Theatre.* Ed. John Loftis. Oxford, 1962.

———. *Tracts and Pamphlets.* Ed. Rae Blanchard. Baltimore, 1967.

Stockwell, La Tourette. *Dublin Theatres and Theatre Customs (1637-1820).* Kingsport, Tenn., 1938.

Street, B. *Historical Notes on Grantham.* Grantham, 1857.

The Strolers Pacquet Open'd. London, 1742.

Stroup, Thomas B. "*The Princess of Cleve* and Sentimental Comedy." *RES*, 11 (April, 1935), 200-3.

Summers, Montague. *The Restoration Theatre.* London, 1934.

Summerson, John. *Architecture in Britain, 1530-1830.* London, 1963.

Survey of London. Vol. 16, *Charing Cross.* Ed. G. H. Gater and Walter H. Godfrey. London, 1935. Vol. 35,*The Theatre Royal Drury Lane and the Royal Opera House Covent Garden.* Ed. F. H. W. Sheppard. London, 1970.

Sutherland, James. "Shakespeare's Imitators in the Eighteenth Century." *MLR*, 28,1 (1933), 21-36.

Swift, Jonathan. *Correspondence.* Ed. Harold Williams. 5 vols. Oxford, 1963-65.

Taylor, D. Crane. *William Congreve.* Oxford, 1931.

Taylor, Houghton W. "Fielding upon Cibber." *MP*, 29,1 (1931), 73-90.

Taylor, John. *Records of My Life.* New York, 1833.

The Tell-Tale; or, Anecdotes Expressive of the Characters of Persons. 2 vols. London, 1750.

Thaler, Alwin. *Shakespeare to Sheridan.* Cambridge, Mass., 1922.

The Theatre-Royal Turn'd into a Mountebank's Stage. London, 1718.

Theatrical Correspondence in Death. An Epistle from Mrs. Oldfield, in the Shades, to Mrs. Br——ceg——dle, upon Earth. London, 1743.

Thompson, Francis. *A History of Chatsworth.* London, 1949.

Thomson, Katherine. *Memoirs of the Court and Times of King George the Second.* London, 1850.

Thorndike, Ashley. *English Comedy.* New York, 1929.

Tillotson, Geoffrey, ed. *Augustan Studies.* London, 1961.

Trevelyan, George Macaulay. *England under the Stuarts.* London, 1920.

The Tryal of a Cause for Criminal Conversation between Theophilus Cibber, Gent. Plaintiff, and William Sloper, Esq, Defendant. London, 1739.

Tunbrigalia; or, The Tunbridge Miscellany for the Years 1737, 1738, 1739. London, 1740.

Tupper, F. S. "Colley and Caius Cibber." *MLN*, 55,5 (1940), 393-96.

[Turnbull, George]. *Three Dissertations.* London, 1740.

The Universal Spectator. Ed. Henry Stonecastle [Henry Baker]. 4 vols. London, 1756.

Unwin, George. *The Guilds and Companies of London*. London, 1963.

Vanbrugh, Sir John. *Works*. Ed. Bonamy Dobree and Geoffrey Webb. 4 vols. Bloomsbury, 1927.

Vernon, P. F. "The Marriage of Convenience and the Moral Code of Restoration Comedy." *EC*, 12,4 (1962), 370-81.

Victor, Benjamin. *An Epistle to Sir Richard Steele, on his Play, call'd The Conscious Lovers*. London, 1722.

———. *The History of the Theatres of London and Dublin from 1730 to the present time*. 3 vols. London, 1761-71.

———. *Memoirs of the Life of Barton Booth*. London, 1733.

The Victoria History of Hampshire and the Isle of Wight. Ed. William Page. 4 vols. London, 1911.

The Victoria History of the Counties of England: Rutland. Ed. Archibald Constable. 2 vols. London, n.d.

A View of the Irish Stage. Dublin, 1766.

Vincent, Howard P. "Two Letters of Colley Cibber." *Notes and Queries*, 168 (5 January 1935), 3-4.

Voorde, F. P. van de. *Henry Fielding: Critic and Satirist*. The Hague, 1931.

Wain, John. "Restoration Comedy and its Modern Critics." *EC*, 6,4 (1956), 367-85.

Walford, Edward. *Old and New London*. 4 vols. London, n.d.

Walpole, Horace. *Correspondence*. Ed. Wyndham S. Lewis. 34 vols. New Haven, Conn., 1937-65.

Ward, Adolphus William. *A History of English Dramatic Literature*. 3 vols. New York, 1899.

Waterhouse, Osborn. "Development of the English Sentimental Comedy in the Eighteenth Century." *Anglia* 30 (1917), 137-72, 269-305.

Watkin-Jones, A. "Langbaine's Account of the English Dramatick Poets (1691)." *Essays and Studies by Members of the English Association*, 21 (1935), 75-85.

Weaver, John. *The History of Mimes and Pantomimes*. London, 1728.

Weekly Journal. 1717-19.

Wells, Mitchell P. "Some Notes on the Early Eighteenth-Century Pantomime." *SP*, 32,4 (1935), 598-607.

———. "Spectacular Scenic Effects of the Eighteenth-Century Pantomime." *PQ*, 17,1 (1938), 67-81.

Wells, Staring B. "An Eighteenth Century Attribution." *JEGP*, 38,2 (1939), 233-46.

Wharton, T., ed. *The Oxford Sausage; or Select Poetical Pieces*. London, 1764.

Wheatley, Henry B. *London Past and Present*. 3 vols. London, 1891.

Wheatley, Katherine. *Racine and English Classicism*. Austin, Tex., 1956.

Whincop, Thomas. *Scanderbeg; or, Love and Liberty*. London, 1747.

Whinney, Margaret. *Sculpture in Britain 1530-1830*. Baltimore, 1964.

Whistler, Lawrence. *Sir John Vanbrugh*. London, 1938.

Whitaker, Wilson C. *Sir Christopher Wren*. London, 1932.

[Whitehead, Paul]. *The State Dunces*. London, 1733.

Whiting, George W. "*The Temple of Dulness* and Other Interludes." *RES*, 10, (April, 1934), 205-11.

Wilkes, Thomas [Samuel Derrick]. *A General View of the Stage*. London, 1759.

Wilkinson, Tate. *Memoirs of His own Life.* 4 vols. York, 1790.

Wilson, Arthur H. *A History of the Philadelphia Theatre, 1835-1855.* Philadelphia, 1935.

Wilson, John Harold. *A Preface to Restoration Drama.* Boston, 1965.

———. "Rant, Cant and Tone on the Restoration Stage." *SP*, 52,4 (1955), 592-98.

Winton, Calhoun. *Captain Steele; the Early Career of Richard Steele.* Baltimore, 1964.

———. *Sir Richard Steele, M. P.; the Later Career.* Baltimore, 1970.

Wood, Frederick T. "The Beginnings and Significance of Sentimental Comedy." *Anglia*, 55 (1931), 368-92.

Woods, Charles B. "Cibber in Fielding's *The Author's Farce*: Three Notes.' *PQ*, 44,2 (1965), 145-51.

Wright, James. *Historia Histrionica; an Historical Account of the English Stage.* London, 1699.

———. *The History and Antiquities of the Country of Rutland.* London, 1684.

Index

Index

240

Index